b.J.Silvan
Orlando
7.84

OPERATION BARBAROSSA

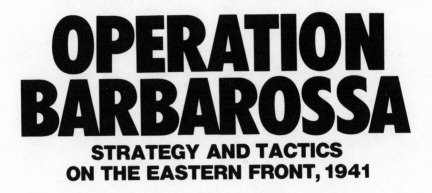

OPERATION BARBAROSSA

STRATEGY AND TACTICS
ON THE EASTERN FRONT, 1941

BRYAN I. FUGATE

PRESIDIO

Copyright © by Presidio Press, 1984
Published by Presidio Press, 31 Pamaron Way, Novato, CA 94947

Library of Congress Cataloging in Publication Data

Fugate, Bryan, 1943–
  Operation Barbarossa.

  Includes bibliographies and index.
    1. World War, 1939–1945—Campaigns—Soviet Union.
  2. Soviet Union—History—German occupation, 1941–1944.
  I. Title.
  D764.F84   1984   940.54'21   84-2035
  ISBN 0–89141–197–6

Maps by Mark Bentley

Sources for photographs:
Nos. 1–10, 12, 13, 15, 17, 19, and 21, courtesy
Bibliothek fur Zeitgeschichte, Stuttgart.

Nos. 11 and 18, courtesy Bundesarchiv, Koblenz,
146/11/724 and 144.

This book is respectfully dedicated to the teachers and students of Russian history who live and work on the outside of the Soviet Union.

They nurture a weak flame of knowledge that, without their ministrations, would die, and the history of a great people would be lost forever within an impenetrable umbra.

O you, Calliope, and all the Muses,
do you, I pray, inspire me: I must
sing of the slaughter and the deaths that Turnus
spread with his sword across the field of battle,
of those each fighting man sent down to hell;
unroll with me the mighty scroll of war.
You, goddesses, remember, you can tell.

Virgil, *The Aeneid*

CONTENTS

LIST OF FIGURES

Unit Designations for Map Interpretation		Unit Designations for Map Interpretation	
GERMAN UNITS		SOVIET UNITS	
Unit Name	*Map Designation*	*Unit Name*	*Map Designation*
Army Group	Army Group Center	Direction	Southwestern Direction
Panzer Army	2 PA	Front	Central Front
Panzer Group	3 PG	Army	21 A
Army	9 A	Rifle Corps	XXV RC
Army Corps	XX AC	Mechanized Corps	XVII MC
Panzer Corps	XXIV PC	Rifle Division	292 RD
Infantry Division	167 ID	Tank Division	102 TD
Panzer Division	10 PD		
Motorized Division	29 MD		
Regiments	448 RGT		
Special Regiments	IR "GD"		
SS Divisions	SS "DR"		

FOREWORD

The historical record revealed in Bryan Fugate's account of the German and Russian strategic planning for Operation Barbarossa, together with his commentary on it, offers a number of lessons to be learned relevant to military operations today. One of the favorite themes of U.S. Army doctrine today is the value of the exercise of initiative by subordinate commanders. Yet we can see in Guderian's activities the other side of this concept at work when a strong-willed commander exercises initiative to pursue his own vision of what is desirable at the expense of his superior's overall concept of operations. Local success can position forces so as to negate or at least drastically alter the original strategic plan. When the military organization is not imbued from top to bottom with a common understanding and unity of purpose with respect to strategic principles and goals the effect of the natural tendency to follow one's own ideas is sure to be magnified. The German officer corps, as highly trained and carefully indoctrinated as it was in a uniform mold based on a single philosophy still harbored the divergence of opinion on critical strategic, operational, and tactical issues that Fugate indicates led to disaster. What might we expect from reliance on initiative to solve problems in a multinational NATO force, when even the U.S. Army alone does not possess such a uniform philosophy or the means to indoctrinate it?

The German high command's activities also bear witness to another all too common reality of war not sufficiently emphasized in textbooks, namely, that personal and institutional rivalries within a military force will lead to disaster. It is easy to say such rivalry must not be tolerated, but unfortunately, in practice it is frequently the authorities who ought not to be tolerating it who are the very ones perpetuating it.

Can we say that our armed forces today are guided by such unity of purpose and understanding of strategic goals as to preclude the problems generated by initiative? Are our institutional and personal rivalries so under control in peacetime that the increased propensity for rivalry during war will not cause a similar disaster? Russell Weigley's book *Eisenhower's Lieutenants* depicts some of the results of rivalry within American forces during WW II. Can we say that the Army, Navy, and Air Force are any less rivals today than they were then?

The institutional rivalry of OKW and OKH and the personal rivalry of various individuals in these staffs are well known. However, Bryan Fugate draws special attention to the way in which Guderian's independence of will and his ability to act accordingly contributed to the fatal lack of unity of strategic purpose so apparent in the execution of Operation Barbarossa. He also reveals in part how the subsequent apologetic memoir literature penned by the guilty generals has attempted to pass all the blame to Hitler.

In today's world all manner of critical decisions for, not only specific operational war plans, but also force structuring and weapons procurement, rest on war games and simulations. Fugate describes the German planning procedure prior to the campaigns in Russia, which also involved war gaming and analysis. General Paulus directed studies that showed that the supply system would not be able to cope with the requirements of a campaign in Russia —yet Halder suppressed these views. The tendency to see such mundane issues as logistics with "rose-colored glasses" remains with us today. One wonders how many inconvenient technical difficulties are being assumed away or suppressed now, especially by people who make a career of always saying they "can do" any mission they are assigned.

Another issue that stands out in Fugate's study is the difference between the operational and tactical levels. This record shows why tactical success does not necessarily lead to operational success and why tactical failure does not necessarily lead to operational or strategic failure. Soviet literature on WW II stresses the claim that their appreciation of the operational art was greater than the Germans and Fugate's account bears this out, at least for this campaign.

Students of Russian military literature and practice are familiar with the extraordinarily pervasive atmosphere of secrecy and deception that has shaped the Russian system for centuries. This secrecy and its counterpart, the effort to achieve surprise, have been ingrained in the Russian national character. A particularly subtle aspect of this is denoted by the term *reflexive control*. This refers to a peculiarly Soviet concept for a plan that attempts to go far beyond the mere springing of surprises through deception to the complete control over the enemy's actions through long-term manipulation of the mind of the opposing leadership. This kind of "control" is difficult to prove in the case of WW II, because secrecy still hampers research and the historical record has been distorted and carefully controlled to serve the same purpose. It is known that Dr. Pavlov of conditioned response fame lectured to the Soviet political/military high command in the 1920s on this concept. One wonders how many of the German moves that now appear as blunders were made in reaction to this kind of Soviet manipulation. The critical switch of the objective from Moscow to the Ukraine and back again comes particularly to mind.

The Soviet military has always had an acute awareness of the importance of space and time and of ways to use one to gain the other. From their point of view the people and equipment lost in the defense of the Ukraine were a necessary sacrifice required to ensure that the loss of that space would cost the Germans even more in terms of time. A premature withdrawal, even if it preserved more forces, would have defeated this purpose—space would have been lost without gained time. Stalin gambled that his first strategic echelon would hold long enough for full mobilization of the strategic reserve, even if mobilization was delayed until after D day. Delayed mobilization was part of the overall deception plan. But the disasters suffered in Belorussia during the first weeks of the war exceeded even Soviet expectations, as the impact of inadequate leadership in the wake of the purges told on Soviet tactical effectiveness. Thus it was essential from the Soviet viewpoint that the German thrust on Moscow be diverted for a time while that city's defenses were prepared.

A lesson that seemingly needs repeated relearning is the inherent weakness of a cordon defense when penetrated by highly mobile attackers. The first Soviet defense line was easily penetrated and defeated. But the Soviet three-echelon system enabled them to position reserves effectively even though they were less mobile than their attackers. The campaign shows the need for operational-level mobile reserves capable of blunting the attacker's penetration and containing it while the third echelon delivers a decisive counterattack.

Among the more narrowly military lessons the Soviets have derived from their study of this campaign is the critical importance of communications and their extreme vulnerability to surprise attack. Much of the Soviet tactical and operational failure can be laid to the chaotic nature of command and control when communications sabotage attack. Since World War II the Soviet armed forces have placed great emphasis on creating an elaborate, highly redundant communications network that is designed to prevent a recurrence of this debacle.

Another lesson vividly impressed on them was the vulnerability of air forces on the ground to surprise attack at the beginning of a war. In reaction to this they have paid especial attention to protecting their airfields and aircraft while at the same time devising methods and plans to strike their opponents a massive surprise air strike as the opening stroke of any future war.

From the German successes and failures at encirclement warfare the Soviets learned the necessity of combining the high speed and mobility of the forces that strike deep to develop an encirclement with the ability to occupy the ground with sufficient density of forces that must fill out the arms of the encirclement. By the end of WW II Soviet forces were regularly achieving encirclements much less porous than those attempted by the Germans during Barbarossa.

Bryan Fugate's organization has brought together several threads heretofore separately treated in accounts of either the German or Soviet side of WW II. Into this contextual framework he has placed a wealth of detail gleaned from careful study of the actual daily records of the German forces and postwar literature on the Soviet forces. Detail and conceptual framework complement each other to make this account a welcome addition to the literature. Individuals concerned with potential warfare in Europe in the future will find much to contemplate in the lessons to be learned here.

John Sloan
20 February 1983
Springfield, Virginia

ACKNOWLEDGMENTS

I wish to thank Col. John F. Sloan, editor of *The International Military Encyclopedia* (TIME), for his continuous support of this project, without which it could never have succeeded. Much credit is also due to Professor James Goff of Mankato State University in Mankato, Minnesota, and to his research assistant Kathryn Newsome. The treatise set forth by Professor Goff in appendix A contains new and important information on Soviet order of battle and deployment in 1941. Rob Conway of Washington, D.C., was a valuable guide for me in the National Archives. In particular, his discovery of the index to German general staff intelligence records was an important milestone. I also wish to thank Robert Wolfe, Chief of the National Archives, Modern Military Branch, and his assistant George Wagner for their help and timely advice. Valuable support was provided also by David R. Jones, editor of *The Modern Encyclopedia of Russian and Soviet History,* and by Dr. Jack Cross of the Center for Strategic Technology at Texas A & M University.

Finally, I want to express special appreciation to Frau Hilde Rittelmeyer, president of the Federation of German American Clubs who, in conjunction with the University of Texas at Austin, graciously provided me a stipend for study at the German Federal Military Archives in Freiburg.

NOTE ON SOURCES

A word must be said regarding the reliability of Soviet sources. In the writing of this book, every possible attempt was made to correlate Russian data with information available in the West. One critical concern for most readers, no doubt, will be how valid the information is regarding Soviet troop deployments in the western regions to counter the German invasion. It has for so long been taken as an article of faith that the Russians were caught by surprise on June 22, 1941, and had no overall defense plan in operation that it seemed at first to be an insurmountable task to convince readers otherwise.

In the last part of Chapter 1 dealing with Soviet defense strategy, a plan is revealed. The revelation can be said to be based largely on conjecture, and in one sense this is true—no one privy to Stalin's war councils ever confided the whole story—but the facts should speak for themselves. When, for example, the deployment of the operational echelon is discussed, in particular the positioning of the Twenty-first Army around Gomel on the southern flank of the Army Group Center, the Russian sources are adequately backed up by contemporary German records. The German maps presented in Figures 1 and 2 are a good case in point: Figure 1 shows what the German army high command thought the Russian deployment would be before June 22, 1941. Notice that the bulk of the Red Army is positioned far to the west and that a breakthrough on both sides of the Biolystok salient would open the way into the hinterland and eventually Moscow—that is, if in fact the Soviet forces were so deployed. Figure 2 shows the situation a few weeks

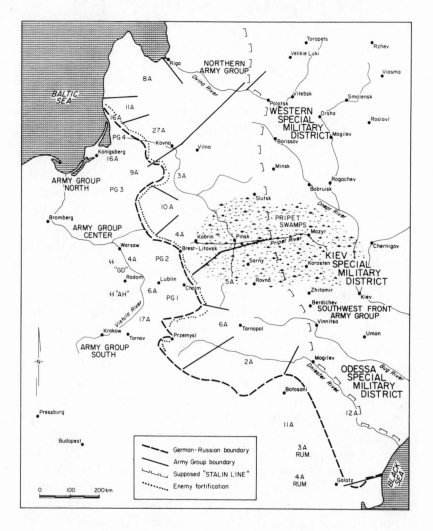

Figure 1. German Map Showing the Supposed Deployment of Russian Forces on July 22, 1941

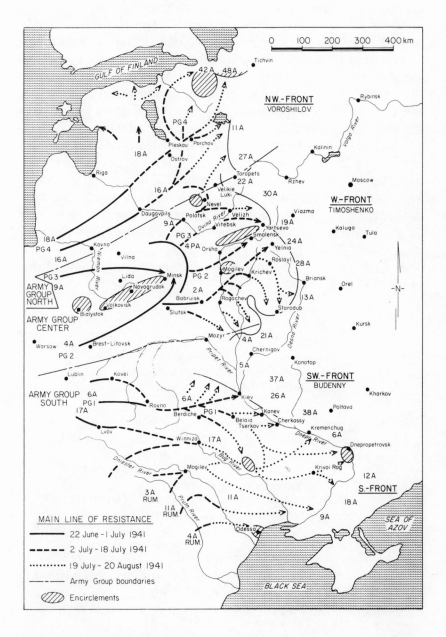

Figure 2. Map showing the Situation on the Southern Flank of Army Group Center, July–August 1941

later after contact with the operational echelon. Note in particular the position of the Russian Twenty-first Army near Gomel on the southern flank of Army Group Center. The war diary of the Second Army command confirms the danger that Army Group Center faced from this direction. Halder's diary also speaks of this threat in specific terms. The Twenty-first Army did not just magically appear, nor was it slapped together in a rush and thrown into battle. It was there in position before the invasion, waiting to perform its mission—which it did with some effectiveness.

Another way to verify the operational deployment of the Red Army is to look at the casualty and prisoner statistics compiled from German sources. An examination of these figures shows where the heavy fighting took place—along the Dnepr line and farther east, not along the frontier where the Russians were supposed to have massed their army according to preinvasion German calculations. The forces along the border represented only a fraction of the Red Army's force in existence in the early phase of the war, as the tables show.

German Casualty Statistics for 1941
(Including all KIA, MIA, and WIA)

Numbers in parentheses indicate percentage of total field army:

July 13, after the end of the Bialystok-Minsk battles	92,120 (3.6%)
August 13, after the elimination of the Smolensk pocket	389,924 (10%)
August 26, after the battles along the Dnepr and Dvina rivers on the flanks of Army Group Center	441,100 (11.6%)
September 30, after the battles around and to the east of Kiev	551,039 (16.20%)
November 13, after the battles of Briansk-Viazma and the resumption of the Typhoon offensive	699,726 (20.58%)
Total for 1941	930,903 (26%)

25.67% of these casualties occurred by the end of July, 74.32% thereafter

Note: From October 1, 1941 to January 31, 1942 during the Typhoon offensive and the Red Army counteroffensive after December 6, 1941, Army Group Center suffered 369,500 losses.

Soviet Prisoner Statistics for 1941

WEST OF DVINA-DNEPR LINE

Battle	Number of Prisoners
Bialystok–Minsk, July 8	287,704*
Uman, August 12	103,000
Total	390,704

Note that only 17.3% of the total of 2,258,535 prisoners were taken in the areas west of the Dvina-Dnepr line.

ALONG THE DNEPR LINE OR FARTHER EAST

Battle	Number of Prisoners
Mogilev, July 16	35,000
Smolensk, August 5	309,110
Roslavl, August 6	38,561
Zhlobin, August 18	50,000
Krichev and Gomel, August 19	78,000
Velikie Luki, August 26	34,000
Kiev, September 26	665,212
Briansk-Viazma, October 19	657,948
Total	1,867,831

Note that 82.7% of the total of 2,258,535 prisoners in 1941 were taken in the areas east of the Dvina-Dnepr line.

*Only 100,000 of these were taken around Bialystok. The rest were captured around and to the east of Minsk.

Field Marshal Fedor von Bock

Colonel-General Heinz Guderian

Colonel-General Franz Halder

Colonel-General Hermann Hoth

Colonel-General Alfred Jodl

General of Artillery Walter Warlimont

Lieutenant-General Friederich Paulus

Field Marshal Gunther von Kluge

Colonel-General Freiherr von Weichs (center, facing)

Lieutenant-General General Geyr von Schweppenburg

Lieutenant-General Hermann Geyer

Field Marshal Albert Kesselring

Reichsmarshal Hermann Göring

General of the Army Georgii Zhukov

Marshal S. K. Timoshenko

General of the Army D. G. Pavlov

Marshal S. M. Budénny

Marshal B. M. Shaposhnikov

Lieutenant-General A. I. Eremenko

Marshal M. N. Tukhachevsky

Lieutenant-General I. S. Konev

Major-General K. K. Rokossovskii

Colonel-General M. P. Kirponos

INTRODUCTION

THE ORIGINS OF RUSSIAN MILITARY DOCTRINE

When one considers the enormous changes that have taken place in the Soviet Union in the sixty-seven years since the Bolshevik Revolution, it seems difficult to believe that certain fundamentals of its character as a nation have remained virtually unaltered. By comparison, the democratic countries of the West and Japan have profoundly reshaped their political and economic ideologies during this period. Think of the world outlook of the United States in the 1920s, when our isolationist foreign policy was concerned with very few major issues abroad, and then mostly in our own hemisphere. The remarkable consistency of Soviet foreign policy and the longevity of the careers of its political leaders has been a great source of power for the USSR, a fact that has been recognized in the West. Since 1924, there have been only four leaders in the Soviet Union as opposed to eleven presidents in the United States. With one minor exception, the heads of the Soviet Communist Party have held their power for a minimum of ten years.[1]

In the realm of military doctrine, the Soviet Union has wavered only temporarily from its basic world outlook since the time of the earlier tsarist imperialism. The primary concern here will not be with the details of doctrinal development or with the lives of the various individuals who contributed so greatly to its evolution (for example, Suvorov, Kutuzov, Trotsky, Frunze, Tukhachevski, Stalin, Zhukov, Sokolovsky, and more recently, Gorshkov). Rather, it will be with those organic characteristics of Russia, the

1

Soviet state, and the Communist system that have created an environment allowing these doctrinal elements to flourish.

Traditionally, the transformation of Russia into a major European and military power is said to have occurred during the reign of Peter I ("the Great," 1682–1725). Certainly, however, there was a history of fighting spirit and doctrinal coherency dating back much earlier, to the time of the Tatar occupation and the rise of the Muscovite principality. These struggles in Russia's infancy were, for the most part, absorptive in nature.

The shock of the Tatar invasion under Batu and Subudai in the mid-thirteenth century could not have been withstood by any force that Kievan Russia could muster. The nature of the Tatar occupation was such, however, that it gave the Russian people a chance to survive as a separate entity; they were not submerged and incorporated as a nation into the corpus of the Golden Horde. There were two main reasons for this: (1) the Tatars did not try to move into the forests and towns in the north, choosing instead to remain in the south feeding their herds on the rich grasslands, and (2) the Tatars, nomadic by nature, did not develop the urban productive base, including metal working and weapons manufacture, that would allow them to keep pace with advancing technology. Economically, the Russians were able to maintain a system isolated from the Tatars, who were content merely to enforce the payment of tribute. In the long run, the relationship of economic and political forces was such that the Tatar rule would "wither away," which it did, in fact, during the reign of Ivan III (1462–1505).

From the military standpoint, the Russian people learned several things from the Tatar occupation. The first lesson was that barriers had to be erected in the east and south to prevent a repetition of those events. Initially, this was done in the reign of Ivan IV ("the Terrible," 1533–1584) by conquering centers of Tatar power in Kazan and Astrakhan and later by erecting fortress cities like Orel for "island defense" and hiring Cossack troops as mercenary guards. Ivan's aggressive liquidation of the Tatar and Turkish menace continued under Peter I and Catherine II ("the Great," 1762–1796). Another lesson the Russians took to heart was the importance of developing a military caste. This process was first begun during the reign of Ivan III with the creation of the *pomestie* system, whereby land grants could be obtained by the nobles from the Moscow government only on the condition that they help raise armies and pay for them. This system of land tenure forced the nobles to tie the peasants to the land as much as possible and keep them from leaving. According to one respected Russian historian, the spread of the *pomestie* system was one of the prime factors in the spread of serfdom throughout Russia.[2] The danger from outside invasion and depredation was much worse than the danger of losing freedom to a crushing system of serfdom that, in many ways, was harsher than the treatment meted out to black slaves in the American South. It is interesting to speculate about what the history of the United States might have been had the American Indians possessed a larger reservoir of manpower and acted as a constant threat to our major population centers the way the Tatars did in Russia.[*] What if Indians had overrun the colonies in the seventeenth century and held the European settlers in subjugation for over a hundred years? Few could doubt that our nation would have developed radically differently.

In Russia, the vestiges of serfdom were not eliminated until 1917, for the threat of the Tatars was quickly replaced by that of other powers with predatory interests, particularly in the rich and bountiful farming area that had supported the old Kievan state— the Ukraine. The military caste and the *pomestie* warrier-estate system provided a practical means for repelling these threats, now from the west from Poland-Lithuania and from Sweden. The ascendency of the Principality of Moscow, the neutralization of the Turko-Tatar threat, the ending of the expansionist aims of Poland-Lithuania, and the institutionalization of serfdom and the military caste were all logically connected and formed the basis for the next stage of military development—the creation of a large national standing army and navy under Peter the Great and the other Romanovs.

Much has been written about the military reforms of Peter the Great, so no attempt will be made here to recount his achievements in detail.[3] Suffice it to say that after the defeat of the Swedish king, Charles XII, at Poltava and the Treaty of Nystad in 1721, Russia emerged as a major European power. Although Peter had gleaned his ideas about military reform from his extensive travels in the West and from numerous Western military advisors import-

*As late as 1571 Moscow was partly burned by the Tatars, and in 1591 another Tatar raid approached the walls of the city.

ed into Russia, such as the Dutch Franz Timmermann, the Scott Patrick Gordon, and the Swiss Francois Lefort, among others, the shape of the new army and its methods of warfare had some uniquely Russian characteristics.

In terms of strategy, Peter did not choose to meet Charles on unfavorable territory. Peter was content to allow the Swedish king to become mired first in a seemingly endless war in Poland. Then, when Charles did strike directly at Russia, the tsar did not try to blunt the offensive too soon but instead allowed the invading army to spend its energy overcoming the countless difficulties in maneuver across great distances and over inhospitable terrain. Peter had learned scorched earth tactics from the Tatars and used them against the Swedes, denying them the use of crops and fodder. Finally, when Charles's offensive force was spent, a relatively easy victory was gained at Poltava at a small cost to Russia.

The commanders of Peter's army were initially drawn from the old nobility *(dvoriane),* which had been expected to serve as the officer caste as well as to staff the ranks of the newly created civil administrations. Since there were no military colleges, the upper-class youth trained in one of the three guards regiments—the Semenovskii, the Preobrazhenskii, and the "Life Regiment" (later the Horse Guards). The growing need for military and civilian officers, however, soon outstripped the supply of hereditary nobles. An attempt at a remedy for this was the enoblement of bright young men who succeeded in making their way upward in the hierarchy. Finally, in 1722, a "Table of Ranks" was instituted that, among other things, granted the title of hereditary noble to every military man who achieved the lowest officer grade. This Table of Ranks remained in use substantially without change in Russia until 1917.[4] Despite the fact that a certain "democratization" was admitted in the opening of a path into noble status, the older aristocracy maintained a firm grip on the higher military posts. The traditional gap between nobles and nonnobles in the military continued to exist, but after 1722, it existed in official bureaucratic form. One of the "outsider" representatives of the new military caste, Alexander Suvorov (1730–1800), became the spiritual father of Russian military doctrine and still is paid high homage by the modern Soviet state in the form of a coveted military decoration that is named for him. In many ways, the privileged officer caste is perpetuated in the USSR, with officers' families intermarrying and attending special schools. The Russian officer even today is a breed apart from the "nonnoble" lesser ranks and civilians.[5]

In the career of Suvorov can be seen many of the elements that pointed the way toward Russia's future greatness as a military power. The essence of the great general's teachings can be found in his book *The Science of Victory:* (1) The offensive is the main weapon of war. (2) Achieve rapidity in attack, use the bayonet. (3) Do not lapse into methodical routine, use objective observation. (4) Full power to the supreme command. (5) Fight in the field, not in fortifications; confuse the enemy. (6) Sieges are wasteful, open assault is best. (7) Do not waste forces in occupation of points, bypass the enemy if possible. Russia sought to play a major role in European affairs for the first time in its history through Suvorov's Italian campaign in 1799, where he astonished some of the best French generals, such as Joubert and Moreau, by long forced marches and rapid deployment for the attack. It was Suvorov's plan never to defend a location for long but always attack whenever the opportunity arose. It was also his plan never to assault a fortress simply for the sake of occupying it; rather, his goal was always "to destroy the enemy's life force and his ability to make war." Suvorov became known as a practitioner of combined-arms tactics; that is, no one branch of arms, such as cavalry or artillery, was given favored treatment or allowed to operate autonomously from the other branches of arms. Suvorov's phased and integrated attacks utilizing all forms of combat, including lavish artillery (so loved by Peter) and the bayonet, earned him a fearsome reputation, especially after the assault of the Turkish fortress of Izmail in 1790. Suvorov's emphasis on training for the battlefield and cultivation of morale, plus his unique methods of march, deployment, and attack, established a theme for the future progress of the Russian national army. As great as Suvorov's legacy was, however, it remained to be seen whether the graft of his genius had actually taken hold on the roots left by Peter's reforms. Had the army been annealed in the campaign of 1799 to withstand an onslaught of the largest European army ever raised, led by one of the most outstanding commanders of all time, Napoleon?

The course of events leading up to Napoleon's invasion of Russia in June 1812 should not concern us here. The outcome of the war and its general pattern are also well known.[6] From the doctrinal standpoint, however, several interesting features need to be pointed out.

In the first place, the Russian General Barclay de Tolly's decision to allow Napoleon's Grand Armée to enter Russia without a serious attempt at resistance caused an enormous political problem, both at court and with Russia's chief ally, Britain. It is important to bear in mind, however, that it is the oldest maxim in war "never to do what your enemy wants you to do" and that Napoleon would quickly have blown the Russian army into chaff had he been challenged close to the frontier. It should be remembered also that Kutuzov (1745–1813), Suvorov's disciple, continued de Tolly's retreat after he became supreme commander. The point is this: the Russian army had to rely on a strategy of retreat and scorched earth despite all the political and economic liabilities of such a strategy. To have done otherwise would have invited complete disaster. In this respect, Joseph Stalin's position was not much different from Tsar Alexander's, as will be seen in Chapter I.

There is another interesting parallel between Alexander's and Stalin's wars: the peasant factor. In both cases, the peasantry remained loyal to the regime and gave their lives in vast numbers to repel the invaders. One might wonder why this was so, considering that conditions for them, both in serfdom and later on collective farms, were so harsh and degrading. Answering this question provides an insight into what has made the heart of Russia, both Communist and before, beat with a singular will to live.

Before his great adventure in 1812, there had been much talk in Russia about what the French emperor might do if he succeeded in unfurling his flag above the Kremlin. There seemed to be a widespread hope among the peasants (and fear among the nobility) that Napoleon would abolish feudalism and serfdom in Russia and encourage the emergence of a small-holder class of farmers, similar to what had emerged in France during the revolution. It is not precisely certain what the origins of this rumor were, but anyone familiar with Napoleon's attitude toward the land question in Poland would have expressed extreme reservations about liberation of the serfs in Russia by the French. Polish peasants were "liberated" in name only in 1807, but no move was made really to free them. The Polish nobles rallied to Napoleon's cause in 1812 because he pointedly refused to liberate the serfs in White Russia and in Lithuania.

Napoleon also used French troops to put down peasant revolts in White Russia at the request of Polish landowners. Once the war began and Napoleon failed to issue an edict freeing the serfs in Russia, the peasantry rallied to the Tsarist cause with a vengeance.

The single most important continuous thread of Russian military history has been that no invader of Russia, from the Turko-Tatars to Hitler, has ever offered the Russian masses anything better than the conditions they already had. Typically, as was the case with Napoleon and Hitler, an enemy victory would probably have resulted in a worsening of conditions for the masses as a whole and the peasants in particular. Russian rulers have used this fact most often to save themselves.

Kutuzov's strategy of retreat without giving battle was, until the fateful confrontation at Borodino, forced by necessity, as in fact most Russian strategic decisions have been. What was unique about Kutuzov was his refusal to destroy the Grand Armée in November 1812 en route back to Poland. The reason for Kutuzov's "parallel pursuit" of the demoralized Grand Armée could be that the French were being destroyed through exposure and starvation anyway, and although it is true that an attempt was made to keep them from crossing the Berezina River, another explanation could be that Kutuzov simply did not consider that ridding Europe of Napoleon was truly in Russia's best interest at that particular point. Russia had not yet reached the stage when massive intervention in European affairs was an all-consuming objective; this characteristic of Russian foreign policy would appear later.

After the Congress of Vienna and the final defeat of Napoleon in 1815, Russia, under Nicholas I and Alexander II, began a long and steady decline in military preparedness. Whereas in 1812 the average Russian army unit was equipped with more cannon than its counterpart in the French army,[*] during the period after 1815 virtually no improvements were made in Russian artillery. This lack of progress became painfully evident during the Crimean War (1854–1856).

The events in the Balkans that preceded the Crimean War are of peripheral importance here. The key points to observe are that Russia by 1854 was interested in obtaining world power status by

---

[*]This French army was much larger, and so the total number of guns at its disposal was greater, although the Russian pieces generally were able to fire heavier shells.

commanding the Bosporus and the Dardanelles and that a joint operation by two major powers, Britain and France, albeit with very limited tactical objectives, was just sufficient to hold the Russian bear in check. The fourth major European power, Prussia, maintained a strained silence; nevertheless, Russia could not overlook the possibility of a threat either from the west or from the north against Saint Petersburg. Russian military doctrine had accounted for the difficulties that might be encountered in a two- or even three-front war, but not against major opponents. The other European powers had coped with this problem many times before, notably Prussia during the Seven Years' War and Britain in its war against Napolean and against America in 1812, but for Russia the problems seemed especially grievous considering the vast distances involved and the poverty of its transportation resources. These problems in fighting multifront wars remained essentially unsolved by Russia in the nineteenth century, and at the same time became ever more important because of the continuous expansion of colonization in Asia, in Turkestan and Siberia. The dangers inherent in such rapid expansion became all too real when Japanese torpedo boats sank the Russian fleet at Port Arthur in late 1904.

In the war against the Japanese, despite the twin catastrophes on land at Mukden and at sea at Tsushima, the army held together and did not crack, even though the homeland seethed with unrest, culminating in the abortive Revolution of 1905. The reasons for the steadfastness of the army under these conditions are instructive, especially when its behavior is contrasted with the inward collapse that occurred in 1917.

First, the Japanese war objectives were clearly limited in scope, and all of the fighting took place on foreign soil, in China and Korea. The point is that the Japanese made no attempt to take what was perceived to be Russian territory proper, nor did they have a political philosophy that they cared to promulgate among the Russian people. Second, the war was a short one lasting only a few months. Had it turned into a protracted conflict, the unrest at home would have worked as a poison among the ranks of soldiers. However, in 1917, by contrast: (1) a political philosophy hostile to the regime was spread through the army by a well-organized group within Russia; (2) the First World War was a protracted conflict, and the heavy losses on the battlefield, coupled with the hope of positive good coming from a change in the regime, resulted in a devastating moral collapse in the military.

Russian military doctrine on the eve of World War I in 1914 had become a virtual prisoner of Allied planning. France, in particular, had been given a full claim in Russia's stake in strategic and tactical theory. Probably never in history has a major power so completely prostrated itself to the goals of its allies. The reasons for this utter abandonment of independent thought are complex and should not be discussed here, but the point needs to be made that by August 1914, Russian military doctrine had become a mere extension of French revanchist dreams. Aside from vague musings about Pan-Slavist causes, which few Russians could ever understand, in the beginning Russia had no publicly voiced strategic objectives in the war. Beneath the surface there were objectives, objectives, that, in the past, had caused Britain's adamant and undying opposition: the breakup of the Austro-Hungarian Empire and the seizure of the Straits from Turkey, Germany's ally. The seizure of the Straits would have transformed Russia immediately into a world power and would have put it squarely into the arena of competition with Britain from Suez to India. In March 1915, Britain formally agreed that Russia could annex the Straits and Constantinople, but after the failure of the British Dardanelles campaign in that year, this seemed to be a moot point. As it was, the agreements with the Allies concerning the Straits were kept secret until December 1916, but by then the overall military situation had deteriorated to the point that the announcement failed to stir any public support whatsoever.[7]

Russia's supporting role in the war, as determined by French requirements, called for it to take up the offensive into East Prussia soon after the commencement of hostilities, a mission for which the army was tragically ill equipped. The inertia of Russia's mobilization schedule alone (and early mobilization itself would have been tantamount to a declaration of war) should have predicated against such a foolhardy scheme as tramping directly into the lair of the strongest enemy. Had Russia waited until the proper moment for full mobilization of its steamroller, and had the army been used properly against Austria-Hungary, an opponent more nearly equal to Russia in fighting capacity in 1914, then good results might have been achieved. As it was, however, the outcome was virtually predestined. As the sun set over the bloody battle-field of Tannenberg, so it set over Russia's hopes for a quick victory. Once the war ground on into an interminable struggle, new forces came into play that brought about the eventual disintegration of the armed forces. The lack of objectives or any sense of moral cause in the war, in addition to the windrows of casualties, themselves probably would not have caused the collapse of the army. The injection, however, of a political "virus"—Bolshevism —into Russia by the German enemy created conditions favorable for the development of a revolutionary fever.

The Bolsheviks—Lenin, Trotsky, Stalin, and the others— were astute enough to realize their chances for success in toppling the regime were directly related to Russia's continued participation in the war. The war provided the catalyst for change, and when the provisional government decided, not only to stay in the conflict, but indeed even to increase the effort, the roof began to cave in on the Russian army.

Russia had given a good account of itself in the war, especially against the Austrians. A. A. Brusilov's offensive into Galicia in the summer of 1916 was a significant success and showed what the army could do when it was given a good plan and was well led against forces more or less its equal. But the army's record against German forces was dismal, even disastrous. This failure is tied to economic developments: Industrialization in Russia in 1914 was still in its infancy, and the country had certainly not kept pace with Germany in any area of manufacture, let alone armaments. In 1913 Germany produced 29.1 million tons of iron and steel and 191.5 million tons of coal; in the same year Russia produced 4.43 million tons of iron and steel and 39.85 million tons of coal.[8] The Russian transportation system was very weak and the methods of supply heartbreakingly slow, this in a country that had undertaken the invasion of East Prussia as its first act in the war. In October 1914, the Russian army needed four weeks to move ten army corps a distance of about 325 kilometers from western Galicia to the middle Vistula. The entire month of May 1915 was needed to deploy an army in Bukhovina, and even after a successful offensive operation was concluded, the army had to pull back because of supply problems. By way of comparison, in March 1918, the French were able to concentrate twelve divisions to defend Amiens within only four days. The Germans needed only a week to pull eight divisions into the Gorlice-Tarnow area in May 1915—a force that was increased to thirty divisions in another two weeks to block a Rumanian intervention and ward off an expected Russian offensive. The Russians themslves calculated that it required two weeks to move one army corps of two divisions from the northern to the southern part of the front.[9] It is clear that the strategic role assigned to Russia by its allies was not in its best interests. But finally, it must be said that the external enemy was not what overcame the army— instead, the forces of adhesion in its ranks began to loosen due to internal propaganda.

The First World War differed from Napoleon's invasion in 1812 in its effect on the Russian people and the army. As has been mentioned, the Russian people felt that they had nothing to gain from a Napoleonic victory in 1812. On the contrary, the peasants felt they had potentially a great deal to lose from the French alliance with the Polish nobility. During World War I, however, the army gradually came to perceive that the survival of the tsarist regime would be a greater evil than revolution at home and a humiliating peace with the enemy. This gradual change in mood came about because the country's war aims, at least publicly, were dictated by the Allies and had little or nothing to do with Russia's interests as a nation or those of the people. The whole way the war was conducted, at both the strategic and the tactical levels, demonstrated eventually even to the lowest private that the army was literally being used up for the Allies' cause, not Russia's. Finally, an ingredient was added in 1917 that had been missing during the earlier invasion of Russia; an internal political movement at home promised something definitely better if the soldiers would turn their guns against the regime instead of the enemy.

The collapse of the Russian army in 1917 must be understood as a breakdown from within. This collapse was the first within the Russian army since the "Time of Troubles" early in the seventeenth century.* Since there has not been a comparable event since 1917, the objective lesson becomes doubly significant. The fact re-

---

*During the "Time of Troubles," the Russian nobility turned against the Tsar and backed a pretender to the throne known as "the False Dimitri." Later, the Poles and the Swedes got into the act and a second pretender emerged. The Poles eventually were ejected by a national uprising led by Kuzma Minin and Dimitri Pozharsky. The political situation in Russia was stabilized after a diet of nobles called the Zemskii Sobor elected Michael, the first of the Romanovs, as Tsar in 1613.

mains as a recurrent theme throughout Russian history: the people and the army will fight tenaciously for a cause they consider in their interest—they will turn on their regime, however, if a better alternative is offered.

The partisan movement, which has existed in Russia at least since the time of Pugachev's rebellion under Catherine the Great, is illustrative of this point. Soviet commentators laud the usefulness of the partisans who operated behind German lines in World War II, but they fail to mention that large bands of partisans, such as the one led by Taras Borovets, fought *against* the Red Army. Some of the Ukrainian nationalist groups, Stepan Bandera's for example, were particularly troublesome to both the Germans and the Soviets and attempted to organize a resistance against both sides in the war. Other disaffected army men and peasants joined the so-called Russian Liberation Army (ROA) headed by General Vlasov, a former Soviet hero who lent his services to the Nazis. In addition, one only has to recall the fierce struggle of collectivization in 1929–1933, which led to the wholesale slaughter of livestock by the peasants, to realize how potentially devastating such disaffection can be.

The remaining chapters are devoted to describing implementation of Soviet strategy and tactics during the early period of the war on the eastern front. Also, close attention is paid to the reasons for the failure of the German Wehrmacht to conquer the Soviet Union. It is hoped that the reader will be able to extrapolate the dangers, the power, but also the potentially fatal flaws, that lie buried within the Soviet system.

CHAPTER 1

PREWAR SOVIET DEFENSE PLANNING AND STRATEGY

THE DEVELOPMENT OF SOVIET MILITARY DOCTRINE

The unique features of what became Soviet military doctrine took time to develop after the October Revolution due to the fact that the new regime had to cope with immediate and pressing problems that did not permit the luxury of long reflection. The most urgent problem, of course, was concluding the war with Germany, and this was done quickly, if haphazardly, by March 1918. The next military task was to build a new Red Army and protect the Soviet state from its enemies at home and abroad. Since by 1918 the lines were being drawn for what would become a full-fledged civil war, it was clear to Lenin that the organizer of the Red Army would have to be a man of rare administrative and military talents. Lenin's choice for this challenging assignment was Leon Trotsky, a man who had not even joined the Bolshevik Party until July 1917 but who had proven himself with his unflinching devotion to the revolutionary cause.

Trotsky's main contribution to the early Soviet state came out of his ability to achieve his goals despite chaotic conditions. The old imperial army had simply ceased to exist, both through attrition ("voting with their feet") and through the virtual collapse of discipline after the Bolshevik decrees of elective command and equalization of rights. In February 1918, Trotsky took over the new Workers' and Peasants' Red Army (RKKA) as the commissar for war. Being ultimately pragmatic, he quickly grasped the situation and became a strong advocate of using former imperial officers in the ranks as "specialists." In doing this, he laid himself open to the charge of adhering to the old, traditional methods of warfare. In fact, Trotsky himself was able to admit this resemblance between the Red and imperial armies, but the expeditious winning of the civil war was what interested him, not meaningless and ill-formed platitudes about revolutionary war. By August 1920, the Red Army had taken in almost forty-eight thousand former tsarist officers, although many of them were in service relatively briefly.[1]

The civil war in Russia got into full swing in May 1918, after the abortive attempt to disarm the Czech Legion. The Czechs soon became a nucleus for the White forces in Siberia, and from then until the end of 1920, the Red Army was engaged in a bewildering and complex series of struggles, with a variety of opponents, that swayed back and forth over the huge country. The main foreign opponents included an Anglo-American expeditionary force, the Japanese, and the French-backed Poles. A detailed discussion of these events here is unnecessary (an inquiring reader can find many sources to draw from); the subject at hand is the development of military philosophy.[2]

One of Trotsky's protégé "specialists" in the Red Army was Mikhail Tukhachevski, an aristocrat educated in the Corps of Cadets and the Alexander Military School—hardly the stuff of which revolutionaries are born. Yet after the revolution, Tukhachevski threw himself with great ardor into the Bolshevik cause and quickly distinguished himself as one of the Red Army's ablest commanders and strongest theoreticians. After winning his spurs against the White general Denikin as commander of the First Red Army on the southern front, Tukhachevski began to strike out on his own and take positions that were in direct opposition to Trotsky's. As might be expected, much of the debate about doctrine and strategy was carried out on two levels—a high, theoretical plane and that of a low, vicious struggle for mastery over the armed forces.

The opening shots in the doctrinal battle were fired essentially over what would later become a side issue: the question of the territorial militia. In their writings, Marx and Engels had espoused the idea that irregular militia-type forces were better than maintaining a large standing army.* Whatever the real significance of these writings may have been, the arguments over them quickly evolved into a bitter and personal feud that turned out to have very high stakes. It was Tukhachevski who initiated the fray by making a number of statements in 1920 calling for an "international general staff of the proletariat," which would lend assistance to the embattled revolutionaries of other countries. In taking this extreme position regarding revolutionary wars and the participation of the Red Army, Tukhachevski preempted the "left" position that Trotsky had sought to carve out for himself with his theory of the "permanent revolution." Trotsky here allowed himself to be outmaneuvered and forced to adopt a position to the "right" of Tukhachevski.

Trotsky had already been in a state of siege defending his use of the "specialists," and now he made matters much worse by saying that nothing was wrong with emulating traditional bourgeois military methods once the Soviets had seized power. Trotsky might have had his way with the upstart Tukhachevski in 1920, but he stayed his hand, probably not realizing how serious was the threat to his power. A new figure now emerged on the doctrinal scene in the role of mediator and holder of the middle ground between the feuding camps. This occupier of the center position had proven himself in the civil war in April–June 1919 in the counteroffensive against Kolchak in the Urals. His name was Mikhail Vasilievich Frunze; his patron was Joseph Stalin.[3]

In March 1921, Frunze and S. I. Gusev, then chief of the political administration of the Red Army, presented twenty-two theses to the Tenth Party Congress in Moscow. Gusev is reputed to have composed the first sixteen points and Frunze the remaining six. Gusev homed in on a few specific ideas, calling in the main for remedying qualitative deficiencies in the Red Army, especially in the command apparatus, and for strengthening the army politi-

---

*Curiously, N. S. Khrushchev advocated a "territorial" concept for the army in 1963 shortly before his ouster.

cal apparatus to enable it to guard against the danger of "Bonapartism"—that is, a potential takeover of the government by a military strongman. For his part, Frunze submitted a range of proposals that were breathtaking in scope. The central part of his idea was that a so-called unified military doctrine should be developed on the basis of Marxist teachings. This development would be undertaken by a general staff or "brain of the army," which would become "the military-theoretical staff of the proletarian state." To the congress, Trotsky objected that the Frunze-Gusev theses were not specific enough and so they were officially withdrawn, but these were merely skirmishing shots, the main battle between the forces of Stalin and Trotsky was yet to come. One might suppose that this debate was nothing more than a smokescreen behind which Stalin was seeking ways to gain political leverage against his rival, but even though the debate only makes sense within this context, the issues were real and they did reflect the turmoil and confusion in the young Soviet state about the future direction of military thought.

The world had a chance to see how far Frunze's thinking had advanced with the publication of his article "A Unified Military Doctrine and the Red Army," which appeared in the July 1921 issue of *Army and Revolution.* Frunze stated that wars were no longer waged by professional armies but by the entire population and productive means of the state and that there was a definite link between military science and the productive forces and class nature of the country. Frunze used Germany as an example; its state goals and foreign policy were aggressive, hence its military doctrine was offensive-minded. It was, by contrast, the basic goal of the dictatorship of the proletariat to smash capitalist relationships. Temporary coexistence with capitalism was possible, but "the common, parallel existence of our proletarian Soviet state with the states of the bourgeois capitalist world for a protracted period is not possible." Frunze, thus, like Lenin, believed that the force of arms must eventually decide the outcome in a battle of class enemies. Frunze favored seizure of the initiative by the proletariat and the carrying out of an offensive against the bourgeoisie. Clearly, he was an advocate of preemptive war. This kind of war had the advantage of surprise and would make up for the Red Army's technical inferiority vis-á-vis the armies of western Europe. Such an offensive should make use of the Red Army's ability to maneuver on a huge scale, enhancing its natural advantages. Should, however, the army of the Soviets not strike the first blow, then it was possible to retreat over great distances, as Kutuzov did in his campaign with Napoleon. The offensive, though, was always the instrument that would defeat the enemy, and a withdrawal should only be carried out while awaiting an opportunity for a counteroffensive when the enemy least expected it. Here, Suvorov was held up as the model for offensive tactics. In particular, Frunze stressed that field-maneuverable armies were more important than static fortifications and that preparations could be made in advance to conduct partisan operations behind the lines of an advancing enemy. Frunze put the strongest emphasis on deep maneuver utilizing cavalry (later, he said armor). And finally, he noted that, for the best effect, the military organization should be patterned after the Communist society: the authority of the officers should not be lessened, and there should be no equality between them and the enlisted masses.

Trotsky's rebuttal appeared in December 1921, in an article entitled "Military Doctrine or Pseudo-Military Doctrinairism?" Trotsky stated that there were no ready recipes in Marx's writings for developing a unified military doctrine for the Red Army. As for the ability of the army to take offensive action, Trotsky pointed out that much of the civil war required maneuvers of defense and retreat—a comment that was bound to spark resentment in the military ranks. He also said that the Red Army used whatever manpower resources were at hand, not just the proletariat. Objective conditions alone shape military doctrine, not some universal laws of military science.

When the Eleventh Party Congress was held in Moscow in March–April 1922, the debate over the military question continued in an even more serious vein between Trotsky and Stalin's proxies. This time it was K. E. Voroshilov, long a hand-picked protégé of Stalin's, who took up the cudgels in favor of a unified doctrine and continued the emphasis on revolutionary wars. Undaunted, Trotsky scored a telling point with the argument that an army primarily made up of peasants could not be trained to support an international proletarian revolution. As for a universal or unified doctrine based on Marxist principles, Trotsky paraphrased Suvorov's "seven laws of war" and proposed that Frunze's ideas were a parody of these. How, said Trotsky, could the serf army of

Suvorov's day compare with the modern, politically conscious Red Army? He also took issue with the notion that the Red Army could participate in offensive wars in support of revolutions beyond Russia's borders. It was all-important that a war be made to appear defensive in nature, otherwise the peasants would not be convinced that the war was a just cause.

This last view of Trotsky's must have been particularly galling to those who cherished the internationalist cause, although it came close to some of the goals stressed later by Stalin in his program of "socialism in one country." Trotsky's assertion that there were no universal laws of war was not in agreement, either, with Lenin, who had put forth six fundamental laws of Soviet military strategy as follows: (1) Understand the significance of choosing the direction of the main blow against the enemy. (2) Create a superiority of forces and resources in the direction of this blow. (3) Change forms and methods of combat depending on the situation. (4) Organize troops depending upon the methods of warfare. (5) Understand the significance of strategic reserves. (6) Stress the importance of strategic leadership. Lenin also said, "To have an overwhelming advantage of forces at the decisive moment at the decisive point— that is the 'law' of military success."[4]

Trotsky's campaign for continued control of the military and its doctrine may have ended in personal tragedy for himself, but it cannot be said that others did not heed his warnings. The fact was that he was right about the peasant composition of the army, and all the ideologues aside, nothing could change that basic reality. The competition between the groups supporting Stalin and Trotsky intensified after May 1922, when Lenin suffered the first in a series of paralytic strokes that would eventually kill him. By then it was obvious that a major struggle for succession would not long be postponed.

The struggle over control of the military became more clear when Trotsky's man, V. A. Antonov-Ovseenko, was removed as the head of Main Military Political Administration (PUR) in January 1924. In January 1925, Trotsky was removed from the Revolutionary Soviet, and in the same month Frunze succeeded him as commissar for war. Frunze's personal triumph was, however, brief. By the summer of 1925 he was seriously ill with an intestinal ailment, and he also suffered from a weak heart. Against his wishes, Frunze submitted to an operation on the orders of the Central

Committee, and by the end of October he was dead. His death was officially said to have been caused by an allergic reaction to chloroform, but there is some reason to believe that Stalin had him killed in order to replace him with Voroshilov. At any rate, in November of that year Voroshilov succeeded Frunze, thus completing another step in locking the support of the military in Stalin's hands. His grasp for power was furthered in November 1927, when Trotsky and his associate Zinoviev were expelled from the Party; soon afterward the former commissar for war was exiled to Central Asia.* By December 1929, after the public condemnation of Bukharin, Tomsky, and Rykov, Stalin became the undisputed *vozhd,* or leader of Russia.

Stalin's accession to power as supreme ruler was heralded by the launching of the Soviet Union into the industrial age through the inauguration of the first Five-Year plan. The military purpose of the Five-Year plans can be seen in the following statement by Stalin: "The basic task of the Five-Year plans was to create such an industry in our country as to be able to rearm and reorganize not only industry as a whole, but also transportation and agriculture—on the basis of socialism." It can be seen from the data currently available that under Stalin defense-related expenditures were given a higher priority than investment in heavy industry. During the period 1928–1952, the years of Stalin's rule, funds designated for military purposes increased by a factor of twenty-six times, while the real investment in heavy industry increased by only half as much.

After 1933 and the rise to power of Hitler and the Nazi party in Germany, even closer attention was paid to defense planning, in terms both of theory and practical application. The relationship of the Soviet Union with Germany was one of both love and hate in the 1920s and 1930s: Love, because both sides had been losers in the First World War and because they had nowhere else to turn but to each other for allies. Hate, because Germany was clearly the Soviet Union's greatest potential rival in eastern and central Europe and because Hitler's Nazi party ideology was unreservedly hostile to bolshevism. The Nazis classified the Slavic peoples as inferior to the Germanic; they described them as suitable only for slavery and their countries as fit only for German colonization. An

---

*Trotsky was assassinated on orders from Stalin in Mexico City in August 1940.

attempt was made by well-meaning Russians and Germans to arrive at some sort of military collaboration, which, after 1921, took the form of joint training exercises in the Soviet Union. The Treaty of Rapallo in 1922 publicly declared the two underdogs' mutual interest in cooperation, but the friendship was always strained and could never last. The social and political systems of Germany and the Soviet Union diverged and then became rabidly antagonistic.

It is against this varied background of turmoil and change in a country in the throes of massive economic upheaval, the consolidation of a rigid personal dictatorship under Stalin, and the growing potential threat from a hostile and rearming Germany, that the development of military doctrine in the Soviet Union in the 1930s must be understood.

By 1922, the main concerns in military theory were twofold: (1) how to make use of the coming economic and political collapse of the West and the resulting revolutionary situation and (2) how to make the most out of the experiences gained by the Red Army in the civil war. It did not take long for the blind faith in the immediate decline of the West to die. It took longer, however, for those who wished to exalt the lessons of the civil war to lose their voice. The first attempt at putting these lessons to practical use came with the issuance of Provisional Field Service Regulations in June 1925. Much of what was said in this document could, it seems, have been taken from Suvorov. These regulations called for close cooperation of all types of arms and described the offensive as the main form of warfare. The goal of any defensive action was to gain time for delivering the crushing offensive blow, to hold the enemy in a static position and smite him on the flanks. Close attention was also paid to the investing and holding of critical zones. The emphasis on the offensive and its relationship to defensive operations, dating back to Suvorov, could be described as uniquely Russian. These teachings were not lost on Zhukov and the general staff in 1941, as will be seen later.

After the implementation of the 1925 provisional regulations, it became clear to some thinkers that it was not enough to study the lessons of the civil war. One expert emerged who began to advocate some patently classical solutions, which is not surprising, since he had earned his credits as an officer in the imperial Russian army. His name was A. A. Svechin and his book, first published in 1927, was entitled *Strategy*. In a very conventional way, reminiscent perhaps of Falkenhayn's strategy at Verdun, Svechin advocated a large-scale war of attrition. One of the interesting aspects of this approach was, so it appeared to Svechin, the possibility of devastating the morale in the enemy camp with a war that dragged on interminably with mounting casualties. This was, of course, precisely what Russia had suffered in the period from 1914 to 1917, and the underlying assumption, however false it might have been, was that the new Communist society in Russia would impart a moral courage to the nation and the people that it had lacked earlier.*

As might be supposed, this theory of attrition flew in the face of logic to many who still cherished the belief that a strong enemy could be vanquished only through force of arms in a great offensive action. One of the parties rankled by Svechin's approach was Tukhachevski, who became very bitter about the criticism of his bungled offensive toward Warsaw in 1920. Tukhachevski also disagreed with A. I. Verkhovskii, the former imperial minister of war, who accepted the ideas of the British military thinker J.F.C. Fuller about tanks and aviation being the new wave of modern warfare. By referring to these new ideas cropping up in Russia as "the small mechanized armies of the type of the Fascist police," Tukhachevski showed himself a strong advocate of the mass concept of armies that Russia had always professed to rely on. When Verkhovskii spoke of the need for small professional armies, as de Gaulle had advocated for France, Tukhachevski said that such an "elitist" concept denied the advantages of mass, mobile, offensively trained armies.

During the course of the 1930s, the "one-weapon elitists" were defeated, largely due to Tukhachevski. Such theories as the overweening reliance on the tank or the airplane ran completely counter to the philosophy of the social-political foundations of the Red Army. In 1941, Zhukov would build on Tukhachevski's ideas and develop a harmonious concept of defense, offense, and attrition that would go beyond the understanding of the leaders of the German Wehrmacht and that is, in fact, poorly understood in the West even today. There are still many in our part of the world who

---

*It should be pointed out that, after 1941, the war on the eastern front did turn out to be a war of attrition, but the moral superiority over the Nazis, though real, was exceptionally narrow and was literally thrust into the hands of Stalin.

believe that the Nazi concept of blitzkrieg would have worked in Russia without a political and economic program that would appeal to the Russian people to back it up. It can be hoped that a clearer understanding of the real situation in the Soviet Union will eventually emerge.

In 1927 the first of three volumes of a major work of military theory was published: *The Brain of the Army,* written by B. M. Shaposhnikov. The subject of this book was the organization and role of the Red Army general staff. There can be little doubt that the book influenced the thoughts of Voroshilov and Stalin; in 1937, Shaposhnikov was made chief of the general staff. The Red Army general staff underwent a gradual evolution, and although it was superseded by the STAVKA, Stalin's personal military staff from 1941 to 1945, it became extremely significant after the war, having much more responsibility and authority than the U.S. Joint Chiefs.[5]

By 1929, the Red Army command was ready to attempt a partial application of some of the new philosophies of war that were then being advanced in the West. The embodiment of this experiment was contained in Field Regulations of 1929 (PU–29). The PU–29 was a document authored mainly by the theoretician V. K. Triandafilov, but the commission that finally approved it had been appointed by Voroshilov. One of the non-Western innovations put forward by PU–29 was the elevation of the political commissars in the hierarchy of the Red Army; they were to be the backbone of military morale. The meat of the new regulations, however, was a flirtation with the opportunities presented by the tank as demonstrated by J.F.C. Fuller. PU–29 went a half-step toward adopting the view that independent armored operations were the wave of the future, but it maintained some of the more traditional features of Russian military doctrine. Some months before his death in a plane crash in 1931, Triandafilov amplified his stand on tactics in a special report to the general staff entitled "Basic Questions of Tactics and Operational Art in Connection with the Reconstruction of the Army."[6]

Triandafilov's report was a curious amalgam of purely Russian doctrine, heavily flavored with the somewhat faddish ideas then current abroad. The Russian elements could be seen in the concern given to combined-arms tactics and the theory of deep battle, whereas the Western elements were visible in the attention paid to the use of armor. Triandafilov envisioned an integration of combined-arms and independent armored operations. He stated that the new forms of technical equipment then available would allow the enemy to be attacked "in the entire depth of his tactical deployment." Several echelons of tanks can attack the enemy's first line of defense in cooperation with infantry supported by artillery and close air support. Conditions could thus be created that would be favorable for simultaneous operations over broad expanses of front and at great depth. Even though the doctrine presented in Triandafilov's report was lacking in specifics and the philosophy behind it was somewhat murky, the general tone it set did have some influence. In February 1933, the war commissariat approved and issued to the armed forces a program entitled "Provisional Regulations Regarding the Organization of Deep Battle," which was based on Triandafilov's work as well as that of the new chief of the general staff, A. I. Egorov, and his operations officer, I. P. Obysov.

The work of Triandafilov and Egorov was carried further toward a workable solution by M. N. Tukhachevski, Trotsky's old foe, who became the deputy chief of the general staff in 1924 after serving as head of the Red Army Military Academy. Although Tukhachevski was a man gifted with a talent for theory, he was, apparently, politically naive. He eventually aroused the suspicion of Stalin (in spite of his rank as marshal) because of his wide contacts in the West, particularly within the German Wehrmacht. He was executed on the dictator's orders in June 1937. His accusation and trial led off what became a blood purge of the officer corps in that year that resulted in the liquidation of about half of the Red Army's commissioned staff.

Key elements in the evolution of Tukhachevski's thinking were the large-scale military maneuvers held in western Russia during the mid-1930s. Some of these exercises, such as the one held in the fall of 1936, were attended by Western observers. In these maneuvers, experiments were conducted with mechanized infantry and armored units used in an independent fashion. Although the information gathered then was not made public, the evidence is that the "bourgeois" theories of small armies and highly mobile armored elite units were rejected by Tukhachevski and the Red Army high command. This decision in favor of a massive armed force built around the assumption of the cooperation of all forms of units utilizing combined-arms tactics was made easier by the fact that the Russian industrial base was too weak to admit a heavy investment in armored vehicles and wheeled transport. Certainly, after the calamitous harvest of 1933, the idea of limiting tractor production in favor of tanks could not have been seriously considered. It is a basic reality of military planning in Russia's centralized economy that a failure in one sector, such as agriculture, will have an immediate and pronounced effect in other areas, such as military production. This is a lesson that the West has repeatedly ignored.

In 1934, Tukhachevski wrote an article entitled "The Character of Border Operations" in which he stated that the traditional method of moving mass armies up to the border areas by rail was now outmoded due to the danger of disruption by air attack.[7] According to Tukhachevski, the previously planned character of battles along the frontier no longer conformed with actual conditions. The only tactic that could succeed would be that of preparing a defense in depth, leading to a protracted conflict with broad fronts and deep operations. The initial struggle along the frontiers would be important but would by no means decide the issue. The new form of deep battle would allow the enemy to be destroyed by a series of actions in a given strategic direction, not just by defending the borders. In this respect, Tukhachevski remained true to the philosophy of Lenin, who believed that wars between states that had the capability of mobilizing their entire productive and population resources would always be protracted conflicts.

Tukhachevski went on to say in the article that, because of the danger of concentrating mass armies in the border sectors, it would be best to place there forward armies only strong enough to be considered the first operational echelon of the main force. In his opinion, the main force armies were to be concentrated secretly in areas that were most likely to be on the flanks of the advancing enemy. He attached much significance to fortified zones positioned along the border, which would serve as the shield, absorbing the initial shock of the enemy's offensive and covering the concentration of second echelon armies—the hammer—which would deliver blows to the enemy's flanks. The fortified regions were to offer more than just passive resistance. In Tukhachevski's plan they were to be organically connected with the maneuvers of the field army and act as support for its carrying out a general offensive operation. It is impossible here to overstate the importance of these conclusions; it was on the basis of them that Zhukov and Stalin implemented a plan for defense against Germany in 1941, as will be seen later in the chapter.

On the use of armor, Tukhachevski's ideas followed Trianda-filov's to a certain extent as he attempted to describe specific ways in which independent tank operations could be carried out. Tukhachevski proposed that armored units be divided into different categories depending upon the operational characteristics of the tank and the specific combat mission that was to be carried out. Essentially, there should be three echelons of tanks: (1) tanks for close support of infantry (NPP), which could be slower models of relatively limited range, (2) tanks for distant support of infantry (DPP), which could move faster and farther, and (3) independent long-range striking armor (DD). In the period before the infantry attack in the offensive operation, the artillery and air cover should be used to support the tanks in their initial breakthrough of the enemy lines. Here, Tukhachevski tried to bridge the gap between a combined-arms philosophy and a new tactic based on independent armored operations. The general tenor of this plan, as one future chief of the general staff would put it, was "to assign a mistaken importance and priority to the tanks." As will be seen, however, events leading up to the German invasion of 1941 compelled Stalin and the then chief of the general staff, Zhukov, to reject this concept and to rely almost totally on close infantry-armor cooperation. It should be mentioned also that a parallel attempt was being made in the early 1930s to come to grips with the use of independent strategic air power, the virtues of which had been extolled by the Italian general Douhet. Triandafilov and B. M. Feldmann had written an article entitled "Characteristics of New Tendencies in the Military Sphere" in which they advocated the creation of a strategic air arm. This approach was roundly criticized by R. P. Eideman, Tukhachevski's successor as head of the Frunze Military Academy, who believed that the air force's major role should be to support the army.[8]

After some degree of debate and study, in December 1934 the defense commissariat decided that the "deep battle" scenario proposed by Tukhachevski was not merely a type of tactic but a wholly new and different strategy that included many tactical variants. During a meeting that month, Voroshilov declared that this new theory should be put into practical use at once. Egorov agreed, saying that tanks were to be considered "core units" in the "deep battle" concept. These theories were, in fact, embodied in Field Regulations of 1936 (PU–36). However one might try to apply the new ideas of using armor, the reality was that Russia still lacked the industrial base to mechanize the Red Army as fully as its potential opponents in the West. Germany had already begun its program of full-scale rearmament in 1934, and there were other ominous clouds on the horizon: the Spanish civil war was being waged in full fury by the summer of 1936, and both Russia and Germany would become progressively more involved in this conflict. A more chilling portent for the future was also visible in 1936; in August the trials began for the so-called Trotsky-Zinoviev center, events that proved to be preludes to the massive purges in the party, in the NKVD state security apparatus itself, and finally, in the military.

PU–36 fully reflected the main ideas about deep battle worked out by Tukhachevski and his colleagues. PU–36 stated, in part, that "The enemy is to be paralyzed in the entire depth of his deployment, surrounded and destroyed." PU–36 seemed in tune with the rest of the world when Heinz Guderian's book *Achtung Panzer* was published early the next year. In the offensive operations, tanks were to be employed on a mass scale in echelons, as Tukhachevski had already proposed. Taking a leaf from the books of the Western theorists, PU–36 called for aviation to be used also on a large scale "concentrating the forces according to the times and targets which have the greatest tactical importance." The new field regulations assigned a leading role to artillery in achieving tactical breakthroughs of enemy defenses.

The day of the "artillery offensive" so effectively employed by the Red Army had not yet arrived, but still, PU–36 attempted to come to grips with the problem of the spatial gaps that would widen between fast-moving armored groups and slower artillery units. The Germans tried to get around this problem by using the JU–87 Stuka dive-bomber in a close support role in cooperation with the tanks. The Russian planners, too, favored this approach for their aviation, but the distances in Russia proved too great for the air force (VVS) to manage. The fact is, neither side had enough aircraft to make up for the lack of self-propelled artillery support for long-distance drives by armored spearheads. The Germans found this out to their sorrow after penetrating to the Dnepr line in July 1941. The Germans paid their price in blood for his lesson and, after the reverses in the Army Group Center area in December 1941, were not able to recoup their offensive posture on this strategic front.

The Soviet General Staff Academy, which was founded in 1936, took the new regulations to heart, but there were those who sensed the need for caution. G. Isserson, then a lecturer at the academy, later pointed out a fatal flaw in the deep battle concept. The whole plan was predicated upon the assumption that it would be the Red Army that would be carrying out the offensives and that a future war would be fought mainly on the enemy's territory. In other words, little or no thought was openly being given to deep battle *defensive* operations. One only had to cast one's eyes to the West—the growing power of Germany and the swelling storm in Spain—to see that this future war might have a different beginning. Isserson's comments about this are very interesting in light of the events of 1941 that will be examined later.

> On the other hand, it was the deepest awareness of the highest officers of the general staff that the beginning period of the war could commence quite differently. In some circles of the general staff and in the General Staff Academy these problems were discussed concretely and the necessary calculations were made. However, these discussions took place only behind closed doors and were not given an official airing.[9]

Isserson also says that Stalin's "cult of personality" was responsible for the gap in defense planning, but clearly the problem was a great deal larger than that. Stalin had not yet grasped firm hold over the military, nor had he succeeded in finding people he could trust who would give him objective advice about the whole direction of military strategy, let alone tactics. Voroshilov turned out to be a plodder and a yes-man as the 1939 war against Finland would show, and Tukhachevski proved to be a gadfly, constantly flirting with his contacts in the West. Eventually, these contacts were used by Reinhard Heydrich of the Nazi SD secret police to fabricate false evidence against Tukhachevski showing him guilty of treason. Whether Stalin actually believed the counterfeit documents prepared by Heydrich or not is immaterial; Stalin came to believe that Tukhachevski had become too immersed in the West and was no longer to be trusted. When the old Bolshevik Karl

Radek was brought to trial in January 1937, a collective shudder went down the spine of the officer corps at the mention of Tukhachevski's name in connection with certain evidence bearing on treasonable activities. The end could not be long in coming. By the summer of that year Tukhachevski had been arrested and shot, and by the end of the year a dreadful blood purge of the officer corps was taking place. The instrumentality for this purge was the NKVD security apparatus then headed by N. I. Yezhov, known as the "bloodthirsty dwarf" (he stood only five feet high), whose reign of terror is called the "Yezhovshchina" in the Soviet Union. By the end of 1937 Stalin ruled the military with an iron hand through the person of Lev Mekhlis, the head of the military main political administration (PUR). Even today, Mekhlis's name is used as a synonym for terror in Soviet military publications. The final figures of the purges reveal the fearful consequences: About thirty-five thousand officers were killed, or roughly half the corps. Three out of 5 marshals were killed, 13 out of 15 army commanders, 57 out of 85 corps commanders, 110 out of 195 division commanders, and 220 out of 406 brigade commanders.[10]

But like the phoenix from the ashes, the officer corps rose again from the ruins of the former organization. The new group of men owed their careers and even their lives to Stalin. Those who had been spared the purge, like G. K. Zhukov, S. K. Timoshenko, and B. M. Shaposhnikov, were able to move up swiftly in rank provided they had the natural instincts and abilities to survive in a very tough environment. The Red Army had not been battle-tested on a large scale since the war with Poland and the abortive advance on Warsaw in 1920, but this peaceful lull was soon to be sharply broken. Russia's old enemy, Japan, had been increasing its forces rapidly in China since 1934, and now it was ready to test the sinews of the Red Army in a place where its supply lines were stretched thinnest: in Mongolia, which had become a Soviet satellite in 1922. First at Lake Khasan in the summer of 1938 and then at Khalkhin–Gol in the spring of 1939, the Japanese strove mightily with infantry, armor, artillery, and air power to push the Red Army back into the Soviet Union proper, but these attempts failed.

The Japanese attack at Lake Khasan was thwarted by Marshal Blukher, a curious man who may have wished to become potentate of Siberia—until he was cut down by Yezhov's henchmen virtually on the morrow of his victory in Mongolia. The Japanese assault at

Khalkhin–Gol, by contrast, was broken by a man who received high awards from Stalin and was much trusted by him, Georgii Zhukov. Zhukov was probably successful under Stalin first of all because, at least in his early years, he was unassuming and unpretentious. Zhukov also had two other characteristics that the dictator valued: he had the habit of telling the blunt truth when asked (as we shall see he did in 1941) and he had the habit of being right.

At Khalkhin–Gol Zhukov used a combined-arms counteroffensive to sweep the enemy from the battlefield. It has been said that here he demonstrated the effectiveness of an independent armored thrust, but this is not really true. There was a freewheeling armored encirclement of some Japanese units, but this was carried out on a narrow front with limited range and depth, hardly to be compared with the great German panzer "cauldrons" of 1941. After Khalkhin–Gol, Zhukov was definitely a comer. He gained more experience in Finland and in Bessarabia in 1940. Finally, he was relied upon by Stalin to pull Russia out of the worst crisis it had faced since the seventeenth century.

As a result of Zhukov's experiences against the Japanese and the tank commander D. G. Pavlov's difficulties in Spain, in November 1939 the order went out to disband the tank corps, which had been first created in 1932 (then called mechanized corps), and use the tanks in close cooperation with the infantry. Pavlov's attempts to employ armor independently had come to grief in Esquivas, south of Madrid, where tanks operating inside a town with narrow streets without infantry support had proven to be quite ineffective.[11] But the controversy regarding tanks was far from over, especially after the failure of the Red Army to achieve a decisive victory in Finland in the winter war of 1939–1940 and after Guderian's rapid blitzkrieg defeat of France in May–June 1940.[12] The debate was stirred anew in an article by I. P. Sukhov entitled "Tanks in Contemporary War" published soon after the fall of France.[13] Sukhov was a senior lecturer, and later head, of the Military Academy for the Motorization and Mechanization of the Red Army in Moscow. He denied that tanks operating in the depths of the enemy's forces, either on his flanks or in his rear, were risking disaster. Also, he discounted the potentially disastrous supply problems armored units might face operating far from their own bases. All of these difficulties could be overcome, he said, by creating masses of motorized infantry that would ride tracked vehicles and would be capable of keeping up with the advancing armor. Motorized artillery also would be necessary, but here the proper use of support aviation would make up for deficiencies in long-range firepower. Sukhov's article is interesting for several reasons. First of all, this was precisely the theory that the Wehrmacht attempted to put into practice in Russia a year later. Secondly, although the Red Army undertook a rapid about-face and tried to implement some of these ideas, precious little time was allowed to acquire the necessary level of motorization for the Red Army. Thirdly, this theory is very close to what the Soviet Army actually is able to do today.

As shall be seen later, the Red Army underwent a powerful wrenching in the second half of 1940 and the early months of 1941 in trying to deal with the problem of the mechanized corps. As has been stated, economic realities forced a certain logic on the Red Army as far as strategic and tactical planning was concerned. Now the question should be asked, What were the Russians doing with their economy? Needless to say, the answer is difficult to find, but it is possible to make a few shrewd guesses. Of all the major branches of military industry on the eve of 1941, the greatest development had been achieved in artillery, especially the production of cannon. This was not an accident, for artillery was considered of primary importance. Aside from a brief episode in 1941, artillery was considered by the army high command to be the main striking weapon in warfare. The real "god of war," as Stalin called artillery, was the superb Soviet 76mm gun, which fired twenty-five 6.21kg shells per minute with muzzle velocity of 680 meters per second. This gun was produced in countless thousands throughout the war in many variations, including being mounted in the T–34 tank with devastating effect. The Soviet artillery arsenal in June 1939 was 45,790 guns, and from May 1940 to the end of June 1941 production of artillery was stepped up 150 percent.[14]

There were some deficiencies in artillery, however. Khalkhin-Gol and Finland had shown the need for more mortars, and the lack of good antiaircraft and antitank artillery was also recognized, but these deficiencies were largely remedied by June 1941. There were also problems with handheld infantry weapons and a need for a good workable submachine gun that could be made in large quantities. This was eventually obtained with the development of the famous PPSh1941 "burp gun." But, try as it might, the Soviet economy was able to increase production of rifles and carbines by only 16 percent above what it had achieved in 1940, clearly an unsatisfactory level, and indicative of the load placed on the industrial base.

With regard to armor, Soviet sources give the following production figures for the latest model tanks before the war:

	1940	First half of 1941
KV heavy tanks	243	393
T–34 "medium" tanks	115	1110

The heavy KVs (Klement Voroshilovs) were produced in the Kirov factory in Leningrad and in the Cheliabinsk tractor factory in the Urals. The T–34s were produced at the Stalingrad tractor factory, which also manufactured diesel motors in large numbers, as did the Kharkov diesel works.[15] The total size of the Soviet tank park in 1941, believed to be the world's largest, is difficult to estimate, but it was clearly greater than the German intelligence estimate of about ten thousand. In July 1941, Stalin sent a letter to Roosevelt giving the figure twenty-four thousand. This figure tallies well with the best current Western estimate (22,700).[16] During the military-oriented Five-Year plans, the Soviet Union had been pouring over 26 percent of its capital investment into defense, which allowed it to accumulate vast stores of arms. By contrast, in 1941 the Germans had equipped twenty-one panzer divisions, each with about 165 tanks. Of this number, seventeen were deployed on the eastern front in June. The Germans began the war in the east with only 3,580 tanks and self-propelled guns, and of these, just 439 were the modern Panzer IVs. For all of 1941 Germany produced only 3,796 tanks and self-propelled guns.[17]

Perhaps the area of greatest deficiency in Soviet armaments was that of motor transport. In 1941 the mechanized corps had approximately a third of their necessary trucks. This lack of vehicles acted as a serious handicap to the Red Army's ability to maneuver rapidly throughout the entire war. At the end of the war Russian tank armies were still 10–25 percent short of vehicles, but even this advance in numbers was not due to indigenous production. In the spring of 1945 the Soviet armed forces were estimated to have about 665,000 motor vehicles of all types; of these, some 427,000 had been shipped to the USSR from the United States through the Lend-Lease agreement. It is believed that in 1945 fully 50 percent of all vehicles actually in service in the Soviet armed forces were American. This aid, plus hundreds of locomotives and thousands of railroad cars, large numbers of aircraft, and other kinds of equipment, such as radios, gave the Russians the transport, the mobility, and the communications they needed to defeat the Wehrmacht. Without this aid, their full and strategic victory would have been made extraordinarily more difficult, if not impossible.[18]*

The huge Soviet investment in weapons manufacture was bound to put a strain on an economy that produced in 1940 only 18.3 million metric tons of steel versus the United States' 62.5 million, Britain's 13.2 million, and Germany's (with its occupied territories) 31.8 million tons. After the war began for Russia in June 1941, even higher levels of armaments were produced. In the second half of 1941, the Soviet Union produced 4,177 tanks. In 1942 Russia produced 25,000 planes to Germany's 14,700, 24,700 tanks and armored vehicles to Germany's 9,300, 29,500 artillery pieces over 75mm to Germany's 12,000, 4,049,000 rifles and carbines to Germany's 1,370,000.[19] These graphic statistics alone spelled doom for Germany after the failure of its blitzkrieg campaign in Russia. The reasons for this failure will be examined in the following chapters.

In summary, the period of the 1920s and 1930s was a dynamic one for the development of Soviet military theory. The advocates of the mass theory of war, such as Svechin, seemed to give way to other theorists, like Verkhovskii and Triandafilov, who were enamored of the concepts of war being advocated by Fuller, Douhet, Liddell Hart, Guderian, and others in the West. There were those, mainly Tukhachevski and Shaposhnikov, who advocated a more nearly Russian approach, relying on the mass army concept and the use of combined-arms tactics. Still, the attempts to bridge the gap between the native Russian way of war and the Western methods proved to be awkward and perhaps largely ineffective. The root of most of this wasted energy rested in Stalin's rigid con-

---

*It should be noted as an aside that some trucks being used in the Afghanistan operations by the Soviet Army apparently were manufactured in the Kama River truck factory, which was built with the help of the United States. They are being so used despite promises by Soviet leaders that vehicles built there would not be used for military purposes.

solidation of personal power, which led to too many conflicts in the society and the economy that could not be patched up in time to allow the Red Army to mechanize properly. How these contradictions were resolved enough for Russia to repel the Nazi invaders will be examined next.

THE STRATEGY FOR THE DEFENSE OF THE SOVIET UNION IN 1941

The astonishing success achieved by the Wehrmacht in the summer and fall of 1941 has prompted most military experts in the West to assume that Russia was caught off guard by the suddenness of the German assault. It has been assumed by the most knowledgeable generals and historians that the USSR did not have a strategy for defense in 1941 and that the Red Army was pushed back by the invaders pell-mell into its own hinterland, where it was eventually saved by the miraculous combination of an early, severe winter and some incredible blunders, mostly Hitler's, on the part of the Germans.[20]

As easy as these interpretations might be to accept, nevertheless they leave several questions unanswered: (1) After suffering severe losses so close to the frontier in June 1941, how was the Red Army able to regroup so rapidly and offer such a tenacious resistance a month later at Kiev-Korosten, Gomel, Smolensk-Yelnia, and Velikie Luki-Staraia Russa? (2) How could the desperate situation that existed in the area of German Army Group South and on the southern flank of Army Group Center in July-August 1941 possibly have permitted the rapid continuation of an offensive in the direction of Moscow? (3) Why did large numbers of the newer T-34 and KV tanks, along with the latest model MiG-3 aircraft and others, begin to appear only in October, after the bulk of the Soviet armor and air force supposedly had been destroyed in the earlier battles of encirclement and annihilation at Bialystok-Minsk, Smolensk, and Kiev? (4) How was the Red Army able to mount a counteroffensive in early December at the very gates of Moscow with a force of seven armies, a force that enabled it to enjoy a 50 percent numerical superiority over the Wehrmacht along some key axes of the attack?[21] If the answers to these questions are ignored or glossed over, then the facts themselves will have to be tossed aside or deliberately distorted. It will not do to offer the weather or Hitler's blunders to explain what happened to the German Army in 1941. Only by probing more deeply into the events of the summer of 1941 will it be possible to explain what led to Germany's disaster.

By the end of 1940, the amalgamated deep operations and combined-arms method of tactics, as developed and modified by V. K. Triandafilov and M. N. Tukhachevski between 1929 and 1936, had come dangerously close to becoming a one-edge sword, honed for cutting at the enemy in sharp offensive thrusts, but ill designed for parrying strokes in a defensive maneuver. The reason for this was that, after the purges in the military in 1937–1938, defense planning was allowed to languish. If the Soviet Union had continued to place its hopes on being able to begin a war with Germany at a time and place of its own choosing, presumably in 1943 or 1944, after Germany had again become locked in a ground war on its western front, then, no doubt, great trouble would have resulted.[22] That the country found its salvation before it was too late was not due to luck or fate—it was due to the steady vision of a remarkable man, Georgii Zhukov. It was Zhukov who took the basic precepts of the combined-arms–deep operations tactics, worked out in many of their essentials in the 1930s, and gave the Red Army a concrete and workable plan for defense in 1941. Zhukov would have only four-and-a-half short months to put his ideas into effect. That the Soviet state exists today is testament to the correctness of his vision, although he received an extraordinary amount of help in the form of egregious blunders made by Hitler and the German high command.

Tukhachevski's theories of offensive action, joining the combined-arms and deep operations tactics, have been discussed many times and in great detail by Soviet historians.[23] There are also some excellent Western commentaries on this subject, but none of them, Eastern or Western, attempt to show the close interrelationship of theory and fact in 1941, for the combined-arms–deep operations tactics provided a unique basis for the formulation of a defensive strategy for the Soviet Union.[24] It is true that the line separating strategy from tactics seems somewhat metaphysical, but the development of the theory of deep operations had already opened the way in Soviet military thought for tactical planning on a grand scale. Due to the efforts of Tukhachevski, by 1936 the USSR had already evolved two separate offensive and defensive strategies founded on the precepts of the deep operations–

combined-arms theories of tactics. But after Tukhachevski's execution in 1937 little effort was spent on the defensive aspect of a future war, or on a war on the territory of the Soviet Union itself. By early 1941, Zhukov had succeeded in uniting these offensive and defensive strategies into one harmonious concept of war that went beyond the simple, straightforward plans of their future adversaries. But all was not to be easy for the Red Army or the Russian people. Zhukov had to make some critical guesses about the Germans' schemes for achieving a strategic victory over their country. He was nearly proven wrong.

In working out the plans for a strategic defense on a large scale, Tukhachevski and subsequent theoreticians made the most of the two commodities that the USSR had in abundance, distance and manpower—much of which could be sacrificed in the beginning (if necessary) in order to regain the initiative and hand the enemy a setback at the proper moment. In developing a suitable method for carrying out a strategic defense against an invasion from the west, Tukhachevski and his successors used the deep operations theory of echeloning the phases of an offensive in reverse. In a deep operations offensive each arm or branch of arms was assigned a position in the attacking echelons according to the characteristics of speed, armament, and firepower they each possessed. The strategy for defense essentially mirrored this concept, envisioning the theater of battle as being divided into three zones of maneuver: (1) the tactical zone of defense, the area initially affected by the enemy's attack; (2) the operational zone of defense, the area behind and up to 250 kilometers to the rear of the main line of resistance; and (3) the strategic zone of defense, in an area from 250 kilometers behind the main line of resistance.[25] In Tukhachevski's original plan the frontier armies positioned farthest to the west, protected by their fortifications, would be only the first, that is, the tactical, zone of defense. It would be the duty of the operational group behind the first tactical zone to attack the flanks of the enemy army as it advanced farther east, exhausting the opponent and draining his strength while awaiting the proper moment for committing the third echelon, the strategic reserve, in an all-out counteroffensive maneuver.[26] The political-strategical situation in 1941 had changed a great deal from what it had been in 1934, but it was on the basis of Tukhachevski's theories that the General Staff Academy began work in 1936 preparing the country's future high military officers for the approaching war.[27] Unfortunately, however, the preparation of a thoroughgoing defense plan prior to 1941 was not possible, for several reasons.

Throughout the year 1940, the political and military leadership of the Red Army was on a false track, guided by the assumption that the most likely kind of operation the armed forces would be required to undertake would be to break through an enemy fortified zone, as had been the case in the winter war in Finland. In an article published in February 1941, Maj. Gen. K. D. Golubev, commander of the Tenth Army, positioned within the Bialystok salient, declared that the Red Army was studying in detail the experiences of breakthrough operations in 1914–1918, 1939–1940, and "the exceptionally rich experience in the breakthrough of the Mannerheim Line."[28] Another factor that delayed proper defense preparations was the momentary panic in the summer of 1940 that affected everyone, apparently also Stalin, following the swift German victory over France. In June 1940, the commissar for defense, S. K. Timoshenko, reported to Stalin on the results of the German blitzkrieg campaign. During this same month Timoshenko ordered, with Stalin's approval, the reestablishment of the large armored units that had been disbanded in November 1939. In February 1941, the formation of twenty mechanized corps was authorized, each to be composed of two tank divisions and one motorized, more or less on the German model. The new mechanized corps were to be particularly large organizations, each tank division having 375 tanks, 11,343 troops, and 60 guns. The motorized division, in addition to two motorized regiments and other units, would have 275 light tanks. The total for the corps was intended to be 37,000 men, 1,025–1,031 tanks, 268 armored cars, and 358 guns and mortars from 76mm to 122mm. By way of contrast, the 1939 tank corps were supposed to have 660 tanks, 118 artillery pieces, and 12,710 men.[29] Such spasmodic, kneejerk reactions to events could not help but have an adverse effect on the coordination of plans for defense. As a matter of fact, the Soviet Union had not nearly enough time to carry out such a massive mechanization of the Red Army; Soviet sources note that in June 1941 only four of the nine existing mechanized corps were fully battle ready.[30] Another more practical solution for countering the German threat had to be found in a hurry.

It is not easy to explain the Red Army's consistent preoccupation with methods of offensive warfare during the years 1939 and 1940 without supposing that Stalin harbored the secret intention to send it, sooner or later, on an advance westward. It has been said that it was Stalin's personal decision that forced the Red Army to base its combined-arms–deep operations tactics on the premise that it would be the Soviet Union that would take the offensive and carry the war immediately into the enemy's territory.[31] For this reason, the controversy over an offensive versus a defensive strategy to meet the German threat was not finally resolved until a series of Kremlin conferences and war games held in late 1940 and early 1941. It was then, during the methodical examination of alternatives available to the Red Army and the playing out of various solutions to tactical problems on the map, that Zhukov came into his ascendancy. In Stalin's eyes, Zhukov had correctly foreseen the course of coming events, and from January 1941 on, this man's destiny and the fate of the Soviet Union were inextricably intertwined.

The first round of conferences was held December 23–31 and was attended by the commanders of the military districts and armies, members of the military councils, the chiefs of staff of the districts and armies, commanders of the military academies, professors of military science, ranking general staff officers, and others, including members of the Politburo.[32] Virtually the entire emphasis of this conference was on the conduct of offensive operations. It is significant that even in Timoshenko's summation report there was not a word on defensive strategy or tactics.[33]

Zhukov, present as head of Kiev Special Military District, had been notified as early as September to prepare a report for the conference entitled "The Nature of Modern Offensive Operations." It is not likely that Zhukov was assigned this topic accidentally, for his reputation as a leader of offensive operations had already been well established at Khalkhin–Gol against the Japanese in 1939, and he had gained more experience in the summer of 1940 when the Soviet Union occupied northern Bukovina and Bessarabia. From the content of this report, it can be seen that Zhukov had progressed a long way toward uniting the combined-arms and deep operations tactics into a new kind of offensive strategy.[34] The reliance on combined-arms "shock armies" to achieve breakthroughs that could be pushed to depths of up to two hundred or three hundred kilometers was far more reasonable than the German plan for exploiting a strategic breakthrough for distances up to a thousand kilometers inside Russia.

The character of Zhukov's assignment also reveals the importance the Kremlin attached to the area south of the Pripet Marshes as an area for a future offensive. This was why the premier commander of offensive operations in the Red Army had been appointed to head the Kiev Special Military District. The concentrations of troops gathered in the Western and Kiev military districts in 1940 were committed to an offensive mission. Soviet sources, of course, do not say the USSR would have begun the war with an act of aggression; nevertheless, they make it clear that the forces in the Lvov and Bialystok salients had an offensive purpose. A German general staff intelligence report of May 20, 1941 forecast a Soviet offensive from Czernowitz–Lvov into Rumania, Hungary, and eastern Galicia, with a supporting operation from White Russia toward Warsaw and East Prussia. The offensive was to occur immediately after the beginning of hostilities with the powerful forces deployed in the two western salients. In assembling a strong force in the Ukraine, Stalin hoped to be able to deprive Germany of 90 percent of its oil at once, if war came suddenly, or to intimidate Rumania for as long as possible, if war were to be delayed.[35] Playing a double game such as this so close to the demarcation line with Germany was, however, playing with fire, for although the Bialystok and Lvov salients were good to occupy in strength from an offensive point of view, from the standpoint of defense these positions were a distinct liability.[36]

Following Timoshenko's summation report at the Kremlin conference, on December 30 Stalin called together a group of generals and began to query them about the war game scheduled for the next day. Although Zhukov, who was present, mentions this meeting, he does not explain Stalin's reason for convening it, but it must have been to discuss some grave matter. It could be that Stalin intervened in the program for the exercise before it got under way and hand-picked Zhukov to play the part of a German aggressor, but Zhukov is vague on this point, stating merely that this choice was made without saying by whom.[37] At the end of the December conference, it is evident that Stalin was beginning to have serious second thoughts about what the Germans were preparing to do in

1941. Stalin had based his plans on the hope that the Red Army would have another two or three years' respite before being committed to a full-scale war, but he must have realized that time was running out. According to a reliable Soviet source, the Russian military attaché in Berlin received detailed information about Hitler's Barbarossa directive (ordering an invasion of Russia) from an anonymous letter on Christmas day, 1940, or a week after it was issued.[38] If it is assumed that Stalin considered this information to be authentic, this could have been the basis for his instructions to Zhukov about his role as a German aggressor in the war games.

Before Stalin's intervention in the war game, it is probable that Zhukov was supposed to participate in a single exercise involving a Soviet offensive from the Ukraine into Rumania and Hungary. The evidence to support this conclusion is circumstantial, but it is a fact that two war games were played out in the first half of January 1941, instead of the one game that Zhukov mentions in his memoirs. In the first game, the one probably ordered by Stalin, Zhukov led a "blue" (German) offensive from the western side of the board against the "red" side led by Gen. D. G. Pavlov, then commander of Western Special Military District. Stalin had now decided to see whether the forward strategy based on using the western salients as springboards for future offensive operations could be adapted for defense in an emergency. If Stalin's advisors such as Pavlov and the chief of the general staff, K. A. Meretskov, were correct, the strong mobile forces grouped in these areas would be able to serve in a defensive operation, if need be, by threatening a German breakthrough from the flanks.[39] Zhukov's brilliant handling of the play and analysis of the two war games demonstrated, however, how catastrophic such a forward strategy would have been.

During the first theoretical passage at arms, Zhukov won a crushing victory over Pavlov, which was not surprising considering the neglect of defense planning for the previous four years. In choosing among the possible avenues of attack against the Soviet Union, Zhukov elected alternatives that apparently closely corresponded to those favored by the German general staff. Zhukov himself is unclear about what his plans for the game were, but reports from other sources indicate that he launched three simultaneous blows against the USSR, with the main weight falling north of the Pripet Marshes. This "German" offensive broke through the Soviet fortified zone along the frontier and destroyed the Grodno and Bialystok groups of the Red Army and then pushed east to the region of Lida. It was at this point that the game was called to a halt because the "blues" had succeeded in establishing the necessary prerequisites for a victory.[40] In a swift series of maneuvers, Zhukov had once and for all exposed the fallacy of a forward strategy that placed the main part of the Red Army too close to the demarcation line with Germany, a policy that did not allow the kind of echeloning needed to ward off a German assault employing strong armored thrusts in the area of the Bialystok salient. After so easily dismantling the Pavlov-Meretskov forward strategy by an attack from the west, Zhukov would now prove how risky this strategy would have been for carrying out an offensive from the east.

In the second game, most likely the only one originally scheduled, Pavlov and Zhukov switched sides, but this time the action was confined to the area of the southwestern front in the Ukraine, and the "blue"-controlled territory across the border. No account has been published of how the second war game was conducted, but it is evident from comments made about it in the subsequent analysis presented to Stalin that an offensive from the Ukraine into Hungary and the Balkans would have been extremely hazardous, considering the small number of modern tanks and transport vehicles the Red Army had at its disposal in 1941. With such limited forces, Zhukov was compelled to maneuver his tanks in a single offensive echelon and was able to gain a superiority in strength in the main direction of attack only by weakening the so-called passive sectors of the front.[41] Zhukov does not say what the results of the "reds' " efforts were during the second game, but he does remark that Stalin was quite perturbed about its outcome.[42]

In his explanation to Stalin of the method of the "red" offensive operation carried out in the second exercise, Meretskov displayed a hypothetical map showing a situation in which sixty to sixty-five Soviet divisions overwhelmed a defending German force of fifty-five divisions. In reply to Stalin's question about how victory could be achieved with such a slight advantage in strength, Meretskov answered that the Red Army did not have a general superiority in manpower and firepower, but a local superiority could be gained in the main direction of an offensive by pulling in units from quiet sectors. Stalin contradicted this and said that the

Germans had enough mechanized forces to maneuver rapidly and redress a temporary unfavorable balance of strength to their favor. He also advised Meretskov to dispense with hypothesis and get down to specifics, asking him, "Who won, the reds?" The chief of the general staff avoided giving a direct answer, however, saying only that the "blues" were very strong in tanks and aircraft. Stalin then sealed Meretskov's fate by dismissing his claims of qualitative superiority for Soviet divisions, particularly the rifle divisions, as being "the stuff for agitators, not realists."[43]

For his part, Pavlov tried to explain the "reds'" failures in the two war games by making a small joke about how things such as unexpected defeat often happen in map exercises, but Stalin was a deadly serious man and his sense of humor was lacking when it came time to decide grave issues.[44] Pavlov would eventually have to pay the ultimate price for his inability to understand this.

After some additional inconclusive or muddled reports by Timoshenko, G. I. Kulik, and others, in what must have been a state of utter frustration, Stalin then asked if anyone else wished to speak. It was Zhukov who answered. The commander of the Kiev district pointed out, quite correctly, that the Bialystok fortified region, crammed far to the west into an indefensible salient, was at the mercy of the enemy forces located around Brest Litovsk and Suvalki. In response to a question from Pavlov, Zhukov replied that he also considered the fortified regions in the Ukraine to be positioned too close to the frontier. It was his earnest recommendation that the first main line of defense be constructed no closer than one hundred kilometers from the border. The importance Stalin attached to these recommendations may be judged by the fact that on the day following the final reports on the war games, January 14, 1941, Stalin announced the Politburo's decision to replace Meretskov with Zhukov as chief of the general staff.[45]

In securing Zhukov's new appointment, Stalin was, in essence, preparing to abandon his plans for the deployment of the Red Army's offensive forces in the exposed regions far to the west. The evidence regarding German intentions in 1941 had been mounting with increasing reliability as spring drew closer, and after early March no thought would be given to massing more men and materiel up close to the demarcation line. The objective now would be to concentrate wholly on means of repelling the imminent invasion. After the war, Stalin, and later Zhukov, came under sharp criticism for failing to position enough strength along the state border to repel the invaders as soon as they set foot on Soviet soil. According to the interpretation put forth by Khrushchev at the Twentieth Party Congress in 1956, Stalin was afraid to heed the warnings of the impending attack and neglected to fortify the border properly because he was reluctant to do anything that might provoke the Germans into aggression.[46] In answer to this charge, Zhukov has argued as follows:

> In recent years it has become common practice to blame the General Headquarters for not having ordered the pulling up of our main force from the interior zone in order to repulse the enemy. I would not venture to guess in retrospect the probable outcome of such an action. . . . It is quite possible, however, that being under equipped with anti-tank and anti-aircraft facilities and possessing lesser mobility than the enemy forces, our troops might have failed to withstand the powerful thrusts of the enemy panzer forces and might, therefore, have found themselves in as grave a predicament as some of the armies of the frontier zone. Nor is it clear what situation might then have developed in the future on the approaches to Moscow and Leningrad and in the southern areas of the country.[47]

Here Zhukov has eloquently refuted the contention that the Red Army could have stopped the Wehrmacht on the frontier in 1941. It is plain to see that Zhukov never intended to place the main body of the Red Army close to the initial shock of the onslaught, depriving it of the ability to maneuver while leaving it in a position highly vulnerable to being cut off and then annihilated. Zhukov knew that the German armored thrusts would have to be continually drained of energy by successive echelons of defense located deep within Russia. After a period of active defense, of absorbing and blunting the enemy's momentum, conditions would become favorable for the launching of a counteroffensive by the last echelon, the strategic reserve. Such a plan, of course, would mean that terrible disaster would befall the forces of the first echelon, which would have to stand their ground while the German armor flowed around them.[48]

It might be wondered how a military strategy could be countenanced that would concede so much territory and place the populations of the occupied zones under such extreme danger. The Jews, in particular, among the Soviet minority nationalities, many of whom lived in White Russia and in the western Ukraine, could be expected to suffer greatly from a Nazi occupation. There is evidence to support the belief that Stalin's general attitude toward the Jews was not much different from that of the Nazis. In August 1939, at the time of the negotiations over the German-Soviet "Treaty of Friendship," which led to the dismemberment of Poland, Stalin told Ribbentrop, Hitler's foreign minister, that the Jews were only tolerated in Russia because there was no native Russian intelligentsia and that, when such a class developed in the Soviet Union, the Jews could be disposed of.[49] With regard to the other nationalities, there may have been other than purely military reasons for Stalin's preoccupation with the defense of the Ukraine. In his secret speech to the Twentieth Party Congress in 1956, Khrushchev remarked that Stalin would have relocated the Ukrainians, the largest non–Great Russian minority in the USSR, as he had done some of the smaller peoples (such as the Kalmyks and the Chechin-Ingush) during the war, but that "there were too many of them and there was no place to which to deport them." Stalin's concern about the loyalty of the Ukrainians to the Soviet regime was justified, as the civilian population there was, in general, well disposed toward Germany. Harsh German occupation policies such as the maintenance of the collective farms and the transportation of forced labor to the Reich, however, quickly used up the reservoir of good will.

Stalin, then, counted on the minority nationalities to fight the Nazis because he believed that the treatment the Germans would mete out to them would cause resentment and fear. In this respect, Hitler made the same mistake as Napoleon, discounting the need for winning a political war in Russia as well as a military one. How could Stalin assume that Hitler and the Nazis would be so stupid as to play right into his hands in such a manner? The answer is that the Nazi leadership had already given evidence in Poland of how it would treat the Slavic and Jewish people, and Hitler had already set down in writing an official policy toward Russia that left little doubt about what kind of occupation would be carried out there.

On March 30, 1941, Hitler addressed his military commanders at the Reich's Chancellery in Berlin and laid down the rules for what eventually became the infamous "Commissar Decree" issued on June 6. In this address, Hitler said that the Red Army political commissars, many of whom were Jewish, were not to be treated as soldiers when captured but were to be turned over to Himmler's

SD (Security Service) organization for execution. The führer went on to say that if the SD could not do the job for any reason, the army itself had this responsibility. Hitler then offered some "justifications" for this edict, stating that, since the USSR had never signed the part of the 1929 Geneva Convention that dealt with the treatment of POWs, German prisoners could not expect to fare well in the hands of the Red Army. Also, he said that the conduct of the Red Army, particularly the commissars, in Poland, in the war against Finland, in the Baltic, and in Rumania showed no reason to spare them.[50]

When the decree was officially issued on June 6, 1941, under Gen. Wilhelm Keitel's signature, it contained the following language:

In the struggle against Bolshevism, we must not assume that the enemy's conduct will be based on principles of humanity or international law. Political commissars have initiated barbaric, Asiatic methods of warfare. Consequently they will be dealt with immediately and with maximum severity. As a matter of principle they will be shot at once, whether captured during operations or otherwise showing resistance. The following regulations will apply: . . . on capture they will be immediately separated from other prisoners on the field of battle. . . . After they have been segregated they will be liquidated.[51]

The German army had already placed itself in a compromising position in Poland by allowing the SS and SD units to operate outside of its jurisdiction. Now, after June 6, Halder, the chief of the German general staff, and Walther von Brauchitsch, the army commander in chief, accepted the Commissar Decree without open dissent. To their credit, they did try to soften its effect by issuing an order that stated that the duty of the troops was to fight and there would be no time for special searches or mopping-up operations. No soldier would be permitted to act on his own; soldiers must always follow the commands of their officers. Even though the Commissar Decree was put into effect only in limited measure in 1941, there can be no doubt that the results of it—the excesses of the "Special Units" (Einsatzgruppen) and the SD in the rear areas, as well as the treatment of the mass of POWs—were catastrophic morally, politically, and militarily. This was especially true during the first weeks and months of the war in Russia; the effect was truly devastating. The following comment is from a report by

"Einsatzgruppe A," which operated in the rear areas of Army Group North, and shows how far things had gone even in the first few days of the war in Russia:

> To our surprise it was not easy at first to set in motion an extensive pogrom against Jews. . . . During the first pogrom in the night from 25 to 26th June, the Lithuanian Partisans (with German encouragement) did away with more than 1,500 Jews, set fire to several synagogues or destroyed them by other means, and burned down a Jewish dwelling district consisting of about 60 houses. During the following nights about 2,300 Jews were made homeless in a similar way.
>
> These self-cleansing actions went smoothly because the Army authorities who had been informed showed understanding for this procedure.[52]

After the Commissar Decree, Stalin could rest assured that his forces would remain true to the Soviet cause, for it showed a total lack of understanding by the Germans of conditions in Russia and of the need to wage a political war. In the first few weeks of battle there were stories of minority army units, particularly Lithuanians, shooting their commissars and going over to fight with the Wehrmacht. Soon after the fall of Vilna in late June 1941, the Lithuanians attempted to found their own provisional government and cooperate with the Germans, but Hitler ordered this group suppressed as soon as he heard about it. Space here does not permit a detailed account of how the Germans lost the political war in Russia; the reader who wishes to inquire further should investigate Alexander Dallin's *German Rule in Russia, 1941–1945,* in which the chronicle of these blunders is more or less complete.

The most immediate problem that Zhukov had to face after becoming chief of the general staff was the critical situation along the Bialystok salient. A way had to be found to make the best use of the troop concentrations already in the salient for defense. Since no force on earth could have saved the Red Army units there from being cut off and surrounded soon after the war began, this would mean that they would have to be sacrificed. If handled properly, however, this sacrifice could be expected to pay big dividends later on, much in the way a "poisoned pawn" is offered up as a victim in a chess game. The loss of a small piece is relatively unimportant if the opponent can be placed in a difficult strategic posture. It would require no small amount of skill, planning, and deception in order to ensure that the sacrifice would cost the Germans a maximum amount while still remaining rather "cheap" for the Soviet side.

In a decision that has remained painful for the Red Army to this very day, Zhukov and Stalin decided that the deception would have to be good enough to deceive not only the Germans but also their own front-line forces. The front-line commanders and their units could not be told in advance what their true role would be or what fate awaited them once Hitler unleashed his army. It could be that even Pavlov, the commander of the Western Special Military District, was not informed of the real defense plan for 1941, but toward the end he may have suspected the truth and attempted to protest, thus explaining Stalin's decision to have him and his chief of staff executed in July. Although the military districts in the west were not officially warned of the impending German attack until 3:00 on the morning of June 22, apparently some front-line commanders had already taken matters into their own hands and had begun to make final preparations for defense before the defense commissariat's warning was issued.[53] Soviet sources have never offered a concrete reason for Pavlov being killed. The fact remains that he was the only front commander on the Soviet side to be liquidated during the entire war, therefore it must be assumed that his case was an extreme one. Clearly, the size of the disaster in White Russia had little to do with Pavlov's fate when the considerably larger catastrophes at Kiev and Briansk-Viazma are taken into account. After these debacles, also in 1941, neither S. M. Budënny nor I. S. Konev received anything worse from Stalin than a reassignment.[54]

Knowing in advance that two panzer groups would lead the main thrust of the German offensive north of the Pripet Marshes in closing off the Bialystok salient, Zhukov decided to allow these armored spearheads to pass around the main body of Soviet infantry relatively unimpeded. Nothing could be done, anyway, to stop the panzer groups along the border; they would have to be dealt with later by specially constructed antitank strongpoints (PTOP) and detached tank brigades in the second echelon.[55] The combined-arms units in the salient, however, could be expected to hold their ground and fight effectively against the German infantry coming in from the west, while at the same time acting as a threat to the rearward areas and supply lines of the rapidly advancing panzer groups. Zhukov's tactics were to allow the German armor to separate itself as much as possible from the following infantry and then deal with each group, armor and infantry, separately.[56] Later, when the larger combined-arms units would begin to disintegrate under intense pressure, smaller formations of infantry and cavalry could be expected to take to the forests and continue to operate in groups as partisans.[57]

In fact, the Germans were never able to seal off the large pockets of Soviet troops successfully, and many formations eventually managed to escape almost intact to the east. The phenomenon of the "floating pockets" that drifted steadily toward the east and south would cause the Germans no end of trouble in 1941, and they constantly acted as a bone caught in the throat of the armored jaws, which could snap shut but not chew or swallow.[58] Surrounded units or groups of units were thus intended to continue to function as organic entities of the tactical echelon and play an important part in checking the German advance. The composition of forces in the Bialystok salient would, therefore, have to contain just the proper balance of tanks, artillery, and infantry if the desired result were to be achieved economically and effectively.

One of the more important questions to be considered in deciding what to do with the Bialystok salient concerned the construction of fortifications in the west, which had been continuing since the occupation of eastern Poland in September 1939. By June 22, 1941, some twenty-five hundred fortified points had been built; however, all but a thousand of them were equipped only with machine guns. The Mobilization Plan (MP-41) approved in February called for accelerating the new construction, but this was not enough to suit some individuals who still believed the German invasion could be checked at the border. In late February–early March, the Supreme Military Council of the Red Army met in Moscow, and G. I. Kulik, deputy commissar for armaments, B. M. Shaposhnikov, deputy commissar for fortified areas, and Politburo member A. A. Zhdanov argued for stripping the fortifications along the old pre-1939 frontier and sending the material to the recently built defense line farther west. Zhukov and Defense Commissar Timoshenko vigorously opposed this action, insisting that the old fortifications could still be useful.[59] The key element of contention was the artillery, which could not be moved easily once it was put into position.

Although Zhukov does not specifically say that he was trying to keep all but the minimum amount of artillery and hauling-equipment out of the Bialystok salient, it is evident that this was his intention. Stalin wavered on this question temporarily and then sided with his chief of the general staff. The question of the artillery was, therefore, partially resolved in favor of the pre-1939 fortifications. This so-called Stalin Line of defense proved to be of little use after the war began, but some of the artillery, at any rate, was saved from certain destruction. As for the artillery already in the salient, much of it was pulled back a considerable distance eastward under the pretext of the need for "firing practice." In addition to artillery pieces and tractor-haulers, most of the engineers and the pontoon bridge battalions of the tank divisions were also sent rearwards for "training missions."[60] It is true that many of the big guns and artillerymen were not in front-line positions on June 22, but this had nothing to do with Stalin's failure to heed the warnings of the imminence of war. Stalin would make several mistakes during the course of 1941, but leaving masses of artillery in the Bialystok salient was not one of them.

After the problem of the artillery was met and solved to a more or less satisfactory degree, the question of what to do with all the armor in the salient still remained. For several reasons it was impossible to shift tanks out of Western District's forward zone. To do this would be to arouse unneccessarily the suspicions of the Germans, who would be sure to discover the redeployment by means of their continuing overflights of Soviet territory. A significant removal of tanks from the salient could also be expected to cause undue panic among the infantry units there by making the officers and men feel as if they were about to be abandoned to fend for themselves, without sufficient artillery or armor to give support in case of a German attack. The three armies in the salient, the Third, Tenth, and Fourth, had to be left with their armor intact if the soldiers there were to be expected to stand and fight, not flee or surrender en masse. According to the official standards set by the State of Military Readiness decree issued in April 1941, each Soviet combined-arms rifle division was supposed to have 16 light tanks and 13 armored vehicles. A Soviet mechanized corps nominally consisted of two tank divisions, each with 375 tanks, and one motorized infantry with an additional 275 light tanks.[61]

It was Pavlov, the tank expert, probably unaware of the true nature of the defense plan being put into effect by Zhukov and Stalin, who unwittingly provided the solution to Zhukov's problem. Pavlov, still convinced that it was Stalin's plan to stop the Germans along the border, proposed that three of the four operational mechanized corps be concentrated on the flanks of the two German panzer groups that were to operate against the salient. The plan was substantially the same one Pavlov had used against Zhukov in the December war game, and Zhukov must have known full well what the outcome of it would be. Nevertheless, Pavlov's proposal suited Zhukov, even though any chance for success it might have had in rolling back German panzer groups was very small.

Pavlov believed that three of his mechanized corps—the VIth and the XIth in the north around Grodno and the XIVth near Kobrin in the south—positioned to threaten the flanks of Hermann Hoth's Panzer Group 3 debouching from Suvalki and Guderian's Panzer Group 2 advancing from the direction of Brest Litovsk, would be sufficient to halt the German drive until enough reinforcements could arrive from the operational echelon and the strategic reserve, if need be, to set up a stable front and drive the invaders back. Zhukov was willing to accept Pavlov's plan for his own reasons, for he had reckoned that the three mechanized corps used in this fashion would cause the Germans some trouble and retard the speed of their armored spearheads, but he had no intention of committing the operational echelon, much less the strategic reserve, to the battle for the Bialystok salient. He was prepared to expend armor so abundantly during the early stage of war because the large mechanized corps, with their many obsolete BT and T-26 tanks were not intended to be the backbone of the Red Army's armored force.[62] The new T-34 and KV model tanks that were being produced would outclass anything the Germans had in the field at the time, so it was decided to reserve them in order to stiffen the back of the operational echelon along the Dnepr-Dvina line and to provide the cutting edge for the eventual counteroffensive by the strategic reserve whenever an opportune moment should arise. Western historians have chided the Russians for not immediately forming the new tanks into proper formations and bringing them to the border areas in June, but there was a method to their seeming madness.[63] In the meantime, in June, July, and August the greatest possible benefit would have to be derived from the use of the older tanks in the tactical and operational echelons to slow down the German panzer groups and harass their infantry.

At the end of March 1941, at Zhukov's request, half a million men were brought up from the reserves held in readiness, ostensibly to intensify their training. Nearly all of these men were sent directly to the four western military districts, a vast territory that included most of European Russia west of a line running between Kharkov and Kiev, then north and east to the west of Moscow and to the east of Lake Onega. In addition, three hundred thousand other reservists were called up a few days later.[64] These reinforcements were not moved right up to the frontier but were deployed in an intermediate zone between the tactical echelon, which was already in place and would have to receive the initial shock of the German offensive, and the operational echelon, which would be brought into its final areas of concentration after mid-May.

In June 1941, on the front line of an area that stretched some two thousand kilometers, were stationed nine armies composed of forty-eight divisions within ten to fifty kilometers of the frontier. In the area immediately behind the front and up to three hundred kilometers east of the border, between the tactical and operational echelons in the intermediate zone, were another fifteen divisions and two brigades, making a total of around sixty-three divisions for the forces that would come into contact with the Germans during the first few days of the war. Zhukov states that only forty-eight divisions were in the first echelon, but another Soviet source gives a higher figure, sixty-three divisions and two brigades. The difference of approximately fifteen divisions stems from the fact that Zhukov does not include the forces in the intermediate zone, behind the forward echelon, in his total. These backup forces for the first echelon could be considered a tactical reserve, and they further enhanced the impression made on the Germans—and probably on Pavlov as well—that the Supreme Command intended to fight a major battle for the Bialystok salient. In White Russia, most of the tactical reserve was located in assembly points west of Minsk.[65]

These units, of course, would be badly overmatched by the 154 divisions the Germans would commit to their attack, and this discrepancy was enhanced by the fact that the tactical echelon was purposely left under strength in firepower, as has been mentioned, and manpower. Of the approximately 170 divisions deployed in European Russia west of Moscow and east of Kiev, most had only eight thousand to nine thousand men each, and several had even fewer, five thousand to six thousand men. Since the beginning of the war caught the forces of the operational echelon still in a stage of deployment, it is likely that most of the divisions that were better fitted out, in manpower at least, were located farthest to the west in the tactical echelon.[66] It was hoped that the operational echelon would be protected from the main thrust of the enemy's blow and could be ready in time and positioned properly to threaten the flanks of the German Central Army Group. The Red Army lacked the mobility to make rapid readjustments in the deployment of the operational echelon, and after the war began there would be precious little time for second guesses.

The question of exactly where to deploy the operational echelon was a problem that caused some concern for Stalin and his general staff. Zhukov notes that in 1940 Soviet strategic planning was based on the assumption that the southwesterly direction, the Ukraine, would be the most likely avenue for a German invasion.[67] The 1940 plan for operations was revised under the supervision of Zhukov and Timoshenko in the spring of 1941, and they, no doubt, were well aware of what the Germans' intentions were, insofar as they had been set down in the Barbarossa directive of December 1940. Zhukov says that the general staff intelligence chief, F. I. Golikov, "accurately summarized the evolution of the 'Barbarossa' plan by late March 1941." According to Guderian, "the plan for operation 'Barbarossa' was almost certainly known to the Russian command."[68] Taking the directive itself at face value, the Soviet Supreme Command logically concluded that the Germans were more interested in reaching Leningrad and seizing the Ukraine before taking Moscow, and Stalin himself was convinced that this would be the most rational course for the Germans to follow. In the spring of 1941, during a discussion of the operational plan for that year, Stalin told Zhukov, "Nazi Germany will not be able to wage a major lengthy war without those vital resources [i.e., in the Ukraine, Donets Basin, and the Caucasus]."[69] Before the war, then, Stalin believed that Hitler would elect to turn his powerful Central Army Group southward and fight a large-scale battle for the Ukraine before allowing the advance on Moscow to continue. This belief was based on his personal estimation of Hitler as a shrewd man who took no unneccessary chances, and was confirmed further by the language of the Barbarossa directive.

On the basis of all the information thus at their disposal, Stalin and Zhukov decided to make the operational echelon very strong in the areas that would threaten the northern and southern flanks of Army Group Center as it pushed through White Russia north of the Pripet. It was hoped that the operational echelon could exert enough pressure on the flanks of the Army Group, from around Gomel east of the Pripet and from Velikie Luki north of the Dvina River, to force the Germans to halt their advance along the Dnepr-Dvina line. In this respect the battle for the Bobruisk-Mogilev-Rogachev triangle northwest of Gomel between the Berezina and Dnepr rivers was considered to be particularly important.[70] In any case, the Soviet Supreme Command was probably well aware that the Germans considered it necessary to allow time for an operational pause in their offensive after reaching Smolensk, a short one, at least, in order to regroup their forces and remedy the supply situation. The Soviet Supreme Command had studied closely the German tactics in France in 1940 and presumably were familiar with the operational capabilities of their opponent's large tank units. If properly handled, it was believed that Soviet attacks from Velikie Luki to the north and from Gomel to the south of Smolensk could transform this operational pause into a major delay.[71]

It was Stalin's conviction that the Soviet forces on the Baltic and in the Ukraine would have to bear the brunt of the German offensive from this point on and that the Red Army units in the tactical and intermediate zones escaping from the German advance in White Russia would be enough to arrest the Germans on the approaches to Moscow.[72] It was for this reason that the decision was made to deploy the most important components of the operational echelon deep within the western Ukraine, west of Kiev, and also due east of the Pripet Marshes, where they could be expected to perform three functions: (1) to intensify the direct assaults on the southern flank of Army Group Center if it were, indeed, checked in its forward movement at the Dnepr-Dvina line, or even if the Germans decided to continue the advance straight on to Moscow; (2) to cut off an expected turn from north to south of part of Army Group Center toward the important industrial areas of the eastern Ukraine and the oil-rich Caucasus region; and (3) to meet head on a German push into the Ukraine from the west if the forces in the Lvov salient proved unable to withstand the pressure from Army Group South.

Much of the careful planning carried out by Zhukov in the spring of 1941 had to be undone by early June for reasons that will be explained later, yet the fact remains that the operational echelon was positioned properly in the interior of the Soviet Union in order best to confront all possible contingencies. Zhukov can be criticized for many things, but he cannot be faulted for his lack of prescience. The German army high command's ability to act independently of Hitler's wishes later caught him by surprise, in just the same way they managed to deceive their own commander in chief.

On May 13, 1941, a general staff directive was issued that ordered the movement westward from the interior of the units destined for the operational echelon. The Twenty-second Army was moved from the Urals to Velikie Luki north of the Dvina, the Twenty-first Army from Volga District to Gomel, the Nineteenth Army from the northern Caucasus to Belaia Tserkov south of Kiev, the Sixteenth Army from the Transbaikal District to Shepetovka in the central-western Ukraine, and the XXVth Rifle Corps from Kharkov District to the Dvina River. When these forces were joined with the Twentieth, Twenty-fourth, and Twenty-eighth armies already in the four western districts' reserves, they would swell the size of the operational echelon to about ninety-six divisions, though not all of these would be fully deployed before June 22. In addition, eleven more divisions were held back as a reserve directly under the Supreme Command.[73]

The hefty size of the operational echelon belies the assumption that the general staff was caught napping by the German attack. Quite the contrary, the careful positioning of operational echelon on what would become the flanks of Army Group Center would cause the Wehrmacht no end of difficulty in the summer of 1941. Army Group Center would have a great deal to contend with, especially from the southerly direction, by the time it reached the Dnepr-Dvina line with its long and exposed flanks. The Soviet Supreme Command could hope for good results from the strong forces located around Gomel, which were shielded from the west by the protective cover of the Pripet Marshes. They also hoped that the German push from the west into the Ukraine could be

contained entirely by the tactical echelon there, a force that included one fully equipped mechanized corps. Had this happened, the
operational echelon in the south would have had full freedom to
maneuver and face the right wing of Army Group Center if, as expected by Zhukov, Hitler attempted to push down into the
Ukraine from the north, east of the Pripet. These plans would be
shattered during the first days of war, but no one, no matter how
farseeing, could have been any wiser in predicting the course of action the Germans would follow after June 22.

The last element in the Soviet Supreme Command's plan for
defense was the strategic reserve. Soviet sources are penurious
enough with information about the size, composition, and disposition of the forces in the tactical and operational echelons, but the
cloak of secrecy that surrounds the strategic reserve is the tightest
of all. Some recent Soviet commentators have attempted to disguise the true defense plan for 1941 by claiming that the only strategic reserve available in the early summer had already been
deployed as the Nineteenth, Twenty-first, Twenty-second, Twentieth, and Twenty-eighth armies, which have been described here
as belonging to the operational echelon, not to the strategic
reserve.[74] To a certain extent these commentators are correct, for
had the tactical echelon been able to cripple or seriously retard the
progress of the German panzer groups, and had the German infantry been delayed for a protracted period in the battles close to the
frontier, the operational echelon could have successfully fulfilled
the role prescribed for the strategic reserve by launching a counteroffensive in the area of the Dnepr and Dvina rivers that could have
rolled the enemy backward. This did not happen, however, particularly because of the savage effect of the Luftwaffe raids on
Pavlov's tank columns and on communications, and so the only
maneuvers the operational echelon could undertake were those
that had a purely defensive character.[75]

The rather primitive state of telecommunications in the USSR
in 1941 cannot be documented in detail here. In general, the com-
munication cable and land lines were operated by the People's
Commissariat for Communications. In other words, to a large degree the Red Army depended on the civilian network to handle its
message traffic, for it was the post office system that managed
long-distance telephone and telegraph communications. There was
a high-frequency net (VCh) that used land lines with a carrier fre-

quency of 6.3 and 25.5 MHz for voice and telegraph. This system, which was manned by the NKVD, had the advantage of being non-interceptable aurally at transmission rates over 15 MHz without special equipment. Shortly after the war started, the management of the high-frequency net was handed over to the military, but access to it was limited to the higher command structures. By and large, the Luftwaffe attacks on the Soviet communications centers on June 22 threw the overland civilian system into confusion and disorder. A very large part of the problem that the general staff and Stalin faced in the first few days of the war was trying to make an intelligible whole from the fragmentary reports that were transmitted. As an example of how bad conditions were, on the day of the invasion only one signal was wired from V. I. Kuznetsov, the commander of the Third Army in the Bialystok salient. Such prolonged silence from the frontier areas was hardly conducive to good planning either at Western Front headquarters in Minsk or in Moscow. Fortunately, the Leningrad radio net command headquarters remained intact and proved invaluable in collecting reports from cut-off Red Army units.[76]

The overall effectiveness of the Luftwaffe may be judged from the damage reports given in Russian sources. Luftwaffe raids were carried out against sixty-six airfields in the western border areas and by midday June 22 fully twelve hundred Soviet aircraft had been destroyed, nine hundred of them on the ground. From June 22 to June 30 the Western Front alone lost 1,163 aircraft or 74 percent of its total complement. By 10:00 A.M. on June 22 all telephone and telegraph communications with the three air divisions based in western White Russia had been completely broken, and this also contributed to the general disorganization and the high rate of loss. But as bad as the situation seemed at first, there was some hope for the future. Only 30 percent of the planes based in the Western Front were newer models such as MiG-3s, IL-2s and YAK 1s. Also, even though many older planes were lost, the number of pilots killed apparently was not great. Soviet sources indicate that, although the aircraft were neatly parked on the fields at the time of the German attack, many of the pilots were elsewhere undergoing training. This charade was worth its high cost because it did succeed in deluding the Germans about the Soviet preparedness. Stalin was willing to take some early losses while not ruining chances for a future rapid buildup of the air force.[77]

The fact remains, however, that the shock of the Luftwaffe assault, especially the effect on communications, was much greater than the Supreme Command had anticipated, and as a result, Zhukov's plans were placed in jeopardy. The true strategic reserve had been only partly mobilized prior to the outbreak of the war, and now the Red Army would have to pay the penalty for this seemingly costly blunder. These delays in mobilization have been attributed to Stalin and his fear of provoking Hitler into attacking the Soviet Union, and there is, no doubt, some truth to this argument. Stalin had intended to wait another two or three years before committing the Red Army to war with Germany, but from December 1940, he had no choice left in the matter. War would come to Russia in 1941 despite all that Stalin had done to avoid facing the conflict so soon.[78]

On June 14, Zhukov and Timoshenko appealed to Stalin to order a full mobilization for the Red Army and asked that the country's military forces be brought to a state of war readiness. Stalin's reply was stern: "That means war! Do you two understand that or not?"[79] He had still not relinquished his cherished hope that Hitler would ultimately decide to avoid a further expansion of the European conflict in 1941. One might say that to rely on such prospects, with all the evidence to the contrary, was to clutch at the slenderest of reeds. Yet Stalin must have known that his country would have been placed in a most serious predicament by a German invasion even if the reserves had been fully mobilized before June 22. The strategic reserve could not have saved the situation along the border for the Red Army anyway, and Stalin believed that the fighting power of the tactical and operational echelons, already in the final stage of deployment by June, would be enough to allow the full mobilization of the strategic reserve in time to deal the Germans a crushing blow before they penetrated into the major population centers and industrial heart of the country.[80]

The risk that Stalin took by not mobilizing the strategic reserve in May or June 1941 must be weighed against the disadvantages such an early mobilization would have had. In the first place, Soviet mobilization might have provoked Hitler into military action if his mind had not already been made up in favor of war. In the second place, if war came, Stalin could reasonably suppose that the Red Army's well-echeloned, in-depth defenses in the tactical and operational zones would act as an effective brake in slowing and perhaps halting the German offensive before substantial damage had been done to the country or the army. Third, the military districts in the west were already bulging with forces, and there was a lack of space to quarter newly created formations. Also there must have been a considerable strain on the carrying capacity of the railroads in the western districts after Zhukov's first call-up of eight hundred thousand reservists in March and the movement forward to the west of four armies and one rifle corps in May–June.[81]

The burden on the railroads may have been increased further by the evacuation of certain key factories and economic enterprises from the west to the east before the war began. Although there is no confirmation that such dislocations took place at this time, one Soviet source testifies that during a three-month period in 1941 (the months are not specified) a total of 1,360 large enterprises, mainly war factories, were evacuated from the western regions. How this feat was accomplished in a country supposedly suffering from the chaos engendered by a surprise attack has never been explained by Soviet historians.[82] Finally, a full mobilization of all reserves in the Soviet Union would have meant forfeiture of the important elements of deception and surprise that the Supreme Command believed would catch the Germans off guard. Everything possible had been done in 1941 to convince the German high command that the Red Army was unprepared for war. A mobilization of reserves would have been easily detected by the Germans and would have made them more cautious in their plans for aggression. The greater the chances the German high command were willing to take to win a blitzkrieg victory, the better the opportunity would be for the strategic reserve to catch the Wehrmacht unawares in a difficult situation.

When all factors are thus considered, it must be concluded that the decision not to mobilize the strategic reserve before June 22 was the correct one at that time. The war mobilization plan worked out in March and April 1941 by the general staff was thorough and provided for a rapid increase in the size of the army immediately after the start of hostilities. For various reasons, however, the strategic reserve would not be used properly, and much of it had to be thrown into battle in an uncoordinated fashion. In all, between June 22 and December 1, 1941, the Soviet Supreme Command was able to send 194 newly created divisions and 94 newly created brigades to the various fronts. In addition, 97 other divisions, including 27 divisions from the Far East, central Asia, and the Transcaucasus, were sent to the western regions from the interior of the Soviet Union. The well-prepared Soviet plan for mobilization enabled the country's military forces to increase in size from 5 million men in June 1941 to 10.9 million in 1942, despite the large number of casualties sustained in the summer and fall of 1941.[83] The German high command never dreamed that such feats would be possible. Had the German advance been held at the Dnepr and Dvina rivers, and had the Russians been able to concentrate their strategic reserves properly on the flanks of Army Group Center, in all probability, the war would have been over for Germany as far as any offensive efforts were concerned. The worsening weather—first rain then ice—in October and November would have been the curtain raiser for the counteroffensive by the strategic reserve against the exposed flanks of the Central Army Group. This counteroffensive, as fate would have it, came neither in October nor in November, nor did it come in the area of the Dnepr and Dvina rivers. Rather, it came in early December and at the very gates of Moscow. By early July 1941, Stalin and Zhukov were forced to make several important changes in the original strategic concept for defense, but the essence of the concept, the idea that Army Group Center must be assailed by attacks on its prolonged flanks as it pushed deeper inside Soviet territory, remained, as fortune would have it, unchanged.

Viewed from any standpoint, the USSR was as well-prepared for war in June 1941 as it possibly could have been, considering the late start the general staff under Zhukov's direction had in implementing a strategic defense plan. The tactical echelon on the frontier, some sixty-three divisions in all, although not well equipped with artillery and modern tanks, was theoretically strong enough to cause the Germans some trouble. The operational echelon was also well positioned to fulfill its mission of weakening the main body of the German offensive north of the Pripet Marshes, mainly by flank attacks, and of arresting the eastward progress of the Wehrmacht at Smolensk in the central area. The operational echelon would also serve to prevent the southern wing of Army Group Center from pushing down into the Ukraine east of the Pripet. The capstone of Soviet defense planning was the strategic reserve, which by some force of logic ought to have been made ready before the war. For reasons put forward earlier in the chapter, however, Stalin delayed mobilization until after Hitler made the first move. This decision nearly lost the war for Russia in the early stages, but later in the summer it paid big dividends as fresh forces were continuously being sent to, or directly behind, the battlefronts. Even as early as July 10, the Soviet Supreme Command could count on reserves of thirty-one divisions. S. I. Bogdanov's Reserve Front alone in mid-July included parts of six armies.[84] The deception of the German high command was greatly enhanced by Russia's delayed mobilization, and it led Halder's general staff to draw many erroneous conclusions about the strength of the Red Army, conclusions that cost the Wehrmacht entire divisions and mountains of material in December. In the words of a German field marshal hanged at Nuremberg, "A mistake in strategy can only be made good in the next war."[85]

CHAPTER 2

GERMAN PLANS FOR THE INVASION OF THE USSR

PRELIMINARY STRATEGIC PLANNING

German strategic planning for the invasion of the Soviet Union, which was referred to under the code names Otto, Fritz, and finally, Barbarossa, began in early July 1940, or shortly after the fall of France.[1] It is unclear exactly when Hitler decided to wage war against the USSR, but it can be said that by July 21, 1940, the German army was committed to finding a military solution for the growing series of problems posed by the Soviet Union.[2] On this date, Hitler held a conference with his service chiefs Brauchitsch (army), Jeschonnek (Göring's representative from the Luftwaffe), Raeder (navy), Keitel, and Jodl (Armed Forces High Command, or OKW) in attendance. During this conference the general framework was established for a future eastern campaign.

There is some question as to who brought up the idea for an invasion of Russia at this conference; it seems that after the war none of the services wanted to take responsibility for it. Certainly Admiral Raeder should not; he left the room before Russia was really discussed.

In the words of an old Irish proverb, "Success has many fathers, failure is an orphan." It is true that at this meeting Brauchitsch first received official notice from Hitler to begin preparations for a Russian campaign, but there are reasons for believing that the army commander in chief's interest in this had some

61

background. It is likely that it was Brauchitsch and not the other service chiefs who delivered this initial report concerning Russia. In the first place, the Army High Command (OKH) had been discussing the Russian problem since at least July 3, 1940. In the second place, it would have been unusual for the other service chiefs to bring up a proposal of this nature, especially since a few days later, on July 29, the OKW rejected the idea that the invasion take place in the fall of 1940 on the grounds of insufficient time to carry out the necessary preparations and the approach of the Russian rainy season.[3] Apparently, the thought of carrying out a four-to six-week campaign in Russia with only eighty to a hundred German divisions against the "fifty to seventy-five good divisions" the Russians supposedly possessed, had given the OKW a severe case of mental indigestion. The figures regarding Soviet strength used in the July 21 conference (presumably by Brauchitsch) were provided by Colonel Kinzel's General Staff Intelligence Department (Fremde Heere Ost) and are indicative of the almost total failure of the German intelligence service to supply accurate information about the Soviet Union.[4]

The bad feelings that existed between the OKW and OKH date back to early 1938, when Hitler assumed the title Commander in Chief of the Armed Forces and created the OKW under Field Marshal Wilhelm Keitel as his own personal military staff. The army had suffered great loss of prestige when Field Marshal von Blomberg, the minister for war, and Werner von Fritsch, head of the army, had both been dismissed from their posts in disgrace. Blomberg was tricked into marrying a notorious prostitute, largely through Göring's doing. The führer himself was publicly embarrassed by this incident, since he had attended the wedding, and he cashiered Blomberg without hesitation. Fritsch's turn came when fabricated evidence supplied by Göring and Himmler showed him to have a homosexual past and to be, therefore, unfit for service in the Nazi regime (although there had been such types in high places in the earlier days of the party). Needless to say, the army felt beleaguered and threatened both by its political masters, the Nazis, and by its military archcompetitor, the OKW. The spirit of jealousy and rivalry between the two German high commands would assume important proportions by the time of the invasion of the Soviet Union in 1941.

On July 29, 1940, the chief of the general staff, Franz Halder, informed Maj. Gen. Erich Marcks, then chief of staff of the Eighteenth Army with headquarters in Bromberg, West Prussia, that he had been selected to perform a special duty for the OKH and the general staff. Marcks's assignment was to "prepare the theoretical groundwork for an eastern campaign strictly on his own, without reliance on any other department of the general staff." Although Marcks was the first general outside the OKH to be charged with this responsibility, he was by no means the only officer to be working on the project. Marcks's study was duly reported to Halder in early August 1940, but even before then, separate reports had been made by Colonel Kinzel and by Colonel Greiffenberg, who was chief of the Operations Section of the general staff, and Greiffenberg's subordinate, Lieutenant Colonel Feyerabend.[5] It is interesting to note that none of these proposals favored pushing directly into the center of the Soviet Union toward Moscow. Colonel Kinzel's study called for the taking of Moscow but only by first maintaining a strong link with the Baltic Sea and then turning southward to force the enemy units in the Ukraine to fight on a reversed front. The Greiffenberg-Feyerabend study called for a total German strength of one hundred divisions, with the main thrust coming in the south because of the particularly strong concentration of the Red Army in the Ukraine.[6]

Halder, however, refused to listen to the proposals of his own operations staff and insisted that the main blow should be in the direction of Moscow; after the fall of the city, a turn to the Ukraine could be made. In advocating such a ramrod push right to the capital of the Soviet Union, Halder betrayed neither a sense of caution nor a feeling for originality. The idea of a single main blow with the goal of taking Moscow above all else is usually referred to either as the "OKH plan" or (less often) as the "general staff plan." It would be more accurate to term it the "Halder plan," for no one else in the general staff originally agreed with it, and Brauchitsch, as commander in chief of the army, was totally under Halder's sway. Apparently, the two men had personalities that were similar to those of Ludendorff and Hindenburg during the First World War, with Ludendorff-Halder providing the brains and Hindenburg-Brauchitsch providing the representation before the head of state.[7] It would not be accurate to say that the OKH and the general staff wanted to invade the Soviet Union while the war against Britain continued in the west, yet the conclusion is inescapable that the underestimates of Soviet strength and the inflated belief in the power of one hundred German divisions to storm Russia in four to six weeks had much to do with influencing Hitler's ultimate decision to begin his campaign in the east.[8]

The final step in making the Soviet Union a military target was taken by Hitler at a conference with the OKH and OKW staffs at his palatial Berghof command post high in the Bavarian Alps on July 31, 1940. Far from exhibiting the rash characteristics often attributed to him, Hitler put forward a plan calling for a five-month campaign beginning in May 1941 that could be considered more conservative than that proposed by the OKH. Hitler saw the need for an eastern army of no less than 120 divisions to be launched in two main directions: (1) in the south toward Kiev and the Dnepr and (2) in the north along the Baltic, then in the direction of Moscow. The last stage of the operation would be undertaken as a giant enveloping movement toward the center of the vast country from the north and south.[9] No one at this conference offered any objections whatsoever to the führer's proposals, although it became known later that the army leaders remained silent in order to delay, at least for a time, a hard-and-fast commitment on Hitler's part to a strategy that placed the flanks above the center in order of importance.[10] Halder's wisdom in waiting to offer his criticisms until after his own studies had been thoroughly completed is not in dispute, although it was of critical importance that all disagreements over basic planning be ironed out as soon as possible. But the continued proscrastination and subterfuge of the OKH and the general staff in regard to the question of a flank versus a central attack on the Soviet Union eventually resulted in not one but two plans being carried out simultaneously. In this respect, the generals must share with Hitler a major proportion of the responsibility for the strategic calamities that resulted from this unresolved conflict.

On August 4, 1940, General Marcks presented to Halder his famous study, which received little notice at the time but has since attracted considerable attention and generated some controversy as well. Marcks, who was the son of the noted historian and biographer of Bismarck, devoted intense effort to his work and managed to complete it within a week.[11] Marcks's so-called Operation

East proposal consisted of twenty-six typewritten pages in two parts: (1) general characteristics of the theater of battle, general order of battle, and certain operational considerations and (2) tasks of the army groups and the armies, Luftwaffe, and navy. Further suggestions for solving specific problems in preparation for the campaign were contained in the second part.[12]

The Operation East proposal contained several interesting features that are also to be found in the other German strategic studies of 1940.[13] Marcks was compelled to divide the operational area into two separate and distinct parts, at least for the beginning phase of the assault. This was because the Pripet swamp and forest region acted as a natural barrier between White Russia and the Ukraine. Thus, from the very first, the German push eastward would lack full coordination and unity of action on either side of the swamps (see Figure 3). This enforced division of forces proved to be virtually an insoluble problem throughout the war but particularly during the first few crucial weeks. Marcks attempted to overcome this difficulty by reuniting the southern wing of the front with the main, central group of armies on the eastern side of the marshes, an idea that would have made the German southern wing essentially a subordinate part of the major force that was to strike directly at Moscow through White Russia. The southern wing was supposed to take Kiev and cross the Dnepr, then move either due east toward Kharkov or northeastward, if necessary, to protect the southern flank of the force moving on Moscow from the west. Marcks did not give much attention, however, to the northern flank of the central group of armies, providing only for a "special task force" to move over the lower Dvina toward Pskov and Leningrad.

For Marcks, the push southward into the Ukraine was unavoidable due to the necessity of protecting the Rumanian oil fields. That he viewed the southern theater as having great importance can be seen in his observation that "if it were possible for the main force of the German army to strike from Rumania along with other forces from northern Hungary, Galicia, and southeastern Poland, then the major assault on Moscow could perhaps be carried out east of the Dnepr, which would decide the war." This statement has led some historians to conclude that Marcks believed a southern approach into the Soviet Union offered the best chance for winning the war in a single decisive stroke and that

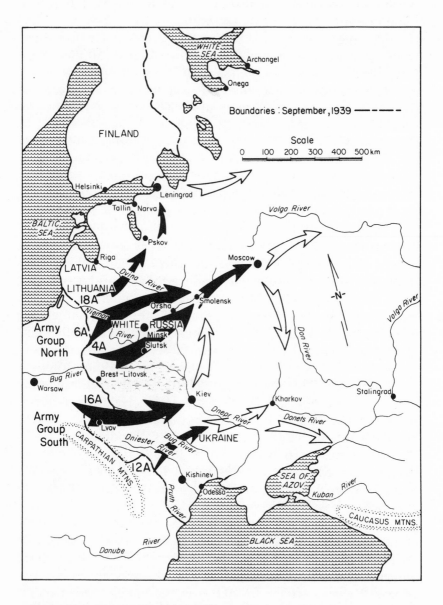

Figure 3. The Marcks Proposal for the Eastern Campaign

66

Moscow should not be taken until after most of the Ukraine had been occupied.[14] More recently, German historians have taken great pains to deny that Marcks's real intention was anything of the sort, pointing out that in the next sentence Marcks stated: "Neither the political situation in the Balkans nor the rail or road communications in Hungary and Rumania will allow the deployment of large German forces before the war begins. Only an attack from Galicia and southern Poland toward Kiev and the middle Dnepr can be undertaken [in the south] with safety."[15]

This controversy over Marcks's real intentions is a matter of more than purely academic interest, for if the Operation East proposal is taken as advocating a maneuver on the southern flank of the Soviet Union as opposed to a major push through White Russia, this would be one more bit of evidence to show that the disagreements over strategy between Halder, the cool, calculating theorist, and Hitler, the impetuous, ignorant meddler, were not at all as one-sided as they have been made to appear in postwar German writings. In order to unravel this tangle, it should be pointed out that Halder had an interview with Marcks on August 1, 1940, that is, four days before Marcks presented his full report. Their discussion revolved around the possibility of a two-pronged attack being launched toward Moscow and Kiev simultaneously, but Halder rejected this suggestion because of the political situation in Rumania and because of his unwillingness to place any other goal in Russia on an equal footing with Moscow in strategic significance.[16] In other words, Marcks's plan as presented on August 5 could not, in strict terms, be considered a study prepared under conditions free from all outside influences, as Halder himself had requested. On the contrary, it appears that Halder's own set of imposed conditions weighed down Marcks's proposals and led to their somewhat contradictory and muddled character. Marcks apparently wanted to give the southern flank an emphasis equal to that of the central sector, but Halder refused to consider the idea even before it was set down on paper.

As for the political situation in Rumania, there were no longer any difficulties to be encountered by September 7, because of the revolt against King Carol. Shortly after the revolt Hitler signed an agreement with the new government under Antonescu, which allowed German troops to take over the reorganization of the Rumanian army and protect the oil fields. Preparations soon be-

gan to ready Rumania for use as a staging area against the USSR.[17]
This plan was known as Construction East and was put into effect
by Jodl on August 9.

The question of the roads and railroads in Hungary and
Rumania must also be put in the proper perspective. The highways
and railroads in Poland, including western Poland, were not a
great deal better than in Hungary and Rumania, and the Germans
were forced to commence extensive improvements of Polish communications as early as August 1940.[18] Although Halder's refusal
to accept Marcks's original proposal was justifiable at the time,
the changed political conditions in the Balkans by early fall of 1940
ought to have led to a serious reconsideration by the chief of the
general staff of the whole subject of a southern strategy, yet
nothing of this kind took place.

Viewed from a general standpoint, the Marcks plan contained
not a trace of pessimism or doubt that the USSR could be speedily
defeated by the qualitatively and quantitatively superior German
forces. This optimism was fostered by the reports of the general
staff intelligence department in early August, which reckoned
Soviet strength in the western regions at ninety-six infantry and
twenty-three cavalry divisions, plus twenty-eight mechanized
brigades. According to these reports, the Russians would not be
able substantially to increase their strength before the first of the
year. Against this Soviet force the Germans should have thirty-five
divisions in the south (eleven motorized or armored) and sixty-
eight divisions north of the Pripet Marshes (seventeen motorized
or armored).

This optimism and confidence in a rapid victory are two of
the areas of agreement between Halder and Marcks; another was
the idea that the coming operations had to be separated into northern and southern parts, with the Pripet Marshes dividing them.
Fundamental to the concept of the blitzkrieg, which both Marcks
and Halder accepted, was the conviction that the mass of the Red
Army would be forced to stand and fight in the western Soviet
Union and could, therefore, be destroyed by a great battle or series
of battles of encirclement and annihilation. Marcks believed that
the Red Army could not afford to retreat beyond the line Dvina-
Berezina-Pripet swamps in the north and beyond the Pruth or
Dnestr rivers in the south. He also believed that the campaign
would be over within seventeen weeks. The persistence of this false

optimism, fanned by erroneous intelligence information about the enemy, until weeks after the invasion had actually begun will be seen time and again. The awakening would come on the banks of the Dnepr River, but even then the OKH would not admit its mistakes.

While the OKH and the general staff were engaged in their labors, the OKW was not content to play a passive role in the planning for the eastern campaign. The head of the OKW Operations Department (later Operations Staff), Col. Gen. Alfred Jodl, first informed his subordinates of the impending invasion on July 29, 1940. Shortly after this date Section "L" (Landesverteidigung) of the Operations Department, headed by Walter Warlimont, began preparing a plan for the invasion of the Soviet Union that became known as "the Lossberg study" after the name of its author, Lieutenant Colonel Lossberg (see Figure 4).[19]

The OKW proposal differed in several major respects from those considered and eventually approved by the OKH. Like Marcks, Lossberg was forced to come to grips with the "Pripet problem" at an early stage in the operational planning. Lossberg considered it to be advantageous to position most German forces north of the swamps, primarily because conditions there for deployment were better and because the Russian railway network in the north ran truer to the axis along which the operations were to be carried out. Lossberg also put much emphasis on a closer cooperation with the Finns, anticipating the willingness of Sweden to allow its railroads to move German troops into Finland. Whereas Marcks had envisioned the formation of only two basic army groups, Lossberg foresaw the need for three, two in the north and one in the south, with the Central Army Group being the strongest. In order to prevent the withdrawal of the Red Army to the east along a continuous front, Lossberg advocated the halting of Army Group Center east of Smolensk and the turning of part of its armored strength northward, thereby threatening the rear of the Russians facing Army Group North. After the turning maneuver, an operational pause would be necessary in order to replenish the exhausted army. Lossberg saw this turn to the north not as being rigidly predetermined in the schedule of events but rather as depending on the development of the general situation—that is, on whether Leningrad fell rapidly enough. Thus, for the first time, a German strategic planner considering the eastern problem

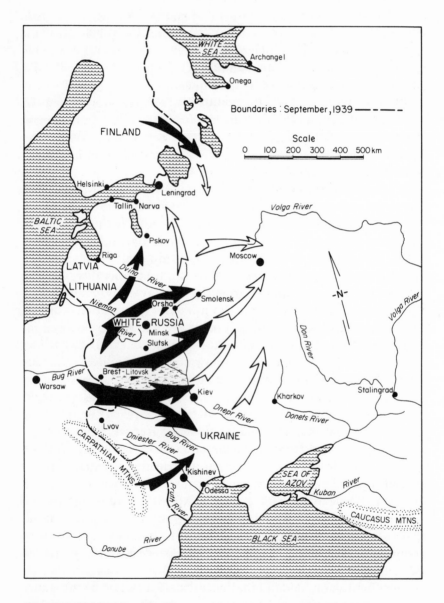

Figure 4. The Lossberg Study

stepped into the true realm of strategy by applying Moltke's dictum: "No operations plan can predict the turn of events after initial contact is made with the enemy's main force," although it is conceivable that Marcks's thinking would have progressed along similar lines had Halder not interfered with his effort.[20]

As for the situation south of the Pripet Marshes, Lossberg was particularly concerned about the possibility of the Russians themselves taking the initiative by leading off with an attack in the direction of the vital Rumanian oil fields. In order to counter this threat, he considered it imperative that forces be sent to Rumania as soon as feasible; first to organize the Rumanian army for defense and then to serve as a nucleus for a larger buildup prior to the German invasion. Once hostilities had begun, Army Group South was to execute a double envelopment maneuver between the marshes and the Black Sea.

It is not clear today how much influence the Lossberg plan had on Hitler, who never actually saw it, but it is evident that several features of the plan were incorporated into what became known as Directive Number 21 or the Barbarossa directive of December 18, 1940. It is possible that the soundness of the OKW study was impressed upon Hitler by Jodl, but this is unlikely because, for reasons of his own that will be explained later, Warlimont apparently kept it out of his superior's hands until mid-November. It is doubtful anyway that the OKW alone could have had a decisive influence over the führer at this time without outside help. There is evidence to show that Göring might have played a part here. Reich Marshal Hermann Göring is best known in his principal role as commander in chief of the Luftwaffe, but he wore other hats as well. As chairman of the Ministerial Council for the Defense of the Reich, in November 1940 Göring commissioned a report from General Thomas, who was chief of the Economic and Armaments Section of the OKW. In this report Thomas advocated a rapid occupation of European Russia for economic purposes (shortages in the Reich) as soon as possible after the start of hostilities, with the Ukraine and the Caucasus being particularly important.[21] It is easy to see how Göring, reinforced by the Lossberg report and the work by Thomas's staff, could have persuaded Hitler to reduce the city of Moscow to secondary importance in the strategic plan for the war against Russia. Halder and the general staff were still working on a solution that would put Moscow ahead as the single most important goal for the coming campaign, but in all probability Hitler's mind had been made up since the end of November. The general staff would now have to offer more evidence favoring Moscow than the OKW could offer against it.

On September 3, 1940, Halder obtained the appointment of Maj. Gen. Friedrich Paulus as Head Quartermaster I (OQI) in the general staff, a post that made Paulus his deputy. This was the same position that Halder himself had occupied before succeeding Ludwig Beck as chief of the general staff after Beck resigned in the fall of 1938 (in a disagreement with Hitler at the time of the Munich crisis over Czechoslovakia). Erich Ludendorff had been OQI during the First World War, but by 1940 the general staff no longer enjoyed the prestige it had once known.[22] Immediately after moving into his office at Army Headquarters in suburban Zossen, fifty-five kilometers southwest of Berlin, Paulus set to work on his new assignment, "to prepare a study, independent of the operational plans of General Marcks and Lieutenant Colonel Feyerabend, dealing with the problems of the distribution and deployment of forces in the east."[23]

The initial work on this project, which envisioned an eastern force of ninety-six infantry, thirty-one mobile, and one cavalry division, was completed and brought before Halder on September 17.[24] Later, at the end of November and early December, the OKH conducted a series of war games under Paulus's direction in which several general staff officers took part. During this time also the staff chiefs of the future army groups conducted games and undertook independent studies of their own. It was Paulus's conclusion, confirmed by the other studies as well, that in case of war with the Soviet Union, provision should first be made for reaching the general line Dnepr-Smolensk-Leningrad. Operations could then be conducted beyond this point only if the supply situation developed favorably. Paulus's appreciation of the supply difficulties was in accord with a study undertaken in November 1940 by the new general quartermaster of the army (this post was functionally different from the one held by Paulus, who was attached to the general staff), Major General Wagner. Wagner believed transportation problems would force a temporary halt in the operations after a line due east of Minsk was reached.[25] The consensus in the Quartermaster's Branch seemed to be that the Red Army would have to be brought to battle and defeated west of the Dnepr line or else the

German forces, spreading out in a fan shape into the interior of the Soviet Union, would lack the density to defeat the Russians.[26]

In any case, Paulus warned against allowing the Red Army to retreat intact into the depths of Russia. The great expanse of the country and the broad fronts meant that opportunities would exist for executing breakthrough maneuvers to prevent this withdrawal. On the other hand, Russia had few natural barriers, such as mountain ranges or large bodies of water, that could be utilized in pinning the enemy down after the breakthroughs had been effected. As a result, Paulus envisioned the possibility of further campaigns that would lead to a final battle to be fought on the basis of a "strategy of annihilation." His plan provided for the military occupation of the important parts of the Ukraine, White Russia, and the Baltic states for use as staging areas and as bargaining chips in future peace negotiations.

Although Paulus's studies were not yet complete (with other war games to be analyzed in mid-December) and although the staffs of the various army groups had not yet made their full reports, the stage was now set for Halder to present the general staff proposal to Hitler. This presentation was made at a conference held on December 5, 1940. Before a detailed discussion of the Halder plan, it would be well to examine briefly the theoretical foundations on which the plan rested.

The three major studies (by Greiffenberg-Feyerabend, Marcks, and Paulus) of an invasion of the Soviet Union that were conducted by the OKH and the general staff during the period from late July to early December 1940 all held two basic premises in common. The first premise was that the Wehrmacht was qualitatively far superior to the Red Army. The second was that there should not be an attack primarily along the traditional or Napoleonic route into Russia. Neither of these common threads of thought should be particularly surprising, though it must be said that Halder's insistence on a direct approach to the Soviet capital amounted to nothing less than a rejection of work done by his own staff and men commissioned by him.

The belief that the Wehrmacht was superior to the Red Army was almost universal in German military circles. This conviction was not just a stock-in-trade of Nazi propaganda but was given wide currency by most serious German military thinkers.[27] Taken in the context of the times, Brauchitsch's estimate that only about half of the Soviet divisions had any fighting ability was not unusual; this opinion had been reinforced by reports from General Köstring, the military attaché in Moscow, and from Colonel Rössing in Helsinki. A report by Guderian about his experiences with the Red Army in September and October 1939 at Brest Litovsk was also held in high regard, especially by Hitler. Guderian characterized the Soviet armaments, particularly the tanks, as "old and antiquated; in particular the communications equipment is very outdated." Guderian, however, neglected to mention this report in his memoirs, where he speaks well of the quality of Soviet tanks. In this regard, certainly, Hitler cannot be blamed for believing what his own experts, including Halder and Guderian, were telling him. In retrospect one should not attempt to find fault here with either Hitler or the generals for believing too strongly in their own technical and tactical superiority. After all, nothing they had seen in Poland or in France could have convinced them otherwise. Britain, of course, was a different matter, but Britain was hardly a threat to Germany's power on the continent in late 1940. It is true that the physical size of the Soviet Union and the country's immense population, over 170 million people,* should have given pause to any German connected with military planning, but they all, Hitler and the generals alike, believed that a rapid surprise attack would balance Germany's inferiority in numbers.[28]

There were several factors besides faulty intelligence information that misled the Germans into believing that Russia was a colossus with feet of clay, including the 1937–1938 purge of the officer corps in the Red Army, the Red Army's lamentable performance in the 1939–1940 war with Finland, impressions from contact with Soviet troops in the 1939 campaign in Poland, the older officers' experience with the Russian army in World War I, the Nazi view that the Russian people were "subhuman," and the belief that the Bolshevik state lacked the organizing ability and the stability to fight a large-scale war.[29] Viewed from the outside, the Soviet Union and its peoples offered a set of paradoxes for Hitler and his generals that they were unable to understand until it was

---

*The 1939 Soviet census put the population of the USSR at 170 million. Since half of the Soviet population was under twenty, the maximum number of men of military age was reckoned in 1941 at 17 million.

too late. The narrow-minded Nazi prejudice about the Russian people was perhaps the biggest problem to overcome, but it was certainly not the only one. Critical errors were made also in the areas of strategy and tactics which were more readily apparent though, in the long run, less fatal.

The idea of retracing Napoleon's march to Moscow through White Russia and Smolensk after crushing the Red Army (which would conveniently mass itself right along the newly erected frontier in eastern Poland, an area that included the tactically indefensible Bialystok salient) will have to rank as the most unimaginative and shortsighted plan for war ever produced by the German general staff. The mistakes made by Count Schlieffen and the younger Moltke before and during 1914 are more understandable, for they at least were ploughing new ground in attempting to make work a unique plan for finding a way out of a strategic impasse. It is a fact, however, that Halder had already shown himself unequal to the task of finding the answer to problems that demanded original solutions. The campaign in Poland, which turned out to be a surprisingly easy task for the Wehrmacht, had presented no difficulties at all. France, though, offered more of a challenge, and here Halder contented himself with presenting Hitler a proposal calling for a strong German right wing to push through central Belgium into the northern part of the country—in other words a maneuver that was nothing more than a reworked version of the old Schlieffen plan. The rapid strategic victory over France was made possible by Manstein* and, on a tactical level, Guderian, who together planned and executed the brilliant armored breakthrough in the Ardennes forest.[30]

For Hitler in December 1940 to have had expectations of much else from Halder beyond his past level of performance seems unlikely, and this undoubtedly is one reason why Hitler was disinclined to place much trust in the general staff.[31] Another reason was that Halder's proposal on December 5 for operations against Russia had no appeal for a man who always had an eye for his opponent's weaknesses. This proposal had not made any good use of the lessons put forth in the studies compiled by men in Halder's own organization; still less had it considered the possibility of un-

---

*At this time Erich von Manstein was chief of staff of von Rundstedt's Army Group "A." He was not allowed by the OKH later to take part in the planning for Barbarossa.

foreseen difficulties on the flanks, something the Lossberg OKW study had not failed to do.

Halder began his presentation to Hitler on December 5, 1940, with a short geographical description of the future theater of war.[32] The entire front was divided into northern and southern zones by the Pripet Marshes. As the roads and railroads in the direction Warsaw-Moscow were better then those in the south, the approaches into the Soviet Union north of the swamps offered more advantages. Continuing with this train of thought, Halder then said that the mass of the Red Army was apparently deployed north of the swamps.[33] This, of course, was pure conjecture on his part and was intended to support his argument that Moscow was the most vital target. As has been noted, the previous Greiffenberg-Feyerabend plan had taken the strong Soviet presence in the Ukraine into account. This same fact was also recognized in a study submitted on December 7, 1940, by General Sodenstern, the chief of staff of the future Army Group South. In Sodenstern's words, "Insofar as we can see, the main buildup of Russian forces has taken place in the Kiev Military District." Halder also noted that so many Soviet units had pulled up westward, close to the current demarcation line in Poland, that their supply bases could not lie too far behind, presumably just beyond the line of fortifications along the old pre-1939 Soviet-Polish border. In more general terms, Halder concluded that "the Dnepr and the Dvina rivers represent the easternmost line behind which the Russians will have to position themselves. If they retreat further eastward, they will no longer be able to protect their industrial areas." In order to prevent the Russians from carrying out a cohesive defensive battle west of the two rivers, Halder recommended the use of mass armored encirclements, especially on the central part of the front in the area Minsk-Smolensk. Finally, Halder proposed the formation of three army groups, two north and one south of the Pripet, which should push toward Leningrad, Moscow, and Kiev. The end goal of the campaign was to be the Volga-Archangel line, and it was to be reached with a force of 105 infantry and 32 armored and mobile divisions, with two armies being held in reserve for the beginning phase (see Figure 5).

In response to Halder's report, Hitler agreed with the general plan but added that the situation on the flanks of Army Group Center would need to be taken care of as the first order of busi-

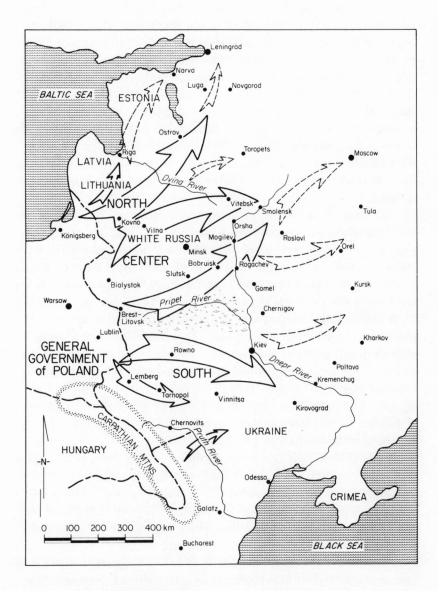

Figure 5. The OKH (Halder) Plan

77

ness. This could be done by encirclements in the Baltic region, aided by forces turned to the north from Army Group Center, if necessary, and encirclements in the south in the Ukraine. After these encirclements were completed, a decision could be made either to take Moscow or to push to the east of the city if circumstances warranted. The choice, at least in Hitler's mind, had now been made. He had elected to place the Baltic and the Ukraine ahead of Moscow in terms of their strategic importance (see Figure 6). In accepting this alternative Hitler also agreed with the innovation first put forward in the Lossberg study, that part of Army Group Center be used to aid Army Group North in securing the Baltic flank before the final drive on Moscow. It seems likely, however, that Hitler could have been more precise in phrasing his rebuttal to Halder's speech. In declaring himself "in agreement with [Halder's] proposed operational considerations" Hitler may have unintentionally given Halder an out for salvaging his own scheme.[34]

In spite of all the propaganda to the contrary, Hitler did not try early in the war to run roughshod over his generals. It could be that here he was trying to be diplomatic and avoid offense to Halder in front of his colleagues. When the war in the east began to develop unfavorably, time and again Hitler shied away from head-on confrontations with his generals. Typically, he would defer a decision for further study, allowing time for people close to him that he trusted to muster their forces and bend his supposed stubborn will to their own whims. This tendency of Hitler's was known by those privileged to have close contact with him and was used to their advantage. This characteristic of the führer had a decisive impact on the way the war was conducted in the east, in particular in the decision-making process in July–August 1941, as will be seen in later chapters.

It is difficult to say what actually passed through Halder's mind at this point, for he let Hitler's comments pass in silence, but actions speak louder than words and we shall see that Halder was a man intent on his purpose. Hitler and the OKW could go to blazes, but Halder would do all he could to see to it that his strategic plan for Russia and no one else's was put into action.

From this point on Halder and his colleagues in the OKH would devote most of their efforts to subverting Hitler's intentions instead of acting in accordance with them. After the war, this atti-

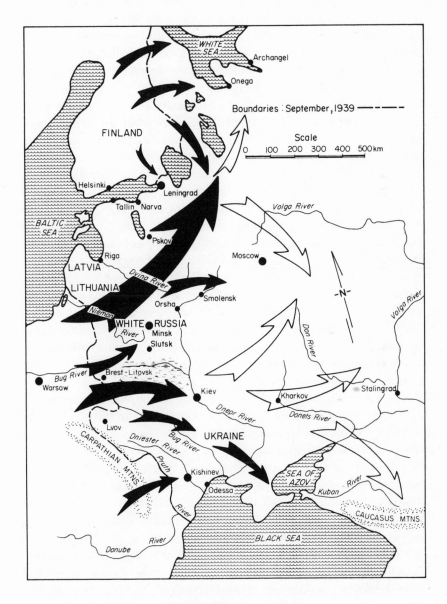

Figure 6. Hitler's Plan for War in 1940

tude would be justified on the basis of Hitler's total irrationality in placing economic goals ahead of purely military concerns in planning the eastern campaign.[35] This justification is only partly valid, however, as Hitler's fears for the flanks of Army Group Center were soundly based on strategical and operational considerations, not economic priorities. As for worrying about the economic aspects of the war in the east, Hitler could hardly be blamed for placing a high priority on the occupation of the Ukraine and the Caucasus, with all their resources.[36] In the year 1940 Germany was dependent on the ten million tons of iron ore imported from Sweden. Germany produced no chrome or nickel, both essential for producing steel of armaments grade. Neither did the country have any tungsten, necessary to make high-speed machine tools, and the supply of molybdenum and manganese could easily be cut off should Stalin decide to end economic cooperation with Germany. Moreover, most of Germany's national stockpiles of copper and tin had been used up in the spring of 1939.[37] Hitler and the Economics and Armaments Branch of the OKW were acutely aware that the only resource Germany had in abundance was coal and that a protracted war, either in the east or the west, would end in a German defeat unless these deficiencies were permanently remedied.[38] To say that Hitler's plan in 1940 was more concerned with economics than strategy is not correct, as an examination of the Lossberg study will prove, yet the plan did not ignore economics, and this feature of it made Hitler's conception of the future campaign more deserving of the name "strategy" than was the proposal put forth by Halder.[39]

After December 5, 1940, the rest of the year was anticlimactic, with little progress being made toward solidifying the basic goals of the Russian plan, let alone finding a way to translate the operational theory compiled in the various studies into a definite scheme of action. Yet, the year 1940 should not be allowed to recede into oblivion without an examination of one other event regarding the Russian problem that occurred shortly before its end; in mid-December the head quartermaster of the general staff, Friedrich Paulus, conducted his final war game.[40]

The second phase of the Paulus games was held between December 17 and 20 and was concerned with two major questions: (1) How would it be possible to coordinate the movements of the mechanized units and the marching infantry, taking into account their differing rates of speed? (2) How would it be possible to supply an army of 3–3.5 million men deep in the interior of the Soviet Union?[41] It should be noted that these questions were fundamental to the whole concept of blitzkrieg warfare. If no satisfactory solutions to these problems could be found, the entire premise that a rapid victory could be won over the Soviet Union would have to be scrapped. In testing this premise, Paulus essentially was exploring new ground, for never before had the general staff been called to expand the blitzkrieg concept into such a vast geographical area. The general staff was now dealing with a problem of truly continental dimensions, and a way had to be found to take a set of strategies and tactics that had been designed for use in countries the size of Poland and France and apply them in a land of virtually limitless space. That the results of Paulus's efforts were not deemed conclusive by Halder and the OKH was not the fault of Paulus; it was, rather, due to their own shortsighted inability to perceive the difficulties with respect to time and space that faced them in the east. The Russians knew perfectly well what time and space meant for military operations in their huge country and were able to use it to their advantage. For the German accustomed to living within the cramped confines of central Europe, the real meaning of distance would have to be learned the hard way.

Despite the fact that the führer had expressed a preference for a flank strategy against the Soviet Union at the December 5 conference, Paulus's last war game was conducted on the basis that Moscow, not Leningrad or the Ukraine, should be the main objective. It is obvious from the summation of the maneuvers written down by Paulus after the war that it was Halder's general staff plan that was being tested and that Hitler's wishes were being disregarded. The participants took the general staff instructions as their starting point, with no independent effort being made to question certain precepts that by now had become articles of faith accepted by everyone connected with Halder and the OKH. It was, for example, assumed for purposes of the maneuvers (1) that the Russians would have to give battle west of the Dnepr-Dvina line in order to protect their vital production centers; (2) that the Russians would commit a significant part of their army to battle close to the frontier in order to protect recently acquired territories and to slow down the German offensive from the very first; (3) that it was necessary to concentrate the largest possible force in the area of Army Group Center in order to take Moscow as rapidly as possible; (4) that the Wehrmacht was decisively superior to the Red Army in artillery, tanks, signals and communications, and in the air. It was taken for granted that the German infantry division was one-third stronger than the Russian in heavy weapons.[42]

The objective posed during the war game was to reach the upper Dnepr–Dvina–Lake Peipus line, not actually to take Moscow itself, although Moscow was considered to be the keystone of the entire operation. Army Group South was to push from Rumania and southern Poland toward Kiev. Army Group Center was to attack from southern East Prussia and from around Brest Litovsk in order to cut off the Russians in the Bialystok salient, which protruded sharply westward. Army Group Center was then to send panzer columns rapidly ahead to a line east of Orsha and Vitebsk, establishing bridgeheads across the Dnepr. Army Group North was to advance from East Prussia toward Leningrad, with the line Velikie Luki–Staraia Russa–Lake Peipus as its first objective. Army Group North was also given the responsibility of protecting the left flank of Army Group Center.

After reaching these objectives on the twentieth day of the theoretical invasion, everyone agreed to call a three-week halt in order to refresh the armored units, bring up supplies, and regroup forces in general. In an evaluation of the situation at this point, the commander of Army Group South, which had been held up in front of Kiev, asked for the loan of some armored units from Army Group Center to aid in cutting off the Russians defending Kiev from the rear. Army Group South would strike northeastward from a bridgehead south of Kiev while Army Group Center would send help from an area near Gomel across the Dnepr and the Desna rivers to Nezhin. The OKH reserve armor near Gomel would also be committed in this maneuver. The commander of Army Group North came forward with a similar request for the loan of Army Group Center's and the OKH's armor in order to stabilize the front held by his right (southern) wing north of Velikie Luki–Lake Ilmen. These requests were argued against by the commander of Army Group Center, who maintained that side issues would not determine the outcome of the war and that his group must preserve its strength intact if a successful assault on Moscow were to be carried out.

The end result of these deliberations was that Army Group

Center was given the go-ahead to carry out its mission while the other two army groups were restricted to more or less supporting roles. Army Group South was to surround Kiev with no outside help while at the same time concentrating the bulk of its forces on its left (northern) wing and cutting off the Russians west of the line Kharkov–Kursk. Once the line Kharkov–Kursk had been reached, the southern flank of Army Group Center would be secured. In regard to Army Group North, Halder himself insisted that the capture of Leningrad and the destruction of the Soviet forces along the Baltic would wait until the task of Army Group Center had been accomplished.[43] In the meantime, Army Group North was to beef up its right wing connecting with the central front in the area of Velikie Luki–south of Lake Ilmen–Lake Peipus.

In his summary of the lessons learned in the war game study, Paulus concluded that the German forces "were barely sufficient for the purpose" assigned to them. Paulus demonstrated that the Wehrmacht would be shorn of its reserves by the time it reached Moscow and that the final assault on the city would have to be undertaken by forces already engaged on the front lines without any follow-up reinforcements at all. Paulus also noted that reaching the Volga-Archangel line was beyond the power of the Wehrmacht to achieve.

Another factor that emerged in varying guises as the biggest problem to be overcome during these exercises was, as has been mentioned, the difficulty associated with time and space in a country as large as the Soviet Union. In order to make the accepted German theory of blitzkrieg warfare serve in this wholly unprecedented situation, the participants in the exercise quickly discovered that some sort of compromise had to be reached between the fast-racing armored units and the slower-moving infantry. It was finally decided to allow the armor to forge ahead in independent thrusts, leaving the infantry alone to mop up the enemy cutoff by the freewheeling pincer movements of the mobile columns. This, of course, left unanswered the serious reservations some commanders had about the lack of flank protection for these independent armored thrusts, but this problem was not solved in 1940. Indeed, it was not adequately dealt with in 1941, either.

The facts of the supply situation seemed to wreak even worse havoc with theory. The distance from the Bug River to Smolensk was seven hundred kilometers, and to Moscow a full one thousand kilometers by air. The games demonstrated that the German supply depots located close behind the original starting point would be adequate to sustain a drive eastward only to the Dnepr–Dvina line. If new supply areas were to be built, they would be dependent on the sparsely connected, mostly one-track, wide-gauge Russian railway system. Even after the destroyed railway lines were rebuilt, taking into account the extra difficulty of correcting the track gauge, the calculation was that shortages and interruptions in supply could not be prevented. In summary, it was concluded that, with the materials available, improvisation would have to be relied upon and that no concrete solution could be found beforehand for the problem of supply.[44]

The Paulus war maneuvers were amazingly accurate in foreshadowing the actual course of events after June 22, 1941. The collapse of the blitzkrieg method of warfare was only a matter of time after the eastern campaign began, as Paulus's exercise demonstrated beyond a doubt. It is to be wondered why, taking all the information at his disposal into account, Halder did not discard his previously submitted operational scheme and offer new, more realistic proposals to Hitler early in 1941, based on the likelihood that the campaign would require a minimum of two seasons in Russia instead of one. Paulus had proven the general staff plan of December 5, 1940, to be bankrupt, devoid of any chance of success. It was now up to Hitler to use what few hard bits of information he had in order to mold a solid cast for an eastern operational directive. This was done on December 18, 1940, in the form of Order Number 21.[45]

DIRECTIVE BARBAROSSA AND ITS IMPLEMENTATION

The similarities of Order Number 21, or Directive Barbarossa to the earlier discussed Lossberg study have already been mentioned, but two of these points should be singled out. First, after the enemy forces in White Russia were crushed, Army Group Center was to prepare to turn northward with strong mobile units and help Army Group North clear the Baltic area of any Soviet threat. Second, with regard to Moscow, "Only after the fulfillment of this first essential task, which must include the occupation of Leningrad and Kronstadt, will the attack be continued with the intention of occupying Moscow." It was further stated that "only a surprisingly rapid collapse of Russian resistance could justify the simul-

taneous pursuit of both objectives [i.e., Leningrad and Moscow]."
In most other respects, however, Directive Number 21 did not dif-
fer materially from Halder's proposal of December 5, especially
on the tactical level. Plan Barbarossa agreed with the general staff
that deeply penetrating armored spearheads could effectively lead
to the destruction of the bulk of the Red Army in western Russia.
It also incorporated the idea that the main weight of the entire
offensive, a force composed of two army groups, should fall north
of the Pripet Marshes. The third army group, Army Group South,
was to push in the direction of Kiev while seeking to destroy all
Soviet forces in the western Ukraine by means of concentric operations (see Figure 7).

An examination of Directive Number 21 reveals nothing to
support the contention that Hitler was obsessed with economic
goals while neglecting the necessary, purely military measures. The
only direct reference to the economic ends of the campaign is contained in the following passage:

> When the battles north and south of the Pripet Marshes are ended,
> the pursuit of the enemy will have the following aims: in the south
> the early capture of the Donets Basin, important for war industry;
> in the north a quick advance to Moscow. The capture of this city
> would represent a decisive political and economic success and
> would also bring about the capture of the most important railway
> junctions.

Directive Barbarossa closed with the statement that the führer
awaited submission of the final plans by his service chiefs in accordance with the guidelines laid down by the directive. The fateful year 1941 was now at hand, and the initial mid-May target date
for Barbarossa was but a short time away. Much had to be done to
prepare for the new war; Halder and Brauchitsch immersed themselves in the tedious but necessary mass of details that had to be
sorted out if the army in the east were to have a coherent organization and a sense of purpose. It has been said of Halder, however,
that his "bureaucratic diligence" was excessive and that he should
have devoted more time to the broader concepts of strategy and
planning.[46] Halder's diary overflows with remarks about petty details that would hardly seem to come within the province of the
chief of the general staff.

On January 31, 1941, Halder and Brauchitsch presented the

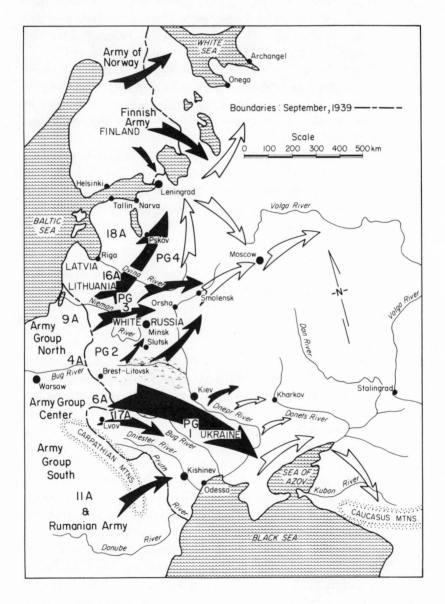

Figure 7. Directive Barbarossa

Deployment Directive Barbarossa to Hitler. This document outlined the basic areas of deployment and operational objectives for
all army groups, panzer groups, and armies on the eastern front.[47]
The OKH had been compelled, no matter how grudgingly, to go
along with Hitler's wishes as expressed at the December 5, 1940,
conference. For this reason the deployment directive provided
that, after Smolensk was reached by Army Group Center, "a
strong portion of its mobile strength should cooperate with Army
Group North in order to destroy the enemy forces along the Baltic
and in the area of Leningrad." A provision was made for an immediate assault on Moscow only if there came about "an unexpected and total collapse of enemy resistance in northern Russia
obviating the necessity of turning [armored forces to the north]."

Actually, however, the deployment directive was a compromise, because the distribution of forces it dictated shows that the
army leadership was trying to prevent a watering down of its own
"guiding concepts." Army Group South was given three armies
and one panzer group in order to achieve its mission of destroying
the Red Army in Galicia and the western Ukraine, but one of these
armies, the Eleventh, was ordered at Hitler's insistence to stand on
the defensive in Rumania. The German force north of the Pripet
Marshes, composed of fifty infantry and twenty-two mobile or armored divisions, was much stronger than the southern force of
thirty infantry and only eight mobile or armored divisions. The
OKH hoped that Army Group North, with its twenty-one divisions
(five mobile), would do well enough against the estimated thirty
enemy divisions on its front so that it could get along without any
outside help. In this way, the OKH calculated that Army Group
North would be able to not only control the situation on the Baltic
but also cover the left flank of Army Group Center's push to
Moscow.[48]

The situation in the south, however, continued to be a vexing
problem. Since the end of 1940 an increasing amount of intelligence information had been filtering out of the Soviet Union that
indicated beyond a doubt that a major shift in the deployment of
the Red Army was taking place.[49] The new area of concentration was the Ukraine, with the buildup there placing Army Group
South decisively in a numerically inferior position. Geographically,
too, squeezed as it was between the Pripet Marshes on its left flank

and the four hundred-kilometer-long barrier of the Carpathian Mountains on its right, Army Group South could not hope to score well in the early battles along the frontier. In March 1941, von Rundstedt, the commander of Army Group South, proposed forming a "Carpathian Group" drawn from the Seventeenth Army that would use Hungarian territory as its base for the attack against Russia. This strategy would avoid clashing head-on with the three Soviet armies in the Galician-Podolian bottleneck between the Pripet swamps and the eastern Carpathians. Hitler refused, however, citing the political reservations of the Hungarian government. Thus, after the German forces in Rumania had been weakened by the Balkan campaign, and contrary to the original plan, Army Group South was to have only one wing of encirclement and the Seventeenth Army would have to advance straight into the enemy's front.[50] The growing feeling of uneasiness about the situation in the Ukraine was manifested in a conference held at the Berghof on February 3, 1941, shortly after the issuance of the Barbarossa deployment directive.

On that occasion, Halder noted, in his report to Hitler dealing with the conduct of operations during Barbarossa, that signs of Russian military activity were on the increase in both the Baltic and the Ukraine.[51] Halder discounted the significance of this new Soviet initiative in strengthening their defenses, however, by downgrading the fighting capability of the Red Army. Halder produced the latest general staff Intelligence Department figures, which estimated the Soviet forces opposing Germany at only one hundred infantry and twenty-five cavalry divisions, plus thirty mechanized brigades.[52] The enemy was credited with having more tanks than the Wehrmacht, but the Russian mechanized units were described as being substantially inferior to the German. As for the tank units operating in the Soviet combined-arms rifle divisions, the chief of the general staff described them as being "wretched, slapped together material." The Russians were conceded to be well provided with artillery, but their equipment was belittled as "of small value." Halder also believed it was pointless even to talk about the leadership of the Red Army, saying only Marshal Timoshenko had any talent to speak of. It would appear from the general tenor of Halder's address that he was going beyond the usual ridicule of the Soviet armed forces, so fashionable in high army circles, and was earnestly trying to convince Hitler that all the

Wehrmacht had to do was walk into Moscow and demand the keys to the Kremlin. The continued attempts by Halder and the OKH to erode Hitler's sense of judgment by supplying him misleading information did not have an immediate effect, but later, after June 1941, the cumulative pressure on the führer from all directions would become very great, and his stubborn will would break with telling results.

In response to Halder's report, Hitler refused to take the bait offered him and said that he was still of the opinion that the Russians would not be easily driven out of the Baltic and the Ukraine. He continued to maintain that the Red Army must not merely be driven back but destroyed wholesale, and that the best way to do this would be by anchoring the strongest German forces on the flanks while holding defensively on the central front. Then after the flanks were secure, the remaining enemy forces in the center could be dealt with by means of concentric operations. Again, and the point must be reemphasized, Hitler based his arguments solely on strategic considerations, not on long-range economic plans or abstruse political dogma as has so often been charged.

The lines of conflict now were firmly drawn between Hitler and the OKH. No further changes in basic goals or strategy were to take place before June 22, 1941. The only major alteration in planning came as a result of the coup in Yugoslavia in late March 1941, which made it necessary for Hitler to clear the southern flank in the Balkans before turning to the main target, the Soviet Union. The Balkan operations, which began on April 6, caused Barbarossa to be postponed by five weeks, from May 15 to June 22, 1941.[53] Hitler agreed to the new timetable in a conference with Warlimont on April 30, 1941. Some have said that this delay was a vital factor in the failure of the German blitzkrieg in Russia to achieve a decisive victory before the onset of winter, but this is not really likely.[54] It is improbable that the attack could have taken place earlier, because of difficulties in deploying the German forces and also because of weather conditions inside the Soviet Union that produced unusually late and extensive spring floods. Nevertheless, it is generally agreed that the wear and tear on the German armored vehicles was severe in the mountainous Balkan region, and this would have an important effect later.[55] The most important reasons for the failure of the blitzkrieg, however, had little to do with the five-week delay, as will be seen.

GERMAN STRATEGIC PLANNING IN RETROSPECT

For their part, the generals in the OKH and the general staff maintained a sullen silence about their real plans and intentions regarding Barbarossa. Halder and Brauchitsch chose not to provoke a clash with Hitler over the question of Moscow versus the flanks in the Soviet Union, but there can be no doubt that a gulf in understanding existed between the two opposing camps—Hitler and the OKW on one side and the OKH, along with its general staff, on the other. It should be said, though, that Warlimont, as head of Section "L" in the OKW was friendly to Halder and the OKH. As has already been noted, it may have been he who attempted to suppress the Lossberg study by preventing Hitler from seeing it; he may also have been responsible for keeping the study out of his superior's (Jodl's) hands for two months in 1940.[56]

It has been argued that the generals were justified in not clearing up the contradictions with Hitler before the campaign because Moscow could be held steadfast as a goal in the political and military sense without formulating the exact operational plans to get there. It was considered, moreover, bad form to plan the latter stages of a campaign even before the war had started.[57] In other words, the OKH and Hitler chose to interpret Moltke's dictum in different ways. Hitler elected to leave the strategic goals undecided until the strategy and power of resistance of the enemy had been tested and to wait until Smolensk and the Dnepr had been reached before making a final commitment. Halder and the OKH wanted to put one basic goal above all else, a strategy that ignored any real possibility of the enemy taking effective countermeasures on the flanks of the Central Army Group. According to this last view, only minor adjustments would have to be made to deal with difficulties on the flanks, whereas the main thrust of the offensive was to be carried out without worrying about enemy concentrations on the Baltic or in the Ukraine. Time would tell which of these views best suited the realities of combat on the eastern front.

Throughout the course of German strategic planning for the eastern campaign in 1940–1941, and especially after the abortive visit by Molotov to Berlin in November 1940, it became a consistent theme in the discussions of high-level military figures with Hitler that Germany had to settle conclusively with the Soviet Union in the immediate future. The necessity for starting a preventive war against the Bolsheviks was something that was not in dispute, either by the OKH, the OKW, or Hitler.[58] On the diplomatic front, the swift Soviet action against the Baltic states and Rumania in June–July 1940, coupled with Molotov's demands for more Soviet influence in Finland and the Balkans in November 1940, convinced Hitler and the German military that the USSR was not going to be content with expansion toward the south and toward the Persian Gulf at the expense of the British Empire, as Ribbentrop and Hitler had wished.[59] Stalin was determined to play a leading role in European affairs, and he had done much since the German-Soviet nonaggression pact in the summer of 1939 to consolidate his country's strategic position in Poland, Finland, the Baltic states, and Rumania.

On the purely military front, by late spring 1941, the Germans had a clearer picture, literally, of the scope of Russian preparations for war in the western areas. A group of specially equipped high-altitude Luftwaffe reconnaissance planes, "Squadron Rowehl," for some weeks had been conducting flights across the German-Russian demarcation line in depths of up to three hundred kilometers.[60] Although the information gathered from these flights was not conclusive, it became obvious that in the event of war the Soviet threat to Rumania and the Wehrmacht's oil supply would become very great. The decision, then, to deal a heavy blow to the USSR before its potential threat could grow much beyond the existing level was one that found easy acceptance among German military leaders. They certainly were not motivated by abstract ideas of "living space" in the east, nor were they dedicated to the grander concept of a "Greater German Reich" stretching from western France to the Black Sea.[61] This is not to deny that the non-Nazi generals favored territorial expansion for Germany, but none of them are on record as having endorsed Hitler's most extreme proposals in this respect. They did believe, however, that after 1941 the relative strength of the USSR, economically, diplomatically, and militarily, could only increase, whereas Germany's could only decline as long as the war dragged on in the west, a war that eventually might well mean the involvement of the United States.[62] Halder himself said after the war that no nation should be denied the ultimate right to launch a preventive war if that is the only alternative left open to it.[63] The Russians, too, are not loath to admit that their country, already under a massive war-oriented economic program inaugurated by Stalin in 1929, would have been in a much stronger position in 1943 than in 1941.[64] The Third Reich's best chance was in 1941, albeit a slender one.

If there is any lesson to be learned from studying the German efforts at developing a plan for war against the Soviet Union, it is that the absence of harmony among the military and political leaders, and among the various military branches as well, produced an atmosphere in which the formulation of a smoothly coordinated program of action was quite impossible. It would be easy to single out one or more individuals—Halder, for example—as blameworthy for having brought this about, but to do so would be an oversimplification. The entire social, political, economic, and military system of the Third Reich can be viewed as an assortment of personal empires and spheres of influence that existed in a state of eternal and sometimes ferocious competition with one another. This point was driven home quite effectively by Albert Speer in his memoir, *Inside the Third Reich.*[65]

The OKH was one of many organizations that had to struggle for a measure of autonomy against the growing spheres of interest of Himmler, Göring, and Bormann. The OKH was also pitted in a struggle against a rival military organization, the OKW, which rightly or wrongly was regarded merely as an extension of Hitler's ego. In the poisoned atmosphere of mistrust and suspicion, rivalry and jealousy, that prevailed in Nazi Germany in the late 1930s and early 1940s, it is easy to understand how Halder and his colleagues could work themselves into a subversive and conspiratorial frame of mind against anything or anyone, including Hitler, who dared encroach upon their own private bailiwick.[66] To go to war under such conditions meant, however, to court disaster. It would also be wrong to condemn the OKH and the general staff out of hand for their slipshod and amateurish handling of Russia as a strategic problem, for they, as has been seen, were operating in an informational vacuum with regard to the prospective enemy. But history is a cruel judge and ignorance cannot be allowed to serve as an excuse.

The real test of the wisdom and good sense of the OKH and its leaders would come on the banks of the Dnepr, Dvina, and Desna in the summer of 1941, at Smolensk, Yelnia, and Kiev. By then enough would be known of the enemy and his tactics for them to make an honest appraisal of a situation that had proven to be a good deal more complex and perilous than they had originally imagined. By drawing the correct conclusions after reaching the Dnepr, the German army could have been spared a catastrophe for another year; precious time could have been won for gearing the country and its economy for total war. But this was not to be.

CHAPTER 3

RACE TO THE DNEPR

THE FORMATION OF THE BIALYSTOK–MINSK POCKETS

The deployment of Hitler's eastern legions began in February 1941 with the arrival in Poland of seven infantry, and one motorized, divisions aboard troop trains from the west. From mid-March to mid-April eighteen large units rolled into western Poland, and from then until the first of May the Reichsbahn had to increase the normal rate of traffic on the Polish railroads by a hundred percent.[1] In addition to the movement of troops, a new, massive bunker complex, called the *Wolfschanze* or "Wolf's Den" by Hitler, was built near Rastenburg in East Prussia to serve as headquarters for the führer and the OKW during the war in Russia. The OKH headquarters was set up in the Mauerwald near Angerburg, about an hour's drive from the Wolfschanze. In a subtle way, the remoteness of this site contributed to the sense of isolation felt by the Army commanders (see Figures 8 and 9).

In all, 2.5 million men were deployed by the Germans along the eastern front by June 22, 1941, with somewhat less than half of them, 1.162 million, positioned in the area of Field Marshal von Bock's Army Group Center. Of the seventeen panzer divisions sent to the east, five were included in Guderian's Panzer Group 2 opposite Brest Litovsk and four were placed around Suvalki in Hermann Hoth's Panzer Group 3.[2] There was no doubt in Halder's mind that Army Group Center was powerful enough to crush all resistance in the Bialystok–Minsk area and then rapidly reach the first important operational objectives on the Dnepr and Dvina rivers.[3]

95

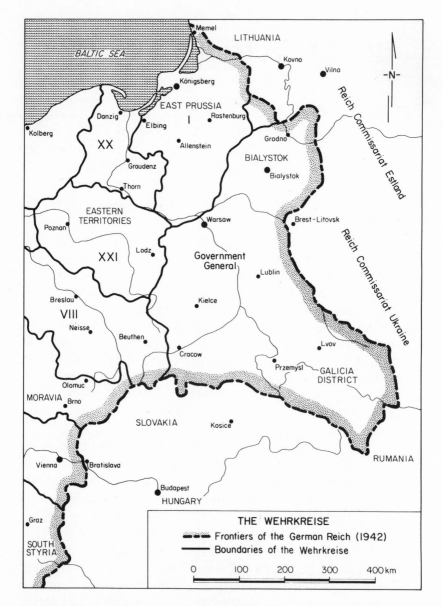

Figure 8. The Eastern Zones of the German Empire

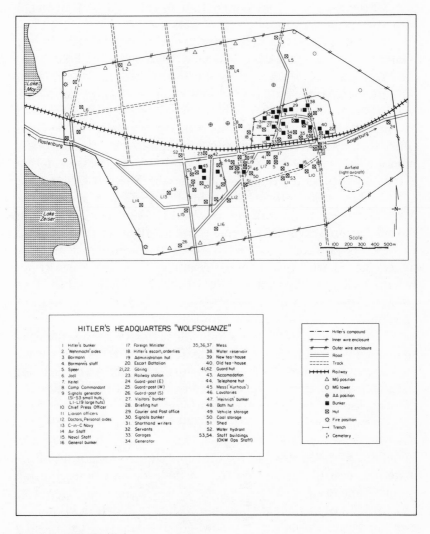

HITLER'S HEADQUARTERS "WOLFSCHANZE"

1. Hitler's bunker
2. Wehrmacht aides
3. Bormann
4. Bormann's staff
5. Speer
6. Jodl
7. Keitel
8. Camp Commandant
9. Signals generator (S1–S3 small huts, L1–L19 large huts)
10. Chief Press Officer
11. Liaison officers
12. Doctors, Personal aides
13. C-in-C Navy
14. Air Staff
15. Naval Staff
16. General bunker
17. Foreign Minister
18. Hitler's escort; orderlies
19. Administration hut
20. Escort Battalion
21,22. Göring
23. Railway station
24. Guard-post (E)
25. Guard-post (W)
26. Guard-post (S)
27. Visitors' bunker
28. Briefing hut
29. Courier and Post office
30. Signals bunker
31. Shorthand writers
32. Servants
33. Garages
34. Generator
35,36,37. Mess
38. Water reservoir
39. New tea-house
40. Old tea-house
41,42. Guard hut
43. Accomodation
44. Telephone hut
45. Mess ('Kurhaus')
46. Lavatories
47. 'Heinrich' bunker
48. Bath hut
49. Vehicle storage
50. Coal storage
51. Shed
52. Water hydrant
53,54. Staff buildings (OKW Ops Staff)

—·—·— Hitler's compound
—#—#— Inner wire enclosure
—#—#— Outer wire enclosure
════ Road
----- Track
+++++ Railway
△ MG position
○ MG tower
⊕ AA position
■ Bunker
▨ Hut
✿ Fire position
⊢—⊣ Trench
¦¦ Cemetery

Figure 9. The Wolfschanze

97

It was the task of the two panzer groups situated on the flanks of Army Group Center to drive into the Bialystok salient from the north and south and link up east of Minsk, thus, according to Halder, creating conditions favorable for the destruction of the enemy forces located between Bialystok and Minsk. After achieving this first goal, Guderian and Hoth were to proceed rapidly toward the line Smolensk–Yelnia–Roslavl across the Dnepr and toward Vitebsk and the upper Dvina area, in order, it was hoped, to prevent the Russians from gaining time to erect a cohesive defense using these two important river barriers.[4]

The two infantry armies assigned to Army Group Center, the Ninth commanded by Colonel General Strauss and the Fourth under Field Marshal von Kluge, were given the task of following behind the two panzer groups as closely as possible and securing the Bialystok–Minsk pocket after the armored ring had closed around Minsk. The Russians then trapped in the pocket were expected either to surrender en masse or to succumb quickly to the greatly superior German force. The Fourth Army was to assist Guderian in crossing the frontier on the southern flank of Army Group Center and then follow along behind his Panzer Group 2, while the Ninth Army was to perform the same function in cooperation with Panzer Group 3. On the extreme southern flank of Army Group Center was positioned the 1st Cavalry Division, which was assigned the difficult task of moving along the edge of the Pripet swamps and guarding against a Soviet thrust from the south. This mounted division would later be reinforced by two infantry divisions.

It was Halder's plan, true to his false theories about the Russian strategy for defense, to subordinate Army Group Center's two panzer groups to the infantry armies during the beginning phase of the attack on June 22. It was believed by the OKH that the Russian fortifications along the demarcation line would be stronger than they in fact proved to be. For this reason, Halder considered it wise to use artillery and infantry to effect the initial breakthrough, saving the armored strength for the rapid exploitation of the anticipated successful rupture of the enemy's defense line. Putting infantry ahead of tanks during the initial assault was, however, just the kind of tactic that Guderian wished to avoid. In his mind's eye, Guderian visualized the few good roads in Russia being choked by marching columns of men and slow-moving motorized and horse-drawn vehicles. Experience in France had shown that fast-moving tank units would encounter delays in passing through such obstacles, so Guderian firmly rejected Halder's proposal when the chief of the general staff visited him at his headquarters in Warsaw on June 6.

Halder made the same proposal to the chief of staff of Army Group North, but it was also rejected by Colonel General Hoepner, the commander of Panzer Group 4.[5] These incidents no doubt contributed to the lack of respect Guderian and the other panzer generals felt for the OKH, a feeling that would grow into a deep and personal enmity when the campaign in Russia began to develop unfavorably. Beyond this, Col. Rudolf Schmundt, Hitler's chief adjutant, was actively trying to persuade the führer to sack some of the older "entrenched" leaders of the OKH and replace them with generals having more recent combat experience. Schmundt especially wanted Guderian to replace Brauchitsch.[6]

The German strategic concept of the disposition of the Russian forces along the eastern front compelled the OKH to assume that the first enemy reaction after the German assault would be to attempt to withdraw all forces from the frontier in a hurried retreat and regroup them along a makeshift defense line farther east, presumably behind the Dnepr–Dvina line.[7] Halder's plan then for using far-reaching armored spearheads to seal off the lines of retreat of the enemy's main force grouped along the border was tailored to suit a situation that did not exist.

At 9:15 P.M. on June 22, Marshal Timoshenko ordered the Northwestern, Western, and Southwestern fronts to take the offensive. No order was given by the Soviet Supreme Command for the Third and Tenth armies to pull back from the Bialystok salient to the line Lida–Slonim–Pinsk until June 25.[8] It was not the intention of the Red Army command to order an immediate retreat for the forces in the Bialystok salient, nor did these units represent anything more than a small part of the military resources at its disposal. (Figure 10 shows how the tactical and operational echelons of the Red Army actually were deployed on June 22. This deployment should be compared with that shown on the general staff map in Figure 1.) Even if Halder's suppositions had been correct about the placement of the Red Army, the probable reaction of the Soviet Supreme Command to the moves by the German panzer groups to cut off the Bialystok salient, other factors would have

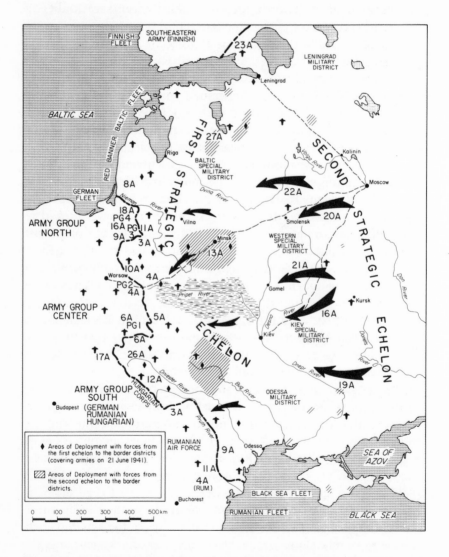

Figure 10. Soviet Tactical and Operational Deployment on June 22, 1941

made the carrying out of such a vast encirclement extremely hazardous.

The scale of maneuver in Russia was to be much larger than anything previously encountered by the OKH, and the Wehrmacht lacked enough mechanized units effectively to manage such great spaces. The distance from the German jump-off line to Minsk was over three hundred kilometers, and Smolensk was seven hundred kilometers distant. By comparison in 1940 German tanks were required to traverse only three hundred kilometers from the border of the Reich to the mouth of the Somme in order to cut off the French army.[9]

Out of Army Group Center's entire allotment of manpower, only eighteen percent was contained in the mechanized units, whereas altogether the Germans were prepared to begin operations in the Soviet Union, on all fronts, with only 3,200 tanks.[10] Although the OKH had committed itself to a strategy that favored rapid movement over long distances, heavy reliance was made on horses, with some 625,000 of them being used to pull everything from field kitchens to artillery pieces. The Wehrmacht began the war in the east with a total of about 600,000 motor vehicles of all kinds; however, many of them were of Czech or French origin and had weak suspensions that could not negotiate poorly surfaced Russian roads, often axle-deep in sand when the weather was dry and impassable quagmires when it rained. Only about 3 percent of the roads in European Russia were hard-surfaced in 1941, and this meant that a great strain would be placed on the German supply system, which would have to depend almost exclusively on wheeled trucks until the Russian railway network could be repaired and converted to the standard European gauge.[11]

When the big guns opened fire in the early dawn hours of June 22 and the first German units crossed over into Soviet territory, reports began to flow into army headquarters that did not conform to Halder's preconceived opinions about the enemy's defense plans. Not only was Russian resistance along the border in most cases surprisingly light, but Soviet artillery activity was scarcely visible. These factors, coupled with the inability of the Luftwaffe to detect any major Russian movement on the roads leading out of the Bialystok salient during the first few days of the war, led some German commanders, particularly those of the larger units, to wonder if the Russians were hiding out in the forests around Bialy-

stok or were much weaker in strength than German intelligence
had estimated. Another possibility also existed, one that Strauss
feared had come true: "Were their masses lying farther east, did
we have a false idea about their deployment?"[12]

The reports about the absence of a Russian retreat from the
Bialystok salient were rationalized by Halder as being due to the
"clumsiness" of the Russian command, which he considered to be
incapable of taking countermeasures on an operational level. It
was his view that the Russians would have to defend themselves in
their current positions, being unable to react properly, because the
Red Army lacked the ability to discern the broad sweep of the
Wehrmacht's movements.[13] The absence of any Russian move to
retreat from the Bialystok salient also made a strong impression on
Guderian, who noted in his panzer group's war diary, "It is possible that the Russian High Command knew about the coming attack but did not pass the information down to the forces actually
doing the fighting."[14] The fact, however, that the number of Russian prisoners brought in during the first day's action was considerably smaller than had been anticipated, along with the noticeable
lack of artillery in the Soviet units, did cause Halder some concern.
These unpleasant developments forced the chief of the general
staff to conclude that large portions of the Russian forces were
located farther east than had at first been thought, but he believed
that the bulk of these forces were no more distant than Minsk and
that after Panzer Groups 2 and 3 linked up around that city, the
breadth of the gap in the Russian front, plus their heavy losses in
the pocket, would allow Army Group Center to achieve full freedom of action.

The feeling of uneasiness in the OKH about what the Russians
were preparing to do to defend themselves was increased by information sent back to headquarters from Army Groups North and
South during the second day of the war. In the Army Group North
area along the Baltic it had become obvious that the Red Army
was making no attempt to defend Lithuania and, in fact, had already begun a withdrawal to behind the Dvina line well in advance
of the German attack.[15] Despite this sign that the Soviet command
had had forewarning about Barbarossa and was implementing a
sophisticated and broad-scale plan for defense, Halder refused to
believe that the "inefficient and sluggish nature of their command
structure" allowed for any kind of planning at all.[16]

Meanwhile, although the Northern and Central army groups appeared to be making fast enough progress, the situation for Army Group South was developing quite differently. There, in the Ukraine, the Wehrmacht had bitten granite because the Red Army was better equipped with the latest model weapons, including T–34 tanks and Mig–3 aircraft, which the Germans had scarcely encountered on the other fronts and had not expected to encounter at all.[17] In a review of the situation on June 24, Hitler told Jodl that the strong Soviet resistance in the Ukraine was confirmation of his belief that Stalin had intended to invade Rumania and the Balkans sooner or later and showed further that Moscow had assigned the protection of the Ukraine the highest priority. Hitler and Jodl were still convinced that it had been Stalin's intention for some time to start a war with Germany on his own initiative, and they were not able to see how the powerful presence of the Red Army in the Ukraine contributed to the overall strategy for the defense of the Soviet Union. Nevertheless, they were on the right track in determining where the strength of the Red Army actually was.

While Hitler, the OKH, and the OKW were busily trying to discover where the Russians were, Army Group Center was hard at work trying to erect a solid wall around the Bialystok–Minsk pocket. The first day of fighting went exceptionally well for Hoth's Panzer Group 3. The Nieman River had four crossing points in Panzer Group 3's operational area, the most important of which were three bridges located between forty-five and seventy kilometers from the demarcation line, and all of them were taken undestroyed. In the case of the bridges at Olita the Russian 126th Rifle Division and the 5th Tank Division tried desperately to defend the Nieman crossings, but the Luftwaffe proved to be very effective in keeping the tank division off balance. The bridges could have been demolished in plenty of time, and Major N. P. Belov of the 4th Pontoon-Bridge Regiment of the Eleventh Army had been ordered to accomplish this task as early as 2:00 P.M. on June 23, but this order was not obeyed immediately, because adequate studies of the bridge's concrete structure had not been made in advance. Later, as the German tanks drew closer, the commander of the units on the west bank refused to let the engineers do their job, which has led at least one Soviet historian to imply that it was an act of treason that opened the way across the Nieman to the Germans.[18] The swift crossing of this potentially troublesome river barrier ensured Hoth's rapid progress toward the Molodechno–Lake Naroch line, and from there an approach could be made on Minsk from the northwest. The failure of the Russian command to hold the Nieman line also led to the rapid fall of Vilna, which was taken by the XXXIXth Panzer Corps in the early morning hours of June 24, (see Figure 11).[19]

The way seemed to be opened also to Vitebsk and the "land bridge" between the Dvina and the Dnepr rivers to the north, a goal that appeared to Hoth, and von Bock as well, to be particularly worthwhile because this area presented itself as the natural pathway to Moscow from the west. In order to further the purpose of securing the Vitebsk–Orsha region, an enterprise that would have left only two motorized divisions available to prevent the Russians from breaking out of the Minsk pocket toward the north, Hoth ordered the LVIIth and XXXIXth panzer corps to stand by to take Molodechno and push toward Glubokoe north of Lake Naroch (see Figure 12).

On June 24, however, Army Group Center informed Hoth that the decision had been made by Brauchitsch to turn his panzer

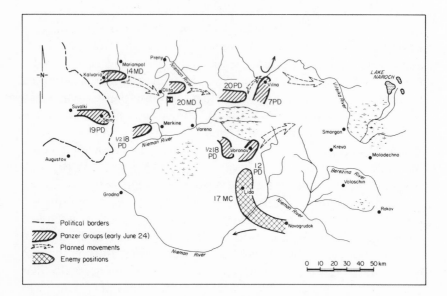

Figure 11. Panzer Group 3 Crosses the Nieman and Captures Vilna

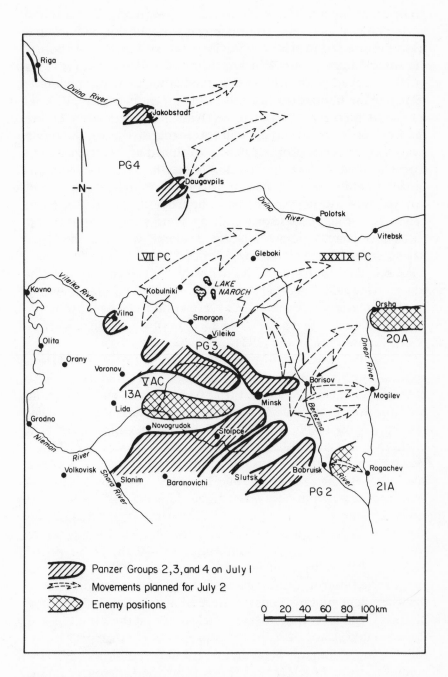

Figure 12. The Dnepr-Dvina Land Bridge between Vitebsk and Orsha

105

group from Vilna to the south and east, toward Minsk, not to the north and east as he and von Bock had wished.[20] Panzer Group 3 was now directed to seize the heights north of Minsk and cooperate with Panzer Group 2 in sealing off the Minsk pocket. This order dismayed Hoth, who viewed the Bialystok–Minsk pocket as relatively unimportant compared to the urgent necessity of securing the "land bridge" between the Dvina and Dnepr rivers before the Russians could group enough forces together along these two rivers to construct a proper defense. Hoth had made an agreement with von Bock before the invasion about the Vitebsk–Orsha approach to Moscow as the first priority of his Panzer Group 3, and now the entire strategy appeared to be jeopardized by what Hoth believed to be an unconscionable delay. Hoth went so far as to dispatch Lieutenant Colonel von Huenersdorff, who was the OKH liaison officer attached to Panzer Group 3, back to East Prussia to plead directly with Halder to try to get this decision changed, but it was to no avail. The OKH remained steadfast in implementing what Hoth acidly referred to as a "safe but time-wasting tactic."[21] Hoth, like Guderian, in the first few days of the war had already begun to lose faith in the OKH.

Actually, Halder's attitude with respect to the Vitebsk–Orsha approach to Moscow was not fundamentally different from those of the panzer generals or von Bock. Nevertheless, Halder saw the need for exercising some restraint in the handling of the vast encirclement now taking place. The biggest problem lay in the area of the Ninth Army after its XXth Army Corps was hard hit by Russian tanks on the eastern side of the Lososna River at Kuznica and Sidra. By the evening of June 24, the XXth Army Corps was being subjected to attacks from three sides by up to a hundred tanks, including some of the newer, heavier T–34s. The German infantry was hard pressed to repulse the massed Russian armor with no tanks of their own and only a few of the highly prized Sturmgeschütz self-propelled artillery vehicles.

To their horror, the German infantry commanders discovered that the 3.7cm antitank guns (PAK) used by the Panzerjaeger tank destroyer regiments were virtually useless against the latest types of Russian tanks. The XXth Army Corps now began to appeal frantically for more antitank weapons and for more armor-piercing ammunition, some of which was flown in by the Luftwaffe. It was von Richthofen's VIIIth Air Corps that saved the right wing of the

Ninth Army from serious damage on June 24 and 25 by respond-
ing quickly to the XXth Corps' pleas for help. The JU-87 Stukas,
in some cases equipped with phosphorus bombs, proved to be particularly effective in disrupting the large Soviet tank columns in
the Lunna–Indura–Sokolka area and also in the area south of
Grodno.

The problems confronting the Ninth Army were caused by the
counterattack by two mechanized corps planned by the commander of the Western Front, D. G. Pavlov, against what he believed
would be the southern flank of Panzer Group 3 advancing from
the direction of Suvalki toward Minsk. Hoth, however, had
crossed the Nieman much sooner than Pavlov could have anticipated for the reasons outlined already, so the bulk of the Russian
tanks ploughed into the right flank of the Ninth Army, merely
brushing Hoth's southern flank. The Soviet XIth Mechanized
Corps was the first to go into action from south of Grodno, and it
was later joined by the VIth Mechanized Corps, which moved
from northeast of Bialystok to southeast of Grodno. The Russian
armor from around Grodno initially achieved some success, particularly the 29th Tank Division commanded by Col. N. P.
Studnev, but the massive German air strikes were too much for
them to overcome.[22] The German air bombardment of Grodno itself wreaked havoc on Russian communications in this area, and
despite all efforts, well-coordinated counterattacks were made
impossible.[23] Pavlov's virtually clean miss of Panzer Group 3
meant that Minsk was left without armored protection, and Hoth's
penetration to that city from around Molodechno on June 26 was
thus left largely unimpeded. Pavlov was under the erroneous impression that Hoth would veer his tanks to the south after reaching
Lida, not Molodechno, as he in fact did. As a result, he did not
prepare an adequate defense of Minsk but instead sent the XXIst
Rifle Corps from the intermediate echelon reserve off toward Lida
from west of Minsk.[24] Pavlov's maneuver in this respect can be
called a mistake, but Hoth's rapid capture of Minsk was not the
only important result of the two mechanized corps' clash with the
Ninth Army.[25]

The gap that was steadily opening up between the motorized
units of Panzer Group 3 and the infantry units of the Ninth Army
was widened further by Pavlov's counterattack, and the Russians
were able to use this delay in the progress of the German infantry

to effect the escape to the north and east of important units that would otherwise have been securely trapped.[26] The holding up of the Ninth Army's right wing near Grodno also meant that Grodno would have to be the turning point for the German infantry to press down to the south to link up with the Fourth Army around Bialystok in order to contain the Russian forces around this city. For the Ninth Army, the ring around Bialystok would initially have to be formed with five infantry divisions, each having a front of approximately twenty-five kilometers. A twenty-five kilometer front would be difficult enough for an infantry division to defend under favorable circumstances, but very troublesome indeed in the thick forests around Bialystok. To try and extend the front of the Ninth Army closer to the main part of Panzer Group 3 farther to the east was, by June 25, an impossibility, yet von Bock was not deterred from ordering one entire army corps from the Ninth Army to turn to the northeast toward Vilna. This turn was planned to aid Hoth's projected drive toward Vitebsk–Orsha but would have seriously impaired the Ninth Army's ability to hold a continuous front around Bialystok. In the afternoon of June 25, Colonel Schmundt, Hitler's chief adjutant, flew to Ninth Army headquarters and informed Strauss that the führer fully agreed with the Ninth Army about the inadvisability of von Bock's action and that Army Group Center, accordingly, had issued an order turning all of the Ninth Army toward the south. Halder remarked that it was "characteristic" of von Bock that he demanded a written order from the OKH before he would execute the closing maneuver around Bialystok. After failing to convince Schmundt of the necessity of carrying out one gigantic encirclement reaching all the way around Smolensk, von Bock then took out his frustrations on Brauchitsch, who visited Army Group Center the following day—again to no avail.[27]

Hitler had already expressed concern to Brauchitsch about the integrity of the Bialystok pocket during a conference in the afternoon of June 24, and this concern was manifested further in an order issued by the führer the following day that forbade the conduct of armored operations by Army Groups Center and South too far to the east without proper precautions being taken to secure the rearward areas. Halder's response to this was to refer to Hitler's order as "the same old song" and further to say that "this will not change our plans at all."[28] What the chief of the general staff had now decided to do was to remedy the serious difficulties facing the Ninth Army, thus placating Hitler, while at the same time giving the panzer generals of Army Group Center a maximum amount of freedom from restraint by any higher authority.

Halder sought to achieve his dual purpose in two ways: (1) by allowing the Ninth and Fourth Armies to turn inward from the north and south to form a tight inner ring around Bialystok and (2) by allowing the panzer groups alone to form an outer ring farther east around Minsk. Thus, by June 28, after Guderian's link-up with Hoth around Minsk, two large pockets had been formed— one around Bialystok, by infantry units that had practically no armor, and the other around Novogrudok-Minsk, with armor but with only six motorized infantry divisions—instead of the one encirclement originally planned (see Figure 13).

In order best to handle this complicated situation, Halder decided to use a clever ploy that was intended at once to increase Hitler's confidence in the OKH while opening the way for Hoth and Guderian to race ahead and reach the Dnepr-Dvina line without waiting for the resolution of the battles around Bialystok and Minsk-Novogrudok. This was done by activating Colonel General von Weichs's Second Army command staff, which was supposed

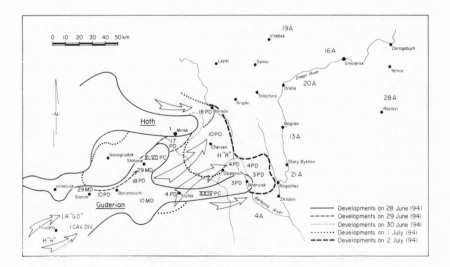

Figure 13. The Minsk-Novogrudok Pocket

to have been held in reserve in Posen until after Army Group Center had reached Smolensk, and giving it command over most of the infantry units of von Kluge's Fourth Army, then operating on the southern side of the Bialystok pocket. When this order was given on June 25, at the same time Panzer Groups 2 and 3 were placed directly under von Kluge's Fourth Army command along with two infantry corps.[29]

Putting the panzer groups under an old-line artillery commander like von Kluge severely rankled the impetuous Guderian, but the arrangement afforded the OKH several advantages. Guderian was so upset by this action that he sent Major von Below, the general staff liaison officer attached to Panzer Group 2, back to the Mauerwald in East Prussia to tell Halder that he preferred to be relieved of his command rather than serve under von Kluge.[30] Halder was not inclined to listen, however, because he hoped that Hitler would accept this action as proof that the OKH was trying to cool Guderian's blood by weakening von Bock's control over him, for it was well known that von Bock, along with Guderian and Hoth, were the strongest advocates of a direct push on Moscow. Von Kluge, by contrast, more conservative and orthodox in his views on such matters, was in agreement with Hitler about the necessity of using the panzer groups to help maintain the Bialystok pocket. It was for this reason that Halder steadfastly refused to give command of both panzer groups to Guderian, a possibility that he talked over with Paulus and Wagner, for he must have known that this action would have unduly excited the führer's suspicions about the activities of the OKH and the staff of Army Group Center. Moreover, Halder probably did not trust Guderian too far, because he had the reputation, frowned upon in army circles, of being loyal to Hitler—if not an out-and-out Nazi. Guderian was one of the few regular army generals—another was von Reichenau—who habitually used the Nazi raised-arm salute.* This distrust prevented Halder from placing Guderian in a position where he could have had more immediate contact with Hitler.[31]

*Guderian's political reputation suffered even more after Stauffenberg's attempt to kill Hitler with a bomb on July 20, 1944. On July 29, 1944, Guderian signed an order directing all general staff officers to either become Nazi "Leadership Officers" or ask for a transfer. Many officers never forgave Guderian for this act, which they considered a betrayal of the army.

Ultimately, Halder hoped that Guderian and Hoth would "do the right thing" by pushing rapidly on to Moscow even though they lacked specific orders directing them to do so. The OKH itself could not give such orders, because Hitler would surely have had them rescinded; the führer had already expressed his wishes in this matter quite plainly to Brauchitsch.[32] It is evident, too, that von Bock was a knowing participant in Halder's plot, for he told Guderian bluntly that he personally wanted to have no responsibility for the panzer general's actions, and he left no doubt in Guderian's mind that the OKH expected the commanders of the panzer groups "to carry out the previously accepted plan" either without orders or even against orders.[33] At this point Guderian must have had the feeling that Halder and Brauchitsch were preparing to leave him out on a limb, asking him to take all the risk involved in disobeying orders while not assuming any responsibility themselves in case something should go wrong. Guderian's misgivings about the motives and actions of the OKH in this way were profoundly increased.

Guderian's push across the Bug River in the area of Brest Litovsk had gone quite smoothly on the morning of June 22, although the stout Russian defense of the Brest fortress itself was an unwelcome surprise. The German 45th Infantry Division had to pay a high toll in blood in order to overwhelm the defenders of Brest, many of whom were new recruits, who managed to hold out for several weeks behind their fortifications. The entire 45th Infantry Division was held up at Brest Litovsk until July 1, and parts of it had to be detained in the area for another three weeks.[34]

Pavlov's attempt on June 23 to organize a thrust against Panzer Group 2 from the Kobrin area toward Brest had come to grief due to the continuous German air and artillery bombardment that dispersed the XIVth Mechanized Corps and prevented it from being employed in a unified fashion. As it turned out, the Russian 22nd Tank Division east of Brest, the 30th Tank Division at Pruzhany, and the 205th Motorized Division near Bereza all were thrown into battle piecemeal. As a result, the Russian Fourth Army had no choice but to fall back to the east.[35] By 2:00 P.M. on June 24 Guderian's XXIVth Panzer Corps had succeeded in crossing the Shchara River near Slonim in the area of the Russian 55th Rifle Division, which had just been pulled up from Slutsk to replace the 205th Motorized Division. After crossing the Shchara and also destroying the last twenty-five tanks of the XIVth Mechanized Corps, Guderian pushed on to Baranovichi on June 25. After the fall of the river crossings at Slonim, the Russian Fourth Army was cut off from retreat. Even though the Fourth Army had now lost the capability of central guidance, its units having broken down into autonomous formations, Panzer Group 2 and the German infantry would have their hands full trying to contain the Russian attempts to break out to the east and southeast. The main job of blocking the Russians attempting to escape from Bialystok toward Slonim devolved on Lieutenant General von Boltenstern's heroic 29th Motorized Division, while the 17th and 18th panzer divisions were thus freed to advance on to Minsk.

During the night of June 24–25 the Russians had already placed the 17th Panzer Division in an "extremely hazardous situation" by a breakout attempt, which included some tanks, from the area of the dense Bialovicha forest reserve through Volkovysk in the general direction of Slonim, and these were the kind of attacks that the 29th Motorized Division would now have to face alone.[36] On June 26 this division was supposed to maintain a sixty-to-seventy-kilometer front from Slonim to the Zelvianka, a stream that flows into the Nieman west and north of Slonim. On this day the Russians mounted repeated attacks with tanks and cavalry against the thin German line. Once again, the German 3.7cm, and even the 5cm, antitank guns had little effect on the Russian armor, and many tanks had to be blown up in the rearward areas by pioneer units with high explosives. During the night of June 29 in the area of Derechin and Zolochieva, a big part of the Russian Fourth Army made a strong push to the east supported by artillery and tanks. The German Panzer Regiment 7 and Infantry Regiment 71 had to pull back to hill 131 west of Derechin where they could still hit the Zolochieva–Derechin road with shellfire, but they could not prevent the Russians from streaming by to the east. Another German battle group was similarly stranded atop hill 191, also west of Derechin, the following night. On June 30 the Russians moved tanks forward to try to open the Zelva bridge across the Zelvianka, but they were pushed back even though there were "very heavy losses" to the 29th Division. The division was finally relieved by infantry on July 1, and the men were given one day's rest near Slonim before being sent on to Baranovichi.[37] Presumably many of the Russian units that escaped were trapped later in the Minsk–Novogrudok pocket farther east, although Guderian's premature weakening of the eastern and southern side of the encirclement front around Minsk led to further Russian breakthroughs between Minsk and Slonim. On June 29 von Bock had expressed grave concern to Guderian about the likelihood of a Russian breakthrough across the line Minsk–Slonim and advised him to move other units, including the SS *"Das Reich"* Division, to this area. Guderian's reply was that Panzer Group 2's units already in the sector were sufficient and that all available forces were needed to reach and cross the Dnepr.[38]

While the 29th Division was heavily engaged in the Zelvianka–Slonim sector, Guderian was locked in a struggle with von Kluge concerning its disposition and that of the 4th Panzer Brigade of the 10th Panzer Division. Von Kluge feared a massive Russian breakout in this area and was determined to keep the 29th Division and the 4th Panzer Brigade in their places, even though most of Panzer Group 2 was pushing on to Minsk. In Guderian's words, "It is unacceptable for this commander to allow a motorized division of this panzer group to remain in the rearward areas for one moment longer than is absolutely required at a time when the armored vanguard does not have enough strength as it is." On June 29 Guderian flew to Hoth's headquarters in order to coordinate their movements in the crossing of the Berezina River and perhaps also to discuss their joint disobedience of any order delaying their eastward progress. On the way back Guderian directed his pilot to fly over the Minsk–Slonim forest and observed "no noteworthy enemy forces" there. Soviet sources, however, confirm the experience of the 29th Division on the nights of June 29 and 30 by revealing that the largest group of the remnants of the Third, Tenth, and Thirteenth armies was attempting to escape from the encirclements in the forested and swampy region between the Nieman, Zelvianka, and Shchara rivers north of Derechin.[39]

Guderian's constant downplaying of the danger of a Russian breakout in the Shchara–Zelvianka sector in order to facilitate the rapid eastward movement of his panzer group must, in retrospect, be viewed as an attempt by him to delude the commander of the Fourth Army, von Kluge, and to provide von Bock with a false excuse to ignore the obvious risk of weakening the encirclement front at Slonim. In his memoirs Guderian lamented the fact that the Fourth Army tried to interfere in "his battle" in the Zelvianka region. Notations in the war diary of Panzer Group 2, however, do not support his statement that he was unaware of the attempted interference at this time.[40] It was well known that the panzer general was ferociously protective of his units and that he would strenuously resist attempts to remove any of them from his command, even for temporary periods. Guderian devoutly believed in keeping his command intact to prevent a watering down of his strength. The personality of this man was such that he ordered every vehicle in his panzer group to be painted with a large white letter "G" for the campaign in France in 1940. This practice was continued in Russia.[41] The problems the high command and the army group would experience with Guderian's unwillingness to part with his units would create profound and far-reaching difficulties in the future.

Von Bock was not, however, in a position to give Guderian the freedom he wanted, because of Hitler's concern about the integrity of the Minsk–Novogrudok pocket. For this reason, the 29th Motorized Division was ordered by Army Group Center to move into the area of the 17th Panzer Division between Minsk and Stolbtsy while this panzer division, along with the 10th Motorized Division, was ordered to push to the west right up to the edge of the Pusha–Naliboka forest. Army Group Center's directive was transmitted by radiotelephone to the XLVIIth Panzer Corps by Panzer Group 2's headquarters on July 2, but due to "faulty reception" the XLVIIth Panzer Corps did not understand the message properly and so dispatched the 17th Panzer Division to Borisov on the Berezina anyway.[42] It is interesting to note that Guderian paid a personal visit to the 17th Panzer Division shortly before this incident took place.[43] This same process was repeated on July 4 when von Kluge ordered the Infantry Regiment *"Gross Deutschland"* to take up a position on the encirclement front in the area of Stolbtsy between the 29th Motorized Division and Machine Gun Battalion 5. By 11:00 A.M., however, *"Gross Deutschland"* along with the last part of the 17th Panzer Division *("Kampfgruppe Licht")* pulled away from the encirclement front and headed toward Borisov after another "misunderstanding" of orders.[44]

In a vain effort to rein in the forceful panzer general, von Kluge had called Guderian into his headquarters early on July 3 and strongly taken him to task, citing certain problems he had experienced with Hoth's units also failing to understand orders. Von

Kluge warned Guderian that he could be court-martialed for participating in a general's conspiracy, but Guderian noted later that
he managed to ease his superior's mind on that score.[45]* Subsequent events would prove, however, that von Kluge was powerless
to control Guderian since his supposed subordinate had the backing of the OKH and the headquarters of Army Group Center. In
the face of such determined resistance on the part of Halder, von
Bock, Guderian, and Hoth, von Kluge could only yield or appeal
directly to Hitler to exert his will over the conspirators. Von Kluge
was not, however, the sort to go outside the normal channels of the
army command in order to seek solutions to problems, no matter
how pressing. He imagined that Hitler himself could not be duped
and manipulated by the OKH for long and that soon the situation
would be rectified, but events were to prove otherwise.

GUDERIAN CROSSES THE DNEPR

The arrival on the Berezina of the 17th Panzer Division at
Borisov was preceded by the rapid push of the 3rd Panzer Division
to Bobruisk, farther to the south along that same river, on June 28
(see Figure 14). It had been the intention of the OKH for the 3rd
Panzer Division to be used to aid Panzer Group 3 in more effectively sealing off the Minsk–Novogrudok pocket, but Guderian already had his eye on a mission farther to the east—the crossing of
the Dnepr River. Halder, of course, had done nothing to dissuade
Guderian from sending the 3rd Panzer on to Bobruisk, a maneuver that opened up the possibility of a rapid breakthrough over the
Dnepr near Mogilev or Rogachev, even though serious problems
were still being caused by Russian breakout attempts in the pocket
farther west in the area of Volkovysk and Novogrudok.[46] Hitler,
meanwhile, on June 29 had again voiced his concern to Brauchitsch
that the wide-ranging panzer operations were endangering the
success of the large encirclements, and he prevailed upon the army
commander in chief to ask Army Group Center not to allow
Guderian to advance beyond Bobruisk but rather have him hold
the city "only for security."[47] Halder, however, would have no
part of this kind of shilly-shallying and hoped that Guderian
would use any opportunity to cross the Dnepr:

*Ironically, it was Guderian who informed Hitler in July 1944 about von Kluge's intention
to negotiate a separate peace with the Western Allies. Thus exposed, the field marshal was
forced to commit suicide in August of that year.

If he did not do that, it would be a great mistake. I hope that today [June 29] he has taken the Dnepr bridges at Rogachev and Mogilev, thereby opening the way to Smolensk and the approach to Moscow. Only in this way will the fortified land bridge between the Dvina and Dnepr be cut off from Moscow.

The move across the Dnepr could not be made immediately, because Army Group Center would need several days, approximately until July 5, in order to resupply and regroup the two pan-

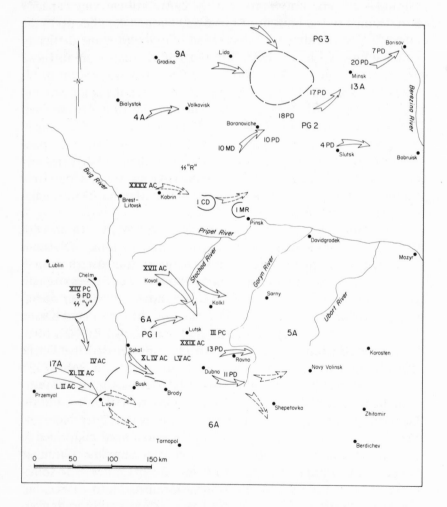

Figure 14. Guderian Reaches the Berezina

zer groups. More time would also be needed to complete the transfer of the command of Panzer Groups 2 and 3 from Army Group Center's direct control to von Kluge's Fourth Army command, a task that was finally accomplished on July 3. It was von Kluge's intention to postpone Guderian's crossing of the Dnepr until the two infantry corps of his new command, the so-called Fourth Panzer Army, could be brought up to lend assistance. Guderian too was worried about the feasibility of cracking the Dnepr line without the help of infantry units being brought forward by train, but the army group could only reply that the entire rail-carrying capacity was strained to the limit in just bringing enough supplies up to the front.[48] Another problem that caused Guderian some difficulty was that his units had already suffered 3,382 casualties up to July 3 and on July 7 he had to report to the OKH that 10 percent of his tanks had been lost and only 35 percent of the tanks in the 3rd and 18th Panzer Divisions were battle worthy. The 10th Panzer Division was in the best condition, with 80 percent of its tanks being in service, but the overall repair and breakdown situation in the panzer group's armored vehicles did not auger well for a blitzkrieg victory over the Red Army.[49] But the Red Army was not passively waiting for Guderian to make the first move. Marshal Timoshenko had plans of his own.

By July 4 the XXIVth Panzer Corps, led by the 3rd and 4th Panzer Divisions and followed by the 10th Motorized Division, had secured several crossings over the Berezina and had come up to the Dnepr near Rogachev and at Stary Bykhov. The Soviet strength west of the Dnepr was, however, far from depleted, as their operational echelon had transformed Rogachev, Mogilev, and Orsha into formidable strongholds. On July 5 a powerful Russian force composed of units of the Twenty-first Army crossed the Dnepr near Zhlobin south of Rogachev and moved toward Bobruisk.[50] This thrust was parried and shoved back across the river by the 10th Motorized Division with some help from the 3rd Panzer Division, but nevertheless, the area between the Dnepr and the Berezina remained hazardous as many Russian units continued to operate here, destroying bridges and causing supply difficulties. On July 12 Guderian pleaded with Army Group Center to do something about putting the Minsk–Bobruisk railroad into service, but the Army Group had to reply that "this area was still too dangerous to work in."[51] Guderian, however, could not wait for these problems to be cleared up; he was determined to force the Dnepr by July 10 and leave the securing of the area west of the river to the infantry of von Weichs's Second Army command, which, for the most part, was still near Minsk.

In order to cross the Dnepr as easily as possible and open the way into Smolensk from the south and west, Guderian made a fateful decision. He decided to bypass the main crossings of the river at Zhlobin, Rogachev, Mogilev, and Orsha, where the largest concentrations of Russian forces were located, and transfer his units over to the eastern bank at Stary Bykhov, to the north of Rogachev, and at Shklov and Kopys between Mogilev and Orsha. This area was covered by the Russian tactical reserve. These Soviet units were banded together with other fragmented forces and given the designation "Thirteenth Army."[52] Guderian's decision to cross the river here looked good on paper because it allowed Panzer Group 2 to push through the Russian line at its weakest points, thereby leading to the capture of Smolensk in a rapid stroke by July 16, the earliest date that the Fourth Panzer Army command had set for the arrival of the mass of the infantry of the Second Army on the Dnepr.[53] Maneuvers of this kind were dear to Guderian's heart—that is, hit the enemy at its weakest link with armor and let the infantry deal with the strong points later. This philosophy was drummed by Guderian into the heads of his subordinate commanders; on July 7 he addressed them all in a briefing session prior to the crossing of the Dnepr: "All commanders of the panzer group and their troops must disregard threats to the flanks and the rear. My divisions know only to press forward."[54]

The idea, however, of pushing across the Dnepr, thus exposing the right flank of the panzer group to the danger of a counterattack by Timoshenko's forces east of the river, while leaving the powerful Russian concentrations around Rogachev–Zhlobin, Mogilev, and Orsha unmolested in the rear, was too much for some of Guderian's own commanders to accept. On July 8 General von Schweppenburg's XXIVth Panzer Corps had captured a Russian map showing the strength of the Red Army at Rogachev–Zhlobin and showing a connection between these forces and the large Russian grouping around Gomel. This map also indicated that a planned Russian counterattack from the southeast would take place as soon as the panzer group crossed the river. As a result of this information, von Schweppenburg earnestly recommended that the attack be postponed either until the infantry had been brought up to Bobruisk or until his panzer corps could be strengthened. The same concern was voiced by von Kluge, who appeared at Guderian's headquarters early on the morning of July 9. He, too, was opposed to Panzer Group 2's crossing the Dnepr without waiting for the infantry and more artillery support, but Guderian would hear nothing of such arguments. He told von Kluge, half truthfully, that the XXIVth and XLVIth Panzer Corps had already been concentrated in their takeoff positions and that to hold them there for too long would be to expose them to the danger of attack by the Russian air force. Guderian went on to say that, if this attack succeeded, then the campaign would probably be decided within the year. After listening to Guderian's barrage of excuses, and knowing full well that he was speaking with the authority of Army Group Center and the OKH, the field marshal reluctantly backed down, though he warned Guderian prophetically, "Your operations always hang by a thread!"

As an illustration of what kind of improvisation was necessary by early July, a battalion of the 255th Infantry Division, without the approval of Army Group Center or the Second Army, was loaded onto trucks provided by the 3rd Panzer Division and moved from southeast of Minsk to Bobruisk during the night of July 9. The main part of the LIIIrd Army Corps, however, could not reach Bobruisk before July 12. The hurried progress of Panzer Group 2 and its consequent lack of infantry support led to another sticky situation on July 4 after the 3rd Panzer Division managed to establish a bridgehead on the Dnepr's eastern bank near Rogachev. Continuous attacks, however, by the LXIIIrd Rifle Corps of the Russian Twenty-first Army, personally decreed by Stalin, forced Lieutenant General Model to order his units back over to the western bank on July 6. Also, on July 8, Guderian's headquarters asked the Fourth Panzer Army to speed up the transfer of ammunition supplies through the Second Army supply area, as both the XXIVth and XLVIth Panzer Corps were reporting shortages, especially of heavy artillery shells.[55] Army Group Center's "Order of the Day" on July 8 announced the end of the Bialystok–Minsk battle and the capture of 287,704 Russian prisoners. Of this number only about a hundred thousand were taken in the smaller pocket around Bialystok.[56]

The fall of Smolensk was now but a short time away, but such haste in the end gained nothing for Guderian. The problems confronting his panzer group from the southeast, and from the rear as well, would absorb ever more of his attention, and the chimera of Moscow would slowly recede into the background as the Russian pressure against his units and against the Second Army coming up from the west gradually intensified.

THE NORTHERN FLANK OF ARMY GROUP CENTER

On the northern flank of Army Group Center events had developed somewhat differently than they had in the south. Hoth's Panzer Group 3 had been more tightly bound to the Minsk–Novogrudok encirclement front than had Panzer Group 2, and no further progress to the east was made there until after June 30, when the OKH ordered both panzer groups to reach the line Rogachev–Mogilev–Orsha–Vitebsk–Polotsk as soon as possible.[57] As far as Panzer Group 3 was concerned, the objective would be to cross the Dvina in the area of Vitebsk–Polotsk, thus helping to secure the seventy-kilometer-wide land bridge between the Dnepr and Dvina rivers. The weather intervened, however, and heavy rains turned the roads into quagmires, especially in the swampy region around the upper Berezina. But since Army Group North had already crossed the Dvina on July 26, there seemed to be a good chance for a similar success by Panzer Group 3.[58]

Due to the weather, the 7th Panzer Division at the head of the XXXIXth Panzer Corps managed to reach only Lepel instead of Vitebsk within the two days originally planned. The vehicle columns of the 7th Panzer Division and the 20th behind it were widely dispersed due to the rain and the sandy roads east of the Berezina. Also, for the first time, the Russians had begun systematically to destroy all bridges in the path of Panzer Group 3.[59] The more northerly route to the Dvina, to the north of Lake Naroch, was better for rapid travel. Part of the 19th Panzer Division leading the LVIIth Panzer Corps covered the two hundred kilometers from Vilna to Disna north of Polotsk in only twenty-four hours and by July 3 had managed to clear the southern bank of the Dvina below Polotsk of all enemy forces. Hoth now hoped to be able to take Vitebsk quickly and also cross the Dvina near Disna, but since Guderian had pulled his panzer units down to the south of Orsha on the Dnepr, this meant that only the 7th Panzer Division coming up on Vitebsk from the southwest remained in the Vitebsk–Orsha land bridge. Moreover, since July 2 air reconnaissance had shown strong Russian movement from the east toward Orsha–Vitebsk and also farther north to Nevel.[60]

Within the next two days long Russian columns would be observed west of Velikie Luki, and more movement would be seen to the north of Lake Ilmen and around Pskov. As Halder observed, the Russian group around Velikie Luki was in a good position to operate either against the southeastern flank of Hoepner's Panzer Group 4 (Army Group North) or against the northeastern flank of Hoth's Panzer Group 3 (Army Group Center). The Red Air Force was also noted to be particularly strong over Velikie Luki. All of this activity, coupled with the heavy concentrations of trains around Briansk–Orel and the Russian movement from there along the roads to the north, caused Halder some concern. Nevertheless, he still concluded that "the strength the enemy has remaining would scarcely permit him to organize an operational reserve."[61]

Although Hoth managed to cross the Dvina easily enough at Disna on July 4 with the 19th Panzer Division, Vitebsk was a different matter. On July 4 Timoshenko ordered the Twentieth Army to launch a counterattack with the Vth and VIIth Mechanized Corps from north of Orsha and southwest of Vitebsk toward Senno and Lepel.[62] This mission was approved by Stalin, who insisted that the infantry of the IInd and XLIVth Rifle Corps support the two mechanized corps by an attack from the area east of Borisov. These attacks were launched at 5:00 A.M. on July 6 and were carried out by a total of nearly a thousand Russian tanks.[63] Panzer Group 3's 7th Panzer Division bore the brunt of these assaults, along with Guderian's 17th Panzer Division on the northern flank of Panzer Group 2. By July 9, the 17th Panzer Division had destroyed one hundred Russian tanks coming from the direction of Orsha, losing few of their own but suffering heavy loss of life.[64] By July 7, however, the 20th Panzer Division had succeeded in crossing the Dvina and begun to press down on Vitebsk from the northwest, and the city fell on July 10. Meanwhile, the 18th Infantry Division had shaken loose from the Russians near Ulla on July 9. It would hit the Russians who were pushing toward Vitebsk from the direction of Gorodok, but the pressure on Panzer Group 3 north of the Dvina would continue to increase after July 12 from the direction of Nevel and Velikie Luki.[65] The growing Russian threat against the left flank of Panzer Group 3, plus other infor-

mation obtained from air reconnaissance, forced Halder (at a conference held on July 13) to advise Hitler to postpone the direct
advance on Moscow. It was Halder's recommendation that Panzer
Group 3 be turned toward Velikie Luki and Kholm to eliminate the
enemy group at Nevel–Velikie Luki.[66] On the eve of the battle for
Smolensk the chief of the general staff was beginning to have serious second thoughts about the potential danger to the flanks of
Army Group Center.

A large part of the problem was that, contrary to German expectations, many Russian units continued to fight after the initial
panzer breakthroughs had been accomplished, as at Brest and in
the Zelvianka–Slonim sector. Even when cut off from the rear,
some Russian units tended to remain remarkably coherent. Part of
the reason for this, no doubt, was the baleful effect of the Commissar Decree. On July 10 Panzer Group 4 of Army Group North
had reported the "liquidation" of 101 Red Army commissars.
By mid-August Panzer Group 3 had "isolated and removed" 170
of them, but the unit's intelligence staff had to report that the
"special measures" taken against the political commissars were
known to the enemy, and this had led to the tougher than expected
resistance. Already Hitler's ideological house of cards had begun
to collapse in Russia, but it would be many months before any
changes were made in the commissar policy.[67]

THE GENERAL STAFF RECONSIDERS THE SITUATION

Earlier, on July 2, Colonel Kinzel of the general staff Intelligence Department reported to Halder on the supposed strength of
the Red Army. It was Halder's belief, fortified by this report, that
the Russians had only fifteen to twenty infantry and six tank divisions remaining in front of Army Groups North and Center. This
fantasy-world conclusion led Halder to make the following statement on July 3:

> In general, one can say that our mission to destroy the mass of the
> Russian Army west of the Dvina and Dnepr has now been fulfilled
> . . . it would not even be too much to say that the campaign in Rus-
> sia has been won within 14 days.[68]

Halder's impressions were further confirmed when on July 8 Colonel Kinzel reported that of the 164 Soviet rifle divisions that had
been identified since the beginning of the war, 89 had been fully or

partly destroyed, and of these only 46 remained on the battle-fronts, while another 14 divisions were tied down facing Finland and 4 more were in the Caucasus. The Russian rearward reserve was reckoned at 11 divisions. Of the 29 Russian tank divisions that had emerged, only 9 were still considered to be battle worthy. From this Colonel Kinzel concluded that the Red Army was incapable of stabilizing a continuous front even behind fortified points and predicted that although the Russians would be able to call up new formations, these units would be deficient in officers, specialists, and artillery. These deficiencies, he thought, would prove to be an especially serious handicap to the Russian armored units. In a review of the situation confronting each Army Group, Kinzel reported decisive German superiority in the areas of Army Groups North and Center and asserted that, with its tactical and operational superiority, Army Group South would soon achieve a numerical advantage.[69] As Halder found these conclusions suitable in every way to bolster his own ideas about how the war should be won, he and Brauchitsch presented them to Hitler in the afternoon of July 8.

After listening to the substance of the Intelligence Department report, Hitler offered his estimate of the situation. The führer's ideal solution to the Russian campaign was to be carried out as follows: (1) Army Group Center was to employ pincer movements and break the last Soviet resistance north of the Pripet, forcing the way open to Moscow. After the Dnepr was reached, Hoth could perhaps aid Army Group North or go around the capital but not use his tanks directly against the city. After reaching Smolensk, Guderian could push either to the south or to the southeast, to work with Army Group South. (2) Moscow and Leningrad were to be razed to the ground by air attacks, tanks were not to be used for this purpose. (3) After the final destruction of the enemy at Smolensk, a push could be made to the Volga. The remaining part of the Soviet Union's industry could then be destroyed either from the air or by mobile ground units. (4) Plans for the construction of winter barracks were to be set in motion. (5) New tank production was to be held back in Germany for use in later operations. The losses in Russia were to be made up by combining the panzer divisions to form new whole units. Hitler also anticipated that some personnel could be sent back to Germany.[70]

It should be noted here that Hitler's grossly overconfident

evaluation of the military situation in Russia in early July was a direct outgrowth of the erroneous information being supplied him by his chief of the general staff. Hitler's overoptimism about the situation in Russia in the summer of 1941 is usually cited by his critics to ridicule his military judgment.[71] It is not possible to say that Halder was purposely trying to delude Hitler as he had already done during the planning phase of Barbarossa, for he still believed the Russians were on their last legs. On July 11 Halder wrote in his diary that "it would be impossible under the circumstances for the Red Army to have any more reserves behind the front lines." To be sure, the large enemy grouping in the Nevel–Velikie Luki area did cause Halder some concern, but he attributed this ominous sign to the Russians' scraping up the remnants of lost divisions, mixing these units with untrained reserves, and throwing them into battle without officers.[72]

By July 12 and 13, however, Halder's attitude had undergone a significant change as the OKH was faced with new evidence that the Red Army was far from finished. Not only was Panzer Group 3 experiencing strong enemy pressure from the direction of Nevel–Velikie Luki, but captured documents proved that new armies were being deployed in the areas Smolensk, Orsha, east of Vitebsk —some of them being brought up from the Ukraine by train. In addition, on the southern flank of Army Group Center a hundred-kilometer-long column of Russian infantry had been observed marching from Gomel to Mogilev, and moreover, there was a huge pileup of abandoned railway cars east of Gomel, many of which had apparently been loaded with vehicles and tanks.[73] It was this new information that caused Halder on July 13 to recommend to Hitler the temporary postponement of the direct advance on Moscow until the flank situation had been remedied.

In a conference on July 15 with Paulus and Heusinger, the general staff chief of operations, Halder reiterated his belief that, although the Russian deployment seemed operational in nature, it in fact was not so, since the Red Army lacked the strength to carry out any effective countermeasures. Paulus, however, was no longer convinced of this and pointed out quite correctly that new Russian concentrations even farther east, around Kalinin and Rzhev, on the Volga northwest of Moscow, and near Briansk on the Desna, might be intended to hit a German push on Moscow from the west on both flanks.[74] Although Guderian's striking success at

Smolensk the following day appeared to be a bellwether for future victories, the OKH remained deeply worried about the Russian activities to the south of Lake Ilmen, between the southern flank of Army Group North and the northern flank of Army Group Center, and at Zhlobin, Rogachev, and Mogilev behind the forward elements of Panzer Group 2. Some officers of the OKH had begun to fear that the worst had happened, that the Russians had been able to deploy an operational reserve along the Dnepr–Dvina–Lake Ilmen line and farther east, although Halder could not openly admit this possibility; yet it is plain to see that by mid-July his faith in his original plan to advance rapidly on to Moscow, after taking Smolensk and crushing the mass of the Red Army west of the Dnepr–Dvina line, had been profoundly shaken.

THE FALL OF SMOLENSK

Guderian's main drive across the Dnepr toward Smolensk, Yelnia, Dorogobuzh, and Roslavl came on July 10–11 and was carried out with only light casualties, as no attempt was made to eliminate the Russian bridgeheads on the western bank beforehand. The Russian bridgehead at Orsha was screened by two battle groups while the XXIVth Panzer Corps was to protect its own flank against attacks from the area Zhlobin–Rogachev and its northern flank against the enemy at Mogilev.[75] The XLVIIth Panzer Corps was given the direct assignment of capturing Smolensk and this was done in remarkably short order by Lieutenant General von Boltenstern's 29th Motorized Division.

The push across the Dnepr by the 29th Division of the XLVIIth Panzer Corps began at 5:15 A.M. on July 11 in the area of Kopys and at Shklov. Although Russian artillery fire was lively, it was soon suppressed with the aid of a nearby Sturmgeschütz self-propelled artillery unit. Even while the enemy artillery was still active, and the Red Air Force as well, the pioneers of the division went to work building a bridge, completing it by 4:00 P.M. that day.[76] After a diversion to the northwest to help the 17th Panzer Division in its crossover near Orsha, the 29th Division made its way straight for Smolensk. The division met no determined resistance until the lead elements of the 15th Infantry Regiment reached Khokhlovo, and here the Russian artillery and air strikes caused heavy casualties. Again, the self-propelled artillery proved its worth in combination with the infantry, and the Russian machine gun nests and strong points were soon overcome. The last resistance near Smolensk was broken in this way, and by the evening of July 15 the battle-hardened Infantry Regiment 15 drove into the southwestern edge of the city. Then, by order of the XLVIIth Panzer Corps, Infantry Regiment 71 (from Khokhlovo) and Artillery Regiment 29 were turned directly into the city's south side. This action was fought on foot and across fields mostly against militia units that had been hastily formed by the Russian Sixteenth Army command. By nightfall this second German group had also entered Smolensk.[77]

Colonel Thomas's Infantry Regiment 71 had taken the Russian heavy artillery positions on the Koniukovo hills southwest of the city and learned from prisoners that Smolensk was strongly defended from this direction. After learning this, the regiment pressed on farther east to the Chislavichi–Nikitina–Smolensk road, escaping observation by the enemy. By 4:00 P.M. they were in the city's outskirts, but within an hour a heavy barrage of Russian artillery fire began to rain down on them. Not until nightfall were the troops of Regiment 71 able to reach the southern bank of the Dnepr. During the night Artillery Regiment 29 brought up some support guns placed at its disposal including 100mm cannon, Nebelwerfer rocket launchers, 88mm flak antitank guns and the regular antitank guns. Infantry Regiment 15 was to the west of Regiment 71, also on the city's south side.

The final assault on Smolensk began at 4:00 A.M. on July 16. Due to the narrowness of the streets, the German artillery could offer the infantry only a little direct help. The main part of the Russian force in the city seemed to be on the northern bank of the river, and other Red Army motorized columns were observed coming in from the north and east. The German artillery opened fire on the Russian reinforcements; the Russians replied in kind and also with an aerial bombardment. Already in the morning of July 16 Smolensk began to take on a shattered appearance as only a few undamaged buildings could be seen protruding from the rubble. By late morning, with the aid of some self-propelled artillery and the flame-throwing tanks of Panzer Regiment 100, a secure foothold was carved out on the southern bank. Around noon Russian artillery fire of all calibers picked up considerably, and in this way many fires broke out among the city's predominantly wooden houses, creating dense clouds of smoke; the cathedral tower with its golden cupolas provided a colorful contrast.[78]

Around four in the afternoon, Infantry Regiments 15 and 71 began crossing the Dnepr in rubber boats, while Artillery Regiment 29 on the southern bank poured fire into the Russian-controlled northern bank. This assault was ordered by von Boltenstern, who had his headquarters in the Hotel Molokhov. After arriving safely on the opposite side, the men of Infantry Regiment 15 soon reached the main railroad station and by 5:30 P.M. had fought all the way into Peter's Church, smoking the Red Army men out of their hiding places as they moved along. Particularly rough fighting occurred at the cemetery on the northern bank where parts of the Russian 129th Rifle Division under Maj. Gen. A. M. Gorodnianskii managed to use the tombstones as effective cover.[79] By 6:00 P.M. the fighting had moved out to the northern city limits, with the struggle growing ever more bitter; the streets had to be cleared systematically block by block, in many cases with grenades, flamethrowers, and machine pistols. Right at the city's northern limits were located some military barracks with well-dug-in field fortifications that proved to be a tough nut to crack. Nevertheless, by 11:00 P.M. the whole city had been subdued. The struggle, however, was far from over. Russian artillery fire continued to rain down on Smolensk from the hills close in on the north side. The stricken city glowed red in the night as Russian attacks, backed up by tanks, persisted until the morning. The next day's mission for the 29th Division would be to hold positions south of Smolensk along the Dnepr line, mainly along the Roslavl road, in order to prevent the Russians from breaking out of the large semi-pocket that had been formed by the two panzer groups around Smolensk from the north and south.[80]

Although the actual taking of Smolensk went well enough, the broad encirclement of the city had been carried out neither smoothly nor with great effectiveness. After Guderian's conversation with von Kluge on July 9 and the panzer general's emphatic statement that his assault over the Dnepr would decide the campaign within the year, von Kluge, the commander of the Fourth Panzer Army, ordered the 12th Panzer Division, since July 8 relieved from duty on the Minsk encirclement front, not to join Hoth's 7th Panzer Division at Vitebsk, but rather to drive through

Senno to cover Guderian's northern flank. Panzer Group 3's assault north of Smolensk was thereby weakened in order to aid Guderian's push toward Smolensk–Yelnia–Dorogobuzh from the southwest, much against the protests of Hoth and von Bock.[81]

Guderian's only thought was to reach the high ground to the east and south of Smolensk between the upper Dnepr and the headwaters of the Desna, thus securing an opening to Moscow from the west, whereas Hoth was more immediately concerned with the integrity of the planned encirclement around Smolensk. On July 10 Hoth ordered the XXXIXth Panzer Corps to swing around Smolensk from the north through the line Lesno–Surazh–Usiavits toward the northeast, hoping that the heaviest enemy resistance would thus be skirted, but destroyed bridges and mines in the roads reduced the speed of the motorized units to that of the infantry.[82] On July 13 the lead elements of Hoth's XXXIXth Panzer Corps reached Demidov and Velizh, and on July 14 the 12th Panzer Division reached Lesno and then turned in a more easterly direction toward Smolensk. The 12th Panzer was checked near Rudnia after being hit by Russian attacks from three sides, but Hoth's 7th Panzer Division managed to hold fast to the Demidov highway northwest of Smolensk while Guderian's northerly XLVIIth Panzer Corps crowded up toward Orsha, leaving a great conglomeration of Russians more or less boxed in from three directions to the north and west of Smolensk. It was at this time that the STAVKA decided to unleash a new and highly secret weapon in the fight for the upper Dnepr. On July 14 the Soviet Twentieth Army fired the first Katyusha rocket salvos against the German 5th Infantry Division, then occupying Rudnia northeast of Smolensk on the Vitebsk highway. The Katyusha truck-borne, rail-launched rockets created extreme havoc in the area of the 5th Infantry Division, largely because the Germans had never encountered them before. If used against a relatively flat or open area, a large salvo of Katyusha rockets would create a veritable blizzard of shrapnel.[83]

THE FORMATION OF THE YELNIA SALIENT

In mid-July, Guderian made a critical choice. He elected not to turn the XLVIth Panzer Corps toward the area west of Yartsevo to link up with Hoth northwest of Smolensk. Instead, he aimed for the heights of Yelnia and Dorogobuzh, thinking ahead about

Moscow, and in the process forfeited the chance of forging a strong wall around the Smolensk pocket (see Figures 15 and 16).[84] The availability of an opening leading out of Smolensk to the east saved the Russian Sixteenth and Twentieth Armies from a complete disaster and led directly to the very precarious situation that would soon develop around Yelnia (the name means "spruce grove" in Russian), a small town eighty-two kilometers to the southeast of Smolensk, near the headwaters of the Desna River. The responsibility for the creation of the conditions that led to the battles around Yelnia, battles that raged with such fury that some of the older officers compared them to their experiences at Verdun in 1916, must be shared equally by Fedor von Bock and Heinz Guderian, although Halder perhaps should be given a portion of the blame. Yelnia is a name that was burned into the collective consciousness of the German army, and the memory of it faded only after the larger disasters outside Moscow and at Stalingrad.

Lieutenant General Schaal's 10th Panzer Division of the XLVIth Panzer Corps received orders to take Yelnia at 9:00 P.M.

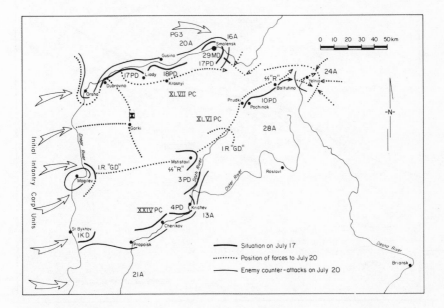

Figure 15. The Dnepr–Desna Area and the Creation of the Yelnia Salient

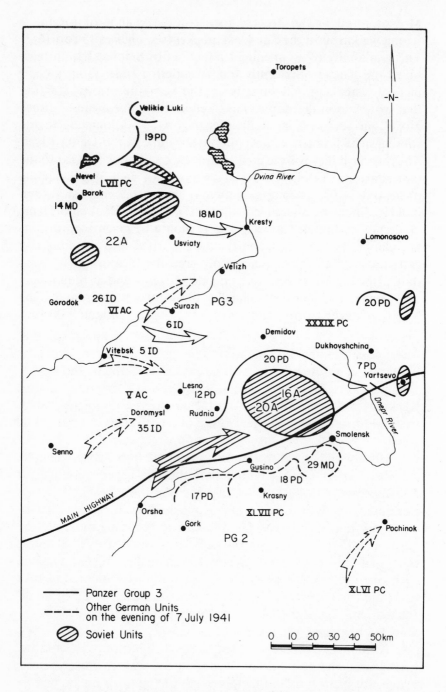

Figure 16. The Failure to Close the Smolensk Pocket

on July 16, before the battle inside Smolensk had been brought to a conclusion. At this time Yelnia was defended by the 19th Rifle Division of the Russian Twenty-fourth Army.[85] It was not until the early morning hours of July 18, however, that the bulk of the 10th Panzer could pull up to Pochinok and to Prudki, at the intersection of the Smolensk–Roslavl and Mstislavl–Yelnia roads. Forward units of the division were held up at Strigino where the bridge over the Khmara had been damaged by a Russian attempt to burn it down. The worries about that particular bridge at least were ended when one of the tanks of Panzer Regiment 7 crashed through it attempting to cross over at 5:45 A.M. Because of this and other delays, Schaal decided to hold the division at Petrova–Berniki and attack Yelnia the following day at 10:00 A.M. The attack had to be further postponed until 1:15 P.M. on July 19, however, because of the bad roads and the collapse of another bridge. During the night of the eighteenth and the morning of the nineteenth, the Russians had used the delay to fortify an antitank ditch that had been dug across the Pochinok–Yelnia road.[86] Two Russian heavy artillery pieces began to shell the road from a long distance in mid-afternoon, making the situation very uncomfortable. Later, by 2:30 P.M., a way was found around the antitank ditch, and Panzer Regiment 7 resumed the advance on Yelnia along the railroad tracks from the northwest, from the direction of Smolensk. Soon the tank men drove into the western and the southern edge of the town.

Hardly had the 10th Panzer penetrated into Yelnia when the XLVIth Panzer Corps command flashed an urgent message for reinforcements to be sent to help the SS *"Das Reich"* Division pushing from Baltutino to Dorogobuzh. Schaal replied that he could not take Yelnia and Dorogobuzh at the same time, but the corps commander, von Vietinghoff, was insistent. As a result, parts of a motorized rifle regiment and an artillery regiment, along with one tank destroyer Panzerjaeger unit, were ordered to take and hold the Dnepr bridge at Dorogobuzh, but it would be an ill-fated attempt, as the Russian pressure around Yelnia and along the Dorogobuzh road was too great.

By 6:00 P.M. on the nineteenth, the 10th Motorcycle Battalion had cleared the east side of Yelnia all the way to the cemetery, which was eight hundred meters north of the town limits, and by 6:30 the church in the center of the town was taken; but a sharp fight was still being waged on the railroad embankment west of the main station. Russian artillery fire now was beginning to pour in at a steady rate from the south and the southeast. Around eight in the evening, the whole south side of the town was under heavy shell-fire from big guns, and the divisional commander had to comment, "It is questionable whether we can take and hold Yelnia."[87] It was not until nearly 10:00 P.M. that the costly battle around the railway station was ended and the combing out of the rest of Yelnia could be completed. This final operation was finished within the next half hour.

It was almost at this precise moment, however, that the 4th Panzer Brigade ran entirely out of engine oil. The shortage of motor oil came about because by mid-July the German tanks were using twice the amount of oil they consumed during normal operations. The dense clouds of dust encountered on the Russian roads ruined the tanks' air filters and increased wear on the engines. By July 22 the 10th Panzer Division had only nine battle-ready tanks remaining (five Panzer IIs and four Panzer IIIs). All the rest had been put out of commission due to breakdowns or enemy action.[88] Now, despite orders to the contrary, Schaal decided to postpone the push toward Dorogobuzh by parts of the three regiments mentioned, for to continue with so many of his tanks immobilized would mean his division would have a difficult time hanging on to Yelnia, much less expanding its area of control. On July 21 von Vietinghoff reported from the XLVIth Panzer Corps headquarters that despite the most strenuous efforts the 10th Panzer could not be supplied with oil or, for that matter, with ammunition, which also was in great demand. Because of the supply problem and because of the strong Russian presence south of Yelnia, behind the Desna, with well-emplaced artillery positions, it was decided by von Vietinghoff and Schaal to pull the stalled SS *"Das Reich"* Division back from the road to Dorogobuzh and use it to guard the 10th Panzer's northeastern flank while the armor pushed further out to the east and south. On July 20 a tank battalion of the 10th Panzer Division, along with some infantry, overran a few Russian artillery positions to the east and south of Yelnia. These emplacements were reported to have been especially well constructed, with accommodations for both men and horses, and had obviously been completed for some time.[89]

The infamous "Yelnia salient" had now been created, and it would soon become a holocaust of fire and steel that would consume the lives of tens of thousands of German and Russian soldiers. The battles around Yelnia would be more costly than any the German army had fought since 1918 and reminiscent of that earlier war in many ways. For the first time the Wehrmacht would have to face the Red Army across a static front lined with trenches and foxholes, enduring almost continuous artillery barrages and having to beat back savage infantry attacks, sometimes supported by armor. In the summer of 1941 at Yelnia, it was the Red Army that came out the victor, with the last stage of the battles coming under the personal direction of Georgii Zhukov, an ominous foreshadowing of the fate of the German army.

On July 19 Guderian issued Panzer Group Order Number 3, which stated that "after reaching the area southeast of Smolensk [i.e., around Yelnia] Panzer Group 2 will come to a halt for refitting and replenishing supplies." However, on July 20 this order was canceled due to the "changed situation."[90] Guderian was now ready to give his battle-worn panzer group a much-needed rest after reaching Smolensk-Yelnia, but the Wehrmacht had set only one foot inside Great Russia, and the Red Army had just begun to bring the main part of its force into action. Halder and the generals in the field had wondered about the absence of large quantities of Russian artillery in the Bialystok–Minsk pockets, but by the third week in July they wondered no longer. The Russian thunder was on the Dnepr River.

CHAPTER 4

BATTLES FOR THE
UPPER DNEPR

THE SOVIET RESPONSE

The dimensions of the battles that developed around the upper Dnepr in mid-July 1941 were large by any standard. Overall, the battle for the Dnepr in the area of the Army Group Center encompassed 600–650 kilometers of front, stretched from Sebezh and Velikie Luki in the north to the Loev and Novgorod–Severski in the south; from Polotsk, Vitebsk, and Zhlobin in the west to Toropets, Yartsevo, and Trubchevsk in the east. Not only was the physical setting of the struggle immense, but the duration of it was protracted, from July 10, when Guderian succeeded in crossing the Dnepr, to the last days of September, when the advance toward Moscow was resumed under the code name Operation Typhoon.[1]

After D. G. Pavlov's sudden dismissal as commander of the Western Front (and his subsequent execution), Marshal S. K. Timoshenko, the commissar for defense, was picked by Stalin on July 1 to serve as Pavlov's successor. It had been said that Timoshenko's assignment was due to Stalin's desire to take direct control over military affairs, yet the evidence seems to show that in early July Stalin was still somewhat shaken by the turn of events and was relying heavily on his close advisors to run the government and the military. The Soviet dictator went into seclusion after June 22 and made no public appearances of any kind until his radio address to the nation on July 3.[2] Whatever Stalin's role at this point might have been, it was Timoshenko who had to answer for the success or failure of the Western Front and he must have been aware that he, too, could share Pavlov's fate.

The situation that confronted Timoshenko when he and his staff arrived at Smolensk on July 2 was anything but enviable. Pavlov's counter-attacks with three mechanized corps had not worked the desired effect on the two German panzer groups coming into the Bialystok salient from the north and south; nor had the enemy failed to take advantage of its overwhelming air superiority close to the frontier. Communications in the forward areas of the Western Front were in shambles; it was difficult for a commander to make intelligent decisions under such conditions.

By June 26 it had become obvious to Zhukov, still the chief of the general staff, and Timoshenko that emergency measures must be taken by the operational echelon if the German armor were to be checked before a breach was torn in the Dnepr line of defense. Zhukov could not have foreseen how rapid the advance of the German tanks was to be after the bridges over the Nieman were captured intact and after the Luftwaffe had made short work of the large Russian mechanized corps. Zhukov acknowledged one other mistake in his memoirs: "We did not envisage the nature of the blow [on June 22] in its entirety. Neither the People's Commissar [Timoshenko], nor myself . . . expected the enemy to concentrate such huge numbers of armored and motorized troops, and, on the first day, to commit them to action in powerful compact groupings in all strategic directions." Zhukov evidently believed beforehand that the Germans would be more cautious in crossing the border, putting infantry and artillery ahead of the tanks, as Halder had proposed.[3] A decision had to be made at once to strengthen the Dvina–Dnepr line in the area of the operational echelon of the Western Front. A delay or postponement of this decision was not possible, because no one could predict how long the forces within the encirclements could resist the strong German pressure. One bright spot in the picture, however, was that the Russian forces, parts of three armies cut off by the Germans west of Minsk, were continuing to put up a stiff fight. The tactical reserve was, in actuality, fulfilling its function by holding its ground while the German armor passed on to the east, and as has been seen, many German units were tied down by the Bialystok–Minsk encirclement operation until after July 8.[4] But Zhukov could not count on the German infantry being held west of the Dnepr for long. Positive action was required to ensure the position of the forces on the upper Dnepr.

On the evening of June 26 Zhukov was summoned to Moscow from the Southwestern Front to discuss the situation with Timoshenko and Vatutin, who was then chief of the Operations Section of the general staff. It was decided at this conference that the forces of the operational echelon already on the Dvina–Dnepr line in the area of the Western Front—the Twentieth, Twenty-first, and Twenty-second armies, plus other units—would now have to be augmented by other armies taken from the main part of the operational echelon in the Ukraine and from the reserves directly controlled by the Supreme Command. The final recommendation made to Stalin on June 27 called for the Thirteenth, Nineteenth, Twentieth, Twenty-first, and Twenty-second armies to defend the line Dvina–Polotsk–Vitebsk–Orsha–Mogilev–Mozyr. In addition, the Twenty-fourth and Twenty-eighth armies from the Supreme Command reserve were to be held in readiness near and to the south of Smolensk. The recommendation also called for the immediate formation of two or three more armies from the Moscow militia. Stalin approved of this proposal without objection.[5]

On July 10, the day Guderian succeeded in forcing the Dnepr, the units of the Russian Western Front were distributed along a line stretching from north of the Western Dvina River to south of Gomel. From Idritsa to Drissa and farther along the Western Dvina, on the extreme northern flank of the Western Front, was the Twenty-second Army under Lieutenant Gen. F. A. Ershakov. This army occupied a 210-kilometer front and had been heavily engaged with Hoth's Panzer Group 3. Slightly to the rear and to the south of the Twenty-second Army was Lieutenant General Konev's Nineteenth Army, which had been brought up by rail from Belaia Tserkov to the Rudnia–Demidov–Vitebsk area. Konev's force had to be thrown into a counterattack toward Vitebsk as soon as it had left the trains, but this counterthrust was largely wasteful, although Hoth's push from Vitebsk to Orsha was slowed somewhat. In the area from Vitebsk to Orsha was Lieutenant Gen. P. A. Kurochkin's Twentieth Army with fifteen divisions that had just arrived from the Orel Military District. This army was in the best shape, numerically, and was the best deployed, with each division having only a 10–12 kilometer front. The remnants of the Vth and

VIIth Mechanized Corps, which had carried out the ill-fated counteroffensive in the Lepel–Orsha area on July 6, were also part of
the Twentieth Army's complement. The many tanks lost by these
two corps at Orsha and Lepel were sorely missed when the battle
closer to Smolensk began to develop.[6]

Deployed in the city of Smolensk itself was the Sixteenth
Army, with two rifle divisions, which had been brought west hurriedly from the interior. The Sixteenth Army was commanded by
Lieutenant Gen. M. F. Lukin, but later, by the time of the assault
on the city by the German 29th Motorized Division, all units
around Smolensk were subordinated to Kurochkin. Many of the
divisions, especially those of the Sixteenth and Nineteenth armies,
which had been brought from the south and east, were rushed into
the front lines in a rather haphazard fashion, and the soldiers,
in many cases, were given very little training and advance
preparation.[7]

South of Smolensk along the front Shklov–Mogilev–Stary
Bykhov was the Thirteenth Army under Lieutenant Gen. P. M.
Filatov. The condition of this army was not good, since many of
its troops had just managed to escape from the encirclement
around Minsk. It was now the front of the Thirteenth Army that
Guderian chose for his breakthrough toward Smolensk and Yelnia.
Each of the Thirteenth Army's four divisions had a 20–25 kilo-
meter front, and its XXth Mechanized Corps had no tanks remain-
ing. Behind the Thirteenth Army south of Smolensk, occupying
the high ground around Yelnia, was Maj. Gen. K. I. Rakutin's
Twenty-fourth Army. Rakutin's neighbor to the south along the
Desna River was Lieutenant Gen. V. Ia. Kachalov's Twenty-eighth
Army. Both of these units had recently been created from the Supreme Command reserves.

On the extreme southern wing of the Western Front, along the
line Stary Bykhov–Rogachev–Rechitsa, and also around Gomel,
was the powerful Twenty-first Army that Zhukov had expected to
play a key role in slowing down Army Group Center by the time
the Germans reached the Dnepr. Shielded as it was from the west
by the Pripet Marshes, Col. Gen. F. I. Kuznetsov's Twenty-first
Army was in an excellent position to fulfill all of Zhukov's expectations; it was composed of three rifle corps placed in two echelons
along a 140-kilometer front.[8] Also filtering east were strong elements of the Fourth Army that had escaped the Bialystok encircle-

ment and were retreating under fire toward the Thirteenth and Twenty-first armies.[9]

In general, the forces which the Red Army managed to assemble on the upper Dnepr by July 10 made an imposing array. Still, however, there were serious shortages of equipment. The four armies in the forefront of the Western Front had, by official estimate, only 145 tanks, 3,800 guns and mortars, 389 usable aircraft, and only a few antitank and antiaircraft weapons. Zhukov knew that manpower alone would not be enough to halt the German advance, so by July 14, the Supreme Command began to deploy the armies of the strategic reserve as soon as they became mobilized along lines east of the Dvina–Dnepr behind the Western Front.[10]

This action, and the movement northward of important units of the operational echelon from the Ukraine, represented a partial breakdown of the careful strategy that Zhukov and Stalin had plotted before the war. By July 8 the former tactical reserve of the Western Front had ceased to exist, and what the Supreme Command had intended to be the operational echelon along the Dnepr–Dvina line was now transformed into the new tactical echelon, with fronts that were becoming rapidly less flexible and maneuverable as the German pressure toward the east continued. As a result of the Supreme Command's decision to deploy the strategic reserve on and immediately behind the Western Front, the strategic reserve would be unable to fulfill the function for which it had originally been intended, that is, launching a counteroffensive as soon as the German army had been halted, presumably along the Dvina–Dnepr line. Now, instead of holding back the strategic reserve and using it all at once against the Wehrmacht in a massive counteroffensive, the Supreme Command had decided by mid-July to use it piecemeal, to deploy it as soon as the mobilization schedule would allow, in order to supplement the armies already on the Dvina–Dnepr line and to establish other lines of defense farther east between the battlefronts and Moscow.[11]

The situation with regard to the large armored formations, the mechanized corps, also had to be brought sharply into focus. The Luftwaffe's work had been so effective against them in White Russia that Zhukov's intended plan to hold the new models back for a counteroffensive by the strategic reserve also had to be given up. Pavlov's failure in White Russia also meant that many factories, including tank factories, had to be dismantled and moved eastward as quickly as possible. For example, the Kirov factory in Leningrad, the Kharkov Diesel Works, and the "Red Proletariat" Factory in Moscow were all moved to Cheliabinsk in the Urals. Eventually, part of the Stalingrad Tractor Factory was moved there, causing the vast complex at Cheliabinsk to be nicknamed "Tankograd."[12]

The combination of higher than expected initial losses coupled with production interruptions in key tank factories forced the STAVKA on July 15 to order the breakup of the mechanized corps. A few tank divisions were kept, but most were split up into their component regiments. The motorized divisions were at the same time made into rifle divisions. The goal was to concentrate on building smaller armored units that could be used more easily to support the rifle divisions in a combined-arms role.[13] The point is that Zhukov was forced to fritter away the new tank production piecemeal in order to shore up the tattered operational echelon. Despite this seemingly desperate situation, however, Soviet industry managed to rise to the occasion and produce 4,800 newer model tanks in the second half of 1941. Some Western commentators have remarked about the severity of the economic dislocations resulting from evacuations of factories to the east, but it should be remembered that the Russians produced more tanks in the last six months of 1941 than the Germans did during the whole year—3,796, including self-propelled guns. This impressive feat not only allowed the Red Army to keep pace with the numbers of German tanks on the front despite continuous heavy losses, but it also permitted Zhukov the luxury of being able to concentrate 774 tanks, including 222 T–34s and KVs, along the key axis of the Moscow counteroffensive against the flanks of Army Group Center in December.[14] It should also be said that the enforced reliance on combined-arms tactics and the forsaking of the large armored formations in the end proved to be an advantage for the Red Army. As will be seen in the next chapter, the Germans would have done well to have taken a leaf from Zhukov's book at Yelnia and themselves learned more about combined-arms tactics, especially in defensive situations. Later in March 1942, after an increase in the numbers of tanks, the Red Army was able to recreate the tank corps, which added significantly to its ability to exploit breakthroughs. The basic reliance on combined-arms operations and the close mutual support of tanks, artillery, and infantry was, however, not discarded.[15]

The important strategic decisions that the Supreme Command made in late June and in the first half of July, to strengthen the approaches to Moscow as rapidly as possible with armies from the interior and from the Ukraine, should not be understood to have canceled out the prewar strategy entirely. A large, uncommitted part of the original operational echelon was still located in the Ukraine, and although Panzer Group 1 of Army Group South had broken through the "Stalin line" of fortifications south of Novograd–Volynskii on July 7, another month was to pass before Army Group South could bring the Uman battle of encirclement to a close. Although Brauchitsch really wanted Panzer Group 1 to cross the Dnepr and take Kiev on its own, he agreed with Hitler that the Uman encirclement should be carried out beforehand because this was a "safe" decision and because he wished in this way to try to conceal from Hitler the true danger of the Kiev situation. The OKH portrayed the situation in the area of Army Group South in brighter colors than the truth warranted because of their desire to influence Hitler in favor of Moscow.[16]

The powerful Russian Fifth Army, operating just south of the Pripet Marshes and west of the Dnepr around Korosten did not begin with its withdrawal over to the eastern bank of that river until after August 21.[17] As the huge mass of prisoners gathered in by the Germans during the Kiev encirclement would show, the Russian Supreme Command had not yet completely cast overboard its hopes of using the operational group in the Ukraine to good advantage against the flanks of Army Group Center. It is true that the prewar strategy of the Supreme Command had been placed in jeopardy by mid-July, but it had not been changed entirely. In mid-July the war was less than a month old and the mobilization of the strategic reserve was still in its first phase. Bigger things could be planned for the coming weeks once mobilization got into full swing. Despite the altering of their strategy, Zhukov and Stalin were not yet faced with a crisis, even after the abrupt fall of Smolensk on July 16.

On July 12, the Supreme Command ordered Timoshenko to prepare a defense of Mogilev and to launch a counterattack from the direction of Gomel toward Bobruisk in order to hit the rearward areas of Panzer Group 2 advancing across the Dnepr.[18] The main blow of this attack was carried out by the LXIIIrd Rifle Corps of the Twenty-first Army. Guderian's push over the Dnepr had caused a gap to open between the Russian Thirteenth and Twenty-first Armies after the units of the Thirteenth Army south of Mogilev were forced to abandon Krichev and withdraw to the east and southeast, leaving the units at Mogilev and Orsha completely surrounded. On July 14, after the taking of Mstislavl to the east of Mogilev, an interpreter from the German 10th Panzer Division made a telephone call over the open line to Krichev and was asked if he needed any more (Russian) troops in Mstislavl. The interpreter replied, politely, "No, thank you."[19]

The counterattack by the Twenty-first Army was begun on July 13 with a force of about twenty divisions, and it achieved some initial success by forcing the Dnepr, retaking Rogachev and Zhlobin, and pushing on toward Bobruisk against the southern flank of Guderian's XXIVth Panzer Corps. These attacks, which were strong enough to cause the commander of the XXIVth Panzer Corps to fear for the loss of his rearward communications, were no deterrent whatsoever to Guderian, who was determined to reach the high ground around Yelnia as soon as possible.[20] Since, however, the XLVIth Panzer Corps was unable to advance toward Dorogobuzh and link up with Hoth's Panzer Group 3 after taking Yelnia on July 19, a significant portion of the strength of the Russian Sixteenth and Twentieth armies succeeded in making its escape eastward through Dorogobuzh. According to Hoth, "To Panzer Group 2 the taking of the heights of Yelnia for the later continuance of the advance eastward appeared more important than the completion of the Smolensk encirclement."[21]

THE CLOSING OF THE SMOLENSK POCKET

Guderian would have liked to have been able to close the Smolensk pocket, but he was unable to do so for two reasons: (1) the strong pressure exerted on the XLVIth Panzer Corps by the Russian Twenty-fourth Army and (2) the strong pressure exerted on the southern flank of his panzer group and against von Weichs's Second Army by the Russian Twenty-first Army. Guderian could have taken Dorogobuzh and linked up with Hoth only by forfeiting his position around Yelnia, but this he would not do. On the morning of July 20, von Kluge, still the nominal superior of both

Hoth and Guderian as commander of the Fourth Panzer Army, telephoned Guderian and asked him if the XLVIth Panzer Corps should not be withdrawn from Yelnia. Guderian replied in the negative because "this would stiffen the beaten enemy and would not be understood by our own troops."[22]

When von Bock received notice on the morning of July 20 of the fall of Yelnia, a success that Guderian described as an "advantage which must be used," he replied that nothing else mattered except that the Smolensk pocket be hermetically sealed. Von Bock went so far as to dispatch a general staff liaison officer to Guderian with a personal message to this effect. In the words of the commander of Army Group Center to Guderian: "You must be reasonable. A push further to the east is now out of the question." Von Bock's reference to the impossibility of an immediate resumption of the Moscow offensive was made because of the delays experienced by the German Second Army in dealing with the threat to the southern flank of Army Group Center. Von Bock was not happy with von Weichs's failure to force the Dnepr; nevertheless, the commander of Army Group Center would have little luck in hurrying the divisions of the Second Army up from the south toward the north and east to relieve Guderian at Yelnia so his tanks could close the Smolensk pocket. Guderian's southern flank was also in danger, and as will be seen, he had other ideas about how the Second Army would have to be used. The commander of Army Group Center was not inclined to attribute his failure to forge a tight, armored ring around Smolensk to Guderian, who, he believed, was fundamentally correct in his desire to hold Yelnia as a springboard for an operation against Moscow. Instead, he blamed everything on von Kluge because he was Guderian's immediate superior, though he had no real power over the panzer general. This awkward command system had been designed by Halder to give Guderian the maximum amount of freedom to strike for Moscow. Guderian's independence was now eroding von Bock's ability to control his army group, as it would later erode Halder's ability to influence the overall situation. Heusinger, Halder's chief of operations, was closer to the truth when he telephoned von Bock and attributed the failure of Army Group Center to close the pocket around Smolensk to the strong Russian pressure against the flank of Panzer Group 2 from the east, southeast, and south.

In order to seal the Smolensk pocket, it was Guderian's plan to send the 18th Panzer Division from Gusino on the upper Dnepr to relieve the Infantry Regiment *"Gross Deutschland"* thirty-five kilometers north of Roslavl and then use the infantry regiment for the move on Dorogobuzh from the south. Guderian recorded in his memoirs that von Kluge did not approve of this plan, because he was afraid of the danger to the northern flank of Panzer Group 2 along the Dnepr if the 18th Panzer Division were to be pulled out of line.[23]

In reality, however, the panzer general's criticism of von Kluge was unjustified, because the 18th Panzer Division could not be used in this fashion before the infantry of the IXth Army Corps arrived to take its place; this corps did not come into position until after July 21.[24] Later, when the 18th Panzer Division arrived to relieve *"Gross Deutschland"* on July 24, both units were immediately hit and pinned down by strong Russian attacks from the direction of Roslavl, a factor that Guderian failed to mention in his memoirs other than to say that the crisis at Roslavl arose because infantry units were held up by the OKH on the Dnepr west of Smolensk.[25] In the end, Guderian was prepared to carry out the assault on Dorogobuzh from the south with only the 17th Panzer Division from Yelnia and the SS *"Das Reich"* Division, a move that would then have been extremely risky. At the last minute, on July 25, von Kluge contacted Guderian and advised him to call off the attack if it appeared it would be too costly—Guderian took the advice.[26] The gap between the two panzer groups was not closed until July 27 by Hoth's 20th Motorized Division, but by then the real damage had already been done.

TIMOSHENKO'S COUNTEROFFENSIVE AT SMOLENSK

The punishment inflicted on von Kluge's Fourth Panzer Army around Smolensk during the third week in July and after was caused by the new forces introduced by the Red Army Supreme Command. In order to coordinate the forces rapidly being mobilized, a new Reserve Front had been created on July 14 under Lt. Gen. I. A. Bogdanov. This Reserve Front included not only the Twenty-fourth and Twenty-eighth armies at Yelnia and on the Desna, but also four new armies: the Twenty-ninth, Thirtieth, Thirty-first, and Thirty-second. These units were given the initial assignment of holding the line Staraia Russa–Ostashkov–Belyi–

Yelnia–Briansk, and two armies of this group, the Thirty-first and the Thirty-second, were held in the rear at Torzhok–Kalinin–Volo-kolamsk and at Naro–Fominsk-Maloyaroslavets–Vysokinichi. Later, the Thirty-second Army at Naro–Fominsk was sent to the Mozhaisk line of defense. By July 20, Timoshenko's Western Front had formed five special groups under major generals K. K. Rokossovskii and V. A. Khomenko and lieutenant generals S. A. Kalinin, V. Ia. Kachalov, and I. I. Maslennikov. These units, which were in some cases strong enough to give them local superiority over the Germans, were intended by the Supreme Command to mount a counteroffensive to encircle Smolensk and recapture it from the enemy as well as aid the trapped Russian divisions west of the city (see Figure 17).[27]

In a conversation with Timoshenko on July 20, Stalin told the commander of the Western Front:

> Until now you have been throwing only two or three divisions at a time into the front and this has produced no real results. It must now be the time to give up such tactics and begin building spear-

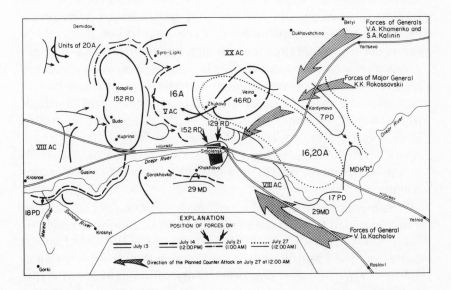

Figure 17. Russian Map Showing the Plans for a Counterattack around Smolensk in July–August 1941

heads on their flanks of about 7–8 divisions with mobile units. It is time to choose our own directions and force the enemy to shift his forces to suit us. I believe that we can now stop pitching pebbles and really throw some big rocks.[28]

It is clear from this statement that Stalin was now a very confident man, in fact too confident. The time was not ripe for the Red Army to be able to choose its own grounds for an offensive without regard for the intentions of the enemy. Stalin would learn his lesson the hard way at Kiev in September, but his basic optimism about the overall situation was not ill-founded. Army Group Center was indeed in difficult straits, especially along its southern flank.

Timoshenko's counteroffensive against Smolensk was unleashed on July 23 with the Twenty-eighth Army striking from the Roslavl area and the Thirtieth and Twenty-fourth armies attempting to advance westward from the area Belyi–Yartsevo. A large group under Rokossovskii, with armor, helped some units of the Sixteenth and Twentieth armies to break out across the Dnepr from south of Yartsevo at this time. On July 29 the Russians assaulted almost the whole front of the German Ninth Army, firing forty guns from one artillery position, and managed to achieve a breakthrough southwest of Belyi. According to von Bock, "The fact is our troops are tired and the high loss in officers has brought about a lack of staying power." On August 2 air reconnaissance reported to Army Group Center that the Russians had built a bridge on the eastern side of the Smolensk pocket and that their troops were "streaming out to the east."[29] After Hoth succeeded in closing the Smolensk pocket, what was left of the Sixteenth Army, including its headquarters staff, joined Rokossovskii's group, which took on the designation "Sixteenth Army" after August 5.[30]

Subsequent to the sealing of the Smolensk pocket, Russian units continued to make their escape eastward. During the night of August 3–4 Rokossovskii pushed forward the Vth Mechanized Corps and the 229th Rifle Division to open the Dnepr crossing at Solovev. On the same day other units of the Twentieth Army crossed over in the area of Zabor on a twenty-kilometer front, and the withdrawals went on for some days under heavy German fire. Field Marshal Kesselring of the Luftwaffe estimated that over one hundred thousand Russian troops managed to escape from the Smolensk pocket to form new divisions. In his words, "The failure to wipe out these forces—I merely recall the costly battles in the Yelnia salient between 30 July and 5 September—could not be laid to the charge of the German troops or their commanders. Our divisions, including the Luftwaffe, were simply overtaxed, at the end of their tether and far from their supply centers."[31] Kesselring was only partly correct in his assessment of the German failure to win a decisive victory at Smolensk. It is true that the Wehrmacht was seriously overburdened, but the Smolensk pocket could have been sealed effectively if Guderian had been willing to give up his position at Yelnia. In his eyes, however, forfeiting Yelnia would have been giving up to Moscow, and that was something he would not do.

Guderian's criticisms of the OKH's actions in the battle for Smolensk require closer examination. Guderian has charged, as mentioned earlier, that the OKH purposely held back the infantry units of the Second Army west of the Dnepr and that this mistake led directly to the crisis along Panzer Group 2's southern flank from the direction of Roslavl. It is true that the Second Army was held up west of the Dnepr for a longer time than expected, but the reason for this had nothing to do with the OKH. The delays encountered by the Second Army were due, first of all, to the extraordinary length of time required to clear the Minsk pocket and, secondly, to the damage inflicted on the Second Army's southern flank by the Russian Thirteenth and Twenty-first armies. The progress of the Second Army was also hampered by the confused and contradictory orders it received from above, most notably from von Bock. At the heart of the difficulties faced by Army Group Center was the employment of faulty tactics that left the flank of Panzer Group 2 sparsely covered, stretching from Smolensk to Yelnia to southeast of Mogilev, beyond the reach of marching infantry units for a long period. The commander of Army Group Center had to weigh the relative importance of sending infantry units toward Smolensk to help secure the pocket there or sending them to Guderian's southern flank, particularly to the XXIVth Panzer Corps at Propoisk (now Slavgorod) on the Sozh, which was experiencing strong pressure from the Russian Twenty-first Army. Von Bock, along with Guderian, was motivated above all by the desire to press on to Moscow, but for von Bock this strategy did not call for sending infantry to protect the southern flank of Panzer Group 2; it called for pushing infantry eastward as rapidly as possible along the most direct route to the Soviet capital. After all, had not Guderian himself told the generals under his command not to worry about their flanks or their rear but always to strike ahead for the supreme goal?

ACTION ON THE FLANKS OF ARMY GROUP CENTER

The problems for Guderian in the south began on July 16, the same day as the fall of Smolensk. The XXIVth Panzer Corps reported early in the morning that the 1st Cavalry Division had to repulse repeated assaults by one to two Russian divisions on both sides of the Dnepr eight kilometers south of Stary Bykhov (see Figure 18). The panzer corps also reported that the 10th Motorized Division on the eastern side of the Gomel–Mogilev road was being pressed hard from a northerly direction. The commander of the corps, Geyer von Schweppenburg, urgently requested that the infantry of the XIIth Army Corps from the Second Army be brought up immediately or else the corps was in danger of losing its rearward communications. The next day Guderian telephoned von Kluge and asked him if part of the XIIth Army Corps could not be used to attack Mogilev and thus relieve the XXIVth Panzer Corps. The commander of the Fourth Panzer Army had to decline this proposal because the XIIth Army Corps was already being turned southward to deal with problems on its own flank.[32]

The difficulty confronting von Weichs and his Second Army staff was that too many demands were being made on his infantry by too many people and all at the same time. Von Weichs needed the XIIth Army Corps badly at Stary Bykhov in order to close a gap that had opened up between it and the LIIIrd Army Corps, the latter unit having its own hands full contending with Russian units that were crossing over to the western bank of the Dnepr in the region of Novy Bykhov. In the early afternoon of July 16, the LIIIrd Army Corps estimated that it was being assailed by seven Russian divisions and could not hold out much longer.[33] Although the XIIth Army Corps reached Stary Bykhov just in the nick of time after a strenuous forced march, the Russians still managed to push west of Rogachev on July 18 and retake Strenki from the 167th Infantry Division with rolling artillery fire and tanks.

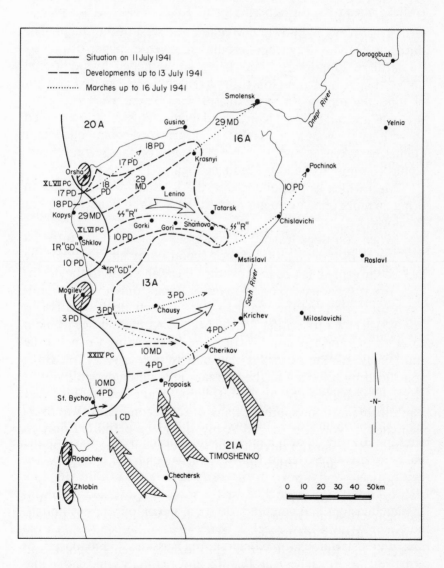

Figure 18. The Southern Flank of Panzer Group 2

149

By July 18, the Second Army had to deal with four groups of Russians: (1) a weak group that had penetrated through the Pinsk swamps, (2) a group of about two divisions, including a motorized division, that had pushed to the south of Bobruisk, (3) the Zhlobin–Rogachev group that had pinned down the LIIIrd Army Corps, and (4) the Russians who had been bypassed by Panzer Group 2 at Novy Bykhov and Mogilev, also west of the Dnepr. The third, or Zhlobin–Rogachev, group had given evidence of powerful artillery support and was being strengthened by additional units brought up from Gomel; its strength was estimated at eight or nine divisions, with more on the way. There were also more Russians around Shklov, Kopys, and Orsha. This situation seemed so serious to von Weichs that he urgently recommended that Gomel be taken at once, or else the flank of the Second Army would continue to be imperiled (see Figures 19 and 20).

Meanwhile, as he pointed out, the Russians would be able to bring up more reinforcements against the XXIVth Panzer Corps at Propoisk.[34]

When von Bock learned of von Weichs's request, he turned a deaf ear to the commander of the Second Army and said that the task of the army must be to cross the Dnepr and push to the northeast, toward Smolensk and Moscow, leaving "only the bare minimum protection for the southern flank." Von Bock then issued von Weichs a written order for the Second Army to move its main force to the northeast and to turn the XIIth Army Corps to the south only insofar as it was "absolutely necessary." Von Bock concluded by referring to the Russian units on Guderian's southern flank as being only "makeshift units" and expressed his belief that the threat to the southern flank of the Second Army was overestimated.[35] Now the Second Army would be permitted only to screen itself from the direction of Gomel, while the bulk of the IXth, XIIIth, and VIIth army corps would have to move toward the northeast.

While the infantry corps of the Second Army were still preparing to cross the Dnepr, Guderian's XXIVth Panzer Corps continued in a state of unrelieved crisis. The corps command fully expected the Russians to cross the Sozh between Propoisk and Krichev and cut off all German units east of the Sozh. Already by July 19, the 1st Cavalry Division had sustained a Russian breakthrough ten kilometers southeast of Stary Bykhov. On this day the

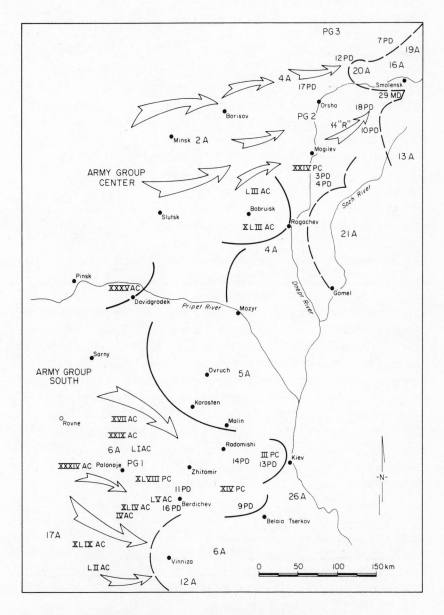

Figure 19. The Southern Flank of Army Group Center on July 14, 1941

151

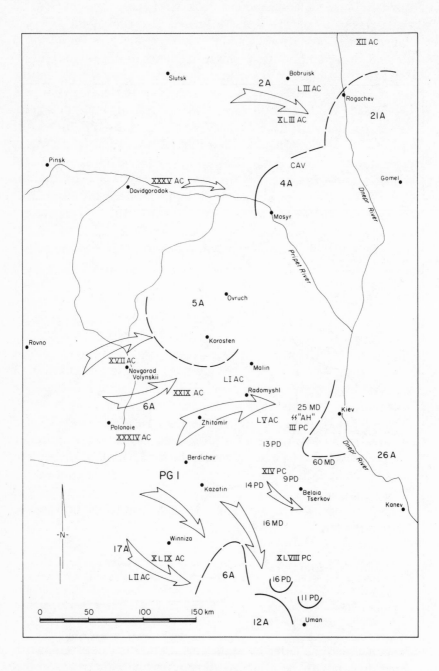

Figure 20. The Southern Flank of Army Group Center on July 21, 1941

Russians made a continuous attack with tanks and artillery all along the front of the 10th Motorized Division of the XXIVth Panzer Corps at Propoisk, and the division was now very close to the end of its ammunition supply.[36] Guderian put in another request to von Kluge for the help of the XIIth Army Corps, but the commander of the Fourth Panzer Army was powerless; von Bock had already rendered a decision. This request for infantry was renewed again on July 21, this time directly from the 10th Motorized Division, but von Weichs replied that he would not turn another division to the south without an express order from Army Group Center.[37] Guderian noted in his panzer group's war diary that the battered German troops at Propoisk "regarded with bitterness" the fact that the XIIth Army Corps was not sent to their aid but turned to the northeast instead. Guderian now realized rather bitterly himself that in order to relieve their comrades at Smolensk, the Russians had taken notice of Panzer Group 2's long, open southern flank.[38]

The predicament of the 10th Motorized Division had become so severe by July 21 that von Bock had to relent and allow the Second Army to send the XIIIth Army Corps to Propoisk: "An impressive result for an enemy already so badly beaten!"[39] This relief operation was carried out by the 17th Infantry Division of the XIIIth Army Corps on July 23, but the battle still raged on northwest of Propoisk. By July 25, other infantry units from the IXth Army Corps had begun to relieve the 18th Panzer Division in the area of Vaskovo, the 29th Motorized Division near Strigino, and the 10th Panzer Division within the Yelnia salient. Guderian's chestnuts had been pulled out of the fire by several redoubtable infantry divisions—a fact that he was not prone to ignore. On July 22 Guderian addressed a personal letter to von Kluge in which he made a most revealing statement:

> The panzer group is locked in a battle in an area over 100 kms. deep and we are forced to operate over huge distances with very poor roads. The securing of the flanks . . . of the widely separated panzer corps has become very difficult and takes away the strength from our spearheads.

He concluded the letter by requesting an infantry corps of two or three divisions to be attached directly to the panzer group that would be used to secure the rearward areas and the flanks.[40] Von

Kluge's reaction to this letter has not been recorded, but he must have reflected grimly on the words that he had said to Guderian on the eve of his rash crossing of the Dnepr on July 10.

While Guderian and von Bock were clumsily trying to solve the difficulties along the Sozh, the battles still raged furiously on the western bank of the Dnepr. The VIIth Army Corps was given the task of assaulting Mogilev, an undertaking that promised to be difficult since the Russians there showed no signs of giving in, even though they had been cut off from the east. Russian planes were still flying in at night and parachuting munitions to the besieged garrison, which was lively enough to launch a counterattack against the German bridgehead on the south side of the city on July 23. During the next day the VIIth Army Corps penetrated into the downtown section of the city with parts of three divisions, and it was then that the roughest kind of house-to-house, block-by-block fighting was encountered, resulting in heavy losses for the Germans. While the battle for Mogilev was underway, von Weichs telephoned von Bock and gave him a dark assessment of the situation of his southern flank, saying that Bobruisk would be endangered if the Second Army pushed more forces to the east. Von Bock took full responsibility on himself and said that the Second Army must cross the Dnepr as rapidly as possible. The battle for Mogilev ended on July 26, ten days after the fall of Smolensk, with the Russian Thirteenth Army yielding thirty-five thousand prisoners.[41]

Even though another Russian stronghold on the Dnepr had been eliminated and even though the Germans had a secure foothold on the Sozh to the east (thanks to the timely arrival of the XIIIth Army Corps), the Red Army showed no evidence of letting up its active defense along either of the two rivers. It still maintained a strong presence on the Dnepr at Rogachev–Zhlobin and on the Sozh at Krichev. In addition, Russian cavalry units were still active far behind the German lines threatening the Minsk–Bobruisk railroad.[42] On July 28, the LIIIrd Army Corps west of Rogachev was raked by a fourteen-hour artillery barrage and a full-scale assault by a Russian division. The XIIIth Army Corps was subjected to similar treatment after it took over the Krichev bridgehead from the XXIVth Panzer Corps. On July 30 the Second Army had to cancel plans for the continuation of the offensive across the Dnepr and the Sozh during the next four to five days because the divisions of the army were 20–65 percent short of their normal supply of ammunition.[43]

Halder's concern about the activities on the flanks of Army Group Center was reflected in the conference he held with Hitler on July 13. In this conference, as has been mentioned, Halder recommended that action be taken to solve the problem of the flanks before resuming the offensive toward Moscow. Halder's views on this subject were transmitted to von Bock through Greiffenberg, the chief of staff of Army Group Center, also on July 13. According to Greiffenberg, Halder favored turning Panzer Group 2 to the south, behind the main group of Russian armies in the Ukraine, after first giving it a chance to rest and refit in the Smolensk area. Greiffenberg added that Hoth should perform a similar maneuver in the north by turning part of his Panzer Group 3 toward Army Group North. The rest of Hoth's panzer group could be used to aid the main drive of the Fourth and Ninth armies on to Moscow.[44] Von Bock reacted swiftly (as could be expected) to this shift in the wind from the OKH. After first conferring with von Kluge, who was still prepared to see Moscow left as the first priority, von Bock dispatched Colonel Schmundt, Hitler's adjutant, who happened to be present at Army Group headquarters, back to East Prussia with a message to Halder protesting this impending decision.[45] Halder, however, was not deterred from putting his plan into effect. During the evening of July 13, the OKH ordered part of Panzer Group 3—it was unclear to von Bock what part was meant—to turn north and cooperate with the southern flank of Army Group North in order to encircle the Russians in the Kholm–Lovat River area south of Lake Ilmen.[46]

In order to clarify the somewhat confused directives emanating from East Prussia, von Bock telephoned Brauchitsch on the afternoon of July 14 and told him that any such wide-ranging operation by Panzer Group 3 would have to wait until after the fall of Smolensk. Brauchitsch agreed to this, but added that a further eastward plunge of the tank units was now out of the question, and that the mass of the German infantry could not then move far beyond the Dnepr, due to the problems of supply. Brauchitsch believed, however, that some sort of armor-infantry combined "expedition-corps" could be used to reach further goals, such as Moscow.[47] But the army commander in chief did not relent on the question of sending Panzer Group 3 northward. On July 16 the

19th Panzer Division was ordered to take Velikie Luki on the Lovat against von Bock's wishes.[48]

The assault on Velikie Luki by the 19th Panzer Division began on July 17. After the Germans took the central railroad station, a Russian train rolled in loaded with tanks, wholly an unexpected gift! On July 18 the Russian Twenty-second Army fought stubbornly to retake Velikie Luki without success, suffering considerable losses in the process. The rest of the LVIIth Panzer Corps —that is, the 12th Panzer Division and the 18th Motorized Division, screening the 19th Panzer Division's southeastern flank at Nevel—was not so lucky. During the night of July 19 the screen front at Nevel was put under strong pressure by a well-organized attack from the west by Russian units being pushed back from the front of Army Group North's Sixteenth Army. In the early morning of July 20 two Russian regiments broke through the LVIIth Panzer Corps' front from west to east at Borok, inflicting some damage. Also on July 19 two Russian divisions set upon Hoth's XXXIXth Panzer Corps and with powerful artillery support broke through the front of its 14th Motorized Division south of the Nevel–Gorodok road.[49] The German attempt to surround the Russians northwest of Nevel by coordinating movements between Army Group North and Panzer Group 3 apparently would not work.[50]

After some discussion, it was agreed by everyone, except Hoth, that Velikie Luki would have to be given up. Hoth later blamed the loss of Velikie Luki on von Kluge and von Bock, both of whom were against the operation from the start because it jeopardized the attempt farther south to close the armored ring around Smolensk. In fairness it must be said that von Kluge and von Bock cannot be blamed for the failure of an operation that they had done all they could to prevent. The real blame, if blame must be assigned, belongs to Halder, for it was he who convinced Hitler that such a maneuver was necessary before the Smolensk pocket was closed.[51] Halder was willing to admit now that Velikie Luki would have to be given up, in spite of the fact that the Russians were bound to turn the city into a strongly fortified position.[52] As Hoth noted, a month later, in August, seven infantry and two panzer divisions would be needed to retake Velikie Luki.[53] The order for the 19th Panzer Division to abandon Velikie Luki and pull back to Nevel was given at 7:00 P.M. on July 20.

VACILLATION BY THE OKH—
TROUBLE BREWING WITH GUDERIAN

On the morning of July 21 Brauchitsch and Heusinger paid a short visit to Army Group Center's headquarters in Borisov in order to clarify the latest views on strategy entertained by the OKH. During a preliminary discussion Brauchitsch set forth the first goal as the sealing off of Smolensk and the elimination of the pocket of trapped Russians. Then he said preparations could be made for sending the Second Army and Panzer Group 2 toward the south and the Ukraine by the beginning of August, a judgment that was unpleasant music to von Bock's ears. During this conversation, when von Bock was temporarily absent from the room, von Kluge took the opportunity to make some disparaging remarks to Brauchitsch about von Bock's methods of command. When the commander of Army Group Center returned, he overheard part of the conversation and flew into a rage, saying that von Kluge had been his enemy for a long time and that his vanity was well known. The origin of the two field marshals' dislike for one another can be traced back to the planning phase of Barbarossa when they argued over the best method for employing tanks.[54]

When Brauchitsch returned from his trip to Borisov that same day, Halder was ready to reveal to the army commander in chief in greater detail his plans for the future conduct of operations by Army Group Center: (1) von Kluge, then the commander of the Fourth Panzer Army, should take command of the southern flank of Army Group Center, that is, over Panzer Group 2 and the southern part of the Second Army; (2) von Kluge's force was then to split off from Army Group Center and push to the southeast and come under the overall direction of von Rundstedt's Army Group South; (3) von Kluge's force would then push eastward with Stalingrad as its ultimate objective; (4) Strauss's Ninth Army would be divided, with its southern wing joining von Weichs's Second Army and its northern wing uniting with Army Group North, which in turn would shift some of its forces to the south, including the Sixteenth Army and Panzer Group 4; (5) Army Group Center, now to be composed of the Second Army and Panzer Group 3, would proceed along a line from Kholm to Bologoe toward the east (approaching Moscow from both the north and south), envelop the city, and reduce it with some help from Army

Group North; and (6) Army Group Center would then move its front to Kazan on the middle Volga before the end of 1941. After the war Halder stated that "the ultimate goal of Hitler was to eliminate Russia as a European power in a brief period of time. This the OKH knew to be a military impossibility, but Hitler was never able to realize this."[55]

In his memoirs Guderian quotes Halder's words in an OKH memorandum of July 23, 1941, in which the chief of the general staff set forth his plans as outlined above. The panzer general attempted to show that Halder favored putting the Ukraine ahead of Moscow in terms of importance, but this certainly was not the case. Von Bock also reacted strongly to this OKH communique and dispatched an immediate objection to East Prussia, saying that his army group command would become "superfluous" if the proposed order went into effect and that his post should be abolished if his army group were to be split up into three separate groups.[56] In fact, the chief of the general staff had been forced to take cognizance of reality and change his original plan so as to alleviate the problems faced by Army Group Center on its southern flank and to remedy the difficulties confronting Army Group South in the Ukraine. The essence of Halder's new strategy was that by early August a general shift of German forces to the south should take place. Important parts of Army Group Center, including Panzer Group 2 and units of the Second Army, should be sent to Army Group South, while portions of Army Group North should also be moved south to supplement the main drive on Moscow by the rest of the Second Army and Panzer Group 3—some parts of the Ninth Army would remain with the Second Army, and some of its units would come under the direction of Army Group North. Presumably, Army Group North would have to forgo the assault on Leningrad until after Moscow had been taken.

By arriving at this solution at such a late date, however, Halder would have serious problems persuading Hitler to go along with it, for he had already convinced the führer once, prior to July 17, of the necessity of sending Panzer Group 3 to cooperate with Army Group North. This idea had been Hitler's all along ever since Jodl, on the basis of the Lossberg study, had shown him the efficacy of it back in December 1940. The setback that Hoth had suffered by July 20 at Velikie Luki would further strengthen Hitler's conviction that the Russians in front of Army Group North would have to be dealt with before any rapid plunge eastward was made in the direction of Moscow. Halder's blunder at Velikie Luki would thus have a double-damning effect, not only on the situation along the northern flank of Army Group Center, but on Hitler as well. The führer had furthermore been unfavorably impressed by Army Group Center's inability to form a tight pocket around Smolensk, a factor due more, however, to Guderian's unwillingness at any cost to give up Yelnia than to any direct fault of Halder's. The course of events had begun to catch up with Halder by the third week in July, for he had already set forces in motion that would shortly prove to be beyond his power to control. Fate would soon play a cruel trick on the chief of the general staff, but it was a fate of his own making.

On July 27, Guderian and his chief of staff, Freiherr von Liebenstein, flew to Army Group Center headquarters at Borisov expecting to hear that the new assignment for Panzer Group 2 would be to advance either on Moscow or Briansk, but to Guderian's surprise, he was told by von Bock that his next order of business, as ordered by Hitler, would be to cooperate with the Second Army and encircle the eight to ten Russian divisions in the direction of Gomel. In Guderian's words this would mean "sending tanks toward Germany."[57] Guderian's reaction to this order was predictable, and it was also a portent of things to come. The panzer general first replied to von Bock that his units would not be ready to undertake any new operations before August 5 and only then if supplies arrived soon enough to allow the repair and refitting of his tanks. In truth, some of what Guderian said did have a basis in fact. On July 29 Panzer Group 2 reported that as of July 25 only 263 Panzer IIs, IIIs, and IVs remained in battle-worthy condition. Up to this same date the panzer group had lost 20,271 men and had received approximately ten thousand men as replacements. Panzer Group 2 had begun the war with 113,500 men and 953 tanks.[58] The overall tenor of his speech, though, was designed to pressure von Bock. Guderian also described the terrain toward the south and southwest as being "impossible" and beseeched von Bock to allow his tanks to continue east.

After von Bock managed to calm Guderian down, he told him that he would not have to send his tanks all the way back to Gomel on the Dnepr, the job of taking that fortified point could be left to the Second Army, which, it might be added, was already having a rough time with Rogachev and Zhlobin. Von Bock then broke the news to the panzer general that Brauchitsch had visited him earlier in the morning and that both had agreed that Panzer Group 2 should be used against Roslavl and not Gomel. In order to sweeten the task for Guderian, the commander of Army Group Center further informed him that two infantry corps, the VIIth and the IXth, were to be placed directly under his command for the Roslavl operation.[59]

The stone was now, at least temporarily, removed from Guderian's heart. The Roslavl operation was similar to the one that he had been advocating ever since July 20 as the best way to secure the southern flank of Panzer Group 2 in a drive toward Moscow.[60] The attacks that had punished the XXIVth Panzer Corps along the Sozh since July 18 had come from the direction of Roslavl, as well as the attacks that had been launched against the XLVIIth Panzer Corps since July 24 along the Stomat River east of the Sozh. Guderian had already made plans before July 27 to finish with Roslavl before going on to Moscow. It was for this reason that on July 23 he ordered the XXIVth Panzer Corps to remain in the Propoisk–Cherikov area after its relief by the XIIIth Army Corps. There the panzer corps could be supplied with the fuel and ammunition that it needed to push on Roslavl.[61] Guderian was further pleased by the fact that two infantry corps would be added to his panzer group instead of the one that he had originally asked for on July 22. With this extra complement, Panzer Group 2 would also be able to take Krichev on the Sozh, another troublesome thorn in the panzer group's southern flank. Guderian had at first told von Bock that he would not be able to move against Gomel before August 5 at the earliest. The operation against Roslavl–Krichev, however, began on August 1.

For Guderian, the major confrontation with Hitler and the OKH could be postponed until after the Roslavl–Krichev operations had been brought to a close. The panzer general knew well enough that the OKH would do what it could to convince Hitler that a rapid drive on Moscow was necessary, but he did not care for the way Halder had outlined his view of things in the OKH communique of July 23.[62] Guderian believed that a wide sweep by his panzer group south of Moscow, perhaps through Briansk and across the Oka, might be necessary, but he strongly disagreed with Halder's plan to take Moscow with only two infantry armies and Panzer Group 3, and to detach his panzer group from Army Group Center entirely and dispatch it to the Ukraine and the lower Volga.[63] The panzer general's vanity was much too great for him to endure the slight being offered to him by the OKH. If Moscow could be taken, Guderian was sure that it could only be done with his panzer group in the vanguard. Guderian's self-esteem was well known to his colleagues, and it was a factor that von Bock had already been forced to take into account.

On July 9, before the crossing of the Dnepr, von Bock had seriously considered the possibility of moving the armored and motorized units in the rearward areas toward Panzer Group 3, which had already crossed the Dvina and was thus in a good position to drive down from the north toward Smolensk and eastward. Von Kluge's chief of staff, Blumentritt, however, had argued von Bock out of this idea, saying that he was afraid of Guderian's reaction at being slighted in such a manner. Earlier, at the time of the operations around Minsk, Guderian had shown himself to be ferociously protective of his units whenever it seemed that some of them, even temporarily, might be taken from under his command.[64] It would have been better for Halder if he had not forgotten this important feature of Guderian's forceful character. After the communique of July 23, the panzer general firmly considered Halder to be hostile to his cause, and he would not hesitate to betray the chief of the general staff in the future if given a chance.

Although Halder had not yet fathomed the depths of Guderian's psyche, Hitler knew his man, so he sent his adjutant, Schmundt, to Guderian on July 29 to present him the Oak Leaves to the Knight's Cross.[65] The award earned the gratitude of the panzer general, who was loyal to the core to the führer. Guderian used the occasion of Schmundt's visit to ask him to carry a personal message to Hitler stressing the importance of Moscow over the Ukraine. Hitler, in the end, was not one casually to brush off Guderian, as he was prone to do with Halder, and this quirk in his character would have a telling effect later on Halder's schemes and on the course of the war.

The stage was now set for the fateful month of August: for the fearful battles along the Yelnia salient, for the operations at Roslavl–Krichev, Rogachev–Zhlobin, Gomel, and again at Velikie Luki. The time was also near for a momentous resolution of forces to take place between Hitler, the OKH, and Guderian. The losers in these struggles were, as they have always been, the men who had to die for their leaders' mistakes.

CHAPTER 5

THE PAUSE OF ARMY GROUP CENTER

THE YELNIA SALIENT

After the formation of the Yelnia salient there was little else the German armored and motorized units of the XLVIth Panzer Corps of Panzer Group 2 could do but hold on grimly to the territory they had won and hope for relief. The marching infantry of von Kluge's Fourth Panzer Army was, however, far to the west, and this army's IXth Army Corps would not arrive in the salient in force until July 28, nine days after the fall of Yelnia (see Figure 21).

On July 24, 1941, the XLVIth Panzer Corps ordered its SS *"Das Reich"* Division and its 10th Panzer Division to rectify the defense line around Yelnia and prepare to hold the area as economically as possible, making the best use of the irregular terrain. By 1:00 P.M. the SS was already fighting off Russian assaults with heavy tanks near hill 125.6. The SS had to defend a long front of over thirty kilometers on the northern side of the salient from this hill to Koloshchina, Vydrina, Lavrova, Ushakova, and the Glinka railroad station. In order to shorten *"Das Reich's"* front, von Vietinghoff, the commander of the XLVIth Panzer Corps, decided to pull the motorized infantry regiment *"Gross Deutschland"* into the salient, also to the northern side, to the immediate left of the SS.[1] The northern front of the salient was particularly dangerous at this time, for the Russian divisions, both inside and outside the

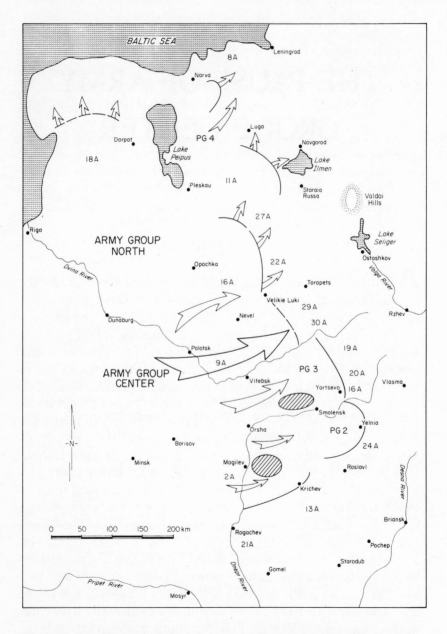

Figure 21. The Situation of Army Groups Center and North on July 21, 1941

164

semipocket around Smolensk, were doing all they could to keep open an escape route to the east.

Early in the afternoon of July 25, the following day, several Russian tanks broke through the seam of the SS and the 10th Panzer Division, three of them penetrating nearly to Yelnia itself. In about an hour this attack was beaten back, with the Russians leaving sixteen broken tanks on the battlefield. Only one German gun position had been overrun, but the damage would have been considerably worse had the Russians sent in infantry behind the tanks.[2] The Russian commanders, especially on the tactical level, still had much to learn, but the Germans would not be able much longer to consider themselves so fortunate. Von Vietinghoff, realizing that the 3.7cm antitanks guns his troops were using were worthless against the big Russian tanks, managed to get one 8.8cm antiaircraft weapon brought in from a Luftwaffe unit. This gun could destroy a Russian tank at over one thousand meters, and it and others like it proved to be indispensable for the prolonged defense of the Yelnia salient. The Luftwaffe also provided welcome support in other ways. JU–87 Stuka dive-bombers were constantly in action over and around the salient disrupting Russian tank columns. Later the Stukas would be gone, for they would follow Guderian during his march to the Ukraine and Guderian would not allow any of his units to remain at Yelnia. When the panzer general left, he would not only take the air cover and some artillery away from the salient, he would also remove virtually all of the motorized units, which were critically important behind the lines of a static defense in order to provide a mobile reserve in case of an enemy breakthrough. This was a factor readily appreciated while the XLVIth Panzer Corps was within the salient but ignored when the unit was ordered to pull out and head to the south. As an example of this, on the morning of July 26 the Russians hit SS *"Das Reich"* along its entire front with aircraft and tanks, and the division pleaded for a mobile reserve to be sent by the 10th Panzer Division, which was done in short order.[3]

During the afternoon of July 25, von Geyer's IXth Army Corps received orders from von Kluge's Fourth Army to proceed as rapidly as possible to Yelnia and relieve the forces of Panzer Group 2. On the way into the salient, near and to the east of Voroshilovo, Infantry Regiment 485 of the 263rd Infantry Division was hit hard by the Russian 149th Rifle Division. Two Ger-

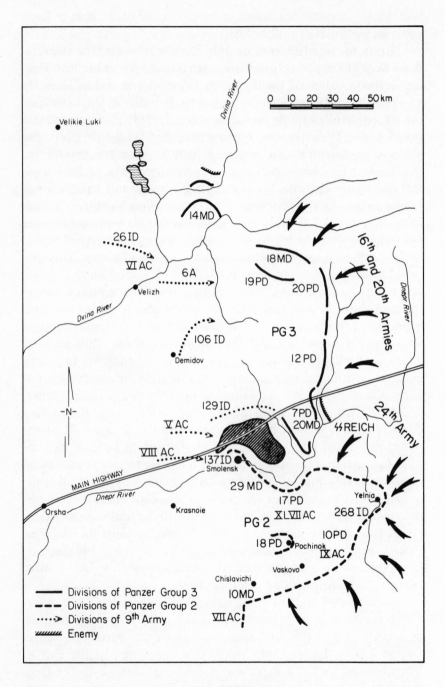

Figure 22. Panzer Groups 2 and 3 on July 27, 1941

man battalions were cut off and had to beat back attacks from all sides by Russian tanks. The division had no reserves, and so the battalions were ordered to fight their way out of the encirclement as best they could; they succeeded in doing so on July 27—"after suffering considerable losses in personnel and materiel."[4] The rest of the IXth Army Corps began the relief of the 18th Panzer Division west of Yelnia and the infantry regiment *"Gross Deutschland,"* an operation that was completed by July 28.[5] The infantry regiment *"Gross Deutschland"* was moved out of line to a position in and generally to the west of Yelnia. The SS Division's western flank was now covered by units of the XLVIIth Panzer Corps, including the 17th Panzer Division; these were then linking up east of Smolensk with Panzer Group 3's 20th Motorized and 7th Panzer Divisions. Meanwhile, the Vth and VIIIth Army Corps of Strauss's Ninth Army were employing four divisions in rounding up the trapped Russians to the north and west of Smolensk (see Figure 22). By the end of July the divisions of the Russian Sixteenth and Twentieth armies caught in the Smolensk pocket were down to about one or two thousand men each. The Twentieth Army had only 65 tanks and 177 guns remaining, yet the battles went on with neither side yielding or expecting quarter.[6] The Smolensk pocket would not finally be eliminated until August 5, when Army Group Center's "Order of the Day" proclaimed that the Russians had lost 309,110 prisoners, 3,205 tanks, 3,000 guns, and 341 aircraft.[7]

After coming into the salient, the IXth Army Corps took up positions on the southern side of the front, with the 292nd Infantry Division being farthest east, next to the 10th Panzer Division, and the 263rd Infantry Division being farthest to the west. The final move by the infantry divisions into the salient was aided by the willingness of General Schaal, the commander of the 10th Panzer Division, to allow his empty trucks to be used for this purpose.

During the next two days, the units of the IXth Army Corps discovered for themselves what others in the Yelnia salient had already come to know: that the Russian attacks with heavy tanks could not be stopped with ordinary antitank weapons. Fortunately, the IXth Corps had a few Sturmgeschütz self-propelled artillery pieces, which allowed it to bolster its front with a mobile reserve of sorts. Without the Sturmgeschütz and some antiaircraft guns brought into action at the end of July, the IXth Corps would have been in serious trouble.[8] Other problems for the corps were caused by the swampy ground around the upper Desna, on the southern side of the salient, and by the thick scrub that grew everywhere and allowed the enemy to creep up close to the front lines without being observed. The worst problem that the German troops had to face at Yelnia was a difficulty that became more troublesome every day: the growing power of the Russian artillery that was being moved into the range of the salient. On July 30, the 10th Panzer Division was subjected to heavy attacks while trying to disengage itself from the front, and the artillery support that the Russians had brought up for these attacks caused some surprise. The 10th Panzer received word from the Luftwaffe that "outside the range of our own artillery large numbers of Russian guns are firing from open country; closer in to our front their guns are well hidden under the low trees."[9] It was taken as an ominous sign by many at Yelnia in late July that the Russians appeared to be so well provided with artillery and ammunition behind the Dnepr. It was also regarded as an ill omen that the Russian prisoners taken during the attacks on the salient were fresh, clean-cut, and had a military bearing, unlike the rather motley prisoners captured in earlier battles.[10] The Russian strategic reserve was already making its presence felt to Army Group Center: so far only the advance elements had arrived; the rest would come soon enough.

When Guderian began to make plans on July 28 for the march southward with Roslavl as the first objective, as ordered by the OKH and Army Group Center, he also made provision for two Army Corps, the VIIth and the IXth, to join him. The IXth Corps was to push its front south and east toward Kovali and Kosaki along the western bank of the upper Desna. This would mean that, for a time, the IXth Corps, augmented by the 137th Infantry Division, would be removed from the Yelnia salient. The corps was compelled to return to Yelnia at a later date, however, after conditions there had deteriorated to a considerable degree.[11]

On August 8 the defense of the Yelnia salient, now some thirty kilometers long and twenty kilometers wide, was temporarily transferred to the XXth Army Corps under General Materna, although Panzer Group 2 retained overall command of the area until August 26. Around the perimeter of the salient, starting from the southwestern end, were the 268th Infantry Division, the SS *"Das Reich"* Division plus one regiment of the 292nd Infantry Division and, along the northern rim, the 15th Infantry Division.[12] The troubles for these units began almost immediately, especially in the hills near Klematina, a small village northwest of Yelnia near the swampy Ustrom rivulet. This area was repeatedly subjected to Russian artillery, tank, and air attacks. On August 10, the Russians shifted their assaults to the Uzha stream, which flows due north from Yelnia into the Dnepr. Here the Russians broke through the seam between the 15th Infantry Division and the SS, retaking a small village. In order to stem this assault, the XXth Corps had to send three thousand rounds of light field howitzer ammunition to its 15th Division. Despite this heavy dependence on artillery, the next day the corps was ordered to give up two artillery regiments to Guderian's XLVIth Panzer Corps, which was preparing to move the *"Das Reich"* Division out of the salient toward the south, along with the regiment *"Gross Deutschland"* and the 10th Panzer Division, which had already moved out. Materna protested violently against this decision, which he described as "a significant weakening of our defense strength," but to no avail.[13] The Russians now attacked the 15th Division in dense waves, losing heavily in the process but bloodying the Germans as well. On August 10–11 alone, the 15th Division lost twenty officers. By August 11, the German shortage of artillery ammunition was critical, and the units of the 292nd Division had been pushed off the hills around Klematina. As a matter of urgent necessity, the SS division was temporarily forced to move back into line along the Uzha. The position at Klematina was soon restored without major difficulty, although the corps command had been seriously worried about the integrity of the front lines. On August 13, the rest of the 292nd Infantry Division began to filter back into line (having returned from the mission northeast of Roslavl) in order to bolster the beleaguered 15th Division and the SS, whose front had been pushed back three kilometers.

When he was informed about the situation along the Uzha and about another breakthrough in the front of the Ninth Army north of Yelnia, von Bock remarked that Army Group Center had no reserves left except the Spanish "Blue Division" and the 183rd Infantry Division, which was scheduled to arrive in Grodno sometime in mid-August; "From Grodno to the front is 600 kms.! . . . I need every man at the front." Von Bock was known to have a low opinion of his country's allies—he had observed that the Spanish were wont to pound their MG–34 machine guns into the ground with shovels instead of using the tripods. There were also stories of them carrying pigs and chickens in their trucks as well as taking women for rides.[14] As amusing as these tales must have been, von Bock would have done better to worry about the behavior of his own countrymen. In a report by *"Einsatzgruppe B"* of the SS operating in the rear areas of Army Group Center it was claimed that by mid-November 1941, 45,467 Jews had already been shot.[15]

In a report dated August 13, Materna outlined the situation of the XXth Army Corps to Army Group Center, describing the heavy losses along the salient, especially the northern perimeter, and stated that it was impossible to respond adequately to the Russian "drum fire" artillery barrages because of the ammunition shortage. The three divisions then under his command, the 268th, the 292nd, and the 15th, had fronts of twenty-five, fourteen, and twenty-two kilometers respectively, in very difficult terrain. At the end of the report, in the gravest possible language, he prophesied that if the Russian attacks were better coordinated and came in larger than battalion strength, then his divisions might not be able to hold on.[16] On August 14, Materna flew to Guderian's headquarters to plead for help: he asked either to be allowed to reduce the size of the salient or for Panzer Group 2 to send forces to the Desna and the Ugra, south and east of Smolensk. Guderian did not give a definite reply to this request, saying only that the decision would be made within the next two days.[17]

The first time the panzer general had been asked to render a decision about maintaining the position at Yelnia had been on July 20, when, in response to a query from von Kluge, he had refused to consider the possibility of abandonment. The next occasion on which Guderian's opinion was solicited came on August 4, when Hitler visited Army Group Center. In order to ensure the smooth running of this conference, Halder had telephoned Greiffenberg, Army Group Center's chief of staff, on August 3 and warned him "to use caution in outlining the Yelnia situation" to Hitler so as to avoid any possibility of interference from the führer.[18] Halder did not need to worry about what Guderian would say about Yelnia, however. The panzer general told Hitler that Yelnia was indispensable for a future operation against Moscow, and even if an offensive against Moscow were not envisioned, "the maintenance of the salient still remains a question of prestige."[19] This was the second time that Guderian had referred to the Yelnia salient as being important for certain metaphysical reasons, such as troop morale or prestige, but Hitler would not listen to any such talk from one of his generals; in his words "Prestige cannot be permitted to influence the decision at all." In his memoirs Guderian mentioned only the first part of his argument—that Yelnia had importance for future operations against Moscow.[20] Hitler, however, was unable to decide the question about Yelnia immediately, and so a final decision was postponed. On August 14, after his confrontation with Materna, Guderian realized that something had to be done.

In a telephone conversation with von Bock on this same day, Guderian said that Yelnia could be held only if (1) the Russians were pushed back to the edge of the great forest east of the Desna; (2) a great deal more ammunition were made available for the salient; and (3) the Luftwaffe concentrated strong forces for use against the Russians around Yelnia. Von Bock decided to pass this thorny problem on to the OKH, telling Brauchitsch essentially what he had heard from Guderian but adding that he doubted that a short push over the Desna would help Yelnia at all. Von Bock also said that he could do nothing more about either the ammunition supply or the Luftwaffe, the latter being in Göring's province. Brauchitsch promised an early answer.[21]

Late in the afternoon Halder telephoned Greiffenberg at Army Group Center and notified him that the OKH would leave the final decision about Yelnia to von Bock, although Halder was of the personal opinion that the salient should be held "because it is harder on the enemy than it is on us."[22] The OKH also left open the possibility of Army Group Center pushing farther east, a possibility that von Bock was "overjoyed" to hear.[23] When von Bock contacted Guderian the next day to ask his advice, the panzer general said the salient should continue to be held, although two infantry divisions of the IXth Army Corps would have to relieve two of his motorized divisions there. Another infantry division could be held behind the salient in reserve. In his memoirs Guderian noted that his plan to push his panzer group to the northeast toward Viazma was rejected by the OKH on August 11 and that soon after that he advocated giving up the Yelnia salient, thus attempting to rid himself of any responsibility for this bloody affair. Notations after August 11 in von Bock's diary and in the diary of Guderian's own panzer group, however, contain no such record that the panzer general wanted to abandon Yelnia. On the contrary, Guderian's advice to von Bock was key to the question of holding the salient.[24] The decision to hold on to Yelnia had thus firmly been made by mid-August, but no one from the OKH or Panzer Group 2 had any reason for doing so other than that the Russians were wasting more lives there than the Germans—a true reversion to Falkenhayn's strategy at Verdun in 1916—or that the location was valuable to hold in case another immediate offensive operation were to be carried out against Moscow, a decision that had been repeatedly put off by Hitler. It is also a sad commentary on the state of German military planning in 1941 that some generals advocated maintaining a position for reasons of prestige. To say that Yelnia was a costly blunder would be to minimize its true horror.

On August 15 at 10:30 A.M. the IXth Army Corps received orders from Panzer Group 2 to move both of its divisions, now the 137th and 263rd Infantry Divisions, back into the Yelnia salient to relieve the elements of the SS *"Das Reich"* Division and infantry regiment *"Gross Deutschland,"* both belonging to Guderian's XLVIth Panzer Corps (see Figure 23). The panzer corps conveniently provided trucks to hurry the infantry into place on the northern side of the salient west of the Uzha.[25] In the area of the XXth Army Corps, IXth Corps' neighbor to the east, the 78th Infantry Division was brought in on August 16 to replace the badly mauled 15th Infantry Division. By August 17, after the XXth Army Corps had been in the salient only one week, its three divisions had lost 2,254 men, including 97 officers.[26]

Taking notice that his IXth Army Corps had a forty-kilometer front and that the infantry units lacked the mobility to react to crises along it (as did the XLVIth Panzer Corps), General von Geyer on August 18 urgently requested Panzer Group 2 to send some self-propelled artillery and heavy artillery units back into the salient. This request was prompted by the fact that on the previous day Panzer Group 2 had ordered nearly all of the heavy artillery and the engineers taken away from the XXth Army Corps.[27] It was the opinion of the chief of staff of the XXth Corps that the loss of this artillery and the engineers, plus the casualties the corps had suffered, had badly weakened the front. On August 20 General Materna drove to see Guderian near Roslavl to tell him personally about the "extremely difficult and threatening situation" faced by

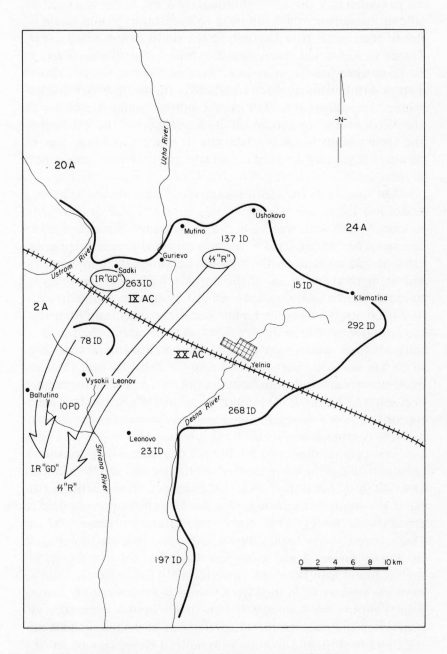

Figure 23. Panzer Group 2 and Second Army, August 17, 1941

173

the XXth Army Corps. The only concession Guderian was willing to make was that the 268th Infantry Division on the southeastern side of the salient would not have to undertake the immediate relief of the 10th Panzer Division to the south of the XXth Corps. Guderian would not relent on the question of artillery—it had to be taken elsewhere.[28] At noon on August 22, von Kluge's Fourth Panzer Army officially took command over the three Army Corps within the salient, the IXth on the northern and western sides, the XXth on the eastern and southern sides, and the VIIth along the Desna front leading to the south. Since von Kluge was ill, however, Guderian retained actual command over the salient until August 26.[29]

On August 23 the 263rd Infantry Division of the IXth Army Corps lost 150 men repulsing a penetration at Chimborasso, a low mountain; the loss was also due to a heavy Russian artillery barrage. The 263rd Division was in a particularly bad position because it was located on the extreme northwestern corner of the salient, right at the "neck of the bottle" the Russians were trying to break off. The division had been losing an average of a hundred men a day for the five days it had been in the salient. By August 24 the line strength of the division's infantry companies had sunk to thirty or forty men. Geyer pleaded for the 15th Infantry Division to be sent back into the salient to help the 263rd Division, but this question was shelved until von Kluge could return and render a decision. On August 25 the 263rd Division suffered another penetration south of Chuvashi, which it could not rectify. The Russian artillery continued to rain shells at a steady rate and the division lost over two hundred men on this one day. Meanwhile, von Bock refused to allow the self-propelled artillery of the SS *"Das Reich"* Division to return to the salient, although more heavy artillery batteries were sent. The self-propelled artillery units were supposed to remain with the SS *"Das Reich"* and infantry regiment *"Gross Deutschland"* because they were due to move south to join the rest of Panzer Group 2 and Guderian did not want to split up his mobile units. Von Bock did agree to allow the 263rd Division to have the artillery from the 15th Division but this was only a small gain.[30] During the next day, the 263rd Division lost another 150 men trying to repair the ruptured front line at Chuvashi. This carnage had to stop, and so both Materna and Geyer flew to see von Kluge at Minsk, the field marshal having just returned to duty, and convinced him that he should visit the salient and gain a first-hand impression.[31]

The first result of von Kluge's visit to the front on August 27 was that the 15th Infantry Division was sent immediately to the relief of the 263rd Division, which by then was down to twenty-five to fifty men in each of its companies. Before leaving its sector of the front for refitting, the 263rd Division finally managed to restore the old front line south of Chuvashi, the Russians leaving three hundred dead behind.[32] The second result of von Kluge's visit to the IXth and XXth Army Corps was that the next day he drafted a report to von Bock with the forecast that if the Russians ceased attacking only in battalion strength and mounted assaults with whole divisions, concentrating on a small area, then, with their bountiful artillery support, they would succeed in permanently cracking the German front. Von Kluge went on to say that Yelnia was originally taken by Panzer Group 2 as an offensive measure and that the position was very difficult for defense. Each division in the salient was losing 50–150 men a day, and only one road led out of the salient to the west, through a zone under German control only eighteen kilometers wide. Von Kluge recommended either rapidly resuming the offensive toward Moscow or giving up the salient.[33]

The conditions von Kluge surveyed on the front lines of his army were indeed depressing. There were no trenches as there had been in the First World War; instead the defense at Yelnia was conducted using "a string of pearls" kind of dugout system, with each small dugout holding one or two men and being spaced ten to twenty meters apart. In most areas there was no depth to the line, such as in the area of the XXth Army Corps' 78th Infantry Division, which was compelled to hold an eighteen-kilometer front. No company or division had any reserves, and the enemy was able to creep up to within twenty-five meters of the German lines. As a result of the close contact with the enemy, movement by daylight was impossible, and all but the most essential movement was prohibited at night, for it was then that the Russians were most likely to attack.[34] Barricade and construction work of any kind was also hindered, and food could be supplied to the dugouts only at night and at some risk. The men in the dugouts had little contact with their comrades to the rear and to either side, a condition that made for shaky morale. During four days' fighting up to August 26, the

78th Infantry Division had lost four hundred men, and the overall casualty rate since the beginning of the war was 30 percent for the division. Most of the losses sustained by the division were caused by twenty-five to thirty Russian guns that were firing with an "unlimited" ammunition supply. A daily average of two thousand shells fell on the 78th Division, and on the night of August 24–25 five thousand shells rained down, mostly of 120–170mm caliber. Two 210mm guns were also used along with many heavy mortar tubes—with telling effect. The Russians were using excellent sighting and ranging techniques and frequently changing the positions of their batteries. On August 26, the commander of the 78th Division, General Gallenkamp, predicted that the division would be "used up" very soon.[35] Similar reports flowed in to Fourth Army headquarters virtually every day. The older officers in the field considered the unsteady static front *(unruhige Stellungsfront)* situation at Yelnia to be worse than conditions during the First World War and wanted either to resume the offensive or give up the position—merely to hold it for reasons of prestige was asking too much.[36]

ZHUKOV DEMONSTRATES HIS SKILL

In late July 1941, after a disagreement with Stalin over strategy that will be explained later, G. K. Zhukov was removed from his post as chief of the general staff and replaced by B. M. Shaposhnikov, who had been the Supreme Command's representative at the Western Front opposite Army Group Center. Zhukov was demoted and given command of Bogdanov's Reserve Front, receiving from Stalin the mission of rubbing out the Yelnia salient.[37] He arrived to take up his new assignment in early August. After taking the measure of the job to be done and the resources at his disposal, Zhukov decided to postpone any major action until later when reinforcements could be brought up to support K. I. Rakutin's Twenty-fourth Army. The main assault on the salient by three Russian divisions was not to begin finally until August 30. All other attacks up to this time were only probing efforts to pinpoint the enemy's artillery positions and to generally find the weak spots in the German defense system. Although these small attacks were not calculated to produce big results, nevertheless they caused the Germans much difficulty, especially the XXth Army Corps.[38] When Zhukov's main effort began, he departed from the tactic of using only battalions in the assault. The Russians would now advance with entire divisions, with armor and artillery support on small fronts, and it was this kind of pressure that finally forced the German lines to give way.[39] These tactics were honed and refined with great effectiveness during the later war years.

The breakthrough of the German defenses was to be undertaken by nine of the Twenty-fourth Army's thirteen rifle divisions, while four other divisions maintained defensive positions on the eastern side of the Uzha. The decisive offensive operation was to be carried out by the group west of the Uzha on the northern rim of the salient. Here was located the 102nd Tank Division and the 107th and 100th rifle divisions. These units had the greatest strength and were deployed on a narrow 4.5-kilometer front. The southern group was composed of the 303rd rifle and the 106th motorized divisions, but these units had to move against a front of eight kilometers around Leonova. Two rifle divisions, the 19th and the 309th, were positioned due east of the salient and assigned the task of pushing straight in toward Yelnia from the leading edge of the salient. The main assault was launched early on August 30 with infantry attacks in certain key areas; then at 7:30 A.M. all of the Twenty-fourth Army's eight hundred guns plus many mortars and some Katyusha rocket launchers opened fire on the salient. Some sixty thousand Russian soldiers were flung against seventy thousand Germans, who were well dug in although spread very thin along a seventy-kilometer front. The attack in the south began first, with limited success. The Russian effort in the north was, however, a different matter.[40]

After the German 263rd Infantry Division, with the help of the 15th Infantry Division, had repaired the crack in the front at Chuvashi, no one seriously expected the Russians to resume the offensive immediately. During the early morning hours of August 30, however, the eastern flank of the 137th Infantry Division on the northern rim of the salient was hit by a surprise attack carried out without any advance artillery preparation. The Russians first made a small break in the German front along the Uzha. Later, the 137th Infantry Division was pounded by a three-hour artillery barrage and six Russian battalions succeeded in opening a bigger gap in the German front at Sadki northwest of Yelnia and west of the Ustrom. In this attack some Russian tanks penetrated a kilometer behind the German front, overrunning several machine gun emplacements in the process. The Germans temporarily lost Sadki but regained it by early dawn of August 31.[41] Still early in the morning of August 31, Zhukov renewed the pressure on Sadki, this time with forty tanks, which were well handled in close cooperation with infantry. Instead of bursting into the German rear areas alone, where they could be picked off singly by the direct fire of enemy artillery, the Russian tanks this time remained in the front-line area and systematically rolled over the German weapons positions. This was where the German infantry dearly paid for its lack of self-propelled artillery, which could have played a vital role in the defense of Yelnia. In the words of the commander of the IXth Army Corps, von Geyer: "The IXth Army Corps could have been spared the loss of hundreds of lives and our achievements would have been much greater . . . had our indispensable Sturmgeschütz unit not been taken away from us."[42]

The new penetration at Sadki and farther east widened the gap in the German front to three kilometers and pushed the salient front inward by two kilometers (see Figure 24). The German commanders now believed that the Russians were trying to pinch in the sides of the salient, from the north along the Uzha and in the south against the 268th Infantry Division of the XXth Army Corps at Leonova. Actually, the attacks against the 268th Division in the south were only designed to draw the German reserves, if any, in the wrong direction while the major blow fell along the Uzha. The Germans believed that the Russians were using poor tactics, failing to coordinate their assaults on both sides of the salient, but Zhukov had not made this mistake.[43] The German army would have a lot to learn from Zhukov during the coming months.

While the IXth Army Corps had its hands full on the eastern bank of the Uzha, the XXth Army Corps was also experiencing extreme difficulties along the other side of the stream. On August 31 the 78th Infantry Division was hit hard north of Gurev, and the division had to pull back about two kilometers. On September 1 the Russians reached Voloskov and cut the railroad south of there. Some Russian units in this area, with infantry and tanks, crossed behind the 78th Division's front and penetrated into the rear area of the 292nd Infantry Division farther to the east, destroying some supplies. The 292nd Division was already hard pressed trying to control another Russian penetration south of Vydrina, on the northeastern side of the salient at its juncture with the 78th

Division. On September 2, the operations chief of the 292nd Division reported to the XXth Army Corps that the division "was close to the limit of endurance."[44] Not only could the gap at Vydrina not be closed, but the Russian group at Voloskovo in the 78th Division area immediately to the west of the 292nd Division could not be dislodged. Thus the entire northwestern flank of the XXth Army Corps was in danger of crumbling inward, while the eastern flank of the IXth Army Corps was under the same threat (see Figure 25).

In his memoirs Zhukov singled out the Voloskovo action for special attention. A rifle regiment of the 107th Rifle Division led by I. M. Nekrassov particularly distinguished itself by continuing to hold out for three days while completely surrounded.[45] In order to close the gap at Vydrina and recapture hill 240.3, General Materna of the XXth Corps ordered every artillery battery in the salient that could reach the hill to direct fire at the target for twenty minutes. By committing its last reserves, the 292nd Division retook

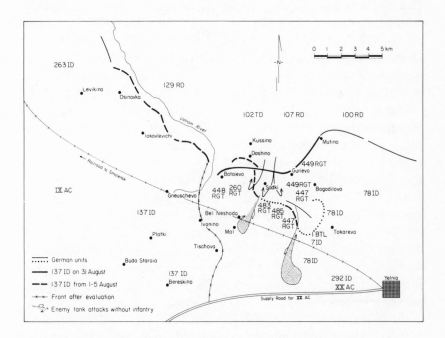

Figure 24. The Sadki Penetration in the Area of the 137th Infantry Division

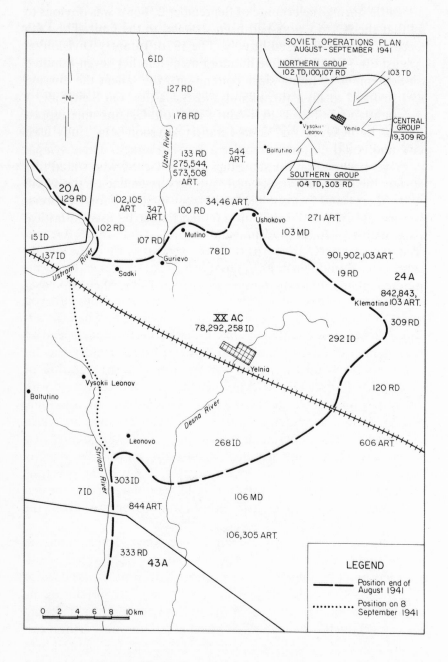

Figure 25. The Yelnia Salient and the Soviet Operations Plan

hill 240.3 during the evening of September 2, but it was obvious to all that the XXth Corps had been strained to the limit. The IXth Corps, too, had suffered heavily. The 137th Infantry Division on August 30–31 had lost five hundred men, another seven hundred on September 1. In all, since coming into the salient the division had suffered at least three thousand casualties. On September 2 the commander of the 78th Infantry Division, Gallenkamp, reported that he believed the 137th Infantry Division was "fully used up" and could no longer repulse a Russian attack. These sympathies were echoed on the same day by von Geyer, who stated that during the past ten weeks each infantry regiment of the XXth Army Corps had lost one thousand men, including forty officers. He urgently requested that infantry no longer be used in critical areas without armored support.[46]

WITHDRAWAL FROM YELNIA

On September 2 Halder and Brauchitsch flew to Army Group Center headquarters at Borisov to review the situation with von Bock. No one at this conference had any idea as to when the advance on Moscow could be resumed; that project would depend on several factors beyond the control of the OKH. Halder was inclined to leave up in the air for the moment the question of Guderian's Panzer Group 2 and whether it could cooperate with Army Group Center in the advance on Moscow. At this time, Halder viewed as possible either a closer-in solution in which Guderian would cooperate directly with Army Group Center or a wider-ranging solution in which Guderian would drive directly from the south toward Moscow on his own. In any event, everyone agreed that no offensive eastward could take place before the end of September, and so a final withdrawal was ordered from the Yelnia salient.[47]

The actual task of pulling out of the salient devolved on von Kluge, and he immediately set to work and conferred with the commanders and the staffs of the IXth and XXth corps. It was decided that the withdrawal would take place in three stages: (1) during the night of September 4 the rearward services and supply units would retreat; (2) during the night of September 5 the troops farthest east would pull back to west of Yelnia; and (3) during the night of September 6 all forces would complete the move westward and take up new positions along the Striana–Ustrom front.[48]

Early on the morning of September 5 the last elements of the 78th Infantry Division east of the Uzha, including fragments of the 137th Division that had been separated from their unit, began to move around the Sadki bulge ("the Russian dumpling") toward the west. The Russians in Sadki probed lightly here and there, but the 137th Division fended off the attacks. Around 6:00 P.M. the Russians laid down a strong artillery barrage against the 137th Division, but this ceased by nightfall. Mercifully, as if sent from heaven, the showers that had fallen the day before turned into a downpour, making the ground treacherous for movement but masking the German withdrawal. A thick fog also blanketed the area, making it impossible for the Russian observers to detect their opportunity to attack the weak German lines.[49] Zhukov reported to Stalin that the Russian forces, particularly the tank forces, were not strong enough to cut off completely the salient from the west, but this probably was not true.[50] If the Germans had not evacuated Yelnia when they did, they most assuredly would have suffered an encirclement of the IXth and XXth army corps. Also, had it not been for the bad weather during the last two days of the withdrawal —a stroke of luck for the Germans—the Russians no doubt would have been able to inflict much heavier losses on the two corps.

The overall cost to the Wehrmacht in terms of lives during the battles around Yelnia in late July, August, and early September is difficult to assess from the German records. Zhukov gives the figure of forty-five thousand to forty-seven thousand German casualties, and this figure may be accurate.[51] The six divisions usually in the salient from July 29 to August 29 probably lost on the average of fifty to a hundred men dead or wounded per day, which would make for around eighteen thousand to thirty-five thousand losses for this period. From August 30 through September 3, however, the casualty rate was much higher, and the figures could easily approach those given by Zhukov. This would certainly be true if the losses suffered by the VIIth Army Corps along the Desna front to the south are taken into account.[52] The total loss to the German army from the battles around Yelnia should not be considered less than three full divisions, a dreadful price to pay for prestige. For that matter, it was a terrible price to pay for a springboard to Moscow, especially since no one knew when such an operation could be undertaken. Some historians have commented on the passivity and slowness to advance of von Kluge's Fourth Army after it reached the Nara River in late November during the Operation Typhoon offensive against Moscow. The fact was that the divisions of the Fourth Army had never recovered from the wounds suffered at Yelnia during the summer. Zhukov may not have completed the destruction of the enemy at Yelnia, but he had done his job well enough so that the results of his efforts would be seen in November and December when the German armies neared Moscow.[53]

During the Yelnia operations the Red Army learned many things about German tactics, and new ways were devised to take advantage of the enemy's weaknesses. In the first phase of the battles the Russians learned that German mobile units by themselves, without strong infantry or extra artillery support, were not able to overcome a stout defense supplied with ample artillery in rugged terrain. This was the situation that prevailed in late July when the SS *"Das Reich"* Division and the 10th Panzer Division were unable either to advance along the Dorogobuzh road or close the gap around Smolensk. These units also could not advance into the high country much beyond Yelnia to destroy the Russian artillery emplacements that were already well dug in along the upper Desna. The Red Army at Yelnia learned how vulnerable German static defenses were if they relied solely on infantry and artillery and lacked a mobile reserve. Once the tanks and self-propelled artillery units were removed from the salient, it could only be a matter of time before breakthroughs were achieved that the Germans would not be able to close. It was important also that the power of artillery in modern warfare was clearly demonstrated to those who might have believed that in a mechanized age cumbersome and heavy artillery pieces had no place on the battlefield. After Yelnia was taken, Zhukov toured the battlefield and was greatly impressed by the destruction artillery and rocket artillery had worked. Zhukov remarked that the main German defense bastion on the Uzha at Uzhakovo was completely smashed, including the underground shelters.[54] This was information that he would file away for future reference, especially for the time in 1944–1945 when the battle lines would cease to be flexible and the Germans would rely increasingly on static defenses.

Finally, Zhukov demonstrated beyond a doubt how close cooperation between infantry, armor, and artillery in a combined-arms operation could achieve excellent results against a strongly fortified enemy. The combined-arms tactics used by Zhukov on a narrow sector of the front proved that these tactics were superior to those being employed by the Germans. If Guderian had allowed the XLVIth Panzer Corps to remain at Yelnia, the battles would have turned out differently, but he did not and so the end was predestined. In 1944 the German army would not have mobile reserves capable of defending hundreds of kilometers of static front, and the end then would be the same.

In several ways, the battles around Smolensk and Yelnia in the summer of 1941 can be said to have been strikingly representative of the entire war on the eastern front from 1941 to 1945. The first phase of the battles took place in the form of wide, sweeping German armored movements that covered tremendous distances in a short time yet failed effectively to cut off or surround the Russian armies between the encircling arms of the two panzer groups. The second phase of the battles developed around a stationary German front line that was increasingly subjected to stronger and more powerful Russian artillery barrages. The Russians also used the pause in the German forward movement to accumulate more reserves, armor and artillery, all the while probing for weak spots in the enemy's defenses. During the third and final phase of the battles, Zhukov directed a powerful combined-arms offensive against a vulnerable German position, and the Red Army carried the day. The battles, then, foreshadowed the war of movement leading up to Stalingrad in 1942–1943 and Kursk in July 1943, as well as the war of stationary fronts from mid-1943 to mid-1944 and the war of massive Russian manpower, armor, and artillery superiority from mid-1944 to 1945 that crushed all German attempts to create defensive barriers in the east.

And now it is necessary to say a word about the Russian strategy of positioning the operational echelon behind the upper Dnepr and the Pripet swamps before and immediately after the beginning of the war. At Smolensk and Yelnia the fruitfulness of this strategy was manifest as the pressure on Guderian's southern flank kept Panzer Group 2 from closing the Smolensk pocket. The wise decisions by Zhukov regarding the operational echelon, coupled with the mistakes of Guderian, Halder, and others, all contributed to the German setback on the upper Dnepr in July, August, and September. The advantages secured by the Russians were not permanent, however, and the tides of war would fluctuate before

Stalin and Zhukov could win a decisive victory over the enemy. Also, Stalin's decisions about the mobilization of the strategic reserve proved to be correct, for Zhukov was able to call on this reserve for extra divisions during the last phase of the battles around Yelnia. Russian losses at Smolensk–Yelnia were high, perhaps three times higher than German losses, but no permanent damage had been done to the Red Army's strategic posture. The German position in July and August, by contrast, was awkward and out of balance. The German flanks in the north and south were easily subjected to strong pressure from the operational echelon, which in mid-July was joined by the first elements of the strategic reserve, and these forces did the job of slowing and then stopping the enemy advance. Stalin had been right: full mobilization had not been necessary before June 22; but in late August and early September he would take his biggest risk of the war, and he nearly lost everything for Russia in the process.

GUDERIAN AND ROSLAVL–KRICHEV

The battles around Yelnia in early August did not concern Guderian as much as did the operations at Roslavl–Krichev, which, in his mind, were absolutely necessary if an advance toward Moscow were to be undertaken. By the end of July, after the fall of Mogilev on July 26, units of the Second Army began crossing the Dnepr in increasing numbers to the north and somewhat to the south of Stary Bykhov. The approach to the Sozh River by the Second Army had actually occured on July 25 when the XIIIth Army Corps reached the Propoisk–Cherikov area. More reinforcements arrived when the XIIth Army Corps relieved the XXIVth Panzer Corps in the Krichev bridgehead east of the Sozh on July 28. Meanwhile, well back to the west, the LIIIrd Army Corps still had not been able to cross the Dnepr due to the strong Russian presence at Rogachev–Zhlobin.[55]

In preparation for the assault on Roslavl, Guderian decided to introduce the commanders of the two army corps recently added to his panzer group, the VIIth and the IXth, to his way of winning a victory. This introduction had an inauspicious beginning when Guderian told General Geyer, the commander of the IXth Army Corps, that the "newly subordinated infantry corps, which up to then had scarcely been in action against the Russians, had to be taught my methods of attacking."[56] Guderian noted that Geyer, his old superior officer at the Truppenamt of the Reichswehr Ministry and while he was stationed at Würzburg in the Vth Military District, disagreed with him at first, but after the Roslavl operation began, according to the panzer general, he came to see the light. Actually, Geyer took Guderian's comment about his troops being untested in battle as a personal insult. Geyer could not refrain from pointing out that the 137th Infantry Division of his IXth Corps alone had suffered 2,050 combat losses since June 22.[57] The panzer general's words with Geyer are illustrative of the attitude that Guderian had toward the infantry units. It was Guderian's position that, since his armored units were always in the forefront of the advance, only they were actively engaged in overcoming the enemy's resistance.

Guderian was not alone in his way of thinking. Infantry units typically were expected to strain themselves to the limits of human endurance in making long forced marches over rough terrain and then defend difficult positions with inadequate weapons. The infantry was no longer considered to be the backbone of the army, and infantry units were more poorly armed, clothed, and equipped and more parsimoniously provided with replacements than any other branch of the military. The OKH constantly overtaxed the infantry and made generally bad use of it during the entire war.[58]

The plan for the encirclement at Roslavl was simple enough to execute. One arm of the trap would be provided by the XXIVth Panzer Corps, which would cooperate with the VIIth Army Corps in a push across the Sozh. The armored units were to cut off Roslavl from the south and east while the VIIth Army Corps approached the city from a westerly and somewhat northerly direction. The other arm of the encirclement was to be provided by the IXth Army Corps, which was to push due south from the Yelnia salient along the Desna toward Kovali and Kosaki. The infantry of the IXth Army Corps and the armor of the XXIVth Panzer Corps would later link up northeast of Roslavl, west of the Desna, forming a relatively small pocket; it eventually netted 38,561 prisoners.[59]

The attack on Roslavl began on August 1 with the advance of the XXIVth Panzer Corps. The movement of the VIIth and IXth army corps did not begin until August 2 (see Figure 26). Guderian was afraid that the infantry of the IXth Corps would be delayed by possible procrastination on the part of General Geyer, so the panzer general went to the corps headquarters in person and stressed to his former superior the importance of cutting and holding the Roslavl–Moscow road.[60] Leaving nothing to chance, Guderian marched along with the troops of the IXth Corps to impress upon them the urgency of their mission and the necessity for haste. The panzer general was a strong believer in the power of his presence to inspire his troops to great achievements.[61] Despite, however, the initial success of the XXIVth Panzer Corps, particularly "Group Eberbach" of the 4th Panzer Division, which approached Roslavl from the south side on August 3, the IXth Army Corps was unable to make fast progress. The 137th and 292nd infantry divisions tried and failed to reach the Roslavl–Moscow road on August 2, for even though resistance was light, the roads were very bad and the 292nd Division became bogged down in the swamps around Kostyri. Both infantry divisions had, however, succeeded in marching thirty kilometers on this warm, sunny day. The next day, August 3, the 4th Panzer Division completed the conquest of

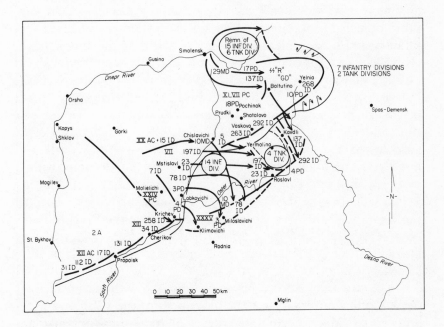

Figure 26. The Roslavl Pocket

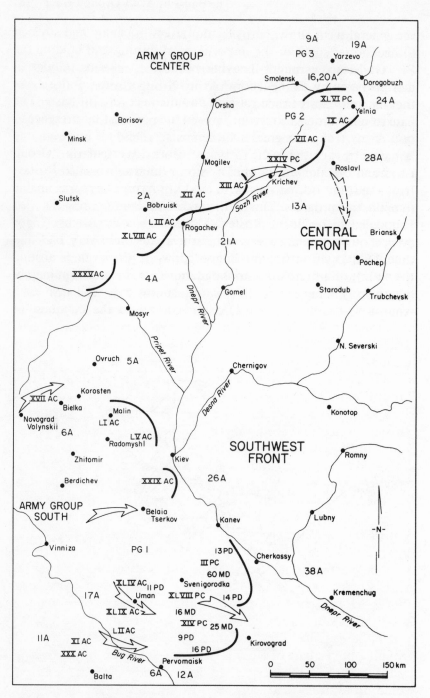

Figure 27. The Soviet Defense of the Dnepr and Sozh Rivers

188

army to push southward along the Dnepr and the Sozh toward Gomel.[68]

Guderian, as might have been expected, reacted violently to this proposal by the OKH and Army Group Center, maintaining that his units badly needed rest. He went so far as to threaten to refuse to obey orders to give up even one panzer division to the Second Army.[69] In his memoirs Guderian defended his objections to this plan by saying that the distance from Roslavl to Rogachev was two hundred kilometers—that is, a four hundred-kilometer round trip—and that his panzer units could not have undertaken such a mission, given the need for refitting the vehicles. Sending tanks to Propoisk on the Sozh, insisted Guderian, would have been very difficult and would have resulted in an unconscionable loss of time.[70] Guderian's memoirs do not, however, give a true picture of the nature of his resistance to the plans of Halder and von Bock in regard to this particular issue. The fact was that Guderian fully realized that something had to be done to hasten the long-delayed advance of the southern flank of the Second Army over the Dnepr. Also, something had to be done about Krichev and Gomel, which acted as thorns in the side of his panzer group.

On August 7, Guderian had asked the permission of Army Group Center to be allowed to send the 3rd and 4th panzer divisions to Krasnopole east of the Sozh and thereby eliminate the Russian strength on the northern flank of the Second Army. The following day, Guderian was ready to send the XXIVth Panzer Corps even farther south, past Krasnopole all the way to Chechersk and Gomel. This idea was only postponed at the time because the XLIIIrd Army Corps on the extreme southern flank of the Second Army was still so far back to the west that the second arm of an encirclement would have been lacking.[71] The key to Guderian's adamant refusal to give up one panzer division to the Second Army was not a fear that the distance was too great for his battle-worn tanks, for two days later on August 9, as mentioned above, he felt confident enough about the capabilities of the XXIVth Panzer Corps to advocate sending it all the way to Viazma, a distance of no less than a hundred kilometers from its grouping points east of Roslavl. The reason for his refusal can be traced to the fact that, as he had done on previous occasions and would do again in the future, he was resistant to any attempt by any authority to remove armored units from his command, even

Roslavl and sent units down the Moscow highway to make contact with the 292nd Division, closing the Roslavl pocket.[62]

The sealing of the Roslavl pocket had proceeded smoothly and with few delays or changes in the plan of operations. The maneuver was a textbook case of the results armor and infantry can achieve through close cooperation. The goals were not set impossibly high for the infantry to reach in a short time and, in contrast to the encirclements at Velikie Luki and Smolensk, Roslavl represented a definite improvement of the tactical situation. This is not to say that the elimination of the Roslavl pocket was accomplished altogether without difficulties. On August 5 the 137th Infantry Division reached the Desna near Bogdanovo, under harsh urging from Guderian, while the right flank of the division was still trying to maintain the northeastern side of the Roslavl pocket along the Oster against strong Russian breakout attempts supported by artillery and armor.[63] Finally, the Russians did manage to break through on the Oster front near Kosaki in the afternoon of August 5 after the 137th Division nearly ran out of ammunition, faced as it was with Russian pressure from the Roslavl pocket from the west and along the Desna front from the east. Elements of the 4th Panzer Division were ordered to help the 137th Division, but they arrived too late to prevent the temporary loss of Kosaki on August 6. It was not until units arrived on the scene from the 292nd Division and from the 137th Division's Desna front that Kosaki was retaken and the pocket finally sealed late in the day on August 6.[64] A closer coordination between infantry and armor could have made for a perfect outcome; nevertheless, the results were good enough, due to the small geographical area in which the encirclement took place.

Guderian was so encouraged by the success of the Roslavl operation that, after an inconclusive conference with Hitler at Borisov on August 4, he ordered his staff to prepare for an advance on Moscow. During the evening of August 9, the panzer general proposed to von Bock that the XXIVth Panzer Corps, then pushing southwest of Roslavl to a position east of Krichev, should reverse its front and advance toward Viazma, to the northeast. Guderian wanted his tanks to press eastward on his southern flank along the Roslavl–Moscow highway while the infantry of his two army corps advanced in the center and on the northern flank. The general direction of the offensive would be through Spas–Demensk toward Viazma. Such a maneuver, according to him, would also aid an advance by Hoth's Panzer Group 3 toward Moscow from the north. It was Guderian's belief that the enemy front was very thin in front of his panzer group and that the Russians here were exhausted and would no longer be able to offer firm resistance. This plan would succeed, he was convinced, because reconnaissance had shown that for a wide area around Roslavl there was no enemy to be found.[65]

Von Bock, too, was aware that there was a gap in the Russian armies around Roslavl and that the 3rd and 4th panzer divisions of the XXIVth Panzer Corps had pushed into this vacuum, seemingly having found a way open for a further thrust to the east. There were, however, other problems that Guderian either could not see or fully appreciate that mitigated against a decision to allow Panzer Group 2 to drive eastward. To the contention that the enemy in front of his units could now offer only a weak resistance, von Bock replied, "The enemy at Yelnia is not exhausted—quite the opposite." The commander of Army Group Center raised the objection that a push from south to north by Panzer Group 2 would be endangered by the strong Russian reserves around Yelnia. Von Bock did not reject the idea totally, but he did say that the enemy facing the Second Army on the Dnepr would have to be defeated first.[66] The Russian pullback on the southern flank of Army Group Center south of Roslavl also made an impression on Halder. He believed it possible that the Russians were drawing all available strength eastward to the line Lake Ilmen–Rzhev–Viazma–Briansk in preparation for constructing a new line of defense.[67]

The situation along the Dnepr front of the Second Army at Rogachev and Zhlobin and also the still open question of what to do about the Russian forces around Gomel (see Figure 27) compelled Halder to fly to Army Group Center and confer with von Bock and von Weichs, the commander of the Second Army, on August 6. A solution to the problem along the Dnepr would have to be postponed, everyone agreed, until the Second Army could build up stronger forces, since at that moment each of its divisions had a twelve-kilometer front to maintain, and only one regiment and a cavalry division remained in the army's reserves. It was Halder's opinion, supported by the others, that Panzer Group 2 should yield one panzer division to the northern flank of the Second Army in order to enable the XIIth and XIIIth corps of that for temporary periods. This consistent behavior on the part of Guderian should have been taken more into account by Halder, for it would cause him much grief in the future.

While smarting from von Bock's and Halder's refusal to allow him to proceed to Viazma, Guderian turned his full attention to the encirclement operation around Krichev on the Sozh that was being carried out by the XXIVth Panzer Corps and the 7th Infantry Division of the XIIIth Army Corps. This operation was begun on August 9 but made slow progress because of the bad roads.[72] By August 12, the Russians at Krichev had been fully cut off, but the fighting there lasted two more days, resulting in the capture of 16,033 Russian prisoners and 76 artillery pieces (see Figure 28). An attempt by the XXIVth Panzer Corps to utilize this success and push rapidly on to Gomel came to grief when the 4th Panzer Division ran into a strong group of the enemy at Kostiukovichi.[73] Guderian had lost one round of his continual battle with Halder and von Bock, but after Krichev a victory was his— the situation on the northern flank of the Second Army had been saved without

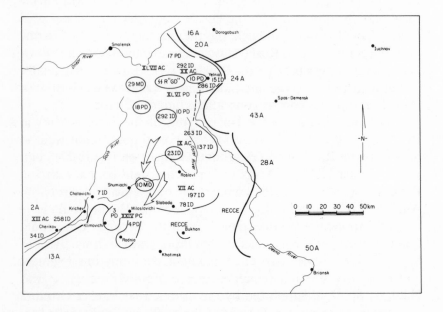

Figure 28. The Krichev Operation

Panzer Group 2 having to surrender any of its units to another command.

THE BELEAGUERED SOUTHERN FLANK OF
ARMY GROUP CENTER

The problem for the Second Army along its southern flank at Rogachev–Zhlobin was, however, far from being solved, although hope was in sight. After the fall of Krichev the Russian Twenty-first Army had begun a deliberate pullback toward the east.[74] Now, nearly two months after the beginning of the war, the front of the operational echelon along the Dnepr north of the Pripet Marshes had begun to give way entirely, but the echelon had fulfilled its function. New Russian armies were already manning lines of defense farther east and, meanwhile, German Army Group South had not yet cracked the Dnepr front south of the marshes. The operational echelon in the eastern Ukraine was still largely intact, although some of its units had been transferred to Timoshenko's Western Front. To Stalin, Kiev seemed to be an unconquerable bastion that would anchor the Red Army's flank in the south while the newly mobilized armies of the strategic reserve could be sent directly to the Western Front. By the third week in August, Stalin could afford to be satisfied with the general situation, for even though the operational echelon north of the Pripet was in its final stage of disintegration, adequate forces were on hand to counter almost any foreseeable German strategy. Overconfidence in war, however, breeds disaster, and the Red Army had not yet suffered its greatest calamity of 1941.

By August 13, the staff of Army Group Center had formulated a plan for effecting an encirclement around Rogachev–Zhlobin and solving the thorny problem of Gomel as well. Von Bock now wanted the Second Army to hold the Russians in check at Rogachev–Zhlobin and press on toward Gomel along the Zhlobin–Gomel railroad (although three army corps that were supposed to participate in the Gomel operation, the XIIth, XIIIth, and XLIIIrd, were forced to halt their movements to the south and east because of Russian pressure from the direction of Gomel and because parts of these three corps had to be used to prevent the Russians at Rogachev and Zhlobin from escaping eastward.)[75]

Early on the morning of August 14, the LIIIrd Army Corps moved directly against Zhlobin with its southern wing of two divisions. To aid the initial breakthrough of the Russian front here, the Luftwaffe supplied a squadron of JU-87 Stukas. By the evening of this same day, these two divisions took Zhlobin after a hard fight and managed to capture both the highway and the railway bridges over the Dnepr intact, although the rail bridge was somewhat damaged.[76] Meanwhile, on the eastern side of the encirclement, the XIIth Army Corps turned its entire front westward to face the Russian breakout attempts coming from the direction of Rogachev. The XIIIth Corps also was unable to proceed southward toward Gomel because the Russians now began stepping up their pressure against the corps' 17th Infantry Division. The Russians used tanks in these attacks, and one assault from the direction of Gomel pushed deeply into the flank of the 17th Division before it was stopped. By August 15 the XLIIIrd Army Corps also had been thwarted in its advance on Gomel even though F. I. Kuznetsov, the commander of the Russian Central Front, which had been created on July 24 from formations of the Thirteenth and Twenty-first armies, now decided to abandon Rogachev and Gomel.[77] As a result of this withdrawal, Rogachev was taken by the German 52nd Infantry Division of the LIIIrd Army Corps in the late morning of August 15, although the Russian rear guard left behind to protect the retreat of the main force eastward toward Novozybkov was strong enough to cause some trouble at Gomel.

By August 16 the Second Army had been divided into four separate parts: (1) the XXXVth Army Corps in the area southwest of the Berezina poised to strike at Mozyr to the south on the Pripet River (if ordered to do so by the OKH); (2) the Rogachev–Zhlobin encirclement front formed by parts of the XLIIIrd, LIIIrd, XIIth, and XIIIth army corps; (3) parts of the XIIIth and XLIIIrd army corps moving toward Gomel; and (4) a group formed by the 167th Infantry Division at the Chechersk bridgehead on the Sozh and a "Group Behlendorff," made up of most of the 258th and part of the 34th infantry divisions, which was moving eastward from the Sozh due north of Gomel.[78] On August 16 both the XLIIIrd and XIIIth army corps were stalled on the way to Gomel, but no forces could be taken from the Rogachev–Zhlobin encirclement front where the Russians were trying to make their escape. During this day, the 267th Infantry Division of the XLIIIrd Army Corps was hit hard by an entire Russian division that succeeded in pushing through German lines between Rudenka and Zavod. Only in a very few cases did the Russians in this area surrender. One company of the 267th Division had only sixty-eight men remaining after trying to fend off the frantic Russian assaults.[79]

In order to help contain the Russians fleeing from Gomel, Guderian decided to send the XXIVth Panzer Corps farther south to Starodub to the east of Gomel. This movement was begun on August 16, also the day on which the 3rd Panzer Division succeeded in capturing the Mglin crossroads. On August 17 the western flank of the XXIVth Panzer Corps came under strong pressure from the enemy, but the 10th motorized and 3rd panzer divisions still managed to cut the Gomel–Briansk railroad.[80] Early in the morning of August 19, however, some units of the 3rd Panzer Division at Unecha were hit hard from the west and were soon surrounded by Russians. In one instance a T–34 tank penetrated the German lines and made its way to the Unecha railroad station, overrunning everything in its path. It was finally stopped when a brave lieutenant jumped up on the tank, pulled off the motor grid and tossed in a grenade.[81] The situation there grew so desperate that some forward elements of the 3rd Panzer Division had to reverse their course and head back northward from Starodub to Unecha. Although the crisis around Unecha soon abated somewhat, the road from Mglin to Unecha was still blocked by the enemy, and the units of the 3rd Panzer Division that were to strike at Novozybkov were held back in readiness, prepared to move toward Unecha or Starodub if necessary. Moreover, the XXIVth Panzer Corps was dangerously near the end of its gasoline supply, and only the timely arrival of Luftwaffe transport planes loaded with oil and fuel for the corps on August 21 averted yet another crisis.[82] Guderian at this point might have welcomed close infantry support for his tanks, as he had enjoyed around Roslavl, but at Unecha such help was far away.

Guderian recalled in his memoirs that on August 17 the Second Army still had not launched its attack on Gomel and that the reason for this delay was that Army Group Center had ordered strong units of the Second Army toward the northeast, far behind the front of the XXIVth Panzer Corps.[83] The commander of the XXIVth Panzer Corps, Geyer von Schweppenburg, said his troops regarded with bitterness the tardy progress of the Second Army, believing their relief at Unecha should have come sooner. This complaint was identical to the one voiced in the third week in July by the same XXIVth Panzer Corps when it desperately required relief at Propoisk. The Germans had to pay a high price for operating their tanks over long distances without close cooperation from the infantry, but this was a lesson that Guderian had not yet taken to heart.

As a matter of fact, on August 16 von Bock had ordered von Weichs's Second Army to leave only the forces barely essential to hold the Zhlobin–Gorodets pocket and to press on to Gomel with all deliberate speed.[84] Yet parts of four army corps were needed to secure this encirclement, which by August 18 had yielded fifty thousand Russian prisoners.[85] The force that had been sent eastward by the Second Army consisted of parts of two infantry divisions, known as "Group Behlendorff," that had left the Chechersk bridgehead on the Sozh on August 16 to provide cover for the northern flank of the XXIVth Panzer Corps when that corps had been ordered by the OKH to turn westward from Starodub and advance on Gomel from the east. For the reasons outlined above, however, the XXIVth Panzer Corps was unable to advance beyond Starodub, a failure that cannot be blamed on the tardiness of the infantry divisions of the Second Army, for they were too far behind to offer any assistance (see Figure 29). The crisis at Starodub was due to Russian pressure at Unecha against the XXIVth Panzer Corps and the difficulties with supplies, as well as to the magnitude of the Russian force doing battle in the Zhlobin pocket—sufficient to tie down several large German units. Unlike the operation at Roslavl, but similar to those at Bialystok–Minsk and Smolensk, the Gomel operation had turned sour because of lack of coordination between the various arms of the German Wehrmacht.

The final assault on Gomel, situated on the Sozh above its confluence with the Dnepr, was begun at 7:00 A.M. on August 19 by units of the XIIIth Army Corps that pushed in toward the center of the town from the northwest and the northeast (see Figure 30). The 17th Infantry Division was first to break into Gomel from the west and north that same day, and there the Germans were forced to engage in the bitterest kind of house-to-house fighting. By the early evening, the Russians had been pressed all the way back to the downtown area and into the southern side; they now used their last opportunity to demolish all the bridges over the Sozh. The struggle around Gomel continued for one more day un-

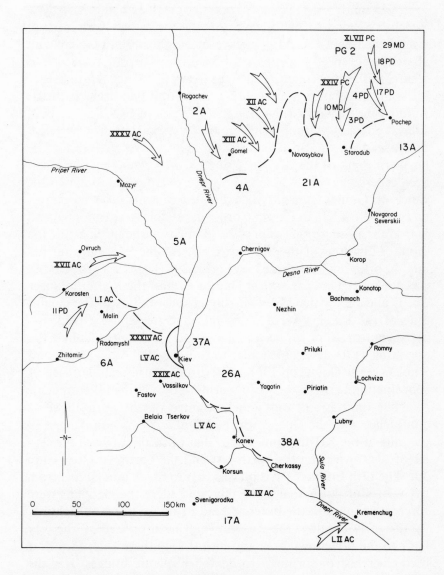

Figure 29. The Exposed Flanks of Panzer Group 2

197

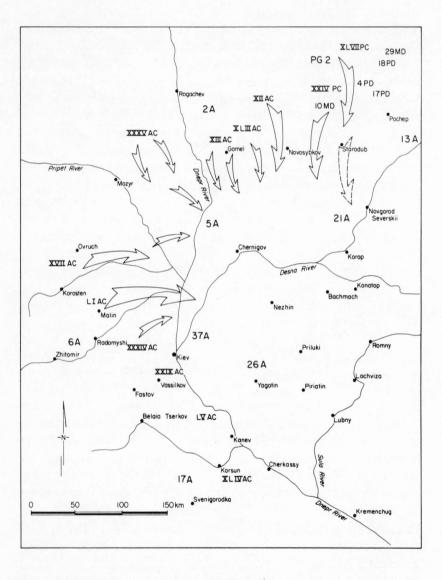

Figure 30. The Fall of Gomel, August 20–21, 1941

198

til the Russians gave up entirely. The 17th Infantry Division continued its advance through the town and began to carve out a bridgehead east of the Sozh while the final clearing of Gomel itself was carried out by parts of the 131st Infantry Division.[86]

The results of the operations at Krichev and Gomel on the southern flank of Army Group Center were satisfactory, at least in the numerical sense, from the German point of view. The two battles cost the Red Army 78,000 prisoners, 700 artillery pieces, and 144 tanks destroyed. The successful conclusion of these battles allowed the Second Army to complete the elimination of the Russian forces between the Dnepr and the Sozh and thus exert strong pressure on the northeastern flank of the Russian Fifth Army facing the German XXXVth Army Corps north of Mozyr. After the fall of Gomel, the Russian Fifth Army began to pull back from Mozyr and from the front on the northern flank of German Army Group South, southwest of the Pripet swamps. Not only was "the specter of Mozyr dead," according to von Bock, but the victories at Krichev and Gomel, coupled with the anticipated success of the resumed advance toward Velikie Luki on the opposite or northern flank of Army Group Center, meant that "the entire army group can begin again the advance to the east."[87] The Velikie Luki operation this time would bring good results, but whether or not Army Group Center would be able to advance east depended on factors beyond von Bock's control.

THE NORTHERN FLANK—VELIKIE LUKI

On August 14 the southern flank of Army Group North south of Lake Ilmen had been hard hit by about seven Russian divisions that crossed over the Polist River and drove westward into a gap between the IInd and Xth army corps. In order to counteract this strong Russian push south of Staraia Russa, Army Group North hurriedly pulled in units of the LVIth Panzer Corps to assembly points east of Dno.[88] Although Halder referred to this Russian breakthrough near Staraia Russa as a "pinprick," on August 15 the commander of Army Group North, von Leeb, reported to Brauchitsch that the Xth Army Corps was no longer able to maintain a front to the east and would now have to pull back the 290th Infantry Division to the west and north. The corps' new front would face southward and it would have its rear abutting on Lake Ilmen.[89] The situation around Staraia Russa seemed so serious that on August 14 Jodl asked for and received permission from Hitler to send Hoth's XXXIXth Panzer Corps from the northern flank of Army Group Center toward Staraia Russa. The crisis for the Xth Army Corps was alleviated, however, by a counterattack on August 19 by Manstein's LVIth Panzer Corps of Army Group North, which succeeded in restoring the front along the Polist River on August 21.[90]

Now that the XXXIXth Panzer Corps was no longer needed in the Staraia Russa sector, it was decided on orders from Hitler not to return it to Army Group Center but to send it on to the northern wing of Army Group North to aid in the assault on Leningrad. This decision to give up part of Panzer Group 3 to Army Group North was deeply resented by von Bock and Hoth, and it must be said that, from their point of view, the splitting up of Panzer Group 3 was largely unnecessary. The sending of this one panzer corps from Army Group Center to the Leningrad front would have an important effect on German strategic planning, as will later be seen. Again, the baleful effects of the failure to close the Smolensk pocket rapidly enough and the inability of Panzer Group 3 to retain control of Velikie Luki in the third week of July made themselves felt. The gap existing between Army Groups North and Center in mid-August had afforded the Red Army an excellent opportunity to drive a sharp wedge westward in the area of Staraia Russa. After the transfer of the XXXIXth Panzer Corps to Army Group North, the problem of Velikie Luki again advanced into the foreground, and a solution of this difficulty was undertaken on August 22 (see Figure 31).[91]

The task of retaking Velikie Luki was given to the Ninth Army and the LVIIth Panzer Corps of Panzer Group 3. Since August 3 the Ninth Army had been occupying defensive positions after having been pressed back from Velikie Luki and Toropets. Despite several attempts to organize a renewed assault on Velikie Luki by the 251st and 253rd infantry divisions of the XXIIIrd Army Corps, the forces of the Ninth Army were simply too weak to move ahead against the determined enemy.[92] It was finally decided by Halder and von Bock on August 9 that no large encirclement around Velikie Luki should be attempted. Instead, a close-in solution with a movement of the Ninth Army from south to north, west of Lake Ilmen, would be undertaken. The tanks of Panzer Group 3 would not be used directly against the city, because the refitting of these units would require eleven more days and it was hoped by Halder and von Bock that the tanks could be held back from a major battle at Velikie Luki and reserved for a push toward Moscow.[93]

The problems faced by the Ninth Army in preparing for an attack by its northern wing were exacerbated by repeated Russian assaults along its long defense front, especially in the area of the Vop River. On August 12 the 5th Infantry Division of the Vth Army Corps suffered an enemy breakthrough of its front that reached all

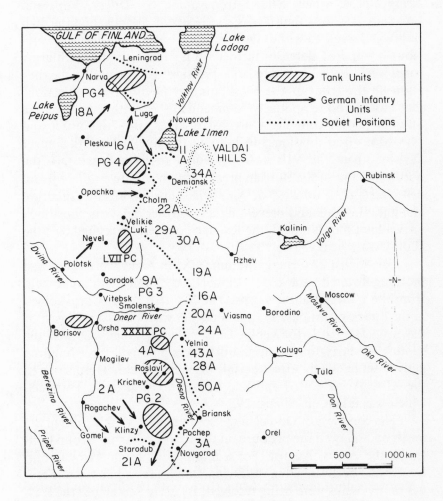

Figure 31. The Valdai Area to the North of Army Group Center

the way into the division's rearward battery positions.[94] The following week, the Russian Thirtieth, Nineteenth, and Twenty-fourth armies intensified their attacks upon the German Ninth Army along a front stretching from the source of the Western Dvina to Yartsevo. K. K. Rokossovski's re-formed Sixteenth Army kept up such continuous pressure on the Ninth Army from around Yartsevo that by mid-August the Russians had succeeded in digging in on the eastern bank of the Vop.[95] On August 18 the German 161st Infantry Division on the northern flank of the VIIIth Army Corps, which held a front along the Dnepr, Vop, and Loiania rivers, was flailed by strong Russian attacks, and the division was forced to withdraw from its front-line positions to previously prepared defenses farther west. The Vth and VIth army corps were also subjected to some pressure. By August 20, the situation on the front of the 161st Infantry Division was so serious that Hoth, who temporarily commanded the Ninth Army because Strauss was ill, committed his last reserves, the 7th Panzer and 14th Motorized divisions, to holding the line.[96] The 7th Panzer Division from the VIIIth Army Corps reserves drove into the northern flank of the Russian breakthrough southwest of Frol and penetrated to southwest of Makovia, thus saving the situation along the Loiania and preventing any further delays in the attack on Velikie Luki, although the Russian counterattacks had cost the Ninth Army heavy losses.[97]

On August 22 General Stumme's XLth Army Corps launched the long-awaited attack on Velikie Luki, along with some help from the LVIIth Panzer Corps. The XXIIIrd Army Corps joined in the attack on August 23, and a pocket was soon formed east of the city. The battle for Velikie Luki ended on August 26 with the capture of thirty-four thousand prisoners and over three hundred guns.[98] Immediately after the fall of Velikie Luki, Hoth ordered the XLth Army Corps and one Panzer division on to Toropets, which was taken on August 29.

The conquest of Gomel in the south and of Velikie Luki in the north had relieved the pressure on the flanks of Army Group Center by the end of August. For a month and a half Army Group Center had been stalled in the Dvina-Dnepr area while the difficulties on its flanks were being resolved. By early September the Russian operational echelon in the Dvina-Dnepr area had largely been exhausted, but new formations were already in place along defense lines farther east. Although Army Group Center was now in a more favorable position with regard to its own flanks, its neighbor to the south, Army Group South, had still not broken the Dnepr barrier in force, and the Kiev stronghold remained a formidable obstacle. The path to Moscow was not yet open, and there would be harsh and complex clashes of personalities among Hitler and his generals before an advance eastward could be resumed. The German military high command structure was chronically incapable of formulating clear and consistent plans for success in the Soviet Union. No important strategic decisions could be made without a contest of wills ensuing among Hitler, Halder, Jodl, von Bock, Guderian, and others. One can only wonder how the German army did so well despite such burdens. No army, however, could withstand the ravages of such jealous, egotistical, contradictory, and ill-informed leadership for long. The foundation of the army had already begun to crack at Yelnia under the weight of the leadership superstructure, a virtual collapse would be barely avoided before Moscow.

CHAPTER 6

HITLER VERSUS THE GENERALS

THE FAILURE OF THE GERMAN COMMAND AND CONTROL SYSTEM

According to the interpretation usually favored by historians and memoirists of the war on the eastern front, the strategy pursued by Hitler in 1941 was erratic and inconsistent, based less on sound military reasoning than on a confused political, social, and economic ideology. By contrast, the policies of the general staff and the OKH are portrayed as having been clear and consistent, but continuously frustrated by incompetent interference from Hitler and from the OKW.[1] However, careful examination of the events that led up to the postponement of the advance on Moscow until after the battle of Kiev in September 1941 does not support the conclusion that Hitler alone was responsible for the confused strategy that led to the German army's shocking reversal of fortunes at the gates of the Soviet capital in December. The general staff, the OKH, the OKW, and some generals in the field, most specifically von Bock and Guderian, must also bear a heavy share of the blame for the blunders that produced the Wehrmacht's first major setback at Yelnia and then the later one at Moscow. Some of these errors and the reasons for them have been discussed in the previous chapters, now close attention must be given to the question of why Panzer Group 2 was sent from Army Group Center to the Ukraine to aid in the closing of the encirclement around Kiev.

The answers to these questions are complex and lie rooted in the unworkable command structure of the German army and in the personalities of the German military and political leaders. In many ways, the errors in strategic planning made by the German high command and the tortured convolutions of policy and underhanded dealings that typified the German military leadership were a reflection of the contradictions that rested deep inside the fabric of the Nazi system.

When Halder first analyzed the strategic problem posed by the Soviet Union during the last half of 1940, Moscow seemed to be the only objective in the country worthy of consideration. In remaining faithful to his first plan to achieve victory, Halder ignored the best advice given to him by members of his own general staff organization (such as Greiffenberg, Feyerabend, and Paulus) and also made bad use of the other strategic studies done by Marcks and Lossberg. Throughout 1941, Halder did not waver from his opinion that Moscow should be considered the primary goal in Russia; but he did, as the battlefront situation deteriorated, modify his operational plans a great deal, and his outlook changed significantly in regard to how the resilient opponent should be defeated.

Before June 22 and the beginning of the war in the east, Halder made it known in no uncertain terms that a consideration of economic objectives had no place in the formulation of strategy.[2] The campaign in Russia was to be a purely military exercise, army against army, which would be conducted with the view that the enemy's main force could be destroyed by vast armored encirclements, with infantry bringing up the rear of the advance to secure the pockets of surrounded enemy formations. These tactics would be effective, he thought, because the Russians supposedly would be compelled to draw up the bulk of their defensive forces along the main approaches to their capital from the west and to give battle west of the Dnepr-Dvina line in order to protect their vital industrial bases.[3] By July 13, however, during the third week of the war, Halder's opinion about the toughness of the Red Army had undergone a fundamental change. It had by then become clear that the Red Army had not exhausted its reserves, as more units were known to have arrived in the Smolensk, Orsha, and Vitebsk areas from the Ukraine. This fact, plus the strong Russian pressure from the direction of Velikie Luki on the northern flank of Army Group Center, compelled Halder to advise Hitler to postpone the direct advance on Moscow until after the problems on the flanks of the Central Army Group had been rectified.[4] The troubles that began after July 13 for Panzer Group 2 and the Second Army on the southern flank of Army Group Center confirmed Halder in his change of mind.

The chief of the general staff had taken great pains before and during the campaign in the east to see that no one interfered with his plans. The OKH's Deployment Directive Barbarossa in January 1941 had set the stage for a major push through White Russia directly toward Moscow, and the creation of the Fourth Panzer Army command under von Kluge in early July had been designed to give the panzer generals Guderian and Hoth the maximum amount of freedom to forge eastward as rapidly as possible.[5] Even though by July 13 Halder was willing to postpone the assault on Moscow for the time being, he was still determined to carry the project through to the finish, although his desire to delay the push on the Soviet capital was increased after the failure of the Fourth Panzer Army to close the gap around Smolensk.

On the morning of July 21, Brauchitsch and Heusinger visited von Bock at Army Group Center headquarters and agreed with him that the army group should continue to press east until the last enemy reserves were crushed, but instead of insisting that Guderian and Hoth have the free rein they had enjoyed in the past, Brauchitsch established the precondition that, first and above all else, the Smolensk pocket would have to be secured and eliminated. The OKH was not in the mood to order Guderian to abandon the Yelnia salient completely, but Brauchitsch and Halder were prepared by the third week in July to exercise a restraining hand over the panzer groups to prevent any further extension of their already badly exposed flanks. Following this explanation of the OKH's policy, the army commander in chief told von Bock and von Kluge essentially what Halder had told Hitler on July 13: after the closing of the Smolensk pocket and after the refitting of Panzer Groups 2 and 3, Guderian should prepare to turn south and east toward the Ukraine; Hoth's Panzer Group 3 alone would remain as Army Group Center's armored force, to support the drive on Moscow by pressing ahead toward the east or the northeast. According to the OKH timetable, Panzer Groups 2 and 3 should have been readied for their new tasks by the beginning of August.[6]

This alteration in the OKH strategic plan was reaffirmed by Halder in a conference held after Brauchitsch returned from his visit. This conference on July 21 was summarized in the communique of July 23, a document that convinced Guderian that the OKH was preparing to throw overboard the entire plan of placing Moscow above all other objectives.[7] This was not, however, the truth of the matter. Halder wished to form a special task force composed of Panzer Group 2 along with part of the Second Army, to be commanded by Field Marshal von Kluge, that would be sent to the Ukraine with Stalingrad on the lower Volga as its ultimate objective. But the main target of Halder's plans was—as it had always been—Moscow. The Soviet capital could be taken, he believed, by the remaining part of Army Group Center along with some help from one army and a panzer group from Army Group North.

On July 23, the day the communique so despised by Guderian was issued, Halder laid his case before Hitler. In his discussion with the führer Halder noted that the infantry of the Second and Ninth armies alone would not be enough to take Moscow after von Kluge's group had been diverted to the southeast. That objective could only be accomplished by Panzer Group 3 first clearing its own flank toward the northeast and then aiding the final drive on both sides of Moscow that could begin between August 5 and 10. Army Group North could continue its advance to the north and east, but with the Sixteenth Army moving its southern wing along the line Kholm-Bologoe, a maneuver that would cover from the north Army Group Center's approach to Moscow.

The chief of the general staff justified his new proposals to Hitler on the basis that it was proving to be impossible to eliminate Russia's military forces without eliminating its economic base. For this reason, he submitted, the Volga line in the south must be reached by von Kluge's group, a force of about ten infantry divisions plus Panzer Group 2. This group would have the mission of moving through Briansk and Gomel toward Kharkov. In terms of territorial objectives, Halder called for reaching the Caucasus-Volga line, a line that could perhaps be extended to Kazan if the situation warranted. In the Army Group North area the territory between Rybinsk and Lake Onega was considered particularly important. Army Group North would have to consolidate its hold here and prepare to send an expedition into the Urals.[8]

In presenting his case to Hitler on July 23, Halder appealed to the führer's sense of reason in terms that, for him, were unusual. Halder had finally realized that Russia's inexhaustible reserves of manpower could not be defeated by the methods heretofore used. The chief of the general staff now advocated the shattering of Russia's economic capacity to make war instead of concentrating simply on destroying the enemy's armed forces.[9] It might be thought that here Halder was resorting to a subterfuge, engaging Hitler's sympathies by advancing a consideration dear to his heart—that is, the importance of economic strategy in winning a victory over the Soviet Union—but there is other evidence to show that this was not the case. The earnestness of Halder's newfound interest in economic matters was manifested in a conference held at OKH headquarters on July 25. In this conference Brauchitsch, who never deviated far from Halder's way of thinking, addressed the chiefs of staff of the three eastern army groups:

> Our main task remains to shatter Russia's capacity to resist. A further goal is to bring their population and production centers under our control. The Russians have a wealth of manpower; we must seize their armament centers before the onset of winter. . . .

> Although their armament production is high, it is limited, nevertheless. If we succeed in smashing the enemy strength before us, their superiority in manpower alone will not win the war for them.[10]

Halder now genuinely believed, in contrast to his earlier and narrower philosophy of war, that economic considerations must be taken into account if the enemy were to be brought to its knees within a reasonable length of time. This change of mind on Halder's part was not, however, a complete departure from the past, for he still had not abandoned the strategy that placed Moscow above all other objectives. In other words, although he now recognized the importance of economic factors in the war in the east, he still stopped short of recommending to Hitler that measures be taken to prepare Germany for a protracted war instead of one short and swift campaign.

Although Hitler was willing to listen to Halder's arguments, he was disinclined to change the wording of a new directive, Directive 33-A, that he caused to be issued that same day, July 23. This directive was a supplement to the Directive 33 that had appeared on July 19, an order that called for armored units from Army Group Center to be used to cover from the south Army Group North's advance on Leningrad and that also made provision for the thrust of part of Army Group Center, mainly Panzer Group 2, into the Ukraine to help Army Group South.[11] Halder badly wanted Hitler to change this directive to assign Moscow priority over Leningrad, although Halder did not disagree with the führer about the necessity of sending Panzer Group 2 to the Ukraine. For this reason, Halder had sent Brauchitsch to Hitler to ask for a clarification of Directive 33. This clarification was ready by July 23 and it did not please Halder. Hitler, however, was adamant, so Directive 33-A stood, providing for the diversion of Panzer Group 2 to the south and the movement of Panzer Group 3 to the north to aid in the capture of Leningrad. The advance on Moscow, according to the directive, would be carried out with only the infantry of the Second and Ninth armies until such time as Panzer Group 3 could be spared from the Leningrad operations.[12]

Although Hitler could not have been more explicit about his wishes, Halder was not a man who could be easily rebuffed, so he sent his minion, Brauchitsch, to Keitel, the head of the OKW, to see what could be done to save the Moscow project there—an undertaking that the chief of the general staff must have known would increase his own sense of frustration—but he realized that he could not now move Hitler save through the OKW. The reaction Brauchitsch encountered in Keitel's office was blunt. Keitel told Brauchitsch that he could do nothing for him and suggested that the army commander in chief himself see Hitler if the matter still needed straightening out.[13] So, for the second time on July 23, Hitler received a representative from the OKH who pleaded with him to reverse his decision placing Leningrad ahead of Moscow.

The path that Brauchitsch took in his audience with the führer was less oblique than that chosen by Halder.[14] Whereas the chief of the general staff had stressed both the need for pressing forward rapidly in the south, thereby striking at the Russian economic capacity to make war, and the importance of taking Moscow ahead of Leningrad, Brauchitsch shifted ground somewhat and put all of his emphasis on the importance of taking Moscow. The army commander in chief backed down from Halder's earlier claim that it was necessary to send Panzer Group 2 and part of the Second Army to the Ukraine. In fact, he even denied that an encirclement operation around Gomel was necessary. Instead of suggesting, as Halder had done a few hours earlier, that one panzer group—that is, Panzer Group 3—was needed in the attack on Moscow, Brauchitsch asserted that, to be safe, both panzer groups would be required. He contended that success would be produced only by continuing the tried and proven tactics of using far-reaching panzer thrusts ahead of and on either side of the advancing infantry armies.

Hitler was unmoved by Brauchitsch's argument and told him that he believed the Russians apparently did not care whether their flanks were endangered by broadly sweeping tank maneuvers or not. The examples of Bialystok, Minsk, and Smolensk were clear to Hitler—the Russians would not surrender even if the German armor cut off their units from the east by wide encirclement operations. Hitler's final comment was that from then on it would be better to plan operations that relied more on the ability of the infantry to close and eliminate the pockets of trapped Russians, rather than to use up the striking power of the armored units for this purpose. In the case of Smolensk, he pointed out, the pocket had not been sealed, nor had it been possible to ready the panzer groups of Army Group Center for further operations.[15] The clash of wills between Hitler and the OKH had temporarily ended, but Hitler would find that Halder would surrender his principles no more easily than the Russians did their lives.

On July 25 Keitel visited Army Group Center headquarters and elaborated on what Hitler had told the army commander in chief two days before. Hitler thought that the tanks were being used up too quickly by Russian flank assaults and that too great a distance separated the tanks from the infantry. The distance had to be shortened if the pockets of trapped Russians were to be eliminated effectively. The führer's "ideal solution," reported Keitel, would be to finish with the Russians on the southern flank of Army Group Center in the area of Gomel–Mozyr by forming several small pockets, as the scope of previous operations planned by the general staff had been beyond the limits of the army to execute. It was also Hitler's view that strongly fortified areas such as Mogilev must be taken with the use of more artillery in order to avoid heavy casualties. Finally, Keitel noted, the führer had become convinced that smaller, more tightly planned operations were needed because Göring had reported to him about the large numbers of Russians escaping from the Smolensk pocket.

The commander of Army Group Center protested this decision charging that Göring's reports were exaggerated and that the enemy had lost considerable materiel at Smolensk. Von Bock also denied that the operation around Smolensk had been carried out on an unmanageable scale, maintaining that the delays in moving the Second Army across the Dnepr to relieve the panzer divisions on the flanks of Army Group Center were responsible for the failure to close the gap at Dorogobuzh. It should be remembered, however, that von Bock himself had been responsible for the decision not to allow the XIIth Army Corps to relieve the XXIVth Panzer Corps along the Sozh.[16] For the moment, von Bock was in the same position as the OKH, powerless to take any direct action to rectify a decision that he considered to be a fatal mistake. But von Bock, like Halder, was a tenacious man, and he would not forfeit his objective, Moscow, without a fight.

When Guderian was told on July 27 that the next goal for he panzer group might be Gomel, he insisted that his tanks would be unable to carry out such a mission in a southerly direction. Although the panzer general's reluctance to move south could perhaps be useful to the OKH in forcing a delay in the implementation of Directive 33–A, such tactics did not fit well with Halder's longer-range plans at this time, for his still believed that Panzer Group 2 would have to go to the Ukraine; it was the departure of Panzer Group 3 to Army Group North that he badly wanted to prevent. On July 26 von Bock had telephoned Brauchitsch to inform him about the results of Keitel's visit the day before, and Brauchitsch used this occasion to ask the commander of Army Group Center to formulate a plan for sending all of Panzer Group 2 to the Kiev area. On the following day, the army commander in chief flew to Borisov and asked von Bock personally to order Guderian to begin his move toward Gomel as soon as possible. Brauchitsch did not, however, tell the commander of Army Group Center that this idea had the approval of the OKH.[17] Halder did not actually want Panzer Group 2 to be used against Gomel—Kiev was his real objective—but he thought it was necessary that Guderian begin his march to the south quickly. Brauchitsch tried to leave von Bock with the false impression that he was merely transmitting Hitler's orders, although his speech to the army group chiefs of staff on July 25 should have tipped off von Bock as to the OKH's intentions. Regardless of whether or not von Bock accepted Brauchitsch's explanation of the order to dispatch Panzer Group 2 to Gomel, he relayed this order to Guderian, saying only that it had Hitler's approval.[18] It is unlikely, however, that Guderian was misled by the attempt to blame Hitler alone for the order for his panzer group to move southward. The panzer general had been attuned to the real feelings of the OKH ever since the general staff communique of July 23.

On July 26 Halder again took his plea before Hitler and argued for conducting broad operations around Moscow and Kiev and not just small maneuvers as had been envisioned around Gomel. On this point Hitler did not yield, and neither did he yield on the question of Army Group Center pressing on to Moscow with infantry alone, although he now altered his previous plan somewhat and no longer spoke of sending Panzer Group 3 all the way to Leningrad. Instead, Hitler came closer to Halder's viewpoint and said that Hoth could concentrate his attack in the direction of the Valdai Hills and cooperate here with the southern wing of Army Group North (see Figure 32).

The debacle at Velikie Luki on July 20, the failure to close the Smolensk pocket, the threat facing Panzer Group 2 from the direction of Roslavl, and the danger to the southern flank of the Second Army from the direction of Gomel, as well as the continued unhealthy situation farther south around Mozyr and Korosten, had all taken their toll on Hitler. The führer now believed that the army groups should strive to effect smaller encirclements than they had in the past, and the areas around Gomel and Lake Ilmen seemed to offer good opportunities for such tactics. Halder did not take this small shift in the wind from Hitler as being very significant and still lamented that Hitler's proposals ignored the importance of Moscow.[19] Nevertheless, it seemed possible to Halder that a delay in the carrying out of Directive 33-A might be brought about now that Hitler was insisting on operations of a smaller scope. Since the führer wanted to send Panzer Group 3 no farther north than the Valdai Hills between Lake Ilmen and Kalinin, an excellent chance existed for retaining Panzer Group 3 close in to the northern flank of Army Group Center and for using it against

Moscow and not to aid the objectives of Army Group North. The chief of the general staff was soon to receive help for his project from an unexpected source.

On July 26, Paulus, the OQI of the general staff, paid a visit to Army Group North to collect information firsthand about the conditions pertaining to the use of tanks against Leningrad. The panzer generals Hoepner, Manstein, and Rheinhardt all told Paulus that the area between Lake Ilmen and Lake Peipus, that is,

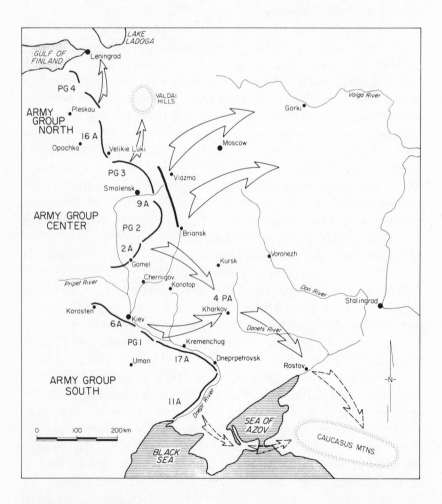

Figure 32. Hitler's Plan as of July 26, 1941

the approach to Leningrad from the south, was not suitable for armor in any respect because of the rugged terrain, the many lakes and thick forests. Manstein's advice was to turn Army Group North's armored units to Moscow instead of Leningrad, saying that a further move northward by his LVIth Panzer Corps would have to be undertaken with massive infantry support in order to clear the enemy from the forests in his path of advance. Paulus agreed that the prospects for employing armor against Leningrad appeared very bad.[20]

In the absence of certain key parts of Jodl's diary and also of the necessary Wehrmacht Operations Staff documents it is impossible to say for certain that Paulus's report to the general staff was made known to the OKW.[21] Jodl's actions on July 27, however, the day following Paulus's visit, would indicate that he had direct knowledge of the conference at Army Group North headquarters. On this day, Jodl met with Hitler and told him that he had now changed his mind about the future course of strategy. Jodl advised the führer to undertake an immediate assault on Moscow after the conclusion of the battles around Smolensk, "not because Moscow is the Soviet capital, but because here will be located the enemy's main force."[22] This alteration of views by Jodl represented a basic deviation from the course of action he had recommended ever since he had been made aware of the Lossberg study in mid-November 1940. It had been an important element of the Lossberg plan that Army Group Center should be halted east of Smolensk and that armored strength should be diverted from it to the north against the flank and the rear of the Russian armies confronting Army Group North. Jodl had gone on record as early as June 29 that he thought the approaches to Leningrad from the west and south would be very difficult for tanks, and by July 27 he had become convinced of the unworkability of this plan, although he was unable effectively to counter Hitler's argument against pushing on to Moscow until the Russian economic base in the Ukraine had been removed from enemy control.[23] Hitler in the past had taken Jodl's advice, however, in fact it was probably Jodl, with some help from Göring, who persuaded Hitler not to carry out the Leningrad operation without aid from Army Group Center. Jodl had favored a provision included in the original Barbarossa directive of December 18, 1940, that called for turning armor from Army Group Center to Army Group North after the Red Army forces in White Russia had been crushed, and now when the chief of the Wehrmacht Operations Staff shifted ground on this matter, the effect on Hitler was profound.

On July 28 Hitler informed Brauchitsch that he had decided to suspend the Leningrad and Ukraine operations as ordered in Directive 33–A. The führer's feelings about the future were so uncertain that, at this point, he was unprepared to order anything other than that the situation on the southern flank of Army Group Center around Gomel be taken care of as soon as possible. Hitler did not give up entirely the idea of sending Panzer Group 3 to help Army Group North, but now, instead of calling for Panzer Group 3 to participate directly in the encirclement of Leningrad, he believed that the panzer group should only screen the southern flank of Army Group North from the direction of the Valdai Hills and move in a northeasterly direction to cut communications between Moscow and Leningrad. An advance to Moscow, according to Hitler, would still have to wait until the successful conclusion of the Leningrad operation.[24] The OKH had not yet won a complete victory for the cause of Moscow, although the confidence of Hitler and the OKW in the feasibility of the original Barbarossa plan, to place Leningrad ahead of the capital in terms of its strategic importance, had been shaken.

The uncertainty that existed in Hitler's mind about future strategy was clearly revealed in his Directive 34 issued on July 30.[25] This new directive officially canceled Directive 33–A and postponed the movement by Panzer Group 3 into the Valdai area for at least another ten days. Army Group Center was ordered to go over to the defensive along its entire front and prepare only for a further operation against Gomel, while the push by Panzer Group 2 into the Ukraine was likewise delayed until proper repairs could be made to the armored vehicles. In discussing the meaning of Directive 34 with Halder, Heusinger, the chief of the general staff Operations Department, described the new directive as being "in conformity with our views"; he commented also that "this solution delivered us all from the nightmare [that the] führer's stubbornness would ruin the entire eastern operation—finally a point of light!"[26] For his part, Brauchitsch was so afraid that Hitler might reconsider Directive 34 that he declined to make any written comment on it whatsoever lest it fall into the wrong hands.[27] Now that Jodl and the OKW seemed to be gradually coming to accept

OKH strategy, Halder could sense that Hitler would sooner or later be forced to give in under the pressure from both command organizations. Hitler had at least decided to delay—for the moment—a firm decision about Moscow, and this was all that Halder needed to make another attempt to regain control of strategic planning for the general staff. Hitler had previously shown himself inclined to defer important decisions if they appeared likely to cause disagreement among his advisors, and it was this weakness in his character that Halder could use to his advantage.

Hitler's tendency to postpone unpleasant decisions was evident in a conference held at Army Group Center headquarters on August 4, with Keitel, Jodl, Schmundt, von Bock, Heusinger, Guderian, and Hoth, in addition to Hitler, all present.[28] The atmosphere surrounding this conference was extremely tense, especially since some officers on von Bock's staff, including his first general staff officer, Henning von Treschkow, had hatched a plot to kidnap the führer, a plan that was forestalled by tight SS security measures.* According to Alan Clark, "The officers privy to this conspiracy were so numerous and occupied positions so close to the army group commander that it is impossible to believe von Bock was unaware of what was going on."[29]

True to his consistent philosophy of divide and rule, each of the participants in the conference was given a private audience with Hitler without being able to know what the others had said.[30] In his memoirs Guderian noted that all the generals of Army Group Center advocated resumption of the offensive against Moscow. He further stated that he told Hitler that the number of tank motors that the führer had promised Panzer Groups 2 and 3 for replacements was inadequate. In his account of the conversation, Guderian recorded that Hitler offered only three hundred tank motors for the entire eastern front, but the führer actually promised four hundred motors for Panzer Groups 2 and 3. There were also two other topics of discussion that Guderian brought up in his interview with Hitler that were not completely or accurately recorded. Regarding the question of Yelnia, as has been mentioned, Guderian advocated holding the salient for reasons of

---

*In March 1943, von Treschkow and his cohorts tried unsuccessfully to explode a bomb aboard Hitler's plane. This plot failed only due to a faulty detonator in the device. Halder and von Treschkow had been close collaborators for some time.

prestige. In regard to the question of resuming the offensive against Moscow, he told Hitler that the Russian front around Roslavl was very thin and that he believed his panzer group should press north and east through Spas–Demensk toward Viazma. He also told the führer that his panzer units and infantry corps had succeeded in overrunning the Russian positions around Roslavl with ease. Guderian gave Hitler the impression on August 4 that the Russians had committed their last "proletarian reserves" and that the enemy henceforth would be unable to offer effective resistance. The panzer general was convinced that he had achieved a full breakthrough of the last line of the Russian main defense force and that the way to the east and to Moscow was now relatively free and open.[31]

This fanciful commentary by Guderian was reminiscent of Halder's speech of February 3, 1941, when the chief of the general staff attempted to persuade Hitler that the Red Army was no worthy opponent for the Wehrmacht and that Moscow could be taken almost with impunity by an assault through White Russia from the west. At that time Hitler had refused to believe that the enemy could be rapidly driven out of the Baltic area and the Ukraine, and he declined to accept Halder's version of a strategic plan. Guderian's testimony on August 4 meant more to Hitler, however, because the panzer general was a front-line soldier and had seen combat at first hand. Deep down, Hitler mistrusted the sophisticated and highly trained staff officers of the OKH, but Guderian was a man of action, a soldier who, in some ways, had experienced the kind of life he himself had known in face-to-face combat with the enemy. A noted historian has written the following words about Hitler:

> The German officer corps was the last stronghold of the old conservative tradition, and Hitler never forgot this. His class resentment was never far below the surface; he knew perfectly well that the officer corps despised him as an upstart, as "the Bohemian Corporal" and he responded with a barely concealed contempt for the "gentlemen" who wrote "von" before their names and had never served as privates in the trenches.[32]

The panzer general was aware of this quirk in Hitler's character and was not above using it to his advantage should an opportunity occur.

After listening to Guderian's report, it seemed possible to Hitler that the Russians were indeed approaching the limit of their ability to conduct large-scale operations after suffering such heavy losses during the first six weeks of the war—although he was still unable to free himself entirely from the conviction that Leningrad and the Ukraine should come before Moscow. Despite the führer's reservations about Moscow, however, Guderian's representations had brought about a change in his attitude. Toward the end of the conference, Hitler announced that he would again consider the possibility of a further—limited—advance eastward by Army Group Center. After hearing a final appeal by von Bock about the necessity of destroying the enemy's main force in front of Moscow, Hitler put off a final decision until a later date.[33] The OKH and the generals of Army Group Center could sense imminent victory in their struggle to force Hitler to accept their view, insofar as they all agreed on the importance of Moscow. There would, however, be disagreements among the generals themselves, particularly between Halder and Guderian, about the Ukraine.

On August 5, the day following the conference with Hitler at Borisov, Halder, Brauchitsch, Heusinger, and Paulus held a meeting at OKH headquarters. In this discussion Halder's opinion held sway: that Moscow would have to be reached before the end of the year if the German forces were to attain full freedom of maneuver. Along with the important goal of Moscow, Halder considered it vital that the Russian economic base in the south be eliminated, "We must penetrate the oil region with strong forces all the way to Baku."[34] Halder was still pursuing the same course he charted in the communique of July 23 and that Brauchitsch had reemphasized in the chiefs of staff conference on July 25, that is, that the economic and manpower reserves of the Soviet Union made the country too strong to defeat by purely military means, that the enemy's power to make war must be reduced by depriving Russia of its resources and war industry. In persevering in this line of thought, Halder was placing himself in a position where he would come into a head-on collision with Guderian. Halder and Guderian could agree on Moscow and Hitler and Halder could agree on the Ukraine, but Guderian would not be prepared to sacrifice Moscow for the Ukraine, for he was positive that the Soviet capital could not be taken without his tanks riding in the vanguard. In the end, the chief of the general staff would try to reach a compromise with

Hitler and Jodl whereby the problem of Moscow and the Ukraine could be solved to everyone's satisfaction—except Guderian's. The last compromise on strategy in 1941, however, would be made without Halder's approval and in a way that would come as a crushing blow to him.

Later in the day on August 5, Brauchitsch conferred with Hitler and subsequently reported to Halder on the results of his conversation. He told the chief of the general staff that Hitler had come to realize that the present tactics would lead to a stabilization of the front as had been the case in 1914. The führer now envisioned three possibilities for a future course of action: (1) the capture of the Valdai highlands by a coordinated maneuver of Army Group North and Panzer Group 3; (2) the clearing of the southern flank of Army Group Center, combined with elimination of the strong Russian force around Korosten; and (3) an operation to eliminate all enemy forces west of the Southern Bug River.

In his discussion with Brauchitsch about the second alternative, Hitler left open the question of a further advance by Army Group Center directly toward Moscow, and he also maintained that the carrying out of the Korosten operation could lead to a solution of the problems east and south of Mogilev and at Kiev. In his diary Halder put special emphasis on the words *Mogilev–Kiev,* and it would be accurate to say that he was excited about the possibility of being able to take Moscow and the Ukraine simultaneously.[35] Halder described the joint Moscow–Kiev plan as "a salvation," although he thought that the inclusion of an attack against the enemy forces around Korosten would be too wasteful in terms of tying up strength. Halder did not want to squander time on winning what he described as tactical victories of the kind that Hitler desired at Gomel and Korosten.[36] Instead, he wished to concentrate on broad grandiose possibilities like those that had seemed to be offered around Bialystok–Minsk and at Smolensk. Halder believed that once the Wehrmacht gained freedom of movement and operations again became fluid, Hitler would give up his notions about concentrating on tactical successes.

Guderian, too, wished to continue wide-ranging maneuvers, but not in the same way that Halder envisioned. The panzer general's stern threat on August 6 to refuse to give up even one panzer division from his command to aid in the Rogachev–Zhlobin operations by the Second Army should have shown Halder the mettle of the man he was dealing with, but he continued to underestimate Guderian's resourcefulness until it was too late.[37] For his part, Guderian was content for the moment to mark time at Roslavl and at Gomel and wait for Hitler to make up his mind about Moscow. Guderian's protest against the OKH decision about Rogachev–Zhlobin on August 6 afforded Halder a chance to confront the panzer general and force him to back down and obey orders, but this was not Halder's way. Instead, Guderian had won a small but important victory over his superiors and he would not be discouraged from seeking bigger successes in the future.

The sign of approval for the Moscow project that Jodl had hesitantly given on July 27 stimulated Halder to renew his attempt to assert his influence over the OKW, an effort he had first made by sending Brauchitsch to visit Keitel on July 23. The chief of the general staff contacted Jodl on August 7 in order to reinforce the latter's already favorable attitude toward an advance on Moscow and to convince him that Russia's economic base in the south must be eliminated at the same time. Halder told Jodl that the forces already in motion in the direction of Leningrad were sufficient and that Hoth's Panzer Group 3 should not be taken from Army Group Center and given to Army Group North. In the first place, Panzer Group 3 was needed to carry out the assault on Moscow, and secondly, Halder insisted that there was no danger to the southern flank of Army Group North from the direction of the Valdai Hills. Finally, the chief of the general staff said that instead of deciding between Moscow or the Ukraine, a decision must be made for Moscow *and* the Ukraine. "This must be done or else the enemy's productive strength cannot be vanquished before the fall."[38]

This conversation on August 7 between Halder and Jodl was of critical importance in influencing the final outcome of events in 1941. In his diary Halder noted: "Overall impression: Jodl is impressed with the correctness of this plan and will move along in this direction."[39] Halder would continue to work on Jodl, who was ever more inclined to accept the OKH view of strategy. By the third week in August Jodl would play a vital role in Halder's plan to gain influence over Hitler. Halder had done his work well in convincing the chief of the Wehrmacht Operations Staff that both Moscow and the Ukraine had to be taken before the onset of winter in 1941. The chief of the general staff now expected Jodl to remain on his side, but Halder's cleverly laid scheme would soon be endangered, for at the end of August conditions would change and Halder would attempt to undo the impression he had made on Jodl about the economic importance of the Ukraine. This attempt would fail, and Halder would be forced to take a new tack with Jodl. For a while, however, after August 7, Halder's confidence in his ability to manipulate the OKW was very great, for now not only had Jodl apparently become a convert to the OKH strategy but Halder also had an important ally within Jodl's own organization, the deputy chief of the Wehrmacht Operations Staff and head of Department "L," Walter Warlimont, a man who had worked diligently on behalf of the Moscow project since the fall of 1940.

On August 10, Warlimont's Department "L" produced a study that called for a resumption of the Moscow offensive at the end of August after first eliminating the immediate threats to the flanks of Army Group Center around Gomel and Velikie Luki–Toropets with the help of Panzer Groups 2 and 3. The study called for using both panzer groups subsequent to the flank operations in a thrust toward Moscow that would "crush the last, inferior, newly formed replacement divisions that the enemy had apparently brought up along the line Rzhev–Viazma–Briansk." After the Rzhev–Viazma–Briansk line had been cracked, Warlimont anticipated that the progress of Army Group Center would take the form of a "pursuit" of the beaten enemy. Thereafter Army Group Center would be able to send support to help the neighboring army groups to the north and south. In particular, Warlimont stated that the forces for the assault on Moscow should be so arranged that during the pursuit stage of the advance Guderian's Panzer Group 2 would be in a position to move along the Don River to the southeast.[40] This study was tailored to fit closely with the OKH viewpoint as it was presented to Jodl by Halder on August 7, and there can be little doubt that Warlimont was acting in accordance with Halder's wishes in preparing it to influence his superior, Jodl.

The impression that Warlimont's study was looked upon with favor by the OKH is enhanced by the fact that on August 8, two days before the Department "L" study, Halder issued a general staff appraisal of the situation confronting the German army.[41] In this report Halder stated that it was clear that the Russians were deploying all of their available strength along the line Lake Ilmen–Rzhev–Viazma–Briansk. The chief of the general staff compared

the position of the Red Army to that of the French in the second
phase of the campaign in 1940, when the enemy relied on strong
"defense islands" located along a new defense line. Halder believed that the Russian attempt to push back the German front in
the Smolensk area by counterattacks was on the verge of complete
collapse. In his words:

> My old impression is confirmed, Army Group North is strong
> enough to carry out its mission alone. Army Group Center must
> concentrate its forces in order to destroy the enemy's main force [in
> front of Moscow]. Army Group South is strong enough to fulfill its
> task, but even so Army Group Center can perhaps lend assistance
> [by sending Panzer Group 2 to the southeast.][42]

In early August Jodl found himself surrounded both within
and without the OKW by generals who were all giving him the same
advice, advice he was prone to accept after he had been made
aware of the problems confronting the armored units in the hill
and forest region on the approaches to Leningrad. Jodl could not
know that the Red Army was far from finished in front of Army
Group Center, although the battles raging around the periphery of
the Yelnia salient should have convinced him otherwise. He also
could not know that the Rzhev–Viazma–Briansk line did not represent the last Russian line of defense in front of Moscow. He could
not know that an advance by Army Group Center beyond this line
would not take the form of a pursuit and that thus the entire premise of the OKH strategy and also of Warlimont's study was wrong.
Halder's general staff appraisal of August 8 listed the relationship
of forces in divisions as follows: in front of Army Group North 23
Russian (including 2 motorized) versus 26 German (including 6
motorized); Army Group Center, 70 Russian (8.5 motorized) versus 60 German (17 motorized); Army Group South, 50.5 Russian
(6.5 motorized) versus 50.5 German (9.5 motorized). No more
than three days later, on August 11, Halder had to admit that these
figures were awry. Instead of the 200 divisions that he believed the
Russians had originally deployed, 360 divisions had been identified
on the entire eastern front. Halder also noted that although the
enemy forces were badly armed and badly led, their preparation to
meet the German invasion had been good and the military strength
of their economy had been seriously underestimated. Halder remarked pessimistically that the Wehrmacht was moving farther

away from its sources of supply while the Red Army was drawing back closer to its own.

On August 12, most probably because of an inquiry from Jodl, now that he had promised Halder that he would work to see the general staff plan carried through, Hitler issued further instructions, Directive 34-A.[43] Its language was optimistic because Army Group South had just concluded the Uman battle of encirclement southwest of Kiev, netting some 103,000 prisoners.[44] This battle was a spur to Hitler's desire to finish with the Russians in the western Ukraine, seize the Crimea, and occupy the Donets Basin and Kharkov. About the army groups north of the Pripet, Hitler stated that the primary goal in the immediate future was for Army Group Center to rectify the situation of its flanks by striking the Russian Fifth Army in the south around Mozyr and using armored units to suppress the enemy in the north around Toropets. The führer also ordered the left flank of Army Group Center, that is, Panzer Group 3 and the Ninth Army, to move northward only far enough to secure the southern flank of Army Group North and enable this army group to shift some infantry divisions toward Leningrad. The directive called for concluding the operations against Leningrad before an advance on Moscow was resumed, but Hitler thought that Leningrad could be dealt with in fairly short order.[45]

Halder's first impression of Directive 34-A was unfavorable, for he disliked Hitler's assertion that the city on the Neva must come ahead of Moscow, and he described the directive as being restrictive and not allowing the OKH the latitude it needed.[46] Two days later, however, he modified his tone somewhat and said that the directive essentially was in agreement with the OKH point of view, namely, that Army Group Center should undertake only two basic tasks. One was to resolve the situation on its flanks and prepare to push on to Moscow, and the second was to make ready to send forces to aid the advance of Army Group South.[47] Halder, a bit late, had come to recognize the subtle change in Hitler's thinking and he could see how the führer's insistence on effecting smaller encirclement operations could be used to the benefit of his plan.

Now that the OKH had gathered new strength by winning over Jodl, and now that Hitler appeared to be on the verge of changing his mind about Leningrad, Halder was emboldened to mount a two-pronged offensive against the führer's negative attitude toward Moscow. This renewed effort by Halder took the form of two studies presented to Hitler on August 18. The first was submitted by Warlimont's Department "L," and the other was delivered by Brauchitsch, the commander in chief of the army. A comparison of these documents leads to the inescapable conclusion that by mid-August the coordination between the OKH and Department "L" of the Wehrmacht Operations Staff had been developed to a high degree.

Warlimont's "Assessment of the Eastern Situation" of August 18, which was probably prepared without Jodl's approval, laid down the goals for the remainder of 1941 as the capture of the Donets Basin, Kharkov, Moscow, and Leningrad.[48] In setting forth the procedure for reaching these objectives, Warlimont deviated from the line most recently espoused by the OKH. The chief of Department "L" described the situation of Army Group South after the battle of Uman as healthy enough so that the turn of Panzer Group 2 all the way to the Ukraine was no longer essential in order to defeat the Russian Fifth Army. The crossing of the Dnepr would also be likely on both sides of Cherkassy, south of Kiev, by early September after the rapid movement eastward of the German Seventeenth Army. The capture of the Crimea, an objective that would soon loom larger in Halder's plans, was not deemed necessary in the near future, a screening force sufficing in that direction. The key to all subsequent operations, according to Warlimont, was to be Moscow, and the approach to this city by Army Group Center had been rendered easier by the successful operations at Roslavl, Krichev, Rogachev–Zhlobin, and Gomel, the latter battle then being in its final stages. On the northern flank, the second attack on Velikie Luki was scheduled to begin on August 21, and it too, Warlimont anticipated, would be brought to a successful conclusion. As a result of the approaching completion of the operations on the flanks of Army Group Center, the resumption of the Moscow offensive was set for early September, this time with the aid of both Panzer Group 2 and Panzer Group 3, not just Panzer Group 3 as Halder had earlier specified.

The reason for the change in plans by the Halder–Warlimont partnership was that Panzer Group 3 had been weakened by the loss of the XXXIXth Panzer Corps, which Hoth had been forced to give up to Army Group North.[49] The XXXIXth Panzer Corps had been sent northward at Jodl's request on August 15 to help prevent a Russian breakthrough on the southern wing of Army Group North south of Lake Ilmen in the region of Staraia Russa. After the crisis around Staraia Russa had passed, Hitler had used the opportunity to dispatch the panzer corps farther north despite Halder's wishes to the contrary. Now, on August 18, both the OKH and Department "L" staffs had to take cognizance of the fact that after being deprived of two panzer and one motorized divisions, Panzer Group 3 alone was too weak to spearhead a drive on Moscow from the northwest. Actually, as will be pointed out, the entire panzer group would have been hard pressed to undertake this task, but the loss of the XXXIXth Panzer Corps to Army Group North was a major factor in compelling Halder to readjust his strategy.

The new OKH proposal was presented by Brauchitsch to Hitler also on August 18.[50] On July 23, as noted earlier, Halder told the führer that it was important to seize both Moscow and the Ukraine before the onset of winter. At that time the chief of the general staff had strongly emphasized the economic necessity of occupying the Ukraine, and it was his opinion that this could best be done by sending a group under von Kluge's Fourth Army command, composed of Panzer Group 2 and part of von Weichs's Second Army, to the south and east. By August 18, however, Halder realized it would be impossible to send all of Panzer Group 2 to the Ukraine and take Moscow at the same time. When thus faced with a choice, Moscow or the Ukraine, Halder, true to his basic conclusion, chose Moscow. The problem that he now faced was, however, a serious one. Hitler had not really needed any convincing prior to June 22 that the economic war was vital and that the south of the Soviet Union was crucially important for Russia's armaments industry. Halder had agreed with the führer on July 26 that the Ukraine must be taken rapidly for economic reasons and had assigned it a priority equal to that of Moscow. Now he would have to backtrack and disassemble the arguments he had made earlier for both objectives.

The chief of the general staff attempted to accomplish this by continuing to place a certain emphasis on economic considerations, though weakening his tone in this respect. He now described the capture of the Moscow industrial area as equal in importance to the economic objectives in the Baltic area and in the south in preventing the Russians from rebuilding their shattered armies.[51]

Beyond this, Halder repeated the case he had made many times before that the enemy's main force was positioned in front of Moscow and that once these units were destroyed, the Russians would no longer be capable of maintaining a continuous line of defense. In order to fortify his point further, Halder made use of Hitler's disinclination to carry out any more wide-ranging maneuvers of the kind that had brought less than desirable results in White Russia around Smolensk.

The ability of the armored units to carry out long-range operations was characterized by Halder as limited, even after repair measures were completed. As a result of the panzer groups' lessened capability to maneuver, Halder advocated using them to traverse shorter distances than had previously been expected of them. It was, therefore, essential that the armored units be used only for decisive and strategic goals and that their strength not be wasted on nonessential tasks. In his operations plan section of the August 18 proposal, Halder set forth restricted goals for Panzer Groups 2 and 3, which would remain positioned on the flanks of Army Group Center. Guderian would move from the area Roslavl–Briansk toward Kaluga and Medyn, west of Maloyaroslavets, while Hoth would push from southeast of Beloe and Toropets toward Rzhev. It should be noted here that the first phase of this planned armored thrust would not have gone far enough to crack the main Russian defense lines running through Mozhaisk and Naro–Fominsk, as will be pointed out in the next chapter.[52] The middle of Army Group Center's front, the infantry armies, were to remain in defensive positions until the enemy began to pull back eastward due to the pressure exerted by the two panzer groups. In any case, Halder called for the infantry in the center of the front to cooperate closely with the armored units in order to achieve maximum results against surrounded pockets of enemy soldiers, for, as he said, "Experience has taught us that infantry alone can perform this task successfully only under exceptional conditions."[53]

In regard to the missions of Army Groups South and North, Halder's new proposal was less clearly defined and objective than his plan for the renewed assault on Moscow. Army Group South was considered by Halder strong enough by itself to force the Dnepr with the Seventeenth Army by September 9, if not, in fact, sooner. After the Dnepr was crossed, Army Group South would be able to speed up its push eastward. As for Army Group North, it would be able to complete the Leningrad encirclement by the end of August and also forge a link with the Finns. Subsequently, Army Group North would be in a position to move into the Valdai Hills and thus protect the northern flank of Army Group Center's drive on Moscow. It was considered possible that Army Group North could send some units of Panzer Group 4 all the way south to Ostashkov, due north of a line from Velikie Luki to Rzhev, and thereby link up directly with the northern flank of Panzer Group 3. The only preconditions set forth by the August 18 study for the offensive against Moscow were that the operations around Gomel, then in progress, and around Velikie Luki, which would begin in three days, should be brought to a successful conclusion.[54]

In announcing his conviction that Moscow and the Ukraine could be taken simultaneously, Halder was remaining true to the plan that he had agreed upon with Jodl on August 7. At this conference, Halder had said that unless both objectives were taken "the enemy's productive strength cannot be overcome before fall."[55] The plan that he had outlined on July 23 and presented to Hitler on July 26 called for the sending of Panzer Group 2 into the Ukraine and, if need be, all the way to Stalingrad. Halder had again, on August 14, expressed approval of the idea of sending Guderian to the Ukraine after Hitler in his Directive 34-A of August 12 had said that the southern flank of Army Group Center would have to cooperate with Army Group South in order to eliminate the Russian Fifth Army's stronghold around Mozyr and south of the Pripet. The proposal of August 18 did not, however, provide for sending any armor from Army Group Center farther south than Novgorod–Severskii, a city on the Desna River south of Briansk in the extreme northern Ukraine (see Figure 33). Even so, Halder wanted no more than two divisions from the XXIVth Panzer Corps to move so far away from the path of the main drive on Moscow. "All thoughts that the crossing of the Dnepr by Army Group South should be hastened by these armored units [from Army Group Center] must be given up, otherwise Army Group Center will not be able to mount a proper assault [in the direction of Moscow] along its southern flank."[56]

The OKH proposal of August 18 represented an about-face by Halder insofar as it made no provision for Army Group Center to help Army Group South in any substantive way. In conceding that two armored divisions could be sent from the XXIVth Panzer

Corps into the Ukraine, Halder was opening up the possibility that Guderian's Panzer Group 2 could be divided if the need arose. This particular feature of the proposal made not the slightest difference to Halder, but it would to Guderian, a man who would go to any length to prevent armored units from being removed from his command. This was a potential difficulty that Halder should have

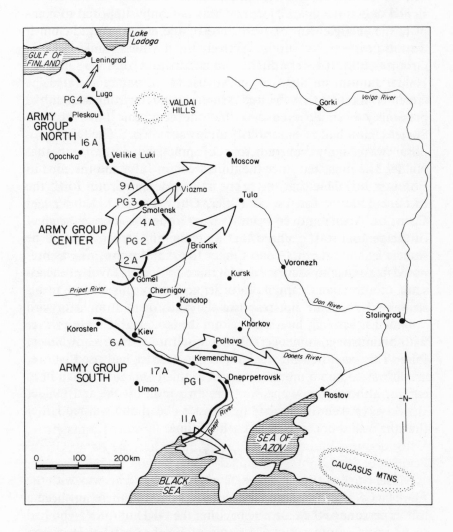

Figure 33. Halder's Proposal of August 18, 1941

been aware of, but for one reason or another, he ignored it until it was too late.

The OKH proposal of August 18 was permeated with optimism that Army Group South could not only effectively handle the enemy on its own front and cross the Dnepr to regain freedom of movement but also play a role in tying down Russian forces that might otherwise be in a position to oppose Army Group Center. The same, or even greater, optimism could be seen in the task assigned to Army Group North. It was not only supposed to complete the encirclement of Leningrad by the end of August, but it was also expected to support actively the northern flank of Army Group Center. It is very difficult to understand what the source of Halder's optimism was, for on August 11, as has been noted, he lamented the fact that the Red Army was much stronger than had previously been believed and that the economic power of the Soviet Union had been seriously underestimated.[57] The OKH proposal was highly contradictory of practically everything that Halder had preached since the third week in July, and the conclusion is inescapable that the proposal was designed, not to fit the facts, but rather to mislead Hitler. Once the XXXIXth Panzer Corps had been removed from Panzer Group 3 and once the chief of the general staff realized that its remaining strength would be insufficient for Army Group Center to take Moscow, he was prepared in essence to sacrifice the Ukraine project in favor of the assault on the Soviet capital. In order to justify this change in his strategy, Halder did not resort to the truth or to straightforward arguments. Instead, he tried to cloud the issue and win Hitler over with optimistic arguments that he himself must have known were false. This was the same technique that Halder had used before, and it was to be no more successful at this point than it had been earlier, although now the war was two months old and Halder should have seen the impending disaster ahead and warned Hitler that the war was going to last a long time.

THE ROLE OF HERMANN GÖRING

The chief of the general staff might have had his way with the führer, now that Warlimont was on his side, had there not been a loftier personage than anyone in either the OKH or OKW who had to be taken into account. The role of Reichs Marshal Hermann Göring in the planning and carrying out of the Russian campaign has never been properly investigated, but several bits of evidence indicate that his influence over Hitler was of crucial importance with respect to several key strategic decisions. Some of Göring's handiwork has already been noted in the planning phase of Barbarossa. Göring at that time, November 1940, may have demonstrated to Hitler through a report that he had commissioned from the chief of the Economic and Armaments Section of the OKW, Georg Thomas, that it was imperative for the Wehrmacht to occupy the Ukraine and the Caucasus as soon as possible after the beginning of the eastern campaign.

It is difficult to judge the significance of Göring's intervention in the strategic decisions made in 1941 in the absence of any personal records that he may have kept; however, as the designated number two man in the state, as the deputy chairman of the Council for the Defense of the Reich, chief of the Luftwaffe, director of economic programs under the Four-Year plan and, after June 29, 1941, economic director of the occupied eastern territories, Göring wielded political, military, and economic power that enabled him to intervene with advice on almost any important question that came up during the campaign in Russia.[58] At first, the marshal concerned himself only with the role and deployment of the Luftwaffe in the east, but gradually, especially at the time of the battles around Smolensk, he began to take a strong interest in the way the entire war was being conducted.

In the opening stages of the Russian campaign, Göring entertained the optimistic idea that his pet project, the so-called Göring Program for the strengthening of the Luftwaffe by a factor of four, could still be put into effect. Among other things, this program as presented on June 26 called for an increase in the labor force allocated for the building up of the Luftwaffe from 1.3 million to 3.5 million men.[59] As the war wore on, however, Göring's hopes for this undertaking began to fade. On August 17 Thomas had to report that the best that could be hoped for would be a doubling of the Luftwaffe's strength, due to the shortage of aluminum and fuel. Also, no increase in the labor force for expansion of the Luftwaffe was possible unless other industries were reduced or unless men were recalled to the factories from the army.[60] By mid-August Göring could see the economic and military ruination of the Luftwaffe if strategy and tactics were not changed.

The marshal's first attempt to exercise some sort of control over strategy in Russia came after Army Group Center seriously delayed closing the Smolensk pocket in the latter days of July. The head of the OKW, Keitel, visited von Bock on July 25 and told him that Hitler believed that the scope of the operations planned by the OKH had been too large and, for this reason, the battle around Smolensk had not been successful. Keitel reported that the führer had been particularly upset after Göring had supplied him information about the numbers of Russians who had escaped toward Dorogobuzh east of the city.[61] The problem that had most concerned Göring and Kesselring at Smolensk was that the fronts were so broad that the Luftwaffe could not be concentrated effectively in any one given area.[62] Göring believed that the army and the Luftwaffe could cooperate better if smaller operations were carried out and goals were set that would not permit dispersion of the ground and air forces over wide distances. The marshal's advice thus may have been decisive in persuading Hitler to undertake smaller and more tightly controlled operations than had been the case at Bialystok–Minsk and at Smolensk.

In regard to the Moscow question, Göring's influence is less evident in the early stage of war, although he did seem to have a certain prediliction for Leningrad, possibly because this objective had been given a higher priority in the original Barbarossa plan and he may have wished to concentrate on as limited a number of goals as possible.[63] The situation in the south of Russia was, however, a different matter, and here Göring's interest became more pronounced after mid-August.

The first time the marshal intervened to favor a southern objective over Moscow came on August 14 when, despite von Bock's protest, Göring withdrew the air units covering Yelnia and sent them to aid the Second Army's push across the Dnepr at Rogachev–Zhlobin.[64] The second intervention came after August 18 when Göring succeeded in imposing his ideas on Hitler and convincing him that it would be a mistake to follow the plan outlined in the latest OKH proposal.

There were actually two rejoinders to the OKH proposal of August 18, one dated August 21 and the other August 22 and both signed by Hitler, although the first, which was short and directly to the point, was drafted by Jodl.[65] The chief of the general staff had been worried about Jodl's reaction to the proposals of August 18, and this was why he dispatched Heusinger to the OKW headquarters at Rastenburg on August 20.[66] Heusinger attempted to convince the chief of the Wehrmacht Operations Staff that it was now impossible to capture Moscow and the Ukraine simultaneously for the reasons outlined in the OKH and Department "L" studies. Halder on August 7 had accomplished his task only too well, however. Jodl was now thoroughly convinced that the goals in the south must be pursued, not only because of the economic importance of the region, but also because the enemy appeared to be very strong east of Kiev and, unless these forces were eliminated, the southern flank of Army Group Center's advance on Moscow would be endangered. Jodl could not be dislodged from the belief that Army Group South alone was too weak to achieve the objectives in the Ukraine that he and Hitler and also, in the last analysis, Halder himself realized were vital. In order to reestablish an area of agreement with Halder, Jodl came to visit the chief of the general staff at his office in the Mauerwald camp in East Prussia on August 21. When this conversation failed to yield anything positive, Jodl drafted on that same day the above-mentioned formal rejoinder to the OKH.[67]

The substance of Jodl's counterproposal was that Army Group Center would have to send forces, meaning Panzer Group 2 and part of the Second Army, to aid Army Group South in the destruction of the Russian Fifth Army around Korosten south of the Pripet. Once Jodl had gone so far as to put his objections into writing, Halder had no choice. He would either have to compromise with Jodl on the Korosten issue, an undertaking that he considered to be too restrictive and wasteful of time, or he would have to forfeit the advance on Moscow in the fall of 1941. Halder now had only a limited amount of time; he would have to work fast if the Moscow project were to be saved for that year.

Halder's problems were multiplied after Jodl submitted his report to Hitler on the OKH proposal. Hitler seized upon Jodl's objections and personally wrote a much longer reply, completed on August 22.[68] In this document Hitler made several revealing comments that demonstrate that his disinclination to accept the proposals of the OKH and Warlimont had been stimulated by Göring. Hitler repeated his conviction that the capture of the Crimea would be vital for the war effort:

Apart from the fact that it is important to capture or destroy Russia's iron, coal and oil resources, it is of decisive *[entscheidend]* significance for Germany that the Russian air bases on the Black Sea be eliminated, above all in the region of Odessa and the Crimea.

This measure can be said to be absolutely essential *[lebenswichtig]* for Germany. Under present circumstances no one can guarantee that our only important oil producing region [that is, Rumania] is safe from air attack. Such attacks could have incalculable results for the future conduct of the war.[69]

There can be little doubt that the commander in chief of the Luftwaffe and Hitler's head economic advisor had been instrumental in stiffening the führer's determination to give the south of Russia the highest priority. Once Hitler had grasped the danger to the Rumanian oil fields, he made the idea his own and held fast to it.

Göring's influence is not only marked in regard to the Crimean question but can also be traced to the remainder of Hitler's answer to Halder. After first setting down the strategic objectives of the war in the east, Hitler then turned to the problem of tactics. The führer was dissatisfied with the way the wide-ranging encirclements had progressed, and he criticized these maneuvers for allowing many Russians to escape the pockets and rejoin other units farther east. The distance between the fast German mobile columns and the slower infantry in the encirclements had been used by the enemy to its advantage, and much time had been lost in trying to contain and destroy the surrounded Russian formations. This impression had originally been conveyed to Hitler by Göring at the time of the battle of Smolensk, and Hitler now firmly believed that smaller operations afforded a better chance of success. Another complaint that Göring voiced about the conduct of the Smolensk operation was also repeated by Hitler: The führer accused the OKH of failing to understand that the panzer groups and the Luftwaffe had to be used in a concentrated fashion in the decisive areas of attack, that is, on the flanks of the entire Soviet Union, against Leningrad in the north and the Crimea in the south not directly on the path to Moscow. The distances in Russia made it impossible for infantry units to be quickly shifted from one area to another wherever reinforcements were needed for an assault. Such distances could only be overcome by the Luftwaffe and the panzer groups, so it was essential that these means of mobile warfare remain under the exclusive control of the highest commanders and not be split up among the various armies and army corps along the front, as, said Hitler, would be the case if the plans of the OKH went into effect.

Hitler's August 22 reply singled out Göring for the highest praise for his ability to understand how the Luftwaffe and the panzer groups should be used, that is, in a unified, concentrated fashion along the main path of attack. He contrasted this "correct" understanding with the rather clumsy efforts that had been made by the OKH.[70] Not surprisingly, Halder took the reply as a personal insult: "The memorandum is full of contradictions and gives prominence to the marshal at the expense of the commander in chief of the army." After the reading of the memorandum, Halder told Brauchitsch that they both should resign at the same time, but Brauchitsch pointed out that this would accomplish nothing as Hitler's policies would remain unchanged.[71]

The third and final section of Hitler's August 22 reply was designated to refute all the remaining arguments that the generals had made in favor of Moscow. Hitler was unable to agree with Halder that Army Group South alone could force the Dnepr and control the situation in the eastern as well as the western Ukraine. It was far better, he believed, to make use of the fact that the battlefront in the Ukraine was three hundred kilometers to the west of the front of Army Group Center; once this Russian "triangle" was eliminated, the advance to Moscow would be made much safer. As for Leningrad, Hitler expected the massed strength of Göring's Luftwaffe, plus some help from Army Group Center along the southern flank of Army Group North, to turn the tide, although he now classified the objectives in southern Russia as being more important. (The Luftwaffe units were already being shifted to the north by the end of August, when they were used against the Russian forces in the area of Smolensk and around Lake Ilmen and east of Velikie Luki).[72] With Hitler's statement in the second half of August, Göring had reached the peak of his power to manipulate Hitler. The Luftwaffe would be as unable to fulfill his promises about Leningrad as it had been unable to force England to its knees, and his influence could thus only decline in the future. Göring's last major inflation of the capabilities of the Luftwaffe would come at Stalingrad. Although the August 22 memorandum had brought Halder to the depths of despair, the chief of the general staff still had one more trump to play for, as has been seen, he was a determined man and did not give up easily. Halder's last hope for 1941 now rested in the hands of Alfred Jodl.

THE HINGE OF FATE—THE HALDER-JODL COMPROMISE

In order to accomplish what he now had in mind, the splitting up of Panzer Group 2, the chief of the general staff had to undertake yet another visit to Army Group Center headquarters, a visit that he saw fit to give only the briefest mention in his diary.[73] After his arrival in Borisov during the afternoon of August 23, Halder presented to von Bock a copy of Hitler's memorandum of the previous day and told the field marshal that at least part of Panzer Group 2 would now have to be sent to fight against the Russian Fifth Army and thereby aid Army Group South in its push across the Dnepr. Halder sought to disguise his true intentions and said that the only recourse was to obey Hitler's orders. This was a trick that the OKH had already tried to use on von Bock, and he was no less wise to Halder on August 23 than he had been to Brauchitsch on July 27. Previously, the chief of the general staff had done nothing to encourage anyone at Army Group Center to knuckle under to Hitler's will, and so such sympathies must have sounded strange emanating from Halder. Von Bock was horrified at the thought of trying to advance on Moscow without all of Panzer Group 2 under his command. The battles then in progress around Yelnia were clear proof to him that the enemy was far from beaten along this front. The commander of Army Group Center decided to muster all the resources at his disposal to force Halder to come to his senses, and so he hurriedly summoned Guderian from the front to participate in this makeshift conference.

The panzer general and von Bock discussed with Halder at some length how Hitler's attitude toward Moscow could perhaps be changed. The chief of the general staff gave the appearance of agreeing that the diversion of Panzer Group 2 to the south would be a great mistake and that to use it in an operation east of Kiev would be folly. Guderian told Halder that his tanks, especially those of the XXIVth Panzer Corps, which had not had a day's rest since June 22, were incapable of carrying out a broad mission to the south. Also, he said, the road and supply situation would make such a maneuver virtually impossible. The real purpose of Guderian's soliloquy on this occasion could be seen in the following comment:

These facts provided leverage which the chief of the general staff could bring to bear on Hitler in still another attempt to make him change his mind. Field Marshal von Bock was in agreement with me; after a great deal of arguing back and forth he finally suggested that I accompany . . . Halder to the Führer's headquarters; as a general from the front I could . . . support a last attempt on the part of the [OKH] to make him agree to their plan.[74]

When Guderian finished his explanation of how he would deal with Hitler and persuade him to see the light about Moscow, Halder must have believed that he had the panzer general right in the palm of his hand. Once it was decided to use Guderian in this fashion, von Bock telephoned Schmundt, Hitler's adjutant, and arranged an interview for Guderian at the Wolfschanze bunker that same evening. The chief of the general staff had prepared a surprise for Guderian at the Wolfschanze, but it was Halder, in the end, who would find that tables could be turned in more than one direction.

It can, at present, be only a matter of conjecture, but several bits of circumstantial evidence point to the fact that Halder and Jodl finally succeeded in ironing out a compromise on strategy sometime during the period August 22–23, probably on August 22. The Halder–Jodl agreement called for the pursuit of both objectives, Moscow and the Ukraine, at the same time, an idea that both generals had agreed upon earlier. This time, however, since Panzer Group 3 had been weakened by one Panzer Corps, the XXXIXth, it was decided to make up this deficiency by removing one panzer corps from Guderian's Panzer Group 2—the XLVIth, then still in the area around Yelnia—and withdraw it behind the front for rest and refitting for use later in von Kluge's Fourth Army command as a spearhead in a renewed thrust against Moscow.[75] The remainder of Guderian's force, the XXIVth and the XLVIIth panzer corps, would then be sent to aid Army Group South in the destruction of the Russian Fifth Army, an undertaking that had been termed essential by Hitler on August 22. The formation of this new *Kraftgruppe* (task force) under von Kluge, a force that included some other infantry units as well as the XLVIth Panzer Corps, would have meant the splitting up of Guderian's panzer group, with two of his panzer corps being sent to the Ukraine (see Figure 34).

This compromise had several features that appealed to Halder and Jodl and, it could be hoped, would appeal to Hitler as well. Aside from answering all of Hitler's objections against renewing the thrust on Moscow and ensuring substantial help for Army Group South, the new strategy would allow the southern flank of Army Group Center's advance on Moscow to enjoy the support of an entire panzer corps. Had the Halder–Jodl compromise been put into effect, von Kluge's Fourth Army could have formed an integrated combined-arms task force, with both armor and infantry

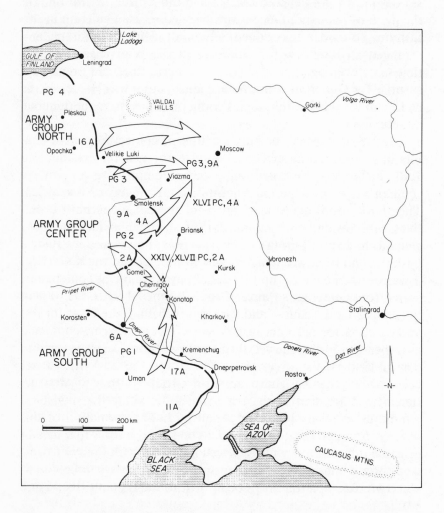

Figure 34. The Halder–Jodl Compromise of August 22, 1941

cooperating in joint objectives. The same would have been true for the operation against Korosten; there, Guderian's armor would be able to concentrate upon a limited goal along with the infantry of von Weichs's Second Army. Halder had called for this kind of cooperation in his proposal of August 18, at that time perhaps cynically, but by August 23 he, too, like Hitler and Göring, may have had enough of Guderian's wide-ranging thrusts by large masses of armor. Another feature of the compromise would have been that parts of the XLVIth Panzer Corps could have been used to brace up the Yelnia salient where, as has been seen, by the end of August severe Soviet pressure was being exerted and where the infantry units were in sore need of armored protection. The Halder–Jodl compromise was the closest thing to good planning that the Wehrmacht was privileged to enjoy in 1941, although it is open to speculation how successful it might have been, since the Russians had plans of their own. Nevertheless, the new plan represented careful thought and was a real effort to deal with tangible facts, not just wishful thinking. The trouble was that Halder's past and continued reliance on intrigue would now ensnare him, and he would be unable to put the new plan into action.

The order for the breaking up of Panzer Group 2 was issued on August 23 before Guderian went to the Wolfschanze, but Halder did not inform Guderian of this in the meeting that afternoon at Borisov. It was for this reason that Brauchitsch instructed Guderian not to mention Moscow in Hitler's presence, that he told the panzer general that the decision about the Ukraine had already been made, and that it would be useless for him to object. It was true, the decision had already been made by the OKH and the OKW that Guderian's command would, in essence, be sacrificed. It had probably also been agreed that Jodl would assume the responsibility for persuading Hitler of the need for the compromise, and probably for this reason no one from the OKH bothered to appear at the last conference on August 23. Guderian's assigned role in all this was simply to go before Hitler and state his case about the condition of his armored units. This speech would confirm the impression that Jodl presumably had already planted in the führer's mind, that Panzer Group 2 could pursue only limited objectives south of the Pripet and that at least part of the panzer group should be retained by Army Group Center and refitted for use later as a spearhead against Moscow.

The possibility exists that von Bock may have received advance warning about the Halder–Jodl agreement and that he may have briefed Guderian about this danger before the panzer general's flight to East Prussia. At 10:30 on the morning of August 23, before the Borisov conference, Greiffenberg, the chief of operations of Army Group Center, telephoned Guderian and told him that some of his units might have to go south toward Nezhin and Konotop. Greiffenberg: "What if this is required of you?" Guderian: "Then I will ask to be relieved." Greiffenberg: "What if your supplies can be sent through Roslavl–Gomel, then could you do it?" Guderian: "That is still too far. . . . By going only half that distance I could be in Moscow. I could take the whole panzer group there. . . . I hope this thing has not been ordered already." Greiffenberg: "It has not been ordered yet."[76]

Actually, by August 23, Guderian's visit to Hitler was superfluous as far as Halder was concerned, and he only agreed to this idea because of von Bock's adamant insistence.[77] Halder may have been afraid to push von Bock too far on this issue, and he may have yielded to the commander of Army Group Center and allowed Guderian to make his fateful journey, hoping that Guderian would be caught unawares by the turn of events. Or he may have believed that the panzer general would merely speak his piece and leave. Yet, knowing that Hitler was highly sympathetic to the views of "front soldiers," he should have been aware of the risk. Brauchitsch's warning to Guderian before his conference with Hitler was another sign that Halder was worried about what the panzer general might do. It is open to conjecture what compelled Halder to go along with von Bock on this matter; it was a decision that Halder would regret for the rest of his life.

GUDERIAN'S COUP IN EAST PRUSSIA

When Guderian arrived at the Wolfschanze, he was ushered into a room where he met Hitler in the presence of a large number of officers, including Keitel, Jodl, and Schmundt. It struck him as peculiar that no one from the OKH was in attendance, not Brauchitsch, Halder, or anyone else. It would not have taken an overclever man to figure out that something very strange was in the wind, and Guderian must have known from the moment he stepped into the conference room that Halder was trying to use him as a tool. The chief of the general staff had, however, met his match in Guderian.

The panzer general began the evening with a report to Hitler about the condition and the situation of his panzer group.[78] When he finished, Hitler asked him if he still thought his units could undertake yet another important task, and Guderian replied that "if the troops are given a major objective, the importance of which is apparent to every soldier, yes." Then Hitler asked whether Guderian meant Moscow when he used the phrase "major objective," and Guderian launched into a long explanation of why he thought Moscow should be the primary target. The panzer general told Hitler that he knew the troops in the field and that it was important for their morale that they be given Moscow as their goal. Guderian also used some other military and economic arguments to support his position as to the importance of the Soviet capital. But it was probably Guderian's insistence on the necessity of taking Moscow in order to bolster the morale of the ordinary soldiers that really affected Hitler. He, too, had been in the trenches and he knew how important morale was, and thus he was not inclined to ignore Guderian's comments.

After listening patiently to the panzer general, not interrupting him a single time, Hitler then repeated some phrases that he must have gotten from Göring about the danger of the "Crimean aircraft carrier" to the Rumanian oil fields. He also charged that his generals knew nothing about the economics of war. Finally, the führer stated that Kiev must fall, and that the capture of this city would be the next primary goal. According to Guderian, "All those present nodded in agreement with every sentence Hitler uttered, while I was left alone with my point of view."[79] The panzer general then recorded that he asked Hitler for permission to keep his panzer group intact so that he could carry out his task in the Ukraine quickly before the beginning of the fall rainy season. Hitler gladly acceded to Guderian's request.

The following day Guderian reported to Halder on the results of the last evening's conference, whereupon the chief of the general staff, according to the panzer general, "suffered a complete nervous collapse" and began to heap all sorts of abuse on his head. Then Halder telephoned von Bock and cursed Guderian for his unwillingness to split up his panzer group.[80] It was very hard for

Halder to believe that Guderian had not pleaded the weakness of his units and insisted to Hitler that Panzer Group 2 was not strong enough to carry out a wide-ranging maneuver around Kiev:

> Guderian's report of yesterday [at the meeting at Borisov on the afternoon of August 23] was designed to give the OKH leverage to restrict the operation to the south. After he saw that Hitler was convinced about the necessity of the operation, he believed that it was his duty to perform the impossible and carry out Hitler's wishes.

> This conversation showed with shattering clarity how irresponsibly official reports have been used.

> The army commander in chief has issued a sharply worded order regarding truthfulness in reports, but this will do no good. A person's character cannot be altered by orders.[81]

On June 29 Halder had boldly stated that he hoped officers like Guderian would disobey orders, if need be, in order to do "the right thing," that is, push ahead to Moscow as rapidly as possible.[82] The command structure that Halder had created in Army Group Center in early July had been intended to give Guderian and Hoth the maximum amount of freedom to forge ahead eastward without interference from above. Halder may have been right about Guderian's character, but the chief of the general staff was himself largely responsible for encouraging him to act in the way that he did. The British historian Alan Clark is correct in writing that Guderian's refusal to allow even a part of his armored strength to stay in Army Group Center while he carried out the Kiev encirclement may have been crucially important during the final push on Moscow, which began only at the end of September. Clark pointed out that Guderian's conference with Hitler on August 23 finished off his relationship with Halder, for the chief of the general staff believed that Hitler's promise to the panzer general not to divide his command amounted to nothing more than a bribe on the part of the führer that Guderian accepted.[83]

Göring and Jodl would still be able to convince Hitler to resume the thrust on Moscow after Kiev, but then it would be too late in the year for the attempt to have any real chance of success. It seems safe to say also that Hitler's final decision about Moscow in September would not have been made had Guderian not given voice to his emotions regarding the intangible importance of the Soviet capital. The damage that had been done to the formulation of strategy and the conduct of the war simply could not be repaired. The mistakes that had already been made up to August 23 would only be compounded later. A major catastrophe, vaster by far than what was in progress at Yelnia, could not be postponed for long.

CHAPTER 7

STALIN AND KIEV,
HITLER AND MOSCOW

STALIN'S MISTAKE

 By the end of July, Zhukov considered the situation along
the western approaches to Moscow to be well in hand. Not only
had additional forces been sent to the Western Front from the
Supreme Command reserves, but units had also been transferred
to the Smolensk area from the Ukraine and the Orel Military
District. Beyond this, the Germans had been temporarily checked
at Velikie Luki, Yelnia, and Gomel and, after July 14, the Supreme
Command had ordered the construction of another line of defense
for Moscow with three new armies: the Thirty-second, Thirty-
third, and Thirty-fourth. These armies would occupy the line
Volokolamsk–Mozhaisk–Maloyaroslavets and later Kaluga. This
barrier would become known as the Mozhaisk line of defense. The
units deployed here, for the time being, were directly subordinated
to the command staff of the Moscow Military District headed by
Lt. Gen. P. A. Artemev.[1] The Mozhaisk line of defense was thinly
manned in August and September, but as the Red Army began to
fall back eastward in October, the density of the forces along the
line began to increase significantly.

 On July 29, Zhukov reported to Stalin in the presence of L. Z.
Mekhlis, the chief of the Main Political Administration of the Red
Army (PRU) and informed him that a continued German advance

245

from the Smolensk area toward Moscow was not likely. The chief of the general staff knew that the German losses around Smolensk had been heavy and he did not believe that Army Group Center had any remaining reserves to strengthen its northern and southern flanks.[2] Zhukov correctly saw that the weakest and most dangerous Russian sector was in the area of F. I. Kuznetsov's Central Front, then covering the approaches to Unecha and Gomel with the Thirteenth and Twenty-first armies.[3] He told Stalin that the Central Front should be given three additional armies, one each from the neighboring Western and Southwestern fronts and one more from the Supreme Command reserve. These units would also have to be given extra artillery, presumably from the reserves. Stalin, however, was opposed to any weakening of the direct route to Moscow, even though Zhukov pointed out that within twelve or fifteen days another eight full divisions, including one tank division, could be brought up from the Far East, which would result in an overall strengthening of the Western Front in a short time. Furthermore, Zhukov said that the entire Central Front should be pulled back behind the Dnepr and no less than five reinforced divisions deployed in a second echelon behind the junction of the Central and Southwestern fronts. In conclusion, Zhukov said, "Kiev will have to be surrendered." He also expressed his opinion that the Yelnia salient ought to be eliminated right away in order to prevent any possibility of a renewed German thrust against Moscow in the near future.

The suggestion to surrender Kiev probably cost Zhukov his position as chief of the general staff. Stalin had no intention of giving up Kiev without a fight, and moreover, he was still convinced that the Wehrmacht was not yet through with Moscow. In order to show his displeasure with Zhukov and at the same time demonstrate his determination not to weaken the Western Front, Stalin dismissed Zhukov from his post and replaced him with Marshal B. M. Shaposhnikov, who was then the representative of the Supreme Command attached to Timoshenko's staff. The demoted Zhukov was sent to command the Reserve Front and given the personal assignment by Stalin to eliminate the Yelnia salient, a task that was, as we have seen, performed with some finesse.

Stalin's preoccupation with the defense of Moscow, despite the push of Panzer Group 2 and the Second Army southward, appeared in a conversation that he had on August 12 with A. I.

Eremenko, then deputy commander of the Western Front.[4] Summoned to the Supreme Command headquarters in Moscow late at night, Eremenko was first given a briefing by the new chief of the general staff. Shaposhnikov explained that the Supreme Command expected a Crimean offensive in the immediate future and also a push by Panzer Group 2 from Mogilev and Gomel toward Briansk, Orel, and Moscow. Stalin then asked Eremenko which assignment he preferred, Briansk or the Crimea. Eremenko replied that he wanted to be sent where the enemy was most likely to use armor, for he himself had commanded mechanized forces and understood mobile tactics. Eremenko was thus dispatched to command the Briansk Front, which was created on August 16, and he was given the specific orders to prepare to stop the resumption of the German offensive against Moscow expected momentarily. The Briansk Front was formed from the Fiftieth and Thirteenth armies and had about twenty divisions, although the Thirteenth Army was far under strength. To the north of the Briansk Front was Zhukov's Reserve Front with the Twenty-fourth, Thirty-first, Thirty-second, Thirty-third, Thirty-fourth, and Forty-third armies, and to the south of it was Kuznetsov's Central Front, now composed of the Third and Twenty-first armies. The original Third Army had been virtually wiped out in the Bialystok salient in June, but it was reconstituted from the Supreme Command reserves in August and assigned to the Central Front. The Fiftieth Army also was a new unit making its appearance for the first time in August, as was the Forty-third Army of Zhukov's command. Altogether, the Briansk Front was assigned a stretch of 230 kilometers, roughly from south of Smolensk to Novgorod–Severskii.[5]

Zhukov's anxiety about the German's intentions grew after Guderian sent the XXIVth Panzer Corps south toward Starodub and Unecha on August 16, after the encirclement at Krichev. On August 17, Guderian broke through the front of the weak Thirteenth Army of Maj. Gen. K. D. Golubev and cut the Briansk–Gomel rail line, placing the entire Briansk Front in a difficult position.[6] Panzer Group 2 had exploited the success at Krichev after August 12 to drive a wedge between the Reserve and the Central fronts, and this gap in the Russian line widened as a result of the pullback of the Twenty-first Army from Gomel. The Supreme Command had created the Briansk Front on August 16 in order to prevent Guderian from passing between the Reserve and Central

fronts and pushing straight to Moscow from the south through
Briansk, as indeed the German panzer general wanted to do, but
contrary to Stalin's expectations, Panzer Group 2 continued its
drive to the south against the hapless Thirteenth Army (see Figure
35).[7]

Eremenko's armies had been supposed to hit the southern
flank of Guderian's panzer group as it moved north and east toward Moscow, but now the Briansk Front itself and the weakest
army in that front had become the direct object of Guderian's
assault.[8] Zhukov sent a warning telegram to Stalin on August 18,
spurred by the threat of disaster to the entire Southwestern Front
in the Ukraine with its Fifth, Sixth, Twelfth, and Twenty-sixth
armies—in all some forty-four divisions.[9] Although Zhukov had
been demoted and was no longer chief of the general staff, he still
was an official member of the Supreme Command staff, and he
now used this position to try to convince Stalin again that his assessment of the situation on July 29 was correct: that Kiev and the
Southwestern Front were in imminent danger of encirclement.[10]

In his message to Stalin, Zhukov contended that the enemy
knew that the main force of the Red Army was now being deployed
on the approaches to Moscow and that the Germans considered it
to be too dangerous to proceed directly toward the capital while a
threat existed to the flanks of Army Group Center from the direction of Velikie Luki in the north and from the Central Front in the
south. Zhukov predicted that Army Group Center would go over
to an active defense against the Western and Reserve fronts and
would turn Panzer Group 2 to the south to hit the Central, Southwestern, and Southern fronts. The goal of the enemy would be to
destroy the Central Front and push to the region of Chernigov,
Konotop, and Priluki and hit the Southwestern Front, defending
Kiev, from the rear. After the fall of Kiev, German mobile units
would be able to bypass the Briansk forests and push on Moscow
from the south and also, at the same time, strike toward the
Donets Basin. In order to foil the enemy's plans, Zhukov proposed
that a powerful group be concentrated in the area Glukhov–
Chernigov–Konotop in the northern Ukraine along the Desna and
Seim rivers, which would thus be in a position to land a hard blow
on Guderian's eastern flank as his panzer group moved south. This
additional force was to be supplied by the Far Eastern Front and
Moscow Zone of Defense (MZO) and other internal military dis-

tricts and should have eleven or twelve rifle divisions, two or three cavalry divisions, no less than a thousand tanks and four hundred to five hundred aircraft. The size of the reinforcements requested by Zhukov show clearly how far the mobilization of the strategic reserve had progressed by mid-August, and there can be little doubt that the thousand tanks and the divisions asked for by him

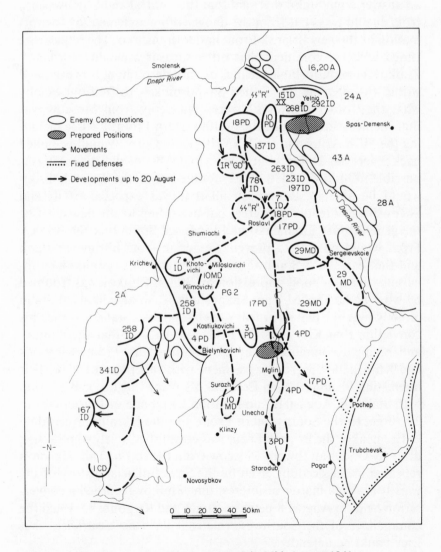

Figure 35. The Position of Panzer Group 2 in Mid–August 1941

were not all that the Supreme Command had at its disposal. The German high command, of course, had no idea of the magnitude of the Russian reserves they would be facing soon and, needless to say, the Wehrmacht could not match the quantities of personnel and material replacements that had begun to appear on the eastern side of the fronts.

Not long after the dispatch of his telegram, Zhukov received an answer from Stalin that said that the Central and Southwestern fronts could be saved from the danger of encirclement by the formation of the new Briansk Front under Eremenko. The return wire ended with the comment that other measures would be taken.[11] Zhukov's uncomfortable feelings did not desert him, however, and within two days he telephoned Shaposhnikov to find out exactly what the "other measures" were. The reply from Moscow was that the northern wing of the Southwestern Front, a force including the Fifth Army and the XXVIIth Rifle Corps, would be pulled back over the Dnepr, but Kiev would be held for as long as possible. Zhukov said that he doubted that the Briansk Front would be able to accomplish all that was expected of it, and Shaposhnikov tended to agree, but according to the new chief of the general staff, Eremenko had promised Stalin that the Briansk Front would be able to prevent Guderian from hitting the flank and the rear of the Southwestern Front and this promise had apparently made a good impression on Stalin. Zhukov was troubled by what he had heard from Shaposhnikov, so he contacted Stalin directly over the high-frequency telephone line. Stalin affirmed his conviction that Kiev must be held, and he said that the military and political commanders of the Southwestern Front, Kirponos and Khrushchev, were in agreement with this point of view. It is interesting to note that in Eremenko's record of his conversation with Stalin on August 12, no mention was made of Panzer Group 2's threat to the Southwestern Front and the Ukraine. According to Eremenko, the Briansk Front was established solely to prevent a drive by Guderian toward Moscow from the south. This version is repeated in the account given by the Soviet official history of the war. It is also a matter of interest that Zhukov recorded a conversation held on August 8 between Stalin and Kirponos in which the commander of the Southwestern Front gave his assurances that Kiev could be defended.[12]

Stalin had made an iron-clad decision about Kiev and he would not yield an inch on the question. Like Hitler, Stalin would take advice from those he trusted, but the Soviet dictator, once his mind was made up, would not waver on important issues. In this way, Stalin's leadership was much stronger than Hitler's; the führer was unable to adhere for long to one plan.

By the second week in July the Russian Supreme Command had come to believe that a greater amount of coordination was needed between the various army fronts that were facing three large German army groups. As a result, on July 10 the Supreme Command ordered the creation of three special "front groups": (1) the Northwestern Direction under Marshal K. E. Voroshilov and Commissar A. A. Zhdanov, which had control over the Northern and Northwestern fronts plus the Northern and Baltic fleets; (2) the Western Direction under Marshal Timoshenko and N. A. Bulganin, which controlled the Western and later the Reserve fronts (Timoshenko still retained direct command over the Western Front); and (3) the Southwestern Direction under Marshal Budënny and N. S. Khrushchev, which controlled the Southwestern, Southern, and later the Central fronts plus the Black Sea Fleet.[13] This command structure would prove to be troublesome in the near future, as friction grew between Moscow and the directional and front staffs and opportunities for misunderstandings multiplied, now that another level of organization had been created.

It was Budënny who convinced Stalin to pull back all of the Southwestern Front to the eastern bank of the Dnepr. The Supreme Command order issued on August 19 directed the Southwestern Front to defend the Dnepr line from Loev to Perevolochna and to prevent the enemy from advancing toward Chernigov, Konotop, and Kharkov.[14] Stalin's assent to Budënny's request demonstrated that he realized the potential threat to the rear of the Southwestern Front posed by Guderian. But in his telephone conversation with Zhukov a few days later, the Soviet dictator reaffirmed his decision not to yield Kiev. Neither Zhukov nor Budënny believed Kiev could be held if Panzer Group 2 continued its march to the south, but for better or worse, Stalin insisted that the Southwestern Front do everything it could to defend the Ukraine. In the meantime, Stalin and Shaposhnikov were mainly concerned about the danger to Moscow, and the Supreme Command continued to do everything it could to protect the capital from the west and the southwest.

In order to allow the Briansk Front more latitude for maneuver, Stalin telephoned Eremenko on August 24 and asked him if he agreed that the Central Front should be abolished and its forces added to those of his command. Eremenko concurred and so the Central Front's Third and Twenty-first armies were combined into one army, the Twenty-first, and subordinated to the Briansk Front. In addition, the Briansk Front received two new rifle divisions made up of about twenty-seven thousand men that had just been brought up to the Desna River. Also on August 24, Shaposhnikov informed the commander of the Briansk Front that Guderian's main blow would fall upon the northern flank of the front, against the 217th and 279th rifle divisions of the Fiftieth Army, probably the next day—first toward Briansk, then Moscow. Guderian's continued movement southward, however, struck at Pochep or at the southern flank of the Fiftieth Army, not at the northern, as Eremenko had expected (see Figure 36). These developments forced him to conclude that the Supreme Command had been taken by surprise by the switch of Panzer Group 2's thrust to the south. This impression was strengthened by the fact that on August 30, the Supreme Command ordered an attack by the Briansk and Reserve fronts that was to begin with an advance of the Fiftieth Army on Roslavl. An attack against Starodub and Guderian's main force was also ordered, but this was to be carried out by the weak Thirteenth Army, and no good result could have been expected from it.[15] Eremenko had been ordered to prepare a defense of the approaches to Moscow from the southwest, not to stop a German push toward Chernigov–Konotop–Priluki and against the northern flank of the Southwestern Front. It was for this reason that the Briansk Front "permitted" Guderian to push southward largely unmolested. Eremenko had been told by the Supreme Command to expect Panzer Group 2 to turn to the north and east, to hit Briansk and then move toward Moscow, and this was what he was trying to prevent.

When the Fifth Army of the Southwestern Front began its withdrawal over the Dnepr, the commander of the army, Maj. Gen. M. I. Potapov, elected not to turn his northern flank toward the north to defend Chernigov—a serious mistake, as von Weichs's

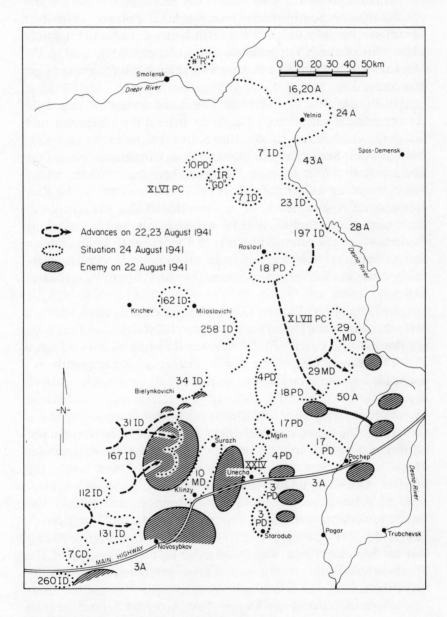

Figure 36. Guderian Continues His March South

Second Army began a push toward that city after August 25.[16] This advance by the German Second Army endangered the rear of the entire Fifth Army, which was trying to establish defenses along the eastern bank of the river from Loev to Okuninov. At the end of August, the Southwestern Front ordered Potapov to protect Chernigov, but by August 31 the Fifth Army was able to send only weak units of the XVth Rifle Corps to this city. Maj. Gen. K. S. Moskalenko was named commander of the XVth Rifle Corps on September 3.[17]

The order that the Supreme Command issued on August 19 for the withdrawal of the Fifth Army behind the Dnepr was not the only action taken to save the Southwestern Front and Kiev from disaster. Soon thereafter the Supreme Command directed the Southwestern Front to create a new army, the Fortieth, which was to be made up, in part, from units first brought to the Kiev area around August 10.[18] The commander of this new army was Maj. Gen. K. P. Podlas, and he was given the task of blocking Guderian along a defense line that ran from north of Bakhmach and Konotop to Shostka and from there along the Desna River to Stepanovki. The problems faced by the Fortieth Army were, however, severe.

On August 26 Panzer Group 2 succeeded in establishing a bridgehead over the Desna near Novgorod–Severskii, and the eastern flank of the Twenty-first Army was thus imperiled (see Figure 37). The commander of the army, Kuznetsov, subsequently ordered his units to continue the retreat begun on August 15 from around Gomel. The first stage of the retreat had carried the Twenty-first Army over the Dnepr, and now it would cross the Desna, seeking to avoid encirclement. Kuznetsov, however, did not inform his neighbor to the east and south, Podlas, the commander of the new Fortieth Army, about his decision.[19] As a result, the Fortieth Army was unable to advance against Guderian's bridgehead near Novgorod–Severskii from Konotop, and Podlas was forced to order a withdrawal toward the southeast. The Twenty-first Army was now completely cut off from the Briansk Front, and on September 6 it was transferred to the command of the Southwestern Front. In this way, a large gap opened between the two fronts.

Kirponos ordered the Twenty-first Army on September 6 to stop its retreat and attack the rearward areas of the 3rd and 4th

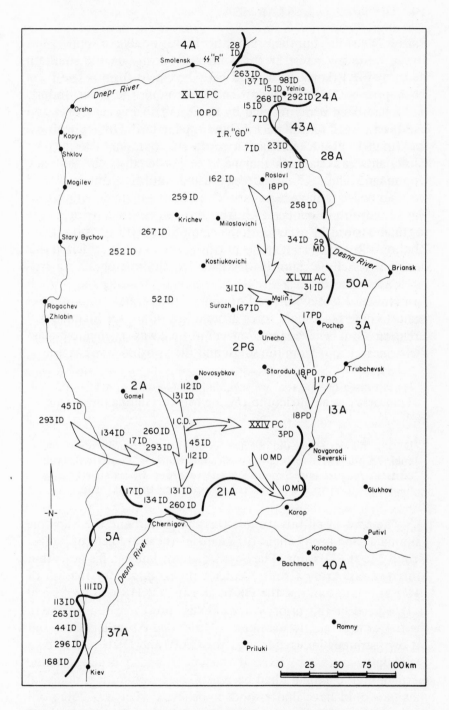

Figure 37. Panzer Group 2 Crosses the Desna at Novgorod–Severskii

255

Panzer Divisions, but the Briansk Front was unable to support this attack.[20] Since August 28 the Thirteenth Army on the southern flank of the Briansk Front had been trying to form a line from Pochep to south of Starodub and then along the River Sudost, but it had been badly mauled by the XLVIIth Panzer Corps and had been forced to pull back behind the Desna.[21] On September 2 the Briansk Front launched a series of counterattacks against Guderian's eastern flank that had been ordered by the Supreme Command. These counterattacks lasted until September 12 and were supposed to have been carried out in two main directions: toward Starodub in cooperation with the Twenty-first Army to the south and toward Roslavl with the help of four rifle divisions from Zhukov's Reserve Front to the north. Eremenko has criticized this decision, which he claimed was made by Zhukov, because it frittered away the Briansk Front's strength by sending the Fiftieth Army toward Roslavl instead of concentrating the counterattacks against Guderian's main force around Starodub (see Figure 38).[22] Eremenko still believed that Panzer Group 2 was striving to bypass the Briansk Front from the south and then push toward Moscow:

> Here it must be said that we regarded the German attack south of Trubchevsk as an attempt to envelop Moscow during the summer of 1941 . . .

> During this period we did not have complete information about the enemy's plans. Therefore, the push southwards by Guderian's tank units in August and September was regarded by us strictly as a maneuver to strip the [southern] flank of the Briansk Front.[22]

The root of all this trouble was that Stalin and the Supreme Command had been caught off guard by the movement of Panzer Group 2 to the Ukraine. The Soviet dictator knew in his heart that Moscow was Army Group Center's prime target for the fall of 1941; after all, had not the OKW and the OKH, with its general staff, agreed on this priority? The ability, however, of a general in the field, Guderian, to manipulate Hitler and essentially carry out his own strategy independent of the OKW and OKH had thrown Stalin into confusion. Even if the underhanded dealings in the German high command had been explained to him, it is doubtful that he would have understood or believed what was going on. Stalin's political police apparatus inspired a wholly different kind

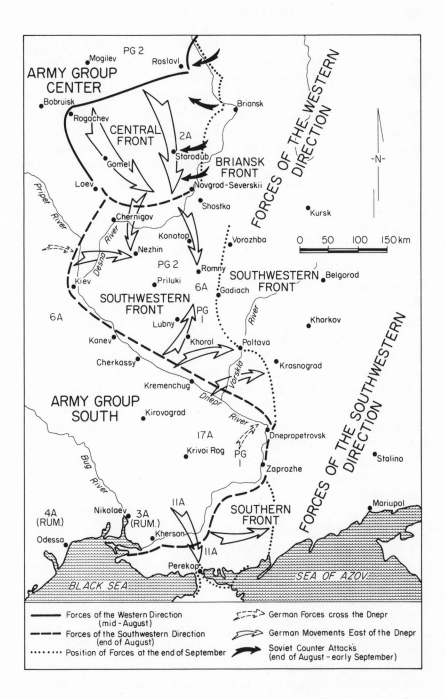

Figure 38. Russian Map Showing the Attacks of the Briansk Front against
Guderian's Left Flank

257

of "loyalty" in the Red Army. He probably could not have imagined that Hitler and the Nazis did not have the same kind of control over the German armed forces.

As for the certainty that Stalin had about the plans of the German high command, there can be little doubt. The *Rote Kapelle* ("Red Choir") Soviet spy network was functioning in high gear inside the OKW, with Hans Schulze–Boysen in the Air Ministry, among others, transmitting streams of high-level intelligence to Moscow. Much of this information was gleaned from OKW cypher clerks who had access to information dealing with military movements and plans at all levels. The penetration of the Luftwaffe staff by Soviet agents was particularly valuable to them since, as we have seen, Göring and his subordinates, such as Kesselring, were not only aware of strategy but were in fact active in making it. The German Abwehr, or counterintelligence agency, under Admiral Canaris was not aware of the *Rote Kapelle* until late 1941 and did not effectively begin to break it up until early to mid-1942, but by then much of the real damage had already been done. One Soviet spy station was caught transmitting details of the Stalingrad operation a month before it was to be carried out. After the war, Abwehr officers admitted that only the surface of the Soviet spy net had been scratched. Other sources, such as "Lucy," who may have been Hitler's party chief, Martin Bormann, continued to function throughout the war and no doubt after the war.[24] Stalin's mistaken belief in the course of German strategy for 1941 would, however, be set right before the end of the year. The German attempt on Moscow would not come in September and October, but rather in November and December, thus the Wehrmacht would play right into Stalin's hands. But first the Red Army would have to suffer for Stalin's error, and suffer it did at Kiev.

THE FALL OF KIEV

Guderian's continued drive southward in the first part of September produced an ever-growing level of uneasiness in the Soviet Supreme Command, but Stalin still could not accept the fact that all of Panzer Group 2 was being used in the Kiev operation and that, temporarily at least, Moscow was in no danger. On September 7 the Southwestern Front had flashed another warning to the Supreme Command and asked for permission to pull back the Fifth Army behind the Desna. Shaposhnikov then contacted

Budënny and found him of the same opinion.[25] The next day Zhukov was summoned to Stalin's office, where he was told that he would be sent to Leningrad; upon Zhukov's recommendation, Stalin selected Timoshenko as Budënny's replacement as commander of the Southwestern Direction. Lieutenant Gen. I. S. Konev was to occupy Timoshenko's position with respect to the Western Front. Just as Zhukov was preparing to take his leave, Stalin queried him about what he thought the Germans would do next. The former chief of the general staff replied that, since Guderian and von Weichs had already advanced as far as Chernigov and Novgorod–Severskii, it would not be long before the Twenty-first Army was shoved back even farther, and the Germans would thus be able to penetrate to the rear of the Southwestern Front. He also prophesied that the bridgehead established by the Seventeenth Army of Army Group South on the eastern bank of the Dnepr near Kremenchug, below Kiev, could be used as the starting place for a mobile strike force that would move to the north and east to link up with Panzer Group 2 (see Figure 39). Zhukov advised Stalin to transfer all Russian forces over to the eastern bank of the Dnepr and deploy all available reserves in the Konotop area for use against Guderian. Stalin then asked, "What about Kiev?" and Zhukov answered, "Sad as it may be, Kiev will have to be given up. We have no other way out." Stalin then telephoned Shaposhnikov and told him what he had just heard. Zhukov did not listen to the entire conversation, but Stalin said that the problem would be discussed later with the Southwestern Front staff.[26]

It is obvious that Zhukov's words had an effect on Stalin, for on the next day, September 9, Shaposhnikov informed the Southwestern Front that the Supreme Command had decided that the Fifth Army and the right wing of the Thirty-seventh Army, defending Kiev, must withdraw to the eastern bank of the Dnepr and turn their fronts to face Panzer Group 2 coming down from the north. This maneuver, however, proved to be very difficult, as on September 7 Guderian crossed the Seim River and drove southward toward Bosna and Romny.[27] Kirponos now called Budënny on September 10 (at a time when the whole northern wing of the Southwestern Front appeared to be caving in) after Chernigov had fallen to the Second Army on September 8, and asked for immediate reinforcements, especially for Podlas's Fortieth Army, which

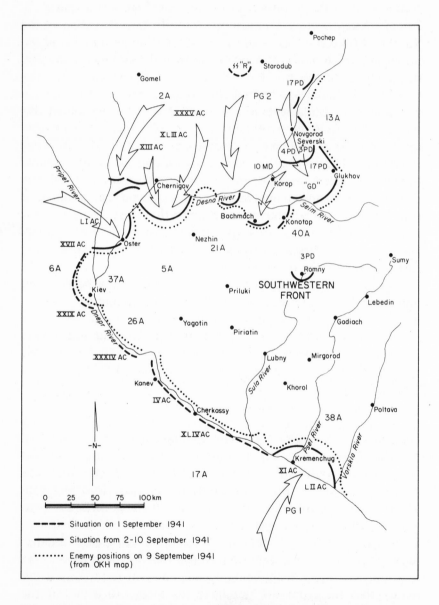

Figure 39. Panzer Group 1 Prepares to Strike North from Kremenchug

260

was now in a desperate situation along the Seim River in the Konotop sector. Already on this day, September 10, the 3rd Panzer Division had taken Romny on the Sula River, well to the south of the Seim and almost due east of Kiev.[28] Budënny had to reply, however, that the Supreme Command had placed no more reserves at the disposal of either the Southwestern Direction or the Southwestern Front. As a stopgap, Shaposhnikov authorized the movement of two rifle divisions from the Twenty-sixth Army, immediately to the south of Kiev, toward the Fortieth Army in order to help stop Guderian's breakthrough in the region of Bachmach and Konotop. Budënny and Kirponos, however, considered this tactic to be wholly unsatisfactory, as this would leave the Twenty-sixth Army with only three rifle divisions to hold a 150-kilometer front. The situation below Kiev was now also worsening rapidly because the Twenty-sixth Army's neighbor to the south, the Thirty-eighth Army, had been unable to eliminate the German bridgehead near Kremenchug between the Psel and Vorskla rivers on the eastern bank of the Dnepr. It was expected that at any moment Panzer Group 1 would burst out of this bridgehead and plunge north and east to meet Guderian.[29]

In the early morning of September 11 the Southwestern Front sent the following telegram to the Supreme Command:

A tank group of the enemy has penetrated to Romny and Graivoron [not far west of Belgorod]. The 40th and 21st armies are not able to check this group. We request that forces be sent immediately from the Kiev area to halt the enemy's movement and that a general withdrawal of the front [to behind the Psel River line] be undertaken. Please send approval by radio.[30]

Around 2:00 A.M. Shaposhnikov telephoned Kirponos and told him that the Southwestern Front had to remain in position, not one division could be removed from Kiev. Kirponos then immediately contacted Budënny. Some hours later, Budënny conversed with Shaposhnikov, but the chief of the general staff was unmoved, describing the requested pullback of the Southwestern Front as "premature." Budënny thereupon dispatched another telegram to Stalin saying that only strong forces could prevent the Southwestern Front from being cut off and surrounded, an eventuality that the front did not have the means to avoid. If the Supreme Command could not deploy the necessary reserves in the area of the Southwestern Front, said Budënny, the front must be permitted to retreat to the east.[31]

Somewhat later in the morning Stalin, Shaposhnikov, and Timoshenko telephoned the staff of the Southwestern Front, Kirponos, Burmistenko, and Tupikov. Stalin said that if the front withdrew from the Dnepr, the Germans would rapidly secure strong footholds on the eastern bank. Consequently, the Southwestern Front, during its withdrawal, would have to face enemy pressure from three directions instead of two; from the west as well as from the north around Konotop and from the south around Kremenchug. Then, he said, the encirclement of the front would follow if the Germans coordinated the thrusts of their panzer groups east of Kiev. Stalin recalled that the earlier withdrawal of the Southwestern Front from Berdichev and Novgorad–Volynskii to behind the Dnepr had resulted in the loss of two armies at Uman, the Sixth and the Twelfth; the retreat had turned into a rout, allowing the Germans to cross the Dnepr on the heels of the fleeing Red Army. A debacle of this sort must not be repeated. Stalin explained that, in his opinion, the proposed retreat of the Southwestern Front would be dangerous for two reasons. In the first place, the Psel River line had not been prepared for defense, and in the second place, any withdrawal would be risky unless something were done first about Guderian's panzer group around Konotop. Instead of an immediate retreat, Stalin made three proposals: (1) that the Southwestern Front use all available forces to regroup and cooperate with Eremenko to hit toward Konotop; (2) that a defense be prepared on the eastern bank of the Psel with five or six rifle divisions and that the front artillery be brought behind this line and positioned to face the northern and southern approaches; and (3) that after the first two conditions had been fulfilled, preparations be made to abandon Kiev and to destroy the bridges over the Dnepr. While the withdrawal was actually underway, a screening force would have to remain on the Dnepr to protect the front from the west.[32]

In his answer to Stalin, Kirponos said that no withdrawal would take place without first discussing the situation with the Supreme Command. However, he did hope that since the front now exceeded eight hundred kilometers the Supreme Command would see fit to send him some reserve forces. Kirponos referred to what Shaposhnikov had said on September 10, that two rifle divisions from the Twenty-sixth Army should be sent northward to help Podlas and Kuznetsov fight Guderian's panzers pushing toward Romny. He stated further that the Southwestern Front had no more units to spare for this task as another two and a half rifle divisions had been sent in the direction of Chernigov to help the Fifth Army. In regard to reinforcements, Kirponos only asked that promises already made by the Supreme Command be fulfilled. Stalin's final statement was that though Budënny favored a pullback to the Psel, Shaposhnikov opposed it, and that for the present Kiev was not to be evacuated or the bridges destroyed without the approval of the Supreme Command. He announced his decision to replace Budënny with Timoshenko as commander of the Southwestern Direction. Budënny's career, however, was far from finished. He was assigned command over the Reserve Front defending the approach to Moscow in the Yelnia–Roslavl region. In 1942 he took charge of the operations in the Caucasus.[33]

Timoshenko had been present when Stalin ordered Kirponos by telephone not to withdraw from Kiev, and the new commander approved of this decision. His optimism on September 11 was partly based on the fact that he knew some reinforcements were on the way. These reserves were, however, inadequate to stem the German tide: only one rifle division and two tank brigades with one hundred tanks. Timoshenko may also have believed that the counteroffensive by the Briansk Front ordered by Stalin against Panzer Group 2 might bring good results, but it is hard to imagine how he could have put much faith in such an operation. The counterattacks by the Briansk Front ordered on August 30 had brought scanty returns because the front had been expected to push in two different directions, toward Starodub and Roslavl, simultaneously. A new counteroffensive ordered by Stalin to begin on September 14 was to be directed solely toward Roslavl and the southern flank of Army Group Center, not toward Konotop at all, as he had promised Kirponos over the telephone on September 11.[34] On September 10 the gap between the Briansk and the Southwestern fronts had widened to sixty kilometers, and Eremenko was correct in saying that the Supreme Command knew there were no forces at hand strong enough to close this breach. All of Eremenko's tank brigades together had only twenty machines remaining in running condition.[35] The question now must be asked: Why did Stalin, Shaposhnikov, and Timoshenko order the Southwestern Front to hold Kiev at all costs, what purpose could this act of mass sacrifice possibly have served?

Stalin had now been forced to use Kiev in the same way that he had used the Bialystok salient in June, only this time the gamble was far more risky. The large hole that would soon be torn in the Red Army's defenses in the Ukraine simply could not be patched up. Too much of the strategic reserve had already been used to bolster the front along the Dnepr and the Dvina ahead of Army Group Center to allow the Supreme Command to save Kiev and Moscow at the same time. The sacrifice of Kiev would, however, exact from the Germans a very high price, greatly exceeding that of the Bialystok encirclement in lives, material, and most importantly, time. Stalin was right when he pointed out to Kirponos on September 11 the impossibility of withdrawing the entire Southwestern Front with its 677,000 troops behind the Psel River line in time to prevent its encirclement by Guderian and by von Kleist's Panzer Group 1. The Southwestern Front would have to stand and fight in the same way that the Third, Tenth, and Fourth armies had fought in the Bialystok salient.

Pavlov, prior to the earlier catastrophe, had not been told what the true task of his forces was to be. Stalin was always a man who played his cards very close to his chest, and he would not tell Kirponos, or for that matter Eremenko, what he really expected of them. Zhukov, Budënny, and Timoshenko, however, were in a position to know Stalin's true intentions and thus Zhukov lost his position as chief of the general staff in late July and Budënny was sacked on September 11. Timoshenko, who had apparently agreed with Stalin in early September, would lose his nerve by September 13 and place Stalin under an intense strain. Stalin could have Pavlov shot, but Zhukov, Budënny, and Timoshenko were men of a different sort. Stalin could put them in their place, but he could not liquidate them.

What if the Germans continued their offensive in the south, through the eastern Ukraine, to the Donets Basin and the Caucasus? What if the entire southern flank of the Red Army were to be rolled up and the offensive against Moscow by Army Group Center postponed until the following spring? What if all the careful defensive preparations to the north, west, and south of Moscow, the massing of the strategic reserves around the capital, had all been for naught? How could the Soviet Union survive without its industrial base in the south while Army Group Center remained intact east of the Dnepr, poised for a spring offensive against Moscow with the aid of three panzer groups? These were questions that Zhukov and the other generals must have put to Stalin, and for them he had no effective answer. His only hope must have been that the Germans would somehow choose to rupture themselves in a final assault on Moscow before the end of 1941. A vain hope, it would seem, after nearly all of Guderian's panzer group had been committed to the Ukraine in early September. If the XLVIth Panzer Corps had remained in Army Group Center, as Halder and Jodl wished, then Stalin's strategy would have seemed unquestionably correct to his generals. But as has been seen, Guderian had his way with Hitler on August 23, and all of his tanks were sent to the south except the 18th Panzer Division of the XLVIIth Panzer Corps, which Halder managed to retain in the rear near Roslavl as an Army Group reserve.[36] In this way, by mid-September, Stalin's plans were placed in extreme jeopardy, for it could not be certain that a German assault on Moscow would be carried out during the remainder of the year. As it turned out, what were probably the Soviet dictator's fondest dreams were realized.

On September 12 von Kleist unobtrusively sent his tanks across the Dnepr near Kremenchug, at a point a considerable distance downstream from Kiev. Panzer Group 1 then unleashed its fury against the 297th Rifle Division of the Russian Thirty-eighth Army and pushed north and east toward Khorol. As Guderian's units were already south of Romny, there could be no doubt about the German intentions (see Figure 40). Altogether on September 12 Army Group South had twenty divisions concentrated against the five rifle and four cavalry divisions of the Thirty-eighth Army on the southern flank of the Southwestern Front. There was no way now for that front to stop von Kleist; all available forces had been sent to the north in a futile effort to block Guderian.[37] North of Kiev, also, the situation had deteriorated badly during the previous two days. Under heavy pressure Potapov's Fifth Army had begun pulling back across the Desna, but when several divisions reached the river, it was discovered that the Germans already held the eastern bank. Some units, such as Moskalenko's XVth Rifle Corps, managed to cross the Desna south of Chernigov relatively unscathed, but for the most part, the Fifth Army suffered heavy

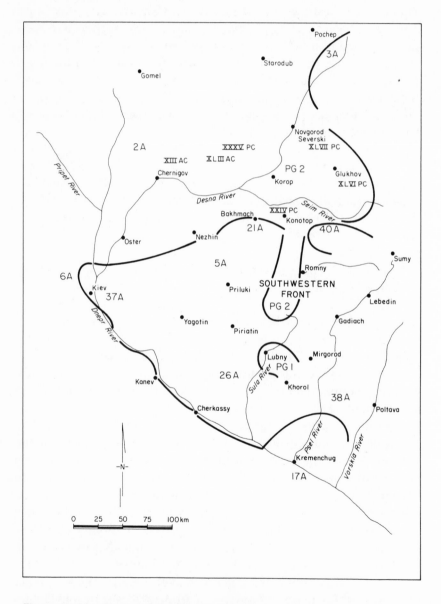

Figure 40. The Closing of the Kiev Encirclement

266

losses. The steadfastness of the Thirty-seventh Army around Kiev saved the Fifth Army from being cut off from the south.[38]

Now that the encirclement of Kiev and the entire Southwestern Front had become all but an accomplished fact, the front staff dispatched telegrams on the evening of September 13 presenting the situation in the gravest possible terms.[39] Somewhat later, in the early morning hours of September 14, the chief of staff of the front, Maj. Gen. V. I. Tupikov, on his own initiative sent a personal wire to Shaposhnikov that ended, "The catastrophe has begun and it should be obvious to you within a couple of days."[40] The chief of the general staff's reply, sent to both the front and directional commands, was immediate and harsh:

> Major General Tupikov has sent a panicky report to the general staff. The present situation demands calmness and self-control at all levels of command. It is necessary not to yield to panic. It is important that all vital positions be defended, especially the flank areas. It is necessary to stop the retreat of Kuznetsov [Twenty-first Army] and Potapov [Fifth Army]. It is vital to impress upon the entire staff of the front the need for continuing the battle. You must not look backwards, you must fulfill comrade Stalin's order of September 11.[41]

Shaposhnikov's answer was nothing less than a death sentence for the Southwestern Front. Now that two German panzer groups were actually linking up east of Kiev, there could be no question about the fate that was close at hand for the forces defending the middle Dnepr, yet faced with the indisputable fact that a disaster of enormous proportions was about to take place, Stalin and Shaposhnikov stood fast. The Southwestern Front would have to stand and fight, to die, in order to drain the Germans of material and deprive them of time—all in order to permit the deployment of the strategic reserve around Moscow to proceed unimpeded. But what if Hitler chose not to attack Moscow in 1941? Would all of Stalin's plans then collapse in ruins? Now that all of Panzer Group 2 had been sent to the Ukraine, it seemed as though Hitler had found the perfect antidote to the strategy that had proven so fruitful at Velikie Luki, Yelnia, Roslavl, and Gomel.

Since July, Stalin and Zhukov had been painstakingly preparing a strong defense of Moscow, a strategy that now appeared to be useless. Zhukov and Budënny believed that Army Group

South, strengthened by an additional panzer group, would have no trouble in overrunning all of the Soviet Union in the south up to the Volga, including the Caucasus. It was for this reason that they broke with Stalin and refused to agree with his adamant insistence not to allow a retreat of the Southwestern Front. Zhukov and Budënny could not accept a strategy that required that the 677,000 troops of the Southwestern Front be used in the same fashion as the three armies that had been sacrificed in the Bialystok salient. The first disaster had cost the Red Army about three hundred thousand casualties, a heavy price, yet not unbearable, but the prospective losses at Kiev might be intolerable. Unless the Germans chose to put around their own necks the noose that had been so carefully prepared for them around Moscow, there could be little hope of winning the war.

At the beginning of the Kiev catastrophe Stalin had relied on Shaposhnikov, Zhukov's replacement, and Timoshenko, Budënny's replacement, to do his bidding, but by September 15 Timoshenko also had begun to break under the strain. On that date the commander of the Southwestern Direction told Shaposhnikov in Moscow that he favored an immediate withdrawal for the front, an attitude that represented a complete reversal of the position he had taken on September 11 when he, Stalin, and the chief of the general staff had telephoned Kirponos and ordered his units to remain in place. The extent of Timoshenko's influence over Shaposhnikov at this point is uncertain, but the next day he returned to the Southwestern Direction headquarters near Poltava and called in I. Kh. Bagramian, chief of the Operations Staff of the Southwestern Front, for a conference.[42] At this conference, with N. S. Khrushchev also present, Timoshenko announced that a decision to allow the Southwestern Front to withdraw behind the Psel River would have to be made without delay while the enemy's ring of encirclement was not yet tight. After pacing the floor for a time, Timoshenko asserted that he was certain the Supreme Command would go along with such a decision, but there was simply no time to waste in securing confirmation from Moscow. Bagramian noted in his memoirs that Timoshenko appeared deeply troubled when he made this statement and obviously doubted the truth of what he had just said, as well he might, considering the language of Shaposhnikov's above-mentioned telegram.

When he finally managed to get hold of himself, Timoshenko ordered Bagramian to fly to Piriatin and give Kirponos an oral command to "abandon the Kiev fortified region and, leaving covering forces along the Dnepr, to begin immediately the pullback of the main force to behind the rearward line of defense [along the Psel River]."[43] Kirponos was also to be instructed not to attempt the withdrawal without first carrying out counterattacks in the Lubny and Romny areas in order to slow down Panzer Groups 1 and 2 as much as possible. There can be no question that Timoshenko lacked the authority to issue such an order, for it clearly violated Stalin's wishes. Hence he refused to give Bagramian any sort of written document, explaining to him that the flight would be very dangerous and no important written orders should be allowed to fall into enemy hands. Timoshenko was right on one point, the flight would be risky and the mission nearly came to grief when German patrol planes gave pursuit, but Bagramian was not fooled by the marshal's artificial excuses. Timoshenko could have been executed for contravening Stalin's orders and Bagramian could have shared his fate for relaying an unauthorized command. It was better not to incriminate oneself any more than necessary, so Timoshenko decided not to commit his order to paper. In the end, Timoshenko was not punished for his disobedience. The Southwestern Direction was abolished at the end of September, and he was made commander of the new Southwestern Front with the Fortieth and the recreated Twenty-first and Thirty-eighth armies.[44]

When the front chief of operations finally met with his commanding officer on September 17 in a forest grove north of Piriatin, Bagramian duly delivered Timoshenko's orders, but Kirponos decided not to act hastily. He asked Bagramian to produce a written command from headquarters. None existed, of course. Then, brushing aside Bagramian's objections, he chose to send a wire to Moscow requesting confirmation of the order instead of accepting his subordinate's word at face value. According to one Soviet general, this action by Kirponos was a fatal mistake.[45] Undoubtedly Timoshenko's order had come too late to save the bulk of the Southwestern Front, but the approval from the Supreme Command did not come for another full day, during the night of September 18 two days after the German encirclement of

Kiev had already occurred (see Figure 41).[46] Stalin had purposely delayed the withdrawal of the Southwestern Front until the German trap had been sprung. What appeared to Eremenko and Kirponos as uncertainty and procrastination and to the Germans as sheer stupidity actually was a desperate gamble on Stalin's part to win the war. The elimination of the Southwestern Front would cost the Germans much in terms of personnel, material, and time. Stalin was now certain that the strategic reserve could be mobilized and deployed in strength around Moscow, but all would depend on the enemy's next move. Stalin's willingness to sacrifice the Southwestern Front may have been foolhardy, as Zhukov believed, but if so, the Soviet dictator was easily surpassed in this respect by the German command. Guderian notes that Potapov, the commander of the Russian Fifth Army, was captured and that he himself had the opportunity to question him. When asked why his army had made no attempt to abandon Kiev until it was too late, the Russian general answered that such an order had been issued but later rescinded (presumably on September 11) and his forces were ordered to defend Kiev at all cost. Guderian and the other generals were amazed at this seeming ineptness on the Soviet side. Although wounded, Potapov survived the war, was freed by the Americans in 1945, and returned to Moscow.[47]

Despite the fact that by September 26 the Southwestern Front would largely cease to exist, some elements of the beleaguered armies did manage to escape eastward. A group of fifty men under Bagramian escaped to Godiach on September 24. Several thousand soldiers of the Fifth and Twenty-first armies also made their way to safety, including five hundred men of the Twenty-first Army staff headed by Kuznetsov. The commander of the Twenty-sixth Army, Lt. Gen. F. Ia. Kostenko, also escaped with a large group, as did a cavalry unit with four thousand men led by A. B. Borisov. Several corps commanders, including major generals K. S. Moskalenko and A. I. Lopatin, evaded the German trap as well. Kirponos and his staff, however, were not so lucky. They were all killed near Shumeikovo on September 20.[48] The Red Army had suffered its worst defeat of the war, but Guderian was right when he said that Kiev was only a tactical, not a strategic, victory even though the Russian losses had been enormous. The official German count of Russian prisoners taken around Kiev was 665,212, but Russian figures are in disagreement with this toll. According to

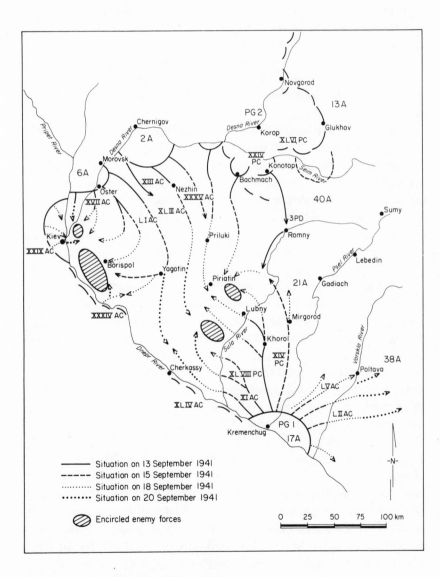

Figure 41. The End of the Battle of Kiev

271

the Soviet official history, the Kiev Military District had 677,085 troops at the beginning of the war. Of this number 150,541 were in the rearward areas, beyond the encirclement, or were among those who managed to escape. The Soviets claim that since the South-western Front suffered heavy losses prior to September 26, the day the battles ended around Kiev, it is unlikely that more than 222,000 soldiers were actually taken prisoner. German losses before and during the battle of Kiev were also heavy. From June 22 to September 28 the Wehrmacht suffered 522,833 casualties, or 14.38 percent of its total strength of 3.4 million. On September 26, the Organization Department of the general staff reported to Halder that the forces in the east lacked two hundred thousand replacements.[49]

The Wehrmacht could perhaps have won a strategic victory in 1941 had the upper-level leadership been decisive and resolute in consolidating the German gains in the southern part of the Soviet Union, but this was not to be. In early September the German high command undertook the planning of an operation that was guaranteed to save Russia—an assault on a strongly fortified Moscow in the fall of 1941.

GUDERIAN—KIEV AND MOSCOW

Once Guderian had made his pact with Hitler regarding the inviolability of his panzer group, von Bock and Halder were powerless to control the situation. The operation east of Kiev would take place on Guderian's terms, with the use of nearly his entire panzer group, and there was nothing his superiors could do now that the panzer general had Hitler's backing. Jodl and Göring were, however, in a different position; they could influence Hitler to change his mind about Moscow, and the evidence shows that they were prepared to so do.

A major alteration in Hitler's mood became apparent during a conversation he had with Brauchitsch on August 30, a week after Guderian's coup at the conference in East Prussia.[50] The army commander in chief's talk with the führer went so well that Halder could say that "all was again love and friendship. Now everything is fine." On August 22 Halder had been on the verge of handing in his resignation and on August 24 Guderian had practically provoked him into a nervous breakdown, but within a few days a thaw had become perceptible in Hitler's attitude. Brauchitsch was informed by the führer on August 30 that the strength of Army Group Center then operating in the Desna area should not be employed for the operation in the Ukraine but rather should be readied for action against Timoshenko in the direction of Moscow. It should be noted here that although Lt. Gen. I. S. Konev took over Marshal Timoshenko's command of the Western Front on September 11, subsequent German documents still referred to the Western Front as "Army Group Timoshenko."[51] The forces on the Desna that Hitler and Brauchitsch discussed were the units of the XLVIth Panzer Corps that had been promised to Guderian on August 23. Hitler had begun to have second thoughts about releasing the XLVIth Panzer Corps to Guderian, for as Halder correctly pointed out, once these divisions were committed to such an operation they would be tied down for some length of time and it would be the enemy who would determine how and when they could be used again for other missions.[52] Guderian, however, would not relent so easily. No matter how much Hitler might vacillate or how hard Halder and von Bock might struggle against him, the panzer general was determined to have his way.

The role of Jodl in bringing about the gradual shift in Hitler's opinion regarding Moscow is not easy to trace. The chief of the Wehrmacht Operations Staff had been convinced of the importance of taking Moscow ever since August 7, and although he had not always agreed with Halder on exactly how this task should be accomplished, nevertheless he had remained dedicated to the project (as his conversations with Halder and the studies produced by his department show). Jodl had found that his compromise with Halder over strategy had been brought to ruin on August 23, but he had not ceased to work to try to change Hitler's viewpoint. On August 31, Halder conferred with his chief of operations, Heusinger, and they discussed a telephone conversation that Halder had just held with Jodl.[53] The chief of the Wehrmacht Operations Staff had referred to the Kiev operation as an "Intermezzo" and said that after the task in the south was fulfilled, the Second Army and Panzer Group 2 should be used against Timoshenko, perhaps in the second half of September. This possibility was also discussed with the view in mind that the northern wing of Army Group Center could be strengthened by some units from Army Group North. It is obvious that Halder was not wholly surprised at Jodl's breakthrough with the führer. On the previous day the OKH had dispatched an order to Army Group Center that declared that all units from Panzer Group 2 and the Second Army that crossed the Desna would come under the command of Army Group South, but it is clear from the way Halder phrased this command that he believed that not all of Panzer Group 2 would have to cross to the southern bank of the Desna.[54] Brauchitsch's talk with Hitler on August 30 seemed to give some substance to this desire. The information Halder received from Jodl the following day appeared to be even more encouraging, although the situation was still indefinite and the chief of the general staff had to tell Heusinger "these things are so unclear that we cannot give Army Group Center any concrete plans."[55]

Von Bock, however, had other sources of information, and he was not left in the dark about the shifts in position of the high command. During the afternoon of August 31, the same day that Halder conferred with Jodl, Kesselring appeared at Army Group Center headquarters with news that probably emanated from Göring.[56] Von Bock was informed that Hitler was considering halting the push southward of the Second Army and of Panzer Group 2 at the Nezhin-Konotop railroad and then allowing all of Army Group Center and part of Army Group North to move eastward toward Moscow. Kesselring advised the commander of Army Group Center that the OKH order of August 30 would now not be put into effect. Considering the problems that von Bock had been having with Guderian over the disposition of the XLVIth Panzer Corps, it is no wonder that he saw the change in orders as a chance to bring Guderian "back under rein."

After listening to Kesselring, von Bock immediately telegraphed Guderian and ordered his units to move no farther to the south or east than the line Borana-Bakhmach-Konotop.[57] But the forceful panzer general had ideas of his own. Guderian had given Hitler a promise that Panzer Group 2 would link up east of Kiev with Panzer Group 1 to destroy the Russian Southwestern Front, and he held to his promise. By fulfilling his end of the bargain, Guderian hoped that Hitler would keep his word and not allow his panzer group to be split. The panzer general had astonished von Bock on August 24 when he told the commander of Army Group Center, rather flippantly, how he had consented to Hitler's wishes and informed the führer that his panzer group could take part in the Kiev operation; in fact, he had insisted that all of his units be sent to the Ukraine.[58] Now Guderian would continue to torment both von Bock and the OKH with constant requests for the release of "his" XLVIth Panzer Corps from Army Group Center. The chief of the general staff was prepared for big trouble from the panzer general, and on August 28 he cautioned von Bock to try to keep Guderian strictly under control.[59]

Guderian had first asked for the release of the XLVIth Panzer Corps from the OKH on August 26 and had received a flat refusal, even though he claimed the spearheads of his panzer group were running into heavy resistance in their push southward.[60] Failing in this approach, the panzer general then turned to Army Group Center on August 27, after the XLVIIth Panzer Corps crossed the Desna near Obolonie and Novgorod–Severskii. During the evening he repeatedly telephoned Greiffenberg, the army group chief of staff, and cursed the Second Army, which, he said, was marching in the wrong direction, that is, due east, perpendicular to his own axis of movement.[61] Guderian again demanded that the XLVIth Panzer Corps, then being held in reserve southeast of Smolensk, be sent immediately to rejoin the main part of his panzer group. Von Bock finally telephoned Halder for instructions, and they agreed, temporarily at least, to do nothing. The commander of Army Group Center referred to Guderian's request as "light headed" ("leichtsinnig") because the 18th Panzer Division was located south of Roslavl, so far behind Guderian's front that he could not help but wonder what use the panzer general could make of it. Matters were complicated even more when Paulus appeared at Army Group headquarters on the evening of August 28. Paulus had been on a short visit to Panzer Group 2 and during this time he had been won over to Guderian's cause.[62] Halder's deputy now went so far as to telephone his chief in East Prussia and plead that, not only should the XLVIth Panzer Corps be returned to Panzer Group 2, but all of the Second Army should be turned to the south and be subordinated to Guderian's command. Halder's decision was emphatic:

> I see the difficulties of the situation but this whole war is made up of difficulties. Guderian wants no army commander over him and demands that everyone in the High Command should yield to his limited point of view. Unfortunately, Paulus has been taken in by him, but I won't give in. Guderian agreed to this mission, now let him carry it out.[63]

The next day, August 29, Guderian again repeated his demands, this time maintaining that the western flank of his XXIVth Panzer Corps was seriously threatened, but von Bock found this difficult to believe, because the panzer corps had already "incautiously" *("unvorsichtigerweise")* reported to the Second Army that its flank was not in danger. Von Bock again contacted Halder for advice, but the chief of the general staff seemed to relish Guderian's predicament. Halder believed that Panzer Group 2 would soon be subjected to attacks from three sides and that Guderian would find himself in a great deal of trouble.[64] In order to ease the situation as much as possible for von Bock, and also to facilitate the splitting up of Panzer Group 2, the OKH issued the directive of August 30 (already mentioned) that would have subordinated the main part of Guderian's force to Army Group South. It was an order, however, that von Bock was happy not to have to put into effect. Kesselring's visit on August 31 had given him new hope that Moscow might once again become the main goal of the German advance. Halder, too, seemed to think things would again be brought onto what he considered the right track. When von Bock queried him about what he had heard from Kesselring about Moscow, the chief of the general staff replied, "I can't confirm it, but it has been talked about!"[65]

Despite the fact that the attacks on the Yelnia salient were growing in intensity and that on August 30 the 23rd Infantry Division of the VIIth Army Corps along the Desna front south of the salient suffered a rupture in its lines up to ten kilometers in depth, Guderian continued his demands for all of the XLVIth Panzer Corps to be sent to the south.[66] Von Bock was of the opinion that the penetration in the area of the 23rd Infantry Division had to be taken seriously and ordered the 10th Panzer Division of the XLVIth Panzer Corps to stand by for an immediate counterattack, which was indeed successfully launched the next day.[67] Although it is hard to imagine what the fate of the 23rd Infantry Division would have been without the timely aid of the 10th Panzer, on August 31 Guderian told the commander of Army Group Center that he would appeal directly to Hitler unless this panzer division and all other units of the XLVIth Panzer Corps were dispatched southward immediately. Halder was further infuriated by Guderian's cheek, which he labeled "unheard-of impudence."[68]

When Halder and Brauchitsch called on von Bock on September 2, the visit that led to the abandonment of the Yelnia salient, there was still a great deal of uncertainty about when the offensive against Moscow could be resumed.[69] Von Bock did not think that his Army Group could renew the offensive unless both Panzer Group 2 and the Second Army were turned toward the east and unless some help was also received from Army Group North. The situation was still unclear, since Guderian had succeeded in so thoroughly wrecking everyone's plans. Halder, Brauchitsch, and von Bock could all agree that Moscow should be taken before the winter of 1941, but as the commander of Army Group Center pointed out, "The Intermezzo, as General Jodl of the OKW referred to the turning of my right flank to the south, can cost us the victory."[70] Until it was decided what to do about Guderian, and about Hitler, no definite plans could be made regarding Moscow. The consensus was that in any event another push toward the Soviet capital could not take place before the end of September.

When Halder returned to headquarters on September 4, he found, to his delight, that the prospects for the Moscow project looked a good deal brighter. Hitler had become very irritated with the way Guderian had carried out his drive to the south, especially his allowing the XLVIIth Panzer Corps to move far to the east of the Desna, causing a big gap to develop between his armored units and the infantry of the Second Army.[71] Keitel finally telephoned von Bock and said that Hitler would personally intervene to bring Guderian back farther west if neither Army Group Center nor the OKH would do so. By this time von Bock had become so fed up with Guderian that he asked Brauchitsch to replace him, but the panzer general still retained too much popularity with the führer for this to be done.[72] Hitler had decided to allow Guderian to continue his movement southward to link up with Panzer Group 1, which would erupt from the Kremenchug pocket south of Kiev on September 12.

Nevertheless, Jodl and Göring had done their work well. Von Bock found out once more what Hitler's future strategy would be from Kesselring, who appeared at Army Group Center headquarters on September 6. In the words of von Bock: "How curious it is that I get all my news first from the Luftwaffe."[73] Hitler was about to make what may well have been the most momentous decision of his life, a decision that would lead directly to the sharpest setback the German army had suffered since 1918 and a defeat of such magnitude that it crippled Germany's chances for victory over the Soviet Union. By September 5 Hitler had become convinced that Russia could not be beaten unless Moscow were taken in 1941.

Shortly before 6:00 P.M. on September 5, Hitler summoned Halder for a conference and revealed to him his plans for the future:

1. The goal of encircling Leningrad had already been achieved; that sector would now become of "secondary importance."
2. The attack against Timoshenko (that is, the Russian Western Front guarding the shortest path to Moscow) could begin within eight to ten days. Army Group North would aid this attack by sending one panzer and two motorized divisions to Army Group Center. Some help could also be provided by Army Group North's Sixteenth Army.
3. After the conclusion of the battles in the Ukraine ("history's greatest battle"), Panzer Group 2 was to be turned north toward Moscow.[74]

This new plan, of course, suited Halder, for he still believed that Moscow was of primary importance if the war were to be won in blitzkrieg fashion, although he thought that the advance eastward could not possibly be resumed for at least three more weeks. That evening Halder conferred with Heusinger and Paulus about the plans for the coming operation. The order for the renewed Moscow offensive, which took the name Operation Typhoon, was issued by Hitler on September 6:

1. On the Central Front, the operation against the Timoshenko Army Group will be planned so that the attack can begin at the earliest possible moment [end of September] with the aim of destroying the enemy forces located to the east of Smolensk by a pincer movement in the direction of Viazma with strong concentrations of armor on the flanks.
2. On the Northeastern Front . . . we must . . . so surround the enemy forces fighting in the Leningrad area that by 15 September at the latest substantial units of the motorized forces and of the 1st Air Fleet . . . will be available for service on the Central Front. Before this, efforts will be made to encircle Leningrad more closely, in particular in the east, and should weather permit, a large-scale air attack on Leningrad will be carried out.[75]

QUESTIONS OF STRATEGY

Göring had promised Hitler that the Luftwaffe could undertake the destruction of Leningrad, a promise that he felt was necessary after the air arm had failed to force England to its knees in 1940. The genesis of the idea that large metropolitan areas in the Soviet Union could be subdued with air power alone goes back to Hitler's conference with Halder on July 8; the idea was further developed in Directive 34 of July 30, which stated that the VIIIth Air Corps was to be transferred from Army Group Center to support Army Group North's advance on Leningrad.[76] Clearly, this was done with Göring's approval. On August 8, Hitler's press secretary, Otto Dietrich, released a statement for publication that said in part, "It is the first time in world history that a city of two million [Leningrad] will literally be leveled to the ground." This statement was made three days after the elimination of the Smolensk pocket and the capture of over 309,000 Russian prisoners, which no doubt contributed to the atmosphere of euphoria in the Reich's Chancellery. Later, on October 7, shortly after the commencement of Typhoon, an OKW directive signed by Jodl stipulated that large Soviet cities such as Leningrad and Moscow were not to be assaulted by infantry or tanks but rather were to be "pulverized" by air raids and artillery. The population of the large cities was to be impelled to flee into the interior of the country: "The chaos in Russia will become all the more pronounced and our administration and utilization of the occupied eastern lands will thus become easier. This desire of the führer must be communicated to all commanders."[77]

This was not the last time that Göring would overestimate the capabilities of the Luftwaffe; the next occasion would come in late 1942 and early 1943 during the battle of Stalingrad. In the summer of 1941 Hitler believed that the air force could neutralize Leningrad, and it was for this reason that he was willing to order the resumption of the Moscow offensive before the metropolis on the Gulf of Finland had actually fallen. That Hitler should have known better, that he should have realized the gravity of the situation should the Luftwaffe be unable to carry out its mission, seems all too clear in retrospect. But Hitler was too dependent on his closest advisors and he was under too much pressure from the army generals to resist the temptation of Moscow in the early fall of the first year's campaign. Göring, like Jodl, had initially been against beginning the Moscow operation so soon, and this had had a telling effect on the führer, but after Jodl's conversion on August 7 and after Göring's reconsideration of strategy somewhat later, Hitler could not deny his generals any longer. On September 10 Kesselring visited von Bock and assured him that Hitler was strongly in favor of all available forces being concentrated against Moscow, including units from Army Group North.[78] By the end of the summer of 1941 Moscow had ceased to be a military target—or even a political or economic goal. The Soviet capital had taken on an air of magical enchantment, it had become the Lorelei that would lure unwary navigators to their death on the rocks.

Once the decision had been made to assault fortress Moscow, all else flowed from the disastrous mistakes that the German leadership had already made. The serious bloodletting at Yelnia had cost the German infantry of von Kluge's Fourth Army heavily, a factor that would become more evident as the fronts moved farther east. Also, the significance of Guderian's refusal to allow one panzer corps of his panzer group to remain behind near Smolensk while the rest of his units were sent to the Ukraine cannot be forgotten. Had the XLVIth Panzer Corps with the 10th Panzer Division, the SS division *Das Reich* and the infantry regiment *Gross Deutschland* remained in the Smolensk–Yelnia area, the battles at Yelnia and along the Desna might have turned out differently. Zhukov's reserves might have been mauled badly in trying to reduce the Yelnia salient, so badly that the defense of Moscow could have been seriously impaired. As it was, however, Guderian had his way, but by the end of September his armor had five hundred to six hundred kilometers to traverse before reaching Moscow instead of the three hundred kilometers that stretched between the capital and Yelnia. Had Moscow fallen in late 1941, the war would have been far from ended. It would have been better for the Wehrmacht to first conquer the south of Russia, then Moscow in the spring of 1942. By the early fall of 1941, however, German strategy had fallen between two stools. The German army could have taken all of the Ukraine or Moscow in 1941, but not both. After Hitler's change of mind about the Ukraine in September, however, and after Guderian's refusal to allow the splitting up of his panzer group, neither goal was attainable. The Red Army was too strong to be so casually bent to its opponent's will. Stalin had done all he could to make Moscow impregnable, a task that might not have succeeded without Guderian's help.

The twin battles of encirclement at Briansk and Viazma in early to mid-October seemed to open the way to Moscow, but von Bock knew that other Russian reserves were positioned even farther to the east.[79] Hitler and the OKH had learned enough from the experiences of Bialystok–Minsk and Smolensk to know that close encirclements that afforded a good opportunity for cooperation between infantry and armor offered the best chance for success. The Briansk–Viazma operation produced spectacular results; the twin battles ended on October 19 with 657,948 Russian soldiers taken prisoner (see Figure 42).[80] But von Bock could sense the troubles that lay ahead. In his view, deeper panzer thrusts were needed in order to cut to the rear of the Russian fortifications and reserves massed to the west of Moscow. In all likelihood, however, such tactics would have led to a worse disaster for the Germans than actually occurred. In the first place, the pockets of surrounded Russians at Briansk–Viazma could not have been effectively contained had the German armored units been sent farther to the east. In the second place, deeper thrusts would have meant longer and more exposed flanks for the armor, dangers that Hitler and the OKH were no longer willing to risk. The toughness of the opponent, too, was obviously growing instead of becoming weaker. The fate of some of the prisoners captured at Briansk–Viazma illustrates why the Red Army would not surrender. On the march route back to a POW camp near Smolensk some five thousand prisoners were machine-gunned before they reached their destination. At Smolensk Camp 126 it is estimated that some sixty thousand Soviet prisoners were killed, mostly under the direction of SS "Special Commander" Eduard Geyss.[81] Why not fight to the death, what was there to lose?

The battle for Moscow in the winter of 1941–1942 did not end the war for Germany in the east, but this colossal defeat went a long way toward sealing the fate of the Wehrmacht. Although the battle served as dramatic proof that Germany's era of rapid victories had come to an end, the actual collapse of the blitzkrieg method of warfare had come during the struggles along the Dnepr River in the summer of 1941. The German high command had not been able to make its strategy and tactics conform to reality. The reality

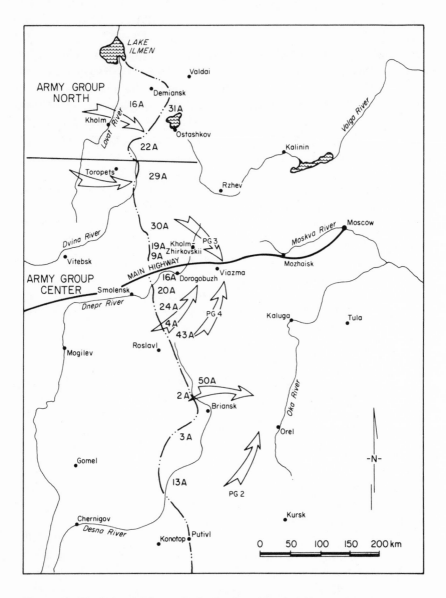

Figure 42. The Briansk-Viazma Twin Battles of Encirclement

of the battles at Smolensk–Yelnia, Gomel, Velikie Luki, and Kiev all pointed to the fact that the war would be a long trial. In the last analysis, however, no one in either of the two military command organizations was willing to take the final step and advise Hitler about the truth of the matter. The ultimate responsibility for Germany's debacle must belong to Hitler, but he should not shoulder this blame alone.

It can only be said that Stalin was right about Moscow, although the price he paid for the victory, the loss of the Southwestern Front, was fearful. Stalin had the ability to force his generals to bow to his will, a task that Hitler, by contrast, would not attempt, however halfheartedly, until Rundstedt, Brauchitsch, and Guderian were dismissed or resigned in November and December 1941. Clearly, much more must be learned about the mechanism of leadership of the Red Army during the war. On the surface it would appear that Russian leadership at the lower levels was inferior to the German, but at the higher strategical-political level, the Soviets were a long distance ahead of their antagonists.

CHAPTER 8

STRATEGY AND TACTICS: A REEVALUATION

BLITZKRIEG VERSUS PROTRACTED WAR

Given the strategic plan for the defense of the Soviet Union and given the faulty strategy and tactics of the Germans, it was impossible for the Wehrmacht to win the war in Russia in a campaign of only one season. Germany could have won a strategic victory over the Soviet Union in 1941, however, by concentrating on gains in the south of the country, in the Ukraine and in the Caucasus, and by forgoing an assault on Moscow in the fall of the year. Whether or not Germany could have won the war in 1942 is problematical. Certainly the task would have been very difficult, but after the collapse of Operation Typhoon in December 1941, the Reich had little hope of achieving a final victory. It is true that the Wehrmacht did not lose the tactical initiative until after the battle of Kursk in July 1943, but the strategic initiative had been lost since the end of the summer campaign in 1941. The German army could have retained the advantage gained by the destruction of the Southwestern Front in September 1941 only by continuing to pursue its successes in the south. To reach for Moscow in the fall of the year amounted to nothing less than suicide, for Stalin had done all he could to transform the capital of the Soviet Union into an unconquerable fortress.

A consistent strategy could have saved the Wehrmacht from disaster in 1941. By holding fast to the Dnepr line, or by moving no farther east than Orel on the Oka River, Briansk on the Desna, Viazma between the Dnepr and Ugra rivers, and Rzhev on the Volga, Army Group Center could have been spared the hammer blows that struck its flanks in early December. But in view of the command structure of the German army, no consistent plans could have been made. From the planning stage of Barbarossa through the decision to undertake Operation Typhoon in early September, the German high command was plagued by divisiveness and intrigue. It was crippled by its own inability to act in a cohesive fashion. Not only did organizations such as the OKW and OKH strive to achieve autonomy in the planning and conduct of the eastern campaign, but individuals such as Göring and Guderian also played decisive roles.

In spite of having made movements to and fro of six hundred kilometers and four hundred kilometers respectively, Panzer Groups 2 and 3 on September 11 were assigned objectives for a renewed push in the direction of Moscow.[1] This time Army Group Center was bolstered by the addition of Panzer Group 4 from Army Group North. At the beginning of October the strength of Army Group Center, including these additional forces, amounted to 1,929,406 men and 1,217 tanks. The Luftwaffe, however, was able to operate less than seven hundred aircraft in the Army Group Center area during Typhoon.[2] By order of Army Group Center on September 26, Panzer Group 4 was subordinated to the Fourth Army command and was given the mission of wheeling around Viazma from the south, from the direction of Roslavl. The beginning phase of Operation Typhoon went well enough, with Guderian's force launching its attack on September 30 and rapidly taking Orel and closing the Briansk pocket with the help of the Second Army. The rest of Army Group Center began its assault on October 2 with Panzer Group 3 from the north and Panzer Group 4 from the south closing an armored ring around Viazma. The Viazma operation was a particular success because there the encirclement took place only 100 kilometers east of Yartsevo and 170 kilometers from Roslavl—in other words, close enough to the starting point of the offensive for the infantry to move in rapidly and help the armored units seal off the pocket (see Figure 43).[3]

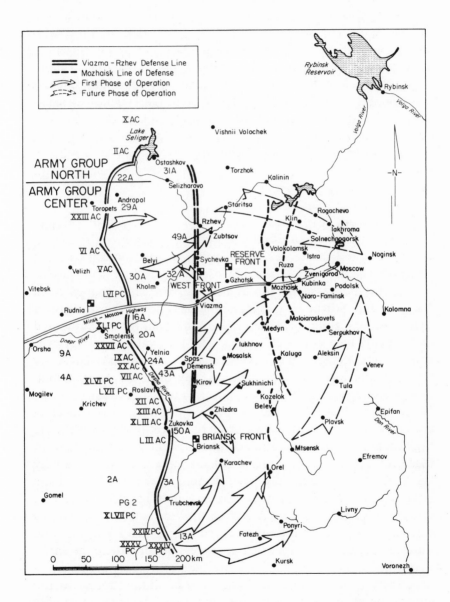

Figure 43. The Operations Plan for Army Group Center During Operation Typhoon

287

In such a manner the battles along the Dnepr, which had lasted from mid-July to late September, were brought to a close. But even after the great victories of Briansk and Viazma, the panzer generals charged with opening a way to Moscow found little to be happy about. Guderian went so far as to say that after the initial success of Typhoon his superiors at the OKH and at the headquarters of Army Group Center "were drunk with the scent of victory." Even before the end of the Briansk–Viazma operations Brauchitsch was confident enough to comment: "Now the enemy has no noteworthy reserves remaining around Moscow. We can, however, expect him to try to build defense lines in and to the west of the city." The army commander in chief went on to describe the advance of the central part of Army Group Center toward Moscow as a "pursuit."

An aura of mystery still hangs over Guderian's thoughts about the resumption of the Moscow offensive in the fall of 1941. In his memoirs, the panzer general gives the impression that he had some doubts about whether such an operation would succeed, yet materials contained in his panzer group's war records show that he was in favor of it.[4] It is generally believed that Hitler alone was responsible for the decision to turn again to Moscow after the battle of Kiev, a decision that probably crippled for all time any chance the Germans might have had for winning the war in the east, but as the previous chapters have shown, this was not the case. Hitler was not strong-minded enough to chart a correct course and hold to it.[5]

The final choice about the deployment and use of the strategic reserve was made by Stalin in the face of intense pressures placed on him by his most trusted commanders.[6] Whether or not the risk the Soviet dictator took in postponing full mobilization until after the war began was justified is a question that still can be debated, as can Stalin's plan to wait until the enemy approached the gates of Moscow before committing the reserves to an all-out counteroffensive. Had the reserves been sent to the Southwestern Front in the fall as Zhukov and Budënny had wished, the defense of Moscow in December would have been seriously jeopardized, if not made impossible.[7] It appears at first glance that Stalin was right and Zhukov was wrong about the reserves, but the issue is too complex to permit a simple resolution.

Zhukov believed that Kiev was to be the stepping stone for a continued German offensive in the south toward the Donbas and the Caucasus. It did not seem plausible to him that Army Group Center would resume the advance on Moscow in late September and that Guderian would attempt to drive on the capital from the south through Orel and Tula. Soon after Guderian reached Orel on October 3, the first snow began to fall and the panzer general himself knew in the marrow of his bones that his troops would never mount a guard on the Kremlin parapets. After Orel, Guderian had only one thought—shift the blame to someone else, accuse the high command of being drunk with the scent of victory. Recall, if you will, the statements that Guderian made to Hitler on August 4 at the meeting in Roslavl. The panzer general told the führer that the Soviets were scraping up their last proletarian levies and had no remaining reserves. Recall, too, how on August 23 Guderian told Hitler and the OKW staff that Kiev could be taken only if his panzer group were not split up or otherwise reduced in strength. At this meeting he also stressed the significance of troop morale and the necessity for making Moscow the near objective of the crusade. It was this intangible foundation so cleverly laid by Guderian that provided the support for Jodl and Göring to press their cause, the Moscow project, with Hitler in September. Guderian was right about the intoxication of the high command after Briansk–Viazma, but it was he who had uncorked this bottle of heady wine and served it to his superiors.

Stalin's strategy of massing the reserves around Moscow while ignoring the encirclement of the Southwestern Front until it was too late should have led to the defeat of the Red Army in the spring campaign of 1942. That it did not was the fault of the German command system. By renewing the assault on Moscow in October, too late in the year for the attempt to succeed given the Russian defense posture, Hitler and the German high command handed away any chance for a victory. Three and a half more years of war confirmed the results of the Soviet Moscow counteroffensive that were visible in the snows soaked with German blood around Kalinin and Rzhev. Stalin's success in saving Russia from an overwhelming disaster in 1942 was due much more to the ineptness of the Germans than to his own genius.

Questions also remain regarding the effectiveness of a strategy that allowed entire fronts to be encircled by the German panzers without permitting a retreat. In the case of the encirclements at Smolensk and Roslavl, no timely retreat was possible, but this was not true at Bialystok–Minsk or at Kiev. It was Zhukov's intention to allow vast forces to be surrounded by the German panzer groups, thus forcing the enemy to spend time and material in the reduction of the large pockets of trapped Red Army units. Zhukov and Timoshenko did not disagree with Stalin about the necessity of sacrificing the three armies in the Bialystok salient, but Kiev was a different matter. Not only were the forces deployed there much larger than at Bialystok, but Stalin went so far as to refuse to order an all-out attack by the Briansk Front on Guderian's eastern flank in late August and early September, preferring instead to conserve the forces of the front in order to blunt a later advance by Army Group Center directly on Moscow. This plan was too much for first Zhukov and then Timoshenko to accept, and so they temporarily parted with their chief over this issue. The German high command, however, set things right for Stalin in Operation Typhoon.

On October 10, Zhukov was named commander of the Western Front, replacing I. S. Konev, who was sent to head the newly formed Kalinin Front.[8] It is evident from Zhukov's postwar statements that after the resumption of the German offensive against Moscow, his faith in Stalin had been somewhat restored. Despite Zhukov's reluctance to submit to Stalin's plan to sacrifice the Southwestern Front, the Soviet dictator had a high respect for his abilities, and he would now call upon him to save Russia in its hour of greatest need.

By the time Zhukov arrived to take charge of his new command, parts of five armies of the Western and Reserve fronts had already been surrounded at Viazma.[9] The twin battles of encirclement at Briansk–Viazma have been described by German historians as great successes brought about by the passivity of the Russian leadership and by the Russian inability to understand the new principles of armored warfare—Why else would the Red Army attempt to ward off powerful German tank thrusts by relying on the kind of static-front tactics utilized during the First World War?[10] Yet there is another possible interpretation. In the words of Zhukov:

> The most important thing for us in the middle of October was to win time in order to prepare our defense. If the operations of parts of the Nineteenth, Sixteenth, Twentieth, and Thirty-second armies and the Boldin Group [a force made up of three tank brigades and

one tank division] encircled west of Viazma are assessed from that point of view, these units must be given credit for their heroic struggle. Although they were cut off in the enemy's rear, they did not surrender. They continued to fight valiantly, attempting to break through to rejoin the main force of the Red Army and thus held down large enemy formations that would otherwise have pursued the drive toward Moscow.[11]

And again:

In the beginning of October the enemy was able to achieve his first objective, taking advantage of his superior manpower and equipment and of errors made by commands of Soviet fronts. But his ultimate strategic objective, the seizure of Moscow, failed because the main forces of the enemy were held down by the Soviet troops surrounded in the Viazma area. The limited forces thrown in by the enemy against the Mozhaisk line with the aim of breaking through to Moscow succeeded in pushing the Soviet troops back to a line running through Volokolamsk, Dorokhovo, the ProtvaRiver, the Nara River, Aleksin, and Tula. They were not able to break through.[12]

The "errors" referred to by Zhukov probably are an indirect criticism of Stalin and Budënny. Some Soviet historians have charged that at the beginning of October the Supreme Command and Budënny had positioned the Reserve Front too close to the rear of the Western Front to allow a true defense in depth or adequate freedom of maneuver for the Western Front. Zhukov's comment about German manpower being superior should be taken to mean superior only on narrow sectors of the front where the German offensive strength was the greatest.[13]

The battles of Briansk and Viazma were fought by the Russian command on the same principles used in the battles of Bialystok-Minsk and Kiev. In 1941, the Red Army lacked the capability of rapid maneuver by its large formations, and it was impossible for Stalin and his generals seriously to entertain the idea of ordering sudden retreats for entire army fronts (although at one point in September Zhukov was prepared to risk the withdrawal eastward of the whole Southwestern Front in order to save it from being cut off). It should be pointed out, however, that the real disagreement between Stalin and Zhukov here concerned the likelihood of a future thrust against Moscow in the fall. Had the Germans failed to live up to Stalin's expectations, had they denied themselves the temptation of Moscow, then Zhukov and Timoshenko would have been proven right. For his part, Zhukov had no qualms about exacting enormous sacrifices from the men under his command if the situation so demanded. This point was proven not only at Bialystok–Minsk and Briansk–Viazma, but also in battles later in the war against Army Group Center in White Russia and Poland. Other generals in history, such as Grant and Nivelle, also had a reputation for producing long casualty lists. In some cases such tactics have been the height of folly (Nivelle), but Grant and Zhukov were winners, however terrible the price. Current Soviet literature on their military history purposely avoids an examination of such problems, not only because many would question the use of such strategy in the past, but because it may have to be used again in the future. Former Marshal I. S. Konev has written the following words about the battle of Viazma:

> Finally, the battle assumed the form of an encirclement. If one is forced to fight such a battle, it is important not to panic but to continue the combat, even in difficult circumstances. In the fortunes of war such situations are always possible and should not be excluded from contemporary military practice.[14]

In the end, more than anything else, the misguided racial prejudices of Nazi ideology toward the Soviet peoples, the minorities as well as the Slavs, dug the grave for the Wehrmacht. Without mass surrender, the blitzkrieg tactics could not succeed in Russia. The German policy toward Russian prisoners did not favor mass surrender for trapped Red Army units. The Prisoner of War Department of the OKW (Abteilung Kriegsgefangenenwesen) issued a report in May 1944 that put the total number of Soviet captured at 5,165,381. Of these, two million deaths were placed under the heading "wastage" whereas another 280,000 were recorded as having died or disappeared in transit camps *(Dulags)*. The number 1,030,157 was given for the total of Soviet prisoners who were either shot while trying to escape or handed over to Himmler's SD for liquidation in special camps. If these figures are extrapolated, it is possible that 5.7 million Soviet prisoners had been captured by the Germans by the end of the war in May 1945. The final count of surviving prisoners is usually approximated at one million. When this number of survivors is added to the number of Russians estimated to be serving with or aiding the Wehrmacht as volunteers *(Hiwis)* or in the Vlasov all-Russian units, together a total of about eight hundred thousand or one million, it can be estimated that about 3.7 million Soviet prisoners simply vanished from the face of the earth.[15] The battle of Kiev required nearly a month to bring to a conclusion; the battles of Briansk–Viazma lasted almost three weeks. These delays in the German advance eastward, coupled with the delays already experienced along the Dnepr and in the Bialystok salient, proved fatal for Germany's hopes, although the Wehrmacht could have been spared ruin in 1941 had its leadership been wiser, more consistent, and less divided than it was.

The time gained by the Red Army in the great battles of encirclement and annihilation that took place during the first four months of the war was used by the Russian command to transform Moscow into a strongly fortified area.[16] Most importantly, time was gained for the mobilization and deployment of the strategic reserve along what would become the northern and southern flanks of Army Group Center as the Germans continued their advance toward Moscow. As has been seen, a considerable portion of the strategic reserve had already been sent to the various fronts, mainly the Western Front, to bolster the forces along the Dnepr, but important elements of the reserves were held back to play a decisive role in December as the Wehrmacht neared the capital.

At the end of November, the Twentieth and First shock armies of the strategic reserve were moved into the Moscow region to join the newly formed Twenty-fourth, Twenty-sixth, and Sixtieth armies.* In addition, the Tenth Army had been concentrated south of Riazan, and the Sixty-first Army had been deployed around Riazhsk and Ranenburg.[17] From the first to the fifteenth of November 1941, the Western Front received one hundred thousand men and officers, three hundred tanks and two thousand guns from the strategic reserve.[18] During the next month, November 15 to December 15, the Moscow Zone of Defense (MZO) was able to send two hundred thousand fully equipped troops to the Western and Kalinin fronts as well as to the remnants of the Southwestern

---

*The original Twenty-fourth Army had been surrounded at Viazma. This unit number was revived by the Russian command and given to a new formation farther east. The designation "shock army" *(udarnaia armiia)* was a new classification given to some field units in the fall of 1941.

Front defending the line Belopole–Lebedin–Novomoskovsk. From mid-November on, Artemev's Moscow Zone of Defense was in actual charge of the deployment of the strategic reserve.[19] Some of the units that Artemev had at his disposal for use around Moscow, at least three rifle and two tank divisions, came from the Far East, thanks to the timely advice sent from Tokyo by Richard Sorge, a master spy who correctly notified the Kremlin on September 14 that the Japanese would make no move against the Soviet Union. In the main, the First Shock Army, which was to play a key role in the Moscow counteroffensive, was made up of men from Siberia, the Urals, and also the Gorki and Moscow regions. It is difficult to say with certainty when the transference of forces from Siberia to the west began, but it is known that this movement had started by mid-June 1941—that is, before the start of the war.[20]

The size of the strategic reserve forces concentrated around Moscow on the flanks of Army Group Center by early December spelled disaster for the Wehrmacht. Not only had the Red Army been able to send seven new armies to the Western Front for the Moscow counteroffensive, but several other armies received substantial reinforcements. Altogether, the Russian forces gathered around Moscow numbered 1.1 million men, 7,652 guns and mortars, 774 tanks (including 222 T–34s and KVs), and 1,000 aircraft.[21] It was Zhukov's goal to use these forces to drive the enemy all the way back to Staraia Russa–Velikie Luki–Vitebsk–Smolensk–Briansk and, if possible, to encircle the Germans in the areas of Rzhev, Viazma, and Smolensk.[22] The main weight of the counteroffensive was to fall north of Moscow, where the Russians were able to achieve an overall numerical superiority. In some areas, such as on the southern wing of Konev's Kalinin Front, their edge rose to 50 percent—more than enough to nullify the superiority in tanks and aircraft of Panzer Group 3 and the Ninth Army.[23] South of Moscow, Panzer Group 2 and the Second Army also were to face an enemy stronger than they were in manpower, although here the difference was not so decisive (see Figure 44).[24]

By the time Army Group Center neared Moscow, the Red Army was prepared to deliver devastating blows to both the northern and southern flanks of von Bock's hapless force. The shocks that compelled Army Group Center to reel backward after December 6 might have succeeded to an even greater extent than they actually did had Stalin followed Zhukov's advice. It had been

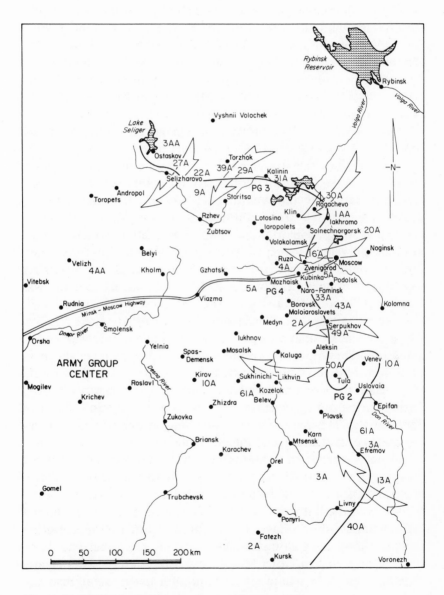

Figure 44. Zhukov's Counterattack near Moscow, 1941

Zhukov's original intention to launch two minor counteroffensives in mid-November against Army Groups North and South, one at Tikhvin and the other at Rostov, in order to prevent Army Group Center from calling for help from its neighbors after the main action got under way around Moscow. It should be noted here that although Zhukov had command over only the Western Front, his position on the Supreme Command staff permitted him to voice opinions about the situation in other areas as well.[25] Stalin, agreeing with this idea in principle, wanted to make the counteroffensives against Army Groups North and South considerably stronger than Zhukov desired (see Figure 45).[26] In this way, the counterattack around Moscow was weakened and the maximum results not achieved. By the end of January 1942, Army Group Center had managed to stabilize its front along the line Rzhev–west of the Staritsa–Iukhnov–Suchinitsi–Belev–Chern, points much farther east than Zhukov had planned (see Figure 46).[27] Had Stalin followed his recommendations, the setback of Army Group Center might have turned into something more significant, but the opportunity was lost. Stalin may have been fortunate in sticking by his guns and refusing to accept Zhukov's dire warnings in September, but he should have listened to him more carefully in November —although even if Zhukov's plan had been carried out the war would still have been far from over.

Nevertheless, the Wehrmacht had suffered serious losses. Although the Germans would retain the tactical initiative in the south until the time of the battle of Kursk in July 1943, never again after Kiev and the commencement of Operation Typhoon would they regain the strategic advantage. The losses incurred by Army Group Center during Operation Typhoon from October 1, 1941, to January 31, 1942, were 369,500 men.[28] The inexorable law "A single mistake in strategy cannot be made good in the same war" could not be repealed. The German high command had thrown away any chance of winning a strategic victory after the battle of Kiev, and the results of the battle of Moscow were a confirmation of this fact: the blitzkrieg had died a natural death. The German high command should have recognized this truth after the development of the struggle along the Dnepr—they should have admitted to themselves and to Hitler that the war was bound to be long and grueling—but they would not or could not make the admission.

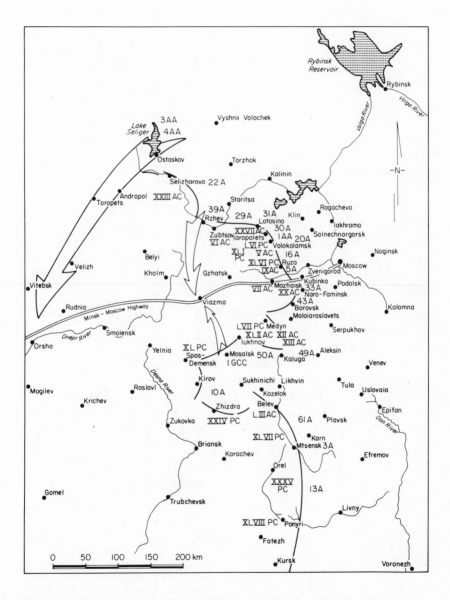

Figure 45. The Far-reaching Goals of the Soviet Moscow Counteroffensive

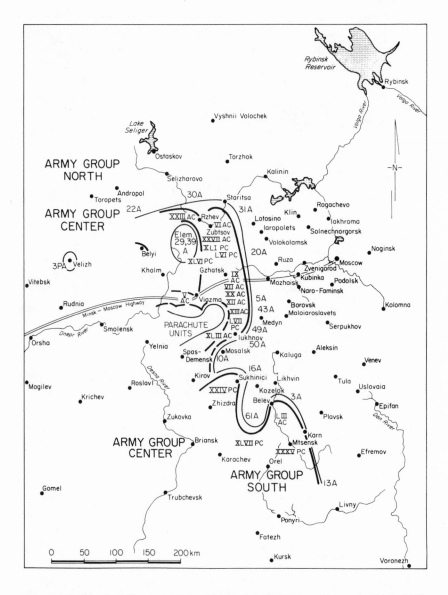

Figure 46. The Stabilization of the Front of Army Group Center in Early 1942

COMBINED-ARMS AS THE WAVE OF THE FUTURE

In regard to tactics, the experience of the first three months of the war bore out the correctness of Zhukov's decision to rely on combined-arms operations to defeat the wide-ranging encirclements of the German panzers. The physical characteristics of the USSR and the ability of the Russian people to support a mass although poorly mechanized army in 1941 seemed to impose natural limitations on defense planning. With the exception of a brief and faltering attempt in late 1940, after the success of the blitzkrieg in the west, the Russians after 1936 had never seriously considered utilizing armor alone in deep maneuvers of penetration. The experiences of the Red Army in Spain in 1936, at Lake Khasan and Khalkhin-Gol against the Japanese in 1938 and 1939, and in Finland in 1939-1940, were convincing proof that tanks could not play a completely independent role apart from infantry and artillery. This was especially true for an army that could put fewer of its infantry units on wheels than the Germans could. In the Red Army's projected field regulations for 1941, tanks were considered part of the complement of the rifle divisions and were thought of as vital for the support of the infantry in the breakthrough of the enemy's tactical zone of defense.

As the war progressed through its early stages, the Russians learned from their mistakes how to neutralize the German armored tactics. In the evolution of Russian antitank operations the battles of Bialystok-Minsk and Smolensk-Yelnia played an important role. The failure of Pavlov's counterattack with three mechanized corps in June, coupled with the German failure rapidly to close the Smolensk pocket in July, confirmed Zhukov in his belief that combined-arms methods would eventually carry the day. His success at Yelnia in late August and early September, a success that rested on the lavish use of artillery and infantry to support tanks in a drive against a well-prepared German position, was crucially important for the development of Russian tactics for the remainder of the war.[29] After the summer of 1941, the command of the Western Front issued instructions forbidding tank attacks without reconnaissance and a careful coordination of the assault with infantry and artillery. In a defensive role, tanks were to be used to support infantry by direct fire from ambush or dug-in positions. Tanks could be used in semi-independent counterattacks, but only to protect the flanks and the seams of the rifle divisions.[30] Throughout the remainder of the war these tactics were not fundamentally changed. After the summer of 1941, when an increased number of tanks were available, some armored vehicles were attached to rifle regiments.[31]

The problems with the use of infantry support tanks (NPP) proved to be so serious that in January 1942 the STAVKA issued a new set of directives, which were followed by further directives from the Defense Commissariat in October of that year. These regulations provided that tanks must support the infantry particularly along "the axis of the main blow." NPP tanks were to carry out their operations never allowing gaps of more than two hundred to four hundred meters to develop between them and the following infantry. Instead of allowing NPP tanks to be flung into battle without proper support, where they had in practice incurred heavy losses, the directives required that artillery be used to counter German tanks. Tank-to-tank battles were to be avoided unless the terrain conditions and number relationships were highly favorable. The role of the infantry was to scout for, mark, and if possible, destroy, enemy antitank mines and obstacles. After the initial phase of an assault, the infantry would then carry out the crucial mop-up operations that had often been neglected. Pockets of resistance would be closed off and annihilated, not left to be troublesome thorns in the rear of an advance. Artillery and support aviation were to coordinate their operations with the armor and infantry as closely as possible.

During the counteroffensive at Stalingrad in early 1942, these tactics were brought to a finely honed point and used with great success. There, tank regiments and brigades were integrated into the rifle division units. Since each tank battalion had at least one artillery battery and an engineer unit, they were able to penetrate and hold positions in the depths of the German defenses. These lessons were incorporated in the Field Regulations of 1943.

However it was not until mid-1943 and the advent of self-propelled guns on the Soviet side—guns like the SU–76, the SU–122, and the superb SU–152 built on the KV tank chassis—that armored close support of infantry came into its own. The renowned German Sturmgeschütz self-propelled gun had proved its usefulness in close cooperation with infantry many times in 1941, but these guns were always in critically short supply. Late in the war Soviet breakthroughs were usually accomplished with tanks and self-propelled guns being distributed to the infantry regiments. Typically, tanks and self-propelled guns would be assembled ten to fifteen kilometers behind the front a couple of days before the attack. In the predawn hours before the assault, these units would move up to their jump-off areas one to three kilometers in back of the main line. If the German resistance was expected to be heavy, the attack would take place in two or three echelons. The first wave would be composed of a battalion of T-34s or a company of KVs. The second wave would move out about two hundred to three hundred meters behind the second line of the first wave. The reserve elements, the motorized rifle battalion, would operate about the same distance in back of the second wave. The goal was to keep about twenty-five to fifty meters spacing between the tanks and self-propelled guns. In practice, however, a density of approximately thirty or forty armored vehicles was achieved per kilometer of front along the main axis of the assault. Usually, this combined-arms attack was accompanied by a rolling artillery preparation at a depth of 1.5–2.5 kilometers. In 1943, a great deal of emphasis was placed on moving forward and shifting fire after the enemy began to pull back. Later, in 1944, the techniques of advancing artillery fire and employing self-propelled guns became refined enough to earn the name "artillery offensive."[32]

THE COLLAPSE OF GERMAN STRATEGIC PLANNING

The answers to questions of German strategy and tactics are less clear and certain. In a real sense, it can be said that the Wehrmacht had no strategic guidance in 1941. Instead, the assault on Russia was launched without a unified and coordinated plan of action for all levels of command on all sectors of the front. In June 1941, essentially two strategies were followed, one favored by Hitler and the OKW, the other by Halder and the OKH. In addition, by mid-July other strategic plans began to emerge that further clouded the situation. Halder and Jodl reached a compromise during the fourth week of August that could possibly have produced some desirable results for the Wehrmacht. However, the nature of this compromise was such that it ran afoul of the plans of Heinz Guderian who, for a variety of complicated reasons, managed to achieve almost total independence from the commands of his superior officers. Guderian's autonomy was due in part to the machinations of Halder, for the chief of the general staff wished to see Guderian gain the cherished goal of Moscow as rapidly as possible, and in order to ensure the panzer general's chance of success, Halder systematically insulated Guderian from interference from above. The creation of the Fourth Panzer Army under the nominal command of von Kluge was an artificial device designed to confuse the command structure and keep Guderian closely tied to the OKH. Hitler was able to issue orders immediately to Army Group Center, but von Bock was unable to issue orders directly to Guderian. By making use of Halder's awkward command system, it was easy for the panzer general to devise delays and to "misunderstand" directives that were sent to him by Army Group headquarters. Von Bock recognized soon enough what Halder and Guderian were trying to do, and he endeavored repeatedly to regain control over Panzer Group 2, but to no avail.[33]

By the end of August the damage wrought by the fundamental contradictions in German strategic planning and the Wehrmacht command structure had come to the surface. By then Halder and von Bock had completely lost control of Guderian after the panzer general managed to gain personal influence with Hitler at the Wolfschanze conference on August 23. The führer went along with Guderian's bad advice and chose not to divide Panzer Group 2 in undertaking the Kiev encirclement in September. Once this decision had been made, it was no longer possible for Moscow to be taken in 1941. Hitler decided in early September, however, that both goals, Kiev and Moscow, were attainable. The führer's greatest strategic mistake of the war was the result of his simultaneous reliance on too many sources of conflicting advice.

Halder had come to realize after mid-July that Moscow could not be taken unless the situation on both the northern and the southern flanks of Army Group Center were remedied beforehand. The chief of the general staff won Jodl over to this point of view on August 7, and eventually they concluded that it was possible for both Kiev and Moscow to be taken, but only by leaving a substantial part of Panzer Group 2 in the Yelnia area instead of committing it to the Ukraine. The question of whether or not this strategy would have worked is an interesting one indeed. It seems unlikely that Army Group Center could have taken Moscow in the fall of 1941 with only one panzer corps on its southern flank. It is highly likely that the Typhoon offensive would have bogged down well before reaching the area near Moscow. Probably the German high command would have chosen to halt the advance along the line Rzhev-Viazma-Briansk-Orel, thus putting Army Group Center beyond the immediate reach of Artemev's reserves massed north and south of the capital. If this had happened, Army Group Center would have been in much better shape to resume operations against Moscow in the spring of 1942 than it was in fact. This is why the Halder-Jodl plan has been described as a possible salvation. It would not have worked in the way that its authors intended, but it very probably would have saved Army Group Center from catastrophe. Had the front been stabilized in November 1941 and had the Wehrmacht been able to withstand the pressures of the Russian reserves Hitler might not have been bold enough to relieve, or accept the resignations of, Brauchitsch, von Bock, von Leeb, Rundstedt, and Guderian in the next few weeks, thus tightening his grip over the army even further. Without this defeat in the winter of 1941-1942 the generals' conspiracy against Hitler and the Nazis would have had more time to succeed. Had Hitler been overthrown, improvements in the Soviet prisoner situation and in the racial policies in general no doubt would have followed, which could have changed the whole complexion of the war on the eastern front. Germany could still not have won the war, but a negotiated settlement with the West could have occurred that would have prevented a Soviet intrusion into the heart of central Europe—a historical fact that may prove to be the biggest threat to world peace, and even the greatest danger to mankind, in our current age.

Guderian's coup at the Wolfschanze was, then, a monumental turning point for Germany and possibly for the Western world. After Guderian's triumph, Halder may have been prepared to see the Moscow project go down the drain entirely in 1941, judging from his conversation with Jodl on August 31, a discussion that demonstrated Jodl's commitment to Moscow even after the debacle he and Halder had suffered on August 23. In the final analysis, it was this commitment by Jodl, plus Göring's promise to neutralize Leningrad with air power, that finally swayed Hitler in the fall of 1941 to attempt the taking of Moscow. Ultimately, too, Guderian's insistence on the importance of the capture of the Soviet capital for troop morale and his willingness to see the pursuit of the Red Army toward Moscow continued by a drive of his panzer group from the south through Orel and Tula—a desire carefully concealed in his memoirs—had a decisive influence on Hitler.[34] Hitler did not trust Halder and the OKH, but he believed Jodl, Göring, and Guderian were men worth listening to. It was a tragedy that Halder was ensnared by such a tangled web of circumstances, but it must be said that he was responsible for creating most of these troubles for himself with his attempts to manipulate Guderian by fashioning an artificial and awkward command structure and to manipulate Jodl through the influence of his deputy, Warlimont. The final element of the equation, Göring, was not subject to Halder's will, and as no record of his private conversations with Hitler exists, the true extent of his role in the strategic blunders of 1941 must be left open to speculation, although the records of Kesselring's discussions with von Bock indicate that Göring's influence in this respect was extensive. This impression is strengthened by Hitler's references to Göring and the Luftwaffe in his answer to Halder's proposal of August 18 and in the Typhoon directive of September 6.

On the tactical level, German plans for the conduct of the war in the east in 1941 were as filled with contradictions as was the making and execution of strategy. The insoluble problems that would arise from the attempt to apply tactics designed for use in France and Poland to a country as large as the Soviet Union were apparent at the time of Paulus's study in December 1940, but neither the general staff nor any other high command organization was able to find new tactical solutions that more closely suited the realities of the campaign in the east. In his excellent study, *The German Economy at War,* Alan Milward points out that Germany was not an economic superpower in 1941 compared with the United States and was also economically inferior to the Soviet Union in certain key military areas. In order to overcome these economic deficiencies, Hitler and his generals were forced to rely on the blitzkrieg concept of war, one that allowed Germany to become a great military power through armament in breadth, not in depth; that is, many different kinds of weapons were produced that were tailored for specific types of warfare, but in insufficient quantities.

In 1939 and 1940, in order to defeat France, German military planners concentrated on the construction of vehicles and armor. After the fall of France, in order to defeat Britain, a switch was made so that the economy could produce more equipment for the Luftwaffe and the navy. Finally, in order to defeat the Soviet Union, a decision was made to increase greatly the size of the army, resulting in a greater output of infantry arms and equipment of all sorts. In retrospect, it seems incredible that Germany was prepared to fight Russia in a life-and-death struggle with only 3,582 tanks and self-propelled guns, but such was the case. Actually, the German war economy was not fully mobilized until after Stalingrad in early 1943, but by then the war was lost.[35]

Thus, the contradictions revealed in the blitzkrieg concept of warfare were reflections of the fundamental contradictions within the German economic system. The blitzkrieg concept was a means whereby a long war could be avoided, and once a long war ensued, the economic inferiority of Germany would have an increasingly telling effect. This is not to say that the Soviet Union did not have its economic contradictions and weaknesses also, but the misguided Nazi race ideology and the harshness to which it led solidified all segments of Soviet society and strengthened the will of the ethnic minorities in the USSR as well as of the oppressed Russian peasant class to repel the invader. The blitzkrieg could triumph in a politically weakened country such as France, but Stalin's Russia was a state of quite different organization. Here blitzkrieg warfare could have worked only had the Nazi leaders been willing and able to exploit the weakest links in the Soviet system, those implicit in the nationalities problem and in the peasant sector.

Had mass surrenders of Red Army units occurred rapidly at Bialystok–Minsk, Smolensk–Yelnia, and at Kiev, blitzkrieg tactics could have produced the desired results. But mass surrenders occurred only after prolonged resistance. Communist agitators were skillfully able to use Nazi propaganda against itself and were able to stiffen the resolve of the minority peoples and the peasants to fight for Mother Russia, despite the fact that the Stalinist system had much to answer for as far as they were concerned. In order to increase the propaganda effort, the political commissars were reintroduced into the Red Army on July 16, 1941, though the system had been abolished in 1940.[36] Nazi ideology, therefore, carried within itself the seeds of its own destruction. Even had this not been so, the strategy and tactics employed by the Germans on the eastern front would have made a total defeat of the Red Army in 1941 extremely unlikely.

In describing the conditions faced by the Wehrmacht in Russia, a German historian has written:

> The troops began to realize by the third day of the offensive that the war in Russia was not going to be the same as it had been in Poland and France. This was not only because the enemy soldier was proving to be tougher than expected, but also because the terrain was a greater problem. Of what use were motorized vehicles when the wheels became stuck in knee-deep sand? Oftentimes when roads were indicated on the maps they were, in fact, nothing more than footpaths through the swamps.[37]

In a way, White Russia acted as a gigantic cocoon for Army Group Center, and soon after June 22, the Wehrmacht began to undergo a remarkable metamorphosis. Gradually, the very color of the German uniforms and vehicles changed from grey to earth brown, and after the supply system began to deteriorate, the diet of the soldier began to change as well and even the lowly sunflower was not overlooked as a source of human energy. By the time of the fall rainy season, crudely built Russian horse-drawn *panye* wagons had assumed great importance for German transportation needs. German construction battalions were set to work to fabricate these primitive vehicles in the autumn, despite the fact that earlier they had been the very symbol of the backwardness of the Red Army.[38] During the winter in 1941 the transformation of the German army continued to progress; the western *muzhiks* found themselves scrambling for Russian padded coats and hats and for the thick and comfortable felt boots that (incidentally) the Red Army issued in only three sizes.

The question of why proper clothing and equipment was not issued to the German troops in time for the onset of winter in 1941 has never been satisfactorily answered. Halder blamed Hitler for this mistake, but Guderian has written that the führer was misinformed, for some unexplained reason, about the issuance of winter clothing by Quartermaster General Wagner. Recently, however, an American historian has charged Brauchitsch with the responsibility for this error.[39]

In 1942, a German general would write:

The external appearance of the troops had been fundamentally altered. . . . The marching columns now resembled the campaigns of the Middle Ages, and the uniforms were now almost unrecognizable as such.[40]

The Wehrmacht had become a "Russian" army.

By late summer and early fall 1941, the war in the east had taken on a more human character; it was a man-to-man struggle to a far greater extent than the German planners had anticipated, and it was at this time that the Wehrmacht began to pay dearly for the neglect the infantry divisions had suffered since 1939.[41] According to one German general, the infantry was misused because it was (wrongly) no longer considered to be the backbone of the army. "The infantry was more poorly armed, clothed, and more poorly provided with replacements than any other branch of the military; it was always thoughtlessly overtaxed by the high command during the course of the war."[42] This general did not deny that the armored units and the Luftwaffe were also overstrained, but not because their worth was underestimated; "In regard to the armored forces, the overstraining and resulting misuse followed as a result of the wrong value placed on the infantry divisions."

Observations of this kind were not confined to lower echelon division commanders. In September 1941, Field Marshal von Kluge submitted a critique to Army Group Center that outlined in some detail his objections to the continued use of blitzkrieg tactics as advocated by Guderian and von Bock.[43] The field marshal began his remarks by saying that he realized motorized units were the wave of the future and their development must be pressed but, he added, in the Soviet Union motorized divisions alone could not achieve decisive victories; the terrain was too difficult and Russian countermeasures too effective. Much was expected of the infantry units, yet their weapons were not as varied and plentiful as in a panzer or a motorized division, a factor that made all forms of combat more difficult. The trouble with the infantry was that it typically did not have the close cooperation with the Luftwaffe enjoyed by the panzer groups. About the battles just concluded around the Yelnia salient, von Kluge stated that armor, particularly the Sturmgeschütz self-propelled artillery, was invaluable for close support of the infantry in both offensive and defensive operations. Much blood could have been saved by utilizing armor to spearhead the main thrust of an infantry attack or to act as a reserve to blunt enemy assaults against static defensive positions. Von Kluge believed that it was wrong to expect infantry divisions to defend fifteen- to forty-kilometer fronts without adequate barriers against coordinated assaults by enemy tanks, artillery, and infantry in rough country. If the war were to be won, he felt the infantry would have to be regarded as something more than an unwanted stepchild; its equipment and personnel would have to be upgraded, and the tasks assigned to it would have to be more reasonable. In essence, the program outlined by von Kluge advocated a reorientation of German tactics toward the kind of combined-arms methods employed by the enemy, whose efficacy had lately been demonstrated at Yelnia. Von Kluge was given a chance to put his ideas into practice when he was assigned the command of Army Group Center in December 1941.

The Kiev encirclement proved to be the last successful mass armored penetration over a long distance that the Wehrmacht would be able to carry out in the Soviet Union. And so with the conclusion of the Kiev operation on September 26, the era of victorious blitzkrieg warfare had ended. After Briansk–Viazma, on October 13, the OKH issued orders for an encirclement of Moscow to be undertaken by the 2nd and 4th panzer groups, but there was little chance that this operation could succeed.[44] The OKH had persuaded itself that the destroyed Russian forces at Briansk–Viazma represented the last main enemy force barring the road to Moscow—a view that did not correspond to reality. After the Moscow debacle in December, neither Hitler nor anyone else in the German high command, including Halder, would ever depend on independent armored thrusts over vast territories to carry the day. This new attitude was made concrete in Hitler's Directive Number 41 of April 5, 1942, which set forth the goals for the second year's campaign:

> Experience has sufficiently shown that the Russians are not very vulnerable to operational encirclements. It is therefore of decisive importance that, as in the double battle of Viazma–Briansk, individual breaches of the front should take the form of close pincers movements.

> We must avoid closing the pincers too late, thus giving the enemy the possibility of avoiding destruction.

It must not happen that, by advancing too quickly and too far, armored and motorized formations lose connection with the infantry following them; or that they lose the opportunity of supporting the hard pressed, forward-fighting infantry by direct attacks on the rear of the encircled Russians.[45]

The blunders made in German strategical planning in the summer of 1941 ensured the prolongation of the war despite anything the Wehrmacht might have done in regard to tactics. The use of combined-arms operations sooner, before the post-Moscow period, might have salvaged at least a partial victory for Germany in the spring and summer of 1942. Once the strategic initiative was lost permanently after Kiev, however, the damage done was irreparable. After Kiev, too, many German officers were afflicted with a "Marne psychosis," a fear that everything must be done to win the war in one campaign or else, as in 1914–1918, Germany would be ground down by its enemies.[46]

Significantly, Soviet criticisms of German tactics center around their misuse of tanks and artillery and the failure of the German command to recognize the importance of combined-arms operations.[47] In retrospect, most of these criticisms appear to be valid. Only 18 percent of Army Group Center's manpower was organized into mobile units, and it became obvious in the early stages of the war that the German transportation system was inadequate to allow artillery to be moved forward rapidly enough to be used properly.[48] During the course of the war, the Wehrmacht suffered greatly from a lack of enough motorized infantry to close swiftly the gaps between fast-racing tank columns and the slower footbound units. The German army in the east had only a few battalions that could properly be called motorized infantry; many units were given this designation, but most of them were "in fact nothing more than infantry units that did not carry their own packs."[49] The few German battalions with armored vehicles that did operate in close coordination with tanks proved themselves to be extremely valuable, but there were not enough of them to make a decisive impact on the outcome of the war.

When the Russians began to employ large numbers of close assault antitank weapons as a defensive measure, the German panzers were increasingly forced to depend on marching infantry for support, as not enough motorized columns were available. By midsummer, 1941, the speed of the German blitzkrieg attack had been slowed to that of a marching man. During the period between June 22 and July 10, 1941, Army Group Center advanced five hundred kilometers, or twenty-five to thirty kilometers per day. During the next sixty days the army group moved only two hundred to three hundred kilometers, or four to five kilometers per day.[50] Mobile columns could still race ahead rapidly to encircle large groups of Russians, and this was dramatically demonstrated at Briansk–Viazma, but these units were unable to continue their advance until the infantry came up to secure and contain the enemy pockets. This phenomenon was observable in all of the encirclement battles fought by the Germans in 1941. In 1943, 80 percent of the German army in the east was still composed of infantry divisions relying mostly on horse-drawn power for transportation, a figure that had not substantially changed since 1941.[51] An attempt to bring about increased mechanization of the infantry was made after Stalingrad, but by then it was too late. Allied bombing would wreak ever-increasing havoc with German industry and the Reich transportation network. The Wehrmacht lost the strategic initiative at Kiev and by resuming the Moscow offensive in the autumn of 1941, fell into the snare that Stalin had so carefully laid. The Red Army would continue to press for a definite tactical superiority also, a goal that was reached after the battle of Kursk in the summer of 1943.

One other matter remains to be dealt with in regard to German strategy and tactics. The question may be asked, Could Moscow have been taken by the German army in 1941 and would this success have led to a defeat of the Soviet Union? Since the war, a twofold myth has been perpetrated by former Wehrmacht commanders such as Halder, Guderian, and Blumentritt and by several German military historians. This myth is (1) that Hitler alone was responsible for the blunders in Russia in 1941 that led to Germany's defeat and (2) that had the blitzkrieg campaign culminated in 1941 with the capture of Moscow, the Wehrmacht would have been victorious.

The first part of this historical misconception has already been discussed. If anything, Hitler was, in 1941, unable to direct personally the strategic development of the war in the east. Intrigues and divisiveness at all levels of command had a telling effect on German planning and operational organization. Whenever Hitler was able to make a decision regarding strategy and tactics, he was all too prone to rely on bad advice from individuals such as Göring and Guderian who were interested in furthering their own causes and not in sacrificing their personal goals for the sake of the common benefit. The führer proved himself time and again to be unable to resist the psychological pressure from those around him who wished to use their influence to change decisions that he had already made. Hitler's answer to Halder's letter of August 18, for example, positively excluded the possibility of a renewed Moscow offensive in 1941, and yet Halder was successful in changing Hitler's attitude (with the help of Warlimont and Jodl). Halder was, in turn, frustrated by the abrupt intervention of another pair of influence-mongers, Göring and Guderian, who succeeded in altering still further Hitler's supposedly stubborn will.

The second element of the myth must now be considered: How could an assault on Moscow actually have taken place during the first year's campaign, and would the fall of the city have meant a German victory? Regarding a siege of the Soviet capital, a German historian has written as follows:

> Thanks to Hitler's unfortunate Far Eastern policy, the Soviets were able to draw on a major part of the strength which had been pinned down by the Japanese. Stalin and Marshal Zhukov had gained time, utilizing the entire power of a totalitarian state, to transform the capital into what would have been an "earlier Stalingrad." In any case, if Army Group Center had commenced an actual assault on Moscow, the fight would have lasted until the last man and the last bullet were spent. It is very questionable whether this struggle would have ended in favor of Germany.[52]

Other German commentators have remarked that the use of blitzkrieg tactics against Moscow in 1941 would have been very risky. In street fighting, tanks could only have been used singly or in small groups and would have had to be close to infantry teams capable of neutralizing the enemy's close-quarter antitank weapons, which were usually concealed in underground bunkers and cellars. "If the enemy had enough time to prepare the defense of a large city, then his fortress-type constructions could only be overcome through the use of strong air and artillery support." Also, "The main burden of battle in a street fighting situation must be borne by the infantryman or motorized infantryman." On several occasions Hitler expressed his fear of using tanks in battles inside large cities, and Guderian too is on record as saying street fighting was outside the operational capabilities of tanks.[53] In other words, Moscow could not have been taken in 1941 by the panzer groups alone; the Russian forces were too well prepared for such an eventuality. Moscow could have been captured only by a combined armor, artillery, infantry, and Luftwaffe assault, which in turn would have meant that the final phase of the attack could not have occurred before enough time had elapsed for men to march from the Bug River to the Moskva. It is no accident of fate that the final storm of Moscow was not attempted before November; such an event could not have taken place sooner even if the German tanks had been in a position to carry out the assault more quickly. The Russian tactic of forcing the German infantry to grapple with large pockets of surrounded Soviet soldiers behind the advancing panzer groups thus paid handsome dividends in the fall and winter of 1941. It was not until after the conclusion of the battles at Briansk–Viazma, in late October and early November, that the German infantry was in a position to assault Moscow.

Another possibility must be taken into account. What if the German tanks had bypassed Moscow and succeeded in cutting off the city from the interior, leaving the infantry and artillery units to assault the city later? This was the kind of maneuver that the panzer generals favored, and it was, in fact, the tactic set forth in the Operation Typhoon directive for the period following the "highly coordinated and closely encircling operations" at Briansk–Viazma. The encirclement of Moscow could only have been accomplished in one of three ways: (1) in late August, as Guderian advocated, without first eliminating the Russian threat to the northern and southern flanks of Army Group Center; (2) in September, as Halder, von Bock, and temporarily, Jodl advocated, after the conclusion of the Kiev operation; or (3) in November or December 1941, with all of Panzer Group 2 participating but also after the fall of Kiev and the neutralization of Leningrad, as at first Jodl and then Göring advocated. The second possibility offered the advantage that the Kiev encirclement would have been accomplished first by dividing Panzer Group 2 and sending two of its three panzer corps to the Ukraine. The rest of the tanks of Army Group Center would be regrouped and refitted for a drive to or around Moscow from the areas of Nevel and Velikie Luki (Panzer Group 3), and from south of Smolensk and near Yelnia (the XLVIth Panzer Corps). Under plan three, supposedly Army Groups South and North would have been able to lend support to the final drive around the capital.

Of these three possible courses of action, the second offered the most advantages, but after the third week in August and the settlement in Guderian's favor of the controversy over the division of Panzer Group 2, this plan could not have been carried out. As pointed out earlier, even if plan two had failed, Army Group Center would have been in the best overall posture for defense during the winter of 1941–1942. The third choice was, of course, the plan that was actually followed, even though the situation at Leningrad had not been resolved at the time. The failure of this plan was predetermined because the operation had to be carried out too late in the year—during bad weather—and also because the delay had allowed the enemy to mobilize fully and deploy its strategic reserve. Only the first possibility then, needs to be discussed, especially since the advocates of this plan were so vocal after the war.

The records of the units in Army Group Center, particularly those of the Second Army and Panzer Group 2 on the southern, and Panzer Group 3 on the northern, flank of the army group, prove that Zhukov's operational echelon in the areas Gomel–Mogilev and Velikie Luki was doing an effective job of pinning down the advancing German forces on the approaches to Moscow. The difficulties experienced by Guderian's XXIVth Panzer Corps at Propoisk in mid-July were symptomatic of the troubles faced by Army Group Center on its southern flank. Guderian was unable to secure the southern flank of the Army Group without help from several infantry divisions, but these same divisions were also desperately needed to aid the XLVIth Panzer Corps in closing the gap in the Smolensk pocket between Dorogobuzh and Yelnia. Guderian had originally intended for his panzer group to push around Moscow from the south, through Briansk across the Oka in August in coordination with a thrust by Panzer Group 3 around the northern side of the capital. But after the abandonment of Velikie Luki on July 20 and after strong Russian pressure developed from the directions of Roslavl–Krichev and Rogachev–Zhlobin, such a possibility appeared to be ever more remote. Guderian was, of course, willing to do something about the Roslavl–Krichev situation before he advanced toward Moscow, but the unbeaten Russian forces on the extreme southern flank of the army group along the Dnepr and the Russian presence at Gomel would have seriously jeopardized the flank of Panzer Group 2 had a deep thrust to the east been carried out through Briansk in August. Guderian himself realized this threat, and on August 8 he asked von Bock for permission to send the XXIVth Panzer Corps all the way to Gomel, if necessary, a request not mentioned in the panzer general's memoirs.

As it was, the Roslavl operation was ended quickly (by August 5) and Krichev was finished by August 12, but Guderian's success here was due primarily to the fact that his panzer group enjoyed the close cooperation of two army corps, a factor not present at Yelnia and Dorogobuzh, where the panzer groups, without infantry help, were unable to close the Smolensk pocket for eleven crucial days after the fall of Smolensk itself.

Given the failure of the German panzer groups to forge a tight ring around Bialystok–Minsk and Smolensk without the help of the infantry, it is hard to imagine how the panzers could have sealed off Moscow from the east. In fact, they could have done so only had the Red Army been totally bereft of reserves and had they prepared no defense of Moscow. By mid-August not only was Army Group Center actively engaged with four Red Army groupings, the Western, Reserve, Briansk, and Central fronts with a total of fourteen armies, but since mid-July a new line of reserves had been in the process of deployment along the Mozhaisk line of defense, a force that included three armies also set to bar the way to Moscow, although this barrier was still inadequately manned even in October.[54]

It would have been theoretically possible for Panzer Groups 2 and 3 to penetrate to or around Moscow in August. Zhukov admitted that such a danger was present in October at the start of the Typhoon offensive, yet what would have been the results of such a breakthrough?[55] In order to accomplish so rapid a push on Moscow, with all of Panzer Group 2's force, as Guderian had wished, the Kiev encirclement would have had to be postponed indefinitely. Zhukov has rendered a judgment on the results of such a rash maneuver:

As for the temporary suspension of the Moscow offensive and the drawing off of part of the forces to the Ukraine, we may assume that without that operation the situation of the German central grouping could have been still worse than it turned out to be. For the General Headquarters reserves, which were used to fill in the gaps in the southwestern sector in September, could have been used to strike at the flank and the rear of the "Center" group of armies advancing on Moscow.[56]

This thesis has been echoed by other Russian commentators:

If the Germans had used the entire strength of the Wehrmacht to support the attack on Moscow, then the pressure would have been reduced on the northern and southern parts of the battlefronts. This would have allowed us to pull in more strength from these areas and also would have enabled us to continue to use the industries in the south, which would have been removed from danger of attack.[57]

The best judgment, in light of conditions existing in the summer of 1941, is that the capture of metropolitan Moscow in August or September by the Wehrmacht would have been impossible for two reasons: (1) the inability of armored units alone, aided by the small number of motorized infantry units the Wehrmacht possessed in 1941, to conquer a large defended urban area and (2) the demonstrated inability of German mobile units without the close cooperation of infantry divisions to seal off effectively large areas controlled by the Red Army. Finally, even if Moscow had fallen in September or October, the Red Army could still have continued the war, utilizing its undamaged position in the Ukraine and around Leningrad. The war would still have been a protracted conflict, the difference being that the Russians would have been able to make better use of their southern economic base during the winter 1941–1942.

It will be the verdict of history that the loss of Germany's best hope for victory over the Soviet Union had two main causes: (1) the incredible blindness of Nazi ideology, which, by discouraging surrender, doomed any chance for the success of a blitzkrieg war and (2) the inner divisiveness in the German command structure, which prevented any coherent or rational plans from being developed or executed. It must also be the verdict of history that the Soviet state under Joseph Stalin was an organism possessing a far greater instinct for survival than that of Hitler's Germany. Stalin's trust in Zhukov was not misplaced. These two men comprised a team that wrote an end to Germany's triumphs on the eastern front.

Appendix A

ORGANIZATIONAL STRUCTURE OF SOVIET UNITS
JUNE 1941

At the start of the war on the Eastern Front (called the Great Patriotic War by the Soviets) the Soviet Union had a well-developed hierarchical military organization. Part I of this appendix reviews that organization down to the division and brigade level. See Figure 1-A for an overview of the Soviet high command structure.

Under the People's Commissariat for Defense, the country was divided into sixteen military districts, each controlling all army ground and aviation units and installations in its area (except for strategic aviation units). The three special military districts along the western border were better prepared than the rest for rapid mobilization as active field commands (fronts). Each special district controlled several armies and independent corps, along with divisions and smaller units of various branches.

On June 22, 1941, the Soviet ground forces had about 24 armies; 62 rifle, 29 mechanized, and 4 cavalry corps; 13 cavalry, 61 tank, 31 motorized, about 168 rifle, and about 30 mountain rifle divisions (about 303 divisions in all); 2 rifle and 10 antitank brigades of the Supreme Command reserve. Of the divisions, 222 were operational and 81 were in the process of formation. On January 1, 1941, the size of the Soviet armed forces was 4,207,000 men. Of these, 80.65 percent were ground troops, 8.65 percent were in the air forces, 7.35 percent were in the navy, and 3.35 percent were in the air defense forces.

The author of appendix A is Professor James Goff, Chairman, Geography Department, Mankato State University, Mankato, Minnesota.

Most armies were responsible for defending wide segments of the border and consisted of one (sometimes two) rifle corps covering an anticipated main axis of enemy advance, a mechanized corps in tactical reserve, usually some independent rifle or cavalry divisions, a composite aviation division, and an array of support and logistical units. In the event of hostilities, each frontier army would be reinforced with one or more rifle corps held in military district reserve in peacetime. Each special military district also had a weak second-echelon army in process

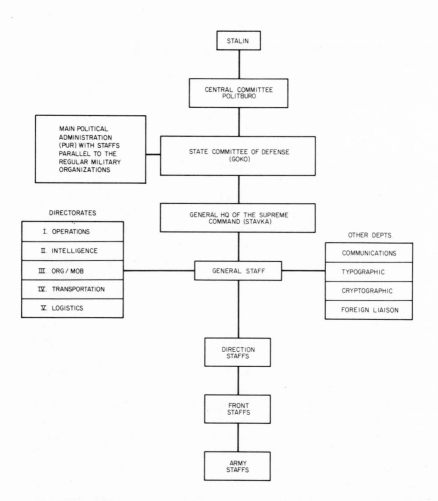

Figure 1-A. Structure of the Soviet High Command, July 1941

of formation, which should be considered the district's main operational reserve.

Rifle troops (the official Soviet term for infantry, the tsarist term for elite infantry being used to indicate the supposed superiority of Soviet units) were the backbone of Soviet combat arms. Rifle troops were organized primarily into rifle corps of 2–3 rifle divisions plus a few support and service units. In frontier armies the rifle corps generally straddled the axes of main advance in the army's sector, with divisions deployed in one echelon. In the interior of military districts were independent rifle corps at a lower state of readiness, deployed in traditional garrison towns.

The rifle division was the largest infantry unit with a fixed *shtat* (TO & E). At the start of the war, three different *shtats* were actually in use, as shown in Table 1–A. It should be noted that the "6,000" divisions in the Far Eastern Military District, and at least some divisions on the western border had a strength of about 7,000 men, intermediate between the two peacetime *shtat* levels.

TABLE 1–A

Rifle Division Strength Levels
June 22, 1941

Shtat Level	Men	Trucks	Horses	Rifles	MMG	HMG	LMG
6,000	5,864	155	905	3,685	691	163	324
12,000	10,291	414	1,955	7,818	1,159	164	371
Wartime	14,483	558	3,039	10,420	1,204	166	392

The Western Special Military District had none of the mountain rifle divisions or rifle brigades. It did include units known as "fortified areas" (UR, or *ukreplennyi raion*), officially considered brigade-sized combined-arms units. A fortified area had variable strength, usually with 2–4 machine gun or artillery–machine gun battalions. These units were numbered and occupied a named physical installation also called a fortified area. The installations were outfitted with obstacles, pillboxes for light artillery and machine guns, and dug-in obsolete tanks.

An airborne corps consisted of three airborne brigades plus support and service units. In strength, it was actually like a division. The number of personnel qualified for parachute use is not known, but shortages of transport aircraft made large airborne operations practically impossible.

Some cavalry was organized into corps of 2–3 divisions plus support and service units. The rest, including mountain cavalry divisions, were directly under district or army control. Cavalry divisions were apparently organized on only one *shtat,* without a separate level for peacetime.

The armored troops were organized primarily into mechanized corps, each consisting of two tank and one motorized divisions, plus support and service units. This organization was based on that of the German panzer corps, also used in American armored corps. Although the mechanized corps had a very strong wartime *shtat* (e.g., 36,080 men, 1,031 tanks, 266 armored cars), the actual strength varied widely. Only one corps in the Western Special Military District was apparently at wartime *shtat,* while the rest seemingly were at about half-strength. The tank brigades from which they were formed appear to have been merely redesignated, and the motorized divisions probably had not yet received tank regiments. The total tank strength of the five western border military districts was at 53 percent of *shtat.*

The armored forces were just starting to replace the old system of light, medium, and heavy tanks (T–28, T–36, BT, T–38, T–35) with a new system (T–40, T–34, KV). The method of assigning the new tank models made sense, however, only from the viewpoint of the Russian combined-arms doctrine, not from the German model. The new tanks were generally doled out as a battalion of fifty-three T–34s or thirty-one KVs to each tank division, rather than being used to reequip totally a few corps. In other words, in a very incompetent way, the Soviets were trying to emulate the hard-hitting German panzer corps but still could not tear themselves away from their more traditional methods of organization, which they would continue to use throughout the war. This attitude toward parceling out the new tanks was illustrative of the deep divisions within the military hierarchy in 1940 and 1941 about the use of tanks in general. These differences were brought into sharper relief after mid-January 1941 and the continuing arguments between Zhukov and Pavlov over the deployment of tanks in the western regions, particularly within the Bialystok salient.

The tank divisions were strong, with 375 tanks by *shtat,* but the variety of tank models in service made it difficult to keep them in operation, especially because spare parts for the older models were no longer being made. The motorized division (mistakenly called motorized rifle or motorized infantry in many Western publications) was to have 275 tanks, attainment of which goal was complicated by production problems with the new T–40 tank. Additionally, the motorized rifle regiments of both tank and motorized rifle divisions required many trucks that were not available.

Anticipating battle with large enemy armored formations, the Soviets were forming highly innovative antitank artillery brigades of the Supreme Command Reserve (RGK). These brigades were strongly equipped with antitank and antiaircraft guns and were motorized, designed to thwart the advance of a panzer division. At the start of the campaign, most of them were still being formed.

Antiaircraft defense, apart from that in combined-arms units, was in the hands of the Territorial Air Defense (PVO, *Voiska protivovozduznoi oborony strany*). This branch was organized administratively into PVO zones, each covering the area of a military district. Each consisted of PVO brigades and PVO brigade areas. The administrative and operational distinction between these two types of units is unclear, but their antiaircraft weapons could also serve in antitank and antipersonnel roles. In a few military districts with more important industrial concentrations, the zone controlled PVO corps or divisions. Only the fighter units assigned to the air defense of Moscow, Leningrad, and Baku were directed by the local PVO commander, and they, therefore, occupied a special position. Elsewhere, the PVO fighter aircraft were subordinated to the air force commanders of the military districts.

The air forces (VVS, *Voenno-vozdushnye sily*), under control of the Commissariat of Defense, had been reorganized some months before the campaign. Its units were controlled by a deputy commander for aviation within each military district. Directly under his control were several attack, fighter, and bomber air divisions and fighter divisions of the PVO. Each army also had a composite air division. Aviation technical and support functions in each military district were provided by a regional system that controlled air base activities.

The navy was organized into four fleets and several flotillas, the last serving primarily on inland waters. The major operational unit of a fleet was the squadron *(eskadr')*, consisting of at least one battleship or cruiser along with smaller surface units. The major permanent operational unit was the brigade, consisting of several ships or smaller vessels of the same type. Each fleet had a naval aviation component that was not part of the army's air force. Among other units, naval aviation still included some brigades, a unit abandoned earlier in the army air force. The navy also included ground branches conducting activities that in other countries would be done by the army or marines. Coast artillery was extensive, organized into area commands containing battalion-sized units. Naval infantry units had the mission of protecting naval bases and conducting small amphibious operations.

The People's Commissariat of Internal Affairs (NKVD) had two types of operational troops trained for combat operations: The border troops guarded the international boundary zone with regiment-sized units. The internal troops had a variety of regiments designed for various internal security activities that could be used for combat emergencies. Some internal troops were organized into divisions.

TABLE 2-A

Soviet Units Opposing Army Group Center.
June 22, 1941

Unit	Location	Commander
I. WEST SPECIAL MD	HQ Minsk	Pavlov, D.G., Army Gen.
(West Front)		

A. ARMIES

Unit	Location	Commander
Third Army		Kuznestov, V. I., Lt. Gen.
IV Rifle Corps		Yegorov, M. Gen.
27th RD	Shtabin Area	
56th RD	Sopotskin Area	Sakhnov, S. D., M. Gen.
85th RD	Grodno	
XI Mech. Corps	HQ Volkovysk	Mostovenko, D. K., M. Gen.
29th TD	Near Grodno	Studnev, N. P., Col.
33rd TD	40 km SE of Grodno	Panov, M. F., Col.
204th Mot.D	Volkovysk	Pirov, A. M., Col.
Direct Army Control		
68th (Grodno)	Fortified Area W of Grodno	
50th RD?	Near Molodechno? (or directly under MD?)	Yevdokimov, V. P., M. Gen.
Fourth Army		Korobkov, A. A., M. Gen.
XXVIII Rifle Corps	HQ Brest	Popov, V. S., M. Gen.
6th RD	Brest	Popsuy-Shapko, M. A., Col.
42nd RD	Brest	Lazarenko, I. I., M. Gen.
XIV Mech. Corps		Oborin, S. I., M. Gen.
22nd TD	E of Brest	Puganov, P. V., M. Gen.
30th TD	Pruzhany	Bogdanov, S. I., Col.
205th Mot. D	Bereza	Kudynrov, F. F., Col.
Direct Army Control		
49th RD	HQ Vysokoie	Vasiliev, Col.
(maybe in 18th Corps?)		
75th RD	Malorita	Nedvigin, S. I., M. Gen
62nd (Brest) Fortified Area	NW of Brest	Puzyrev, M. I., M. Gen.
Tenth Army		Golubev, K. D., M. Gen.
V Rifle Corps	H.Q Lomzha?	
13th RD?		
86th RD?		
89th RD?	Bialystok	
1st Rifle Corps		
I RD	Osovets	Grishin, M. D., Col.
8th RD	Kolno Area	
VI Mech. Corps	HQ NE of Bialystok	Khatskilevich, M. G., M. Gen.
4th TD	Bialystok	Potaturchev, A. G., M. Gen.
7th TD	Volkovysk?	Borzilov, S. V., M. Gen./TK
29th Mot. D	Slonim	

TABLE 2–A

Soviet Units Opposing Army Group Center.
June 22, 1941 (Continued)

Unit	Location	Commander
XIII Mech. Corps	Belsk	Akhlyustin, P. N., M. Gen.
27th TD?		
31st TD?		
4th Mot. D		
VI Cav. Corps	HQ Bialystok	Nikitin, I.S., M. Gen.
6th CD	Lomzha	Konstantinov, M. P.,
		M. Gen.
36th CD	Volkovysk	
Direct Army Control		
155th RD	Baranovichi	Aleksandrov, P. A., M. Gen.
66th (?)		
Fortified Area		?
Thirteenth Army	HQ Minsk	Filatov, P. M., Lt. Gen.
(New understrength HQ		
moving from Mogilev to		
Novogrudok on June		
20–22. No units assigned		
till June 24.)		

B. UNITS UNDER DIRECT DISTRICT CONTROL

	(HQ actually in field near Bialystok)	
II Rifle Corps	HQ Minsk	Yermakov, A. N., M. Gen.
100th RD	Minsk	Russiyanov, I. N., M. Gen.
XXI Rifle Corps	HQ Vitebsk	Borisov, V. B., M. Gen.
17th RD	Lida	
24th RD	East of Lida	Galitskiy, K. N., M. Gen.
37th RD	NE of Lida	
XLVII Rifle Corps	HQ Bobruisk	Povetkin, S. I., Maj. Gen.
121st RD	Bobruisk	Zykov, P. M., M. Gen.
143rd RD	Gomel	Safonov, D. P., M. Gen.
XL Rifle Corps	HQ Smolensk(?)	Yushkevich, V. A.,
		Kom. Div.
64th RD	Smolensk	Iovlev, S. I., Col.
108th RD	Viazma	Mavrichen, M. Gen.
XVIII Mech. Corps	Novogrodek-Baranovichi	Petrov, (M. A.?),
	Area	M. Gen./Tk
25th TD?		
TD?		
209th? Mot. D	Ivye	
XX Mech. Corps	Borisov-Osipovichi Area	Nikitin, A. G., M. Gen.
26th TD	Minsk?	Obukhov, V. T., M. Gen./Tk
38th TD		
210th Mot. D.		

(continued)

TABLE 2–A

Soviet Units Opposing Army Group Center.
June 22, 1941 (Continued)

Unit	Location	Commander
IV Airborne Corps	Marina Gorka	Zhadov, A. S., M. Gen.
7th Abn Brig	"	Tikhonov, M. F., Col.
8th Abn Brig	"	Onufriyev, Col.
214th Abn Brig	"	Levashev, A. F., Col.
Independent Units		
55th RD (or maybe in 47th Corps)	Slutsk?	Ivanyuk, D. I., Col.
161st RD	Mogilev	Mikhaylov, A. I., Col.
6th AT Art. Brig?		
7th AT Art. Brig?		
8th AT Art. Brig? (or in 21st Corps?)	Lida Area?	Strelbitskii, I. S., Col.
Minsk Fortified Area		
Polotsk Fortified Area		
Slutsk Fortified Area		Denisov, N. N., Col.
Mozyr Fortified Area		

C. AVIATION

West Special MD Aviation	HQ Minsk	Kopets, I. I., M. Gen./Avn.
9th Comp AD		Chernykh, M. Gen./Avn.
10th Comp AD	HQ Kobrin	Belov, N.G., Col./Avn.
11th Comp AD		
12th Bomber AD		
13th Bomber AD		
43rd Fighter AD	Minsk area?	
3rd Long Range Avn Corps		Skripko, N. S., Col.
42nd Long Range AD	Smolensk area	
52nd Long Range AD		
II. GROUP OF RESERVE ARMIES	HQ Formed Moscow moved to Briansk June 25, 1941	Budënny, (S.M., Marshal/SU) Marshal
Twentieth Army	HQ Smolensk (26 June '41) Mogilev	Remezov, F. N., Lt. Gen.
LXI Rifle Corps	HQ to Mogilev 29 June	Bakunin, F. M., Gen.
110th RD	Reach Mogilev 29 June	Khlebtsev, V.
53rd RD	Arrive 3 July from Moscow MD	Konovalov, F.
172nd RD	Reach Mogilev 29 June	Romanov, M. T., M. Gen.
LXIX Rifle Corps	HQ from Moscow MD At front by July 6	
153rd RD?	ca. July 1, 30 km S of Vitebsk	Gagen, N. A., Col.

TABLE 2-A

Soviet Units Opposing Army Group Center.
June 22, 1941 (Continued)

Unit	Location	Commander
VII Mech. Corps	HQ in field near Tula	Vinogradov, V. I., M. Gen.
1st Moscow Mot. D	In Camp near Moscow	Kreizer, Ia. G., Col.
14th TD		
18th TD	Kaluga?	
Direct Army Control		
18th RD	At front by 10 July	Sviridov, (K. V.?), Col.
Twenty-first Army	HQ Gomel (July 2)	Gerasimenko, V. F., Lt. Gen.
	Gomel	
LXIII Rifle Corps	Rogachev area	Petrovskiy, L. G., Lt. Gen.
-Org. Dec. '40		
61st RD	Rogachev area by July 7	
117th RD		
167th RD	July Rogachev Area	Rakovskiy, V. S., M. Gen.
LXVI Rifle Corps	Zhlobin area	Rubtsov, F., M. Gen.
232nd RD	July 7–Zhlobin area	
154th RD	July 7–Zhlobin area	Fokanov, Ya. S.?, M. Gen.
XXV Mech. Corps	From Kharkov (or Orel?) MD	
	Novozybkov area July 7	Krivoshein, S. M., M. Gen.
50th TD	From Orel?	Bakharov, B. S.?, Col.
55th TD		
219th Mot. D		
Twenty-second Army	HQ Near Nevel (July 6)	Yershakov, F. A., Lt. Gen.
LI Rifle Corps	Sebezh area	Markov, A., M. Gen.
98th RD	At front by July 9	
112th RD	At front by June 28	Kopyak, I. A., Col.
170th RD	July 7–W of Nevel	Silkin, N. K., M. Gen.
LXII Rifle Corps	HQ at front July 7	Karmanov I., M. Gen.
174th RD	Near Polotsk–in action June 27	Zygin, A. I., Col.
186th RD?	Unloading July 5 at Beshenkovichi	Biryukov, N. I., M. Gen.
In group–Subordination unknown		
XX Rifle Corps	Bogushevsk Area–July 10	Yeremin, S., M. Gen.
144th RD	Unloading July 10	
160th RD	Reach Front July 7 from Moscow MD	Skugarev, I. M., M. Gen.
LXVII Rifle Corps?	Gomel area	Zhmachenko, F. F., Kom. Brig.
137th RD?	At front June 29 Arrive Mogilev July 4	Grishin, I. T., Col.
151st RD	Pre-July 13–Dovsk area	

(continued)

TABLE 2-A

Soviet Units Opposing Army Group Center.
June 22, 1941

Unit	Location	Commander
XLV Rifle Corps	Rogachev area (July 6)	Magon, E. Y., Kom. Div.
148th RD		
187th RD		
132nd RD (Maybe under 20th or 67th Corps)	July 7 Rechitsa area?	Biryuzov, S. S., M. Gen.
III. BALTIC SPECIAL MD Only those units opposing Army Group Center	HQ Riga	Kuznetsov, F. I., Col. Gen.
Part of Eleventh Army		Morozov, V. I., Lt. Gen.
XVI Rifle Corps	HQ Kaunas	Ivanov, M. M., M. Gen.
5th RD	Mostly at Kozla Ruda	Ozerov, F. P., Col.
33rd RD	Mostly at Kozla Ruda	Zheleznyakov, K. A., M. Gen.
188th RD	Mostly at Kosla Ruda	Ivanov, P. I., Col.
XXIX Lithuanian Rifle Corps	HQ Svencionys	
179th RD	Svencionys	
184th RD	Svencionys	
3rd Mech. Corps.	HQ Vilna	Kurkin, A. V., M. Gen./Tk
5th TD	Alita	Fedoruv, F. F., Col.
84th Mot. D	Vilna	Fomenko, P. I., M. Gen.
Direct Army Control		
42nd Fortified Area ⎱	⎰ Alytus Fortified Area	
46th Fortified Area ⎰	⎱ Kaunas Fortified Area	
126th RD	Kalvariya area	?
128th RD	Koptsevo	?
10th AT Art. Brig?		
IV. THE PINSK FLOTILLA	HQ Pinsk	Rogachev, D. D., Rear Admiral

27 Vessels (about 7 monitors, 5 gunboats, 2 patrol boats, 10 armored boats, and 3 patrol ships)
Air Squadron, AAA Battalion, and Naval Infantry Company

PART II

SOVIET TANK STRENGTH OPPOSING ARMY GROUP CENTER, JUNE 22, 1941

At the start of the German-Soviet conflict, the Soviet armored forces were in the midst of a major program of reorganization and reequipment. Many of the new tank divisions were apparently not much more than redesignations of the older tank brigades, equipped primarily with obsolescent tanks generally in need of moderate or serious repair. If the Soviet armored units in the Western Special Military District opposing Army Group Center had been equipped at wartime *shtat* (TO & E), they would have had extraordinary strength in tanks, as shown in Table 3–A.

TABLE 3–A

Shtat **Tank Strength of Western Special Military District Units, June 22, 1941**

Unit	Number	Total Tanks	KV	T-34	Old, Light
Mech. Corps	6	6,186	756	ca. 2,520	ca. 2,910
Cavalry Div.	2	128	—	—	128
Airborne Corps	1	50	—	—	50
Rifle Div.	24	384	—	—	384
Total:	33	6,748	756	ca. 2,520	ca. 3,472

NOTE: Opposing troops of the Baltic Special Military District had a *shtat* of 1,143 tanks (126 KV, 410 T-34, 607 old) in a mechanized corps and 7 rifle divisions.

Most Soviet units opposing Army Group Center, however, were much below *shtat* strength. Just before the war (apparently on June 15), the Western Special Military District's tank strength was 56.7 percent of the *shtat* requirements. Because no Soviet figures for the district's tank strength have been published, this percentage and the *shtat* totals listed in Table 3–A can be used to calculate a total strength of 3,813 (plus or minus 7) tanks.

The calculated tank strength requires some explanation. The Soviets have published data on total tank strength for only a few military districts, and none at all for the entire army. Their purpose, presumably, is to obscure the size of their tank park, which was considerably larger than that of Germany. This is surprising, because many Soviet sources state that most of their tanks were too thinly armored for contemporary warfare and that many were worn out or in need of major repair. Raw figures on total tank strength thus would be very misleading. Nevertheless, those older tanks able to operate made up a sizable force and had the potential to inflict considerable damage if used in dug-in positions or against enemy infantry. They were certainly a match for German Panzer IIs, though they lacked the advantage of air cover.

By contrast, the Soviets have disclosed the number of KV and T-34 tanks for many units. The probable purpose of this disclosure is to emphasize the existence of these new high-quality tanks and to indicate that they were in relatively short supply. Soviet figures presumably include those tanks officially assigned to units, whether or not they were operational. In addition, new tanks awaiting delivery or old tanks sent for repair to military district motor vehicle and armor depots were possibly counted as part of the district tank park. It is uncertain whether those assigned to schools, such as the one at Borisov, were included. The 193 T-18 (MS-1) tanks used as pillboxes in the fortified areas of the Western Special Military District were probably not included, because they had been decommissioned as tanks.

Regarding the geographic aspect of deployment, Soviet statistics take on an interesting pattern. A strong relationship exists between the strength figures published for units in a military district and the quality of Soviet armor in that area. On the one hand, in the Ukraine, where Soviet armor activity was fairly well handled and greatly retarded the German advance, relatively great detail is available on the tank strength of various units. In White Russia, on the other hand, where the mechanized corps failed to have much impact on rapid German armor penetration, details on tank strength are in short supply.

The general lack of Soviet data regarding tank strength of units in the Western Special Military District can be compensated for by using the available and calculated data. Published data is available for tank strength in the VI, XI, and XIV mechanized corps. The VI was the only mechanized corps in the district that is listed as both combat ready and at full strength. The XI Corps supposedly had only 290 tanks, primarily because its XXXIII Tank Division was weak. This strength seems unusually low, particularly because only the XIII, XVII, and XX mechanized corps are listed as having "few tanks." In one source, the XIV Corps is stated to have only T-26 tanks, but another source says that one of its tank divisions had at least one medium tank battalion. If the above figures are taken at face value, these three corps account for about half of the district's calculated tank park. Some of the remaining tank strength could be accounted for by the rifle and cavalry divisions and the airborne corps. Although no tanks are mentioned for such units in sources covering the Western Special Military District, it is known that the rifle divisions in the Baltic Special Military District's Eighth Army each had about 6–8 tanks. If each of the district's rifle divisions had 10 tanks and each cavalry division about 60, this would account for another 360 old light tanks (primarily T-26, BT, and probably some T-38s). To represent their low strength, the three remaining mechanized corps should be weaker than the XI, or each have about 300 tanks. However, the figures fall several hundred short of accounting for the district's calculated level.

Refinement of the above figures requires a closer look at the XI Corps. Its tank total seems far too low, considering it is not singled out in Soviet sources as being weak. It is reasonable to assume that its listed strength includes only those tanks actually concentrated in the corps' main sector on June 22, excluding those still en route or in for repairs. Thus, it may well have had another 200 tanks.

The VI Corps presents a problem regarding specific tank models. One Soviet source gives exact, but low, figures for its KV and T-34 tanks, yet another says over half the tank park in its two tank divisions consisted of these two models. Because one of its divisions is listed as having 355 tanks, the corps should have had about 360 KV and T-34 tanks.

The preceding analysis should be useful in interpreting the data on Soviet tank deployment opposing Army Group Center, shown in Table 4–A.

TABLE 4–A

Probable Tank Strength Opposite Army Group Center, June 22, 1941

Formation	Total	NEW			OLD				
		Total	KV	T-34	Total	T-28	BT	T-26	T-38
Western Spec. MD:	3813?	≤379	≤149	≤230	—	—	—	—	—
6th Mech. Corps	±1000	360?	≥10	≥21	—	—	—	—	—
11th ″ ″	≥290	≥27	≥3	≥24	—	—	—	—	—
13th ″ ″	300?	—	—	—	300?	—	—	300?	—
14th ″ ″	±508	—	—	—	±508	30?	478	—	—
17th ″ ″	300?	—	—	—	—	—	—	—	—
20th ″ ″	300?	—	—	—	—	—	—	—	—
rifle divisions	±240	—	—	—	±240	—	—	—	—
cavalry divisions	±120	—	—	—	±120	—	±120	—	—
airborne corps	≤50	—	—	—	≤50	—	—	—	≤50
Baltic Spec. MD (part of 11th Army)	≤465	82	30	52	≤383	—	—	—	—
	4278	461	179	282	1601	30	598	300	501

Table 4–A reflects a reinterpretation of the new tank strength for the VI Corps. A tally of the KV and T–34 tanks definitely assigned to the other four western border military districts and their mechanized corps shows that about 149 KV and 230 T–34 are unaccounted for. Assigning about 360 of these to the VI Mechanized Corps would give it the strength indicated in the earlier analysis. The total tank strength and its deployment is generally confirmed by German claims that, as of July 8, 1941, they had captured over 2,585 tanks in the Bialystok pocket, and through July 11 the total for both the Bialystok and Minsk pockets had reached 3,332 tanks.

The probable deployment of Soviet tanks facing Army Group Center is shown in Figure 2–A. Many of the older model tanks never actually made it into action, because they needed significant repairs. Although the map seems saturated with tanks, those assigned to rifle divisions were too susceptible to German planes and infantry antitank guns. They were also too dispersed to be much of a threat. Although several mechanized corps were properly located to block or hit the flanks of German armored thrusts along the shortest routes to Minsk, the location of the VI Mechanized Corps is puzzling. It was part of the Tenth Army, the one least likely to confront a strong armored blow. It was well located to shift toward either Grodno or Brest, but too far from either. A more reasonable location for it would have been farther east near Minsk, the probable goal of any armored thrust. If Soviet policy prevented rebasing such large formations in the west, then the new tanks it apparently received in such numbers in 1941 would have been better allocated to the newer mechanized corps in more strategic locations.

The deployment of the new model tanks raises an important question about the effectiveness of the German intelligence system. The appearance of the T–34 was an unwelcome surprise to the Germans for two reasons: first, because they had nothing comparable to it and, second, because the German standard antitank guns were ineffective against it. The T–34's speed, cross-country mobility, and sloping armor clearly put it in a class by itself. A German infantry division had 60–70 antitank guns (PAK, *Panzerabwehrkanone)* as standard equipment, but in the summer of 1941 nearly all of these were of the 3.7cm variety. The 5cm antitank gun was just coming into service then, but it too was ineffective against the T–34. Before the Russian campaign, a 7.5cm gun was developed that had great penetrating power, but it was not put into production because no need for it was foreseen. The two smaller antitank weapons were deemed to work well enough against the Soviet T–26 and BT tanks. Moreover, the need for powerful hauling equipment for the heavier 7.5cm gun meant it was considered not worth the effort.

When the first reports of the T-34 came in from Army Group North in its first clashes with Soviet armor in Lithuania, a commission from the Army Weapons Agency *(Heereswaffenamt)* was hurriedly flown in to investigate. The report that emerged from this investigation called for the immediate production of the 7.5cm PAK, but despite strenuous efforts, the gun did not reach the eastern front in large numbers until early 1942. In the meantime, as described in the text, German units dealt with T-34s by blowing them up with satchel charges or by improvising with the 8.8cm antiaircraft gun depressed into a horizontal antitank role. In the summer of 1941 the T-34 was engaged largely singularly, but the number of them encountered increased alarmingly in the fall and winter.

The appearance of the T-34 also fundamentally changed the course of the German tank-building program. Before the Russian campaign the main role of the tank was seen as antiinfantry, especially in overcoming machine gun emplacements. After the appearance of the T-34 it was realized that the most critical task was to destroy enemy armor at the greatest possible range. The success of all other combat missions depended on the suppression of the T-34. A race now began to arm all tanks

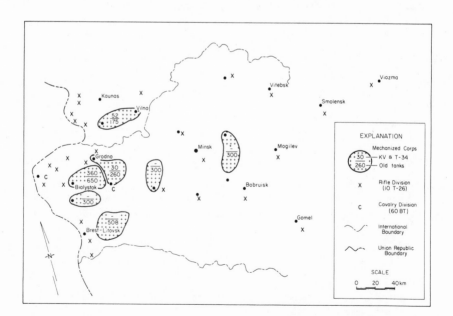

Figure 2-A. Probable Soviet Tank Deployment opposite Army Group Center on June 22, 1941

with a long-barreled cannon of at least 7.5cm. Phase I of this program was to rearm the Panzer IV with a long 7.5cm gun in place of the short-barreled version incorporated in its original design (much, it must be said, against the wishes of Guderian). The "L" version of the Panzer IV was available in significant numbers by the time of the summer offensive in the south of Russia in the summer of 1942. The Germans also began crash programs to develop radically new tank designs such as the Panzer V ("Panther"), first introduced in February 1943, and the Panzer VI ("Tiger"), first introduced in June 1942.

Heinz Guderian in *Panzer Leader* states that his troops were much surprised and frustrated by the KV and T-34 tanks they encountered for the first time in early July. On July 3, Nehring's 18th Panzer Division was hit hard on its left flank near the Berezina River on the Smolensk highway by units from the Borisov Tank School and from Kreizer's 1st Moscow Motorized Rifle Division. Guderian himself did not see a T-34 until July 10, when he went to this area and took photos of one that had run off into a ditch. That Guderian had not seen a T-34 earlier is evidence of the sparse deployment of them in and around the Bialystok salient and evidence that the XIV Mechanized Corps' 30th Tank Division, directly in the path of Guderian's Panzer Group 2 near Brest, must have been equipped with the older T-28 medium tanks.

PART III

ORDER OF BATTLE AND DEPLOYMENT OF SOVIET
FORMATIONS OPPOSING ARMY GROUP CENTER
SEPTEMBER 1, 1941

By September 1, Army Group Center's sector was fairly quiet and stable, with most activity now in the sectors of adjacent army groups. As a result, most Soviet, German, and other Western sources say very little about Soviet strength and order of battle in this sector. Most order of battle has to be interpolated from order of battle known from the fighting around Smolensk (July) and the German drive on Moscow (late September). Information about Soviet order of battle in the Army Group Center area is generally less reliable for this time than for any other period during 1941.

Soviet units and stragglers were still breaking through to the east to rejoin Soviet forces and, on a day-to-day basis, were being rebuilt into operational units. Soviet command and control had improved since July, but some divisions still may have been functionally controlled by an army different from the one to which they were officially assigned. Some chaos is evident from the fact that, shortly after September 1, there were two 160th rifle divisions, which coexisted until one became a guards unit.

Attempting to make Table 5-A accurate specifically for September 1 causes ambiguities. By this time, corps headquarters in the "operational army" (those forces subordinated to active fronts) had generally been eliminated. The operational army was now receiving many newly mobilized rifle and cavalry divisions and the just-formed tank brigades. These new formations were apparently being allocated to armies on a day-to-day basis. Some units in Table 5-A may not have been formally allocated until a few days after September 1, and some other units that do not appear may actually have been allocated by them, but still en route.

The newly mobilized rifle divisions (generally numbered higher than 240th) were organized according to the July 29 *shtat* 04/600-16, with significant reductions in manpower, materiel, and organizational complexity. Existing divisions apparently adjusted to this *shtat* by attrition rather than by planned reorganization, except for the removal of surviving howitzer regiments and antitank battalions from some divisions. The motorized divisions, having lost their tanks and trucks, had been or were being converted into rifle divisions. The surviving pre-June tank divisions were being inactivated or converted into tank brigades. In July, new tank divisions had been formed on a reduced *shtat* (217 tanks), formed primarily by reorganizing units of the mechanized corps in the interior military districts. Several of these had been deployed to the Army Group Center sector, and because of combat losses, several had already been converted into motorized rifle divisions (retaining their numerical designations, which conflicted with those of some existing rifle divisions). The many cavalry divisions formed during the summer were weak (strength less than half the prewar *shtat*), but were needed because tank production was too low to provide an adequate mobile force. Newly produced tanks were given to the armored brigades, which had just started forming in August and were just starting to reach the front.

TABLE 5-A

Soviet Units Opposing Army Group Center.
September 1, 1941

Unit	Location	Commander

I. WEST THEATER

  A. West Front — Kasnia — Timoshenko, S. K., Marshal/SU

Unit	Location	Commander
16th Army	Yartsevo area	Rokossovski, K. K., M. Gen.
1st Moscow Mot. RD		Lizyukov, A. I., Col.
38th RD	Yartsevo area	Kirillov, M. G., Col.
152nd RD		Chernyshev, P. N., Col.
64th RD	Yelnia area	Gryaznov, A. S., Col.
108th RD		Orlov, N. I., Col.
101st TD	Dubrovo area?	Mikhailov, G. M., Col.
27th T. Brig.?		Remizov, F. T.
50th RD	N of Yelnia	Lebedenko, N. F., M. Gen.?
129th RD		
158th RD?		
19th Army		
134th RD?		Konev, I. S., Lt. Gen.
89th RD?		
91st RD?		
166th RD?		
20th Army	Dorogobuzh area	Lukin, M. F., Lt. Gen.
153rd RD	Rachino area	Gagen, N. A., Col.
161st RD?	W of Rudnia	Moskovitin, P. F., Col.?
229th RD?		
22nd Army (Only those units opposing Army Group Center)	Toropets area	Iushkevich, V. A., M. Gen.
98th RD?		
214th RD	Andreapol area?	
186th RD?		Biryukov, N. I., M. Gen.?
179th RD	Velikie Luki area?	
112th RD?		
126th RD?		Sorokin, V. Ye., Col.
170th RD?		Silkin, N. K., M. Gen.?
174th RD?	Velikie Luki area?	Zygin, A. I., M. Gen.?
29th Army	Toropets area	Maslennikov, I. I., Lt. Gen.
252nd RD?		
245th RD		
254th RD		
256th RD		
253rd RD		
243rd RD		

(continued)

TABLE 5-A

Soviet Units Opposing Army Group Center.
September 1, 1941 (Continued)

Unit	Location	Commander
30th Army	Olenino area	Khomenko, V. A., M. Gen.
119th RD		
242nd RD		
107th Mot. RD?		
251st RD	Belii area?	
51st TD (probably inactivated by Sept.)		
162nd RD? (or in 19th Army?)		
West Front direct control or subordination unknown		
Western Military District (Probably had only replacement units and perhaps supply installations)		
69th Mot. RD?		
69th TD		
101st Mot. RD?		
II. RESERVE FRONT		Zhukov, G. K., Gen.
24th Army	Yelnia area	Rakutin, K. I., M. Gen.
103rd Mot. D	Pozhogino	
105th Mot. D.	E of Marino	
19th RD	NW of Varaksina	
107th RD	SW of Mitino	Mironov, P. V., M. Gen.
120th RD	Konoplianka	Petrov, K. I., M. Gen.
133rd RD		
127th RD	Glukhov?	Akimenko, A. Z., Col.
194th RD		
248th RD		
100th RD	W of Ushakovo	Russiyanov, I. N., M. Gen.
309th RD	Moving toward Yelnia	
102nd TD	N of Marino	
106th Mot. D.	S of Bol. Lipnya	
303rd RD	SW of Bol. Lipnya	
6th Moscow DNO		Sidelnikov, A. D., Col.?
4th Moscow DNO	Yelnia area	Orlov, F. M.
31st Army	HQ Rzhev?	Dolmatov, V. N., M. Gen.
244th RD? (Or in 19th Army)		
246th RD		
247th RD		
249th RD		
119th RD		

TABLE 5–A

Soviet Units Opposing Army Group Center.
September 1, 1941 (Continued)

Unit	Location	Commander
32nd Army	Around Mishutino; HQ Viazma?	Fedyuninskiy, I.I., M. Gen.
2nd Moscow DNO		Vashkevich, V., M. Gen.
7th Moscow DNO	Dukhovshchina area?	Zaikin, I. V., Kom. Brig.
8th Moscow DNO	Dorogobuzh area	
13th Moscow DNO	NW of Viazma	
18th Moscow DNO	Khotnya area	
33rd Army	HQ Spas-Demensk	Onupriyenko, D. P., Kom. Brig.
1st Moscow DNO		Pronin, N. N., M. Gen.?
5th Moscow DNO	Moving to Kirov area	Presnyakov, I. A.?, M. Gen.
9th Moscow DNO?	Yelnia area	Bobrov, B. D., M. Gen.
17th Moscow DNO	Furmanovka area	Kozlov, (?) Col.
21st Moscow DNO	Kirov area	Bogdanov, A. V., Col.
43rd Army	Near Yelnia; HQ Kirov	Seleznev, D. M., Lt. Gen.
38th RD		
53rd RD		Konovalov, F. (?)
145th RD		
149th RD	In fragments	Zakharov, F. M., Lt. Gen.?
211th RD		
217th RD		
222nd RD	Korovets area	
279th RD		
303rd RD		
104th TD (Probably inactivated in Aug.)		Burkov, V., Col.
109th TD		
49th Army		Zakharkin, I. G., Lt. Gen.
194th Mtn. RD		
220th Mot. RD		
248th RD		Yerokhin, M. Ye., Col.
4th Moscow DNO		
Reserve Front direct control or subordination unknown		
73rd RD		
178th RD?		
III. BRIANSK FRONT	HQ SE of Briansk	Yeremenko, A. I., Lt. Gen.
3rd Army		Kreizer, Ya. G., M. Gen.
219th RD?		
280th RD?		

(continued)

TABLE 5-A

Soviet Units Opposing Army Group Center.
September 1, 1941 (Continued)

Unit	Location	Commander
13th Army		Gorodnyanskiy, A. M., M. Gen.
269th RD	SE of Pochep	Garnich, Col.
6th RD	Ochkino	Grishin, M. D., Col.
282nd RD	NE of Trubchevsk	
50th TD	Novgorod-Severskii area	Bakharov, B. S., Col.
132nd RD	NE of Novgorod-Severskii	Biryuzov, S. S., M. Gen.
137th RD	E of Trubchevsk	Grishin, I. T., Col.
143rd RD	NE of Novgorod-Severskii	
148th RD	Rudnia	Cherokmanov, F. M., Col.
160th RD	Novozybkov area?	Skugarev, I. M., M. Gen.
307th RD	SW of Trubchevsk	Terentyev, V. G., Col.
21st Mtn. CD		Kuliyev, Ya. K., Col.
52nd CD	SE of Novgorod-Severskii	Yakunin, N. P., Col.?
61st Avn. D.	Novgorod-Severskii	Ukhov, V. P., Col.
41st T. Brig.? (or later in Sept.?)		Nikolaiev, N. P., Lt. Col.
121st RD?	Gulki area?	
155th RD (or maybe in 21st Army)	S of Trubchevsk	Aleksandrov, P. A., M. Gen.
21st Army		Kuznetsov, V. I., Lt. Gen.
219th RD		Korzun, P. P., M. Gen.
187th RD		
5th CC		Kamkov, F. V., M. Gen.
3rd CD		Maleyev, M. F., M. Gen.?
14th CD		Kruchenkin, V. D., M. Gen.
154th RD	Fragmented	Fokanov, Ya. S., M. Gen.
151st RD?		
167th RD?		
117th RD		
102nd RD?		
24th RD	Korop area	
50th Army	Desna & Sudost R. S., HQ Vygonichi?	Petrov, M. P., M. Gen./TK
217th RD	Aug. Roslavl area?	
258th RD	Aug. Roslavl area	Trubnikov, K. P., Kom. Brig.?
260th RD	Aug. Pochep area	Khokhlov, V. D., Col.?
269th RD	Aug.	
278th RD	Aug.-Oct.	
279th RD	Aug.-Oct.	
280th RD	Aug. Pochep	Danilov, S. Ye., M. Gen.?
290th RD	Aug.-Oct.	Ryankin, N. V., Col.?
55th CD	Aug.	Fiksel, K. V., Col.?

TABLE 5-A

Soviet Units Opposing Army Group Center.
September 1, 1941 (Continued)

Unit	Location	Commander
Briansk Front direct control or subordination unknown		
204th RD?		
232nd RD		
283rd RD		
287th RD		
299th RD		
11th Avn D		
47th Avn D		
Front Mobile Group	SE of Trubchevsk	Yermakov, A. N., M. Gen.
121st Tk. Brig.?		
108th TD	Trubchevsk area	Ivanov, S. I., Col.
150th Tk. Brig.		
141st Tk. Brig.		Chernov, P. G., Col.
4th CD		
IV. SW THEATER		
A. SW Front		Kirponos, M. P., Col.-Gen.
40th Army	HQ Konotop	Podlas, K. P., M. Gen.
135th RD		
293rd RD	Novgorod-Severskii area	Lagutin, P. F., Col.
2nd Abn Corps		
10th TD	Glukhov area	Semenchenko, K. A., M. Gen.
5th AT. Brig.		
V. STAVKA RESERVE		
54th Army	NW of Moscow	Kulik, G. I., Marshal/SU
285th RD		
286th RD		
310th RD		
314th RD		
27th CD		
122nd Tk. Brig.		
119th ind. Tk. Bn.		
4th Abn. Corps	Near Moscow	
7th Abn. Brig.		Leschinin, V. A., Maj.
8th Abn. Brig.		Onufriyev, A. A., Col.
5th Abn Corps?		
9th Abn. Brig.		
201st Abn. Brig.		
In existence Subordination unknown		
31st CD		Pivnev, Ya. N., Col.

BIBLIOGRAPHY FOR APPENDIX A

SOVIET SOURCES

Anifilov, V. A. *Bessmertnyi podvig: issledovanie kanuna i pervogo etapa Velikoi Otechestvennoi voiny.* Moscow: Izdatelstvo Nauka, 1971.

Baklanov, G. B. *Veter voennykh let.* Moscow: Voennoe izdatelstvo, 1977.

Borba za Sovetskuiu pribaltiiu v Velikoi Otechestvennoi Voine: 1941-1945. Vol. 1: *Pervye gody.* Riga: Liesma, 1966.

Dorofeev, M. "O nekotorykh prichinakh neudachnykh deistvii mekhanizirovannykh korpusov v nachalnom periode Velikoi Otechestvennoi voine." *Voenno-istoricheskii zhurnal,* March 1964, pp. 32-45.

Galitsky, K. N. *Gody surovykh ispytanii: 1941-1945.* Moscow: Nauka, 1973.

Golubovich, V. "Sozdanie strategicheskikh rezervov." *Voenno-istoricheskii zhurnal,* April 1977, pp. 12-19.

Ivanov, S. P. *Nachalnyi period voiny.* Moscow: Voennoe izdatelstvo, 1974.

Krasnosznamennyi Dalnovostochnyi. Moscow: Voennoe izdatelstvo, 1974.

Krupennikov, A. "Severo-zapadnyi Bresta." *Voenno-istoricheskii zhurnal,* June 1966, pp. 29-66.

Lisov, I. I. *Desantniki.* Moscow: Voennoe izdatelstvo, 1968.

Malanin, K. "Razvitie organizatsionnykh form sukhoputnykh voisk v Velikoi Otechestvennoi voine." *Voenno-istoricheskii zhurnal,* August 1967, pp. 28-40.

Moskva Frontu: 1941-1945. Moscow: Nauka, 1966.

Ordena Lenina Zabaikalskii. Moscow: Voennoe izdatelstvo, 1980.

Pern, Lembit. *V Vikhre Voennykh Let.* Tallin: Eesti Raamat, 1976.

Rokossovskii, K. K. *Soldier's Duty.* Moscow: Progress, 1970.

Rotmistrov, P. A. *Vremia i tanki.* Moscow: Voennoe izdatelstvo, 1972.

Sandalov, L. M. *Na Moskovskom napravlenii.* Moscow: Nauka, 1970.

Simakov, E. "Sovershenstvovanie organizatsionnoi struktury Voenno-Vozdushnykh Sil." *Voenno-istoricheskii zhurnal,* Sept. 1978, pp. 25-31.

Sovetskaia Voennaia Entsiklopediia, 1976-1980. S. V. "Belorusskii voennyi okrug," "Pinskaia voennaia flotiliia," "Yelninskaia operatsiia 1941," "Zapadnyi front," "Zona P.V.O.," and articles on the 3rd, 4th, 9th, 11th, 13th, 16th, 19th, 20th, 21st, 22nd, 24th, 28th, 29th, 30th, 31st, 32nd, 33rd, 40th, 43rd, 49th, and 50th armies.

Sovetskie tankovye voiska: 1941-1945. Moscow: Voennoe izdatelstvo, 1973.

Strusevich, A. "Razvitie organizatsionnoi struktury Voisk PVO Strany v khode voiny." *Voenno-istoricheskii zhurnal,* Oct. 1978, pp. 35-42.

V plamenei srazheniia. Moscow: Voennoe izdatelstvo, 1973.

Zhukov, G. K. *Memoirs of Marshal Zhukov.* New York: Delacorte Press, 1973.

GERMAN SOURCES

Carrel, Paul. *Hitler Moves East.* New York: Ballantine, 1968.

Germany. Heer. Generalstab. Operations Abt. Fremde Heere Ost (IIC). *Der Feldzug gegen Sowjet-Russland.* Vol. 1, *Operationen Sommer Herbst 1941.* Berlin(?), 1942(?).

_____ . *Truppen-Übersicht und Kriegsgliederungen. Rote Armee. Stand August 1944.* Nr. 7000/44 Geheim.

_____ (?). *Panzer-Divisionen.* April 1942 or later. Apparently F.H.O. document; contains no bibliographic information except the title.

Germany. Heer. Heeresgruppe Kurland. *Der Feldzug gegen Die Sowjet-Union der Heeresgruppe Nord: Kriegsjahre 1941-1943.* Vol. 1 (1941). (1944?)

Guderian, Heinz. *Panzer Leader.* London: Michael Joseph, 1952.

U.S. War Department. TM 30-430. *Handbook on U.S.S.R. Military Forces.* Washington, G.P.O., November 1945.

OTHER WESTERN SOURCES

Erickson, John. *The Road to Stalingrad.* New York: Harper and Row, 1975.

_____ . *The Soviet High Command: 1918-1941.* London: Macmillan, 1962.

Grove, Eric. *Russian Armour: 1941-1943.* London: Almark, 1977.

Lundstrom, John. "The Great Retreat: The Soviet Army 22 June-1 December 1941."

Part I. *Little Wars,* Vol. 1:4 (Sept.-Oct. 1976), pp. 4-12;

Part II, *Little Wars,* Vol. 1:3 (Dec. 1976), pp. 4-15;

Part III, *Little Wars,* Vol. 1:4 (Feb. 1977), pp. 8-15.

Madej. V., and Stanton, S. "The Smolensk Campaign." *Strategy and Tactics* 57 (July-Aug. 1976): 4-19.

Seaton, Albert. *The Russo-German War, 1941-1945.* New York: Frederick A. Praeger, 1971.

Appendix B

ORGANIZATION AND STRUCTURE OF THE GERMAN ARMY, 1941

In an examination of the organization and structure of the German army in 1941 it is important to keep in mind the distinction between the Army *(Das Heer)* and the Armed Forces *(Die Wehrmacht)*. Since it was the Army that bore the brunt of the fighting in Russia, no attempt will be made here to discuss the structures of the other components of the armed forces. A detailed treatise on the Luftwaffe would be more appropriate in a book dealing with the Battle of Britain or the air battle over Germany from 1943 to 1945.

In 1941 much of the army's organizational structure was not at all different from what it had been in World War I. The foundation of the army was the military district *(Wehrkreis)*. In 1941 there were twenty-one districts in the Greater German Reich. Each district was home base to several divisions and their subordinate regiments. When war mobilization began in 1939 there were 51 divisions and 2 brigades. At the time of the Russian campaign, the strength of the army had risen to 208 divisions; of these about 154 were on the eastern front, including 4 German divisions in Finland.

The German war mobilization plan was based on a two-part *Ersatz,* or replacement system. Each peacetime unit that was already at full combat strength was supposed to have a permanent replacement unit behind it. The purpose of this replacement unit was to handle recruiting and training and also to organize the reservists should they be called up. Replacement divisional headquarters were set up that, during peacetime, had purely administrative functions.

This plan allowed for rapid mobilization in event of a war or crisis without causing large transportation or economic dislocations. When war occurred, four waves *(Welle)* of infantry could be raised on relatively short notice: (1) active units, (2) reservists, (3) *Landwehr* territorial units, and (4) men 19–20 years old *(Jahrgänge)* who had undergone a short period of training. The 1921 *Jahrgang* was called up in March 1941, and the 1922 group in May. These forces were brought into the replacement army *(Ersatzheer)*. In June, 1941, 80,000 men were available as immediate replacements for the eastern front, and another 300,000–350,000 were in the *Ersatzheer,* mostly in the 20th *Jahrgang.* In 1939 the population of the Greater German Reich was 80.6 million: 38.9 million men and 41.7 million women. Of the men, 12 million fell into the age group 15–34; of these, the Wehrmacht could expect to claim 7 million. In 1939 the civilian labor force was reckoned at 24.5 million men and 14.6 million women: 18.1 million men were employed in war-related or critical industries. In June 1941, the German Army had 3.8 million men, of which 3.3 million were deployed against the Soviet Union. Of 21 fully equipped panzer divisions, 17 were targeted for Russia, 2 were in the OKH reserve destined for Russia, and 2 were in North Africa. In 1941 the army high command structure was organized as shown in Figure 1–B.

The backbone of the German army was, of course, the infantry division. Of the 154 divisions deployed against Russia, including reserves, there were 100 infantry, 19 panzer, 11 motorized, 9 security, 5 Waffen SS, 4 light, 4 mountain, 1 SS police, and 1 cavalry. A typical infantry division in June 1941 had 17,734 men organized as follows:*

> three infantry regiments with staff, communications units
>> three battalions with:
>>> three light MG companies
>>> one heavy MG company
>> one PAK company (mot.)
>> one artillery company
> one reconnaissance unit
> one Panzerjäger unit with:
>> three companies (twelve 3.7cm guns)
> one artillery regiment
> one pioneer battalion
> one communications unit
> one field replacement battalion
> Supply, medical, veterinary, mail, and police

*Source: Mueller-Hillebrand, *Das Heer, 1933–1945,* vol. II, pp. 161–162.

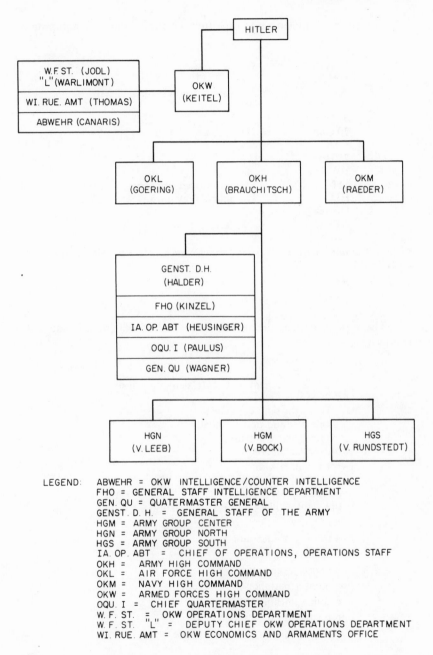

LEGEND: ABWEHR = OKW INTELLIGENCE/COUNTER INTELLIGENCE
FHO = GENERAL STAFF INTELLIGENCE DEPARTMENT
GEN. QU = QUATERMASTER GENERAL
GENST. D. H. = GENERAL STAFF OF THE ARMY
HGM = ARMY GROUP CENTER
HGN = ARMY GROUP NORTH
HGS = ARMY GROUP SOUTH
IA. OP. ABT = CHIEF OF OPERATIONS, OPERATIONS STAFF
OKH = ARMY HIGH COMMAND
OKL = AIR FORCE HIGH COMMAND
OKM = NAVY HIGH COMMAND
OKW = ARMED FORCES HIGH COMMAND
OQU. I = CHIEF QUARTERMASTER
W. F. ST. = OKW OPERATIONS DEPARTMENT
W. F. ST. "L" = DEPUTY CHIEF OKW OPERATIONS DEPARTMENT
WI. RUE. AMT = OKW ECONOMICS AND ARMAMENTS OFFICE

Figure 1-B. Organization of the German High Command, 1941

An infantry division was outfitted with the following equipment:*

LMG	378	
HMG	138	
ATL	90	(antitank rocket launchers)
50 Mtr	93	
81 Mtr	54	
20 Gun	12	
PAK	75	
75 How	20	
105 How	36	
MT	1009	(motorized transport vehicles)
HD	918	(horse-drawn transport vehicles)
Horses	4842	
AFV	3	(armored fighting vehicles)

*Source: *War in the East: The Russo-German Conflict, 1941–1945* (Simultations Publications, 1977), p. 141.

The typical panzer division in 1941 had 15,600 men organized as follows:*

one panzer regiment with staff, communications units
  two panzer units with:
    two light tank companies
    one medium tank company
    one repair company
  one repair company
two battalions with:
  three light MG companies
  one heavy MG company
  one light artillery and PAK company
one infantry artillery company
one reconnaissance unit
one artillery regiment
one Panzerjäger unit
one pioneer battalion
one communications unit
one field-surgical battalion
Supply, veterinary, mail, and police

*Source: Mueller-Hillebrand, *Das Heer, 1933–1945,* vol. II, pp. 182–183.

A panzer division was outfitted with the following equipment:*

LMG	850
HMG	1067
ATL	45
81 Mtr	30
20 Gun	74
PAK	75
75 How	18
105 How	196
MT	2900
Tanks	165

*Source: War in the East: The Russo-German Conflict, 1941-1945, p. 144.

The typical motorized infantry division in 1941 had 16,400 men organized as follows (in 1943, these units were given extra armor and renamed "Panzer Grenadiers"):*

two infantry regiments with staff, communications units
three battalions with:
three light MG companies
one heavy MG company
one motorcycle platoon
one artillery company
one PAK company
two motorcycle battalions with:
three light MG companies
one heavy MG company
one light artillery and PAK company
one reconnaisance unit
one artillery regiment
one Panzerjäger unit
one pioneer battalion
one communications unit
one field-surgical battalion
Supply, veterinary, mail, and police

*Source: Mueller-Hillebrand, Das Heer, 1933-1945, vol. II, pp. 179-180.

A motorized infantry division was outfitted with the following equipment:*

LMG	810
HMG	712
ATL	63
50 Mtr	57
81 Mtr	36
20 Gun	12
PAK	63
75 How	14
105 How	48
MT	2800
AFV	82

Source: War in the East: The Russo-German Conflict, 1941–1945, p. 144.

TABLE 1–B*
Availability of German Armored Vehicles on the Eastern Front, June 22, 1941

Panzer Model	Number
I	ca. 180
II	1518
III	965
IV	439
Armored Command Vehicles	230
Total Tanks:	ca. 3332
Sturmgeschütz Self-Propelled Artillery	250
Total AFVs	ca. 3582

Source: Mueller-Hillebrand, Das Heer, 1933–1945, vol. II, p. 106.

TABLE 2–B
Production of Tanks and Self-propelled Artillery in 1941

Period	II	III	IV	CMD.	Stug.	Total
1Q	155	288	85	60	104	692
2Q	234	400	103	41	151	929
3Q	276	484	128	13	122	1023
4Q	266	541	164	18		1152
Totals:	931	1713	480	132	540	3796

*Source: Mueller-Hillebrand, Das Heer, 1933–1945, vol. II, p. 106.

TABLE 3-B

Tank Availability on the Eastern Front,
September 4, 1941

	Unit	Combat-Ready	In Repair	Total Losses	Initial Strength
	9th PD	62	67	28	157
Panzer Group I	13th PD	96	30	21	147
	14th PD	112	24	21	157
	16th PD	61	26	70	157
Total Panzer Group I		331	147	140	618
(in %)		(53)	(24)	(23)	(100)
Temporarily subordinated to to 6th Army	11th PD	60	75	40	175
	3rd PD	41	157		198
Panzer Group II	4th PD	49	120		169
	17th PD	38	142		180
	18th PD	62	138		200
Total Panzer Group II		190	557		747
(in %)		(25)	(75)		(100)
Temporarily subordinated to 4th Army	10th PD	159	22	25	206
	7th PD	130	87	82	299
Panzer Group III	19th PD	102	47	90	239
	20th PD	88	62	95	245
Total Panzer Group III		320	196	267	783
(in %)		(41)	(25)	(34)	(100)
	1st PD	97	24	33	154
Panzer Group IV	6th PD	188	11	55	254
	8th PD	155	33	35	223
Total Panzer Group IV		440	68	123	631
(in %)		(70)	(11)	(19)	(100)
Temporarily subordinated to 16th Army	12th PD	96	34	101	231
Total for Eastern Front		1596	542	696	3391
			+ 557		
(in %)		(47)	(ca. 23)	(ca. 30)	(100)

*Source: Mueller-Hillebrand, *Das Heer, 1933–1945,* vol. III, p. 205.

PART II

ARMY GROUP CENTER ORDER OF BATTLE, JUNE AND OCTOBER, 1941

The Units of Army Group Center, June 21, 1941

Panzer Group 2 (Guderian)
  XXIVth Panzer Corps (Geyer von Schweppenburg)
    1st Cav. Div., 3rd Pz, 4th Pz, 10th Mot.Div., 267th ID
  XLVIth Panzer Corps (von Vietinghoff)
    SS *"DR"* Div., 10th Pz, Inf. Reg. *"GD"*
  XLVIIth Panzer Corps (Lemelsen)
    17th Pz, 18th Pz, 29th Mot.Div., 167th ID
  XIIth Army Corps (Schroth)
    31st ID, 34th ID, 45th ID
  Reserve: 255th ID

Fourth Army (von Kluge)
  VIIth Army Corps (Fahrmbacher)
    7th ID, 23rd ID, 258th ID, 268th ID, 221st Sec.Div.
  IXth Army Corps (Geyer)
    137th ID, 263rd ID, 292nd ID
  XIIIth Army Corps (Felber)
    17th ID, 78th ID
  XLIIIrd Army Corps (Heinrici)
    131st ID, 134th ID, 252nd ID
  Reserve: 286th ID

Ninth Army (Strauss)
  VIIIth Army Corps (Heitz)
    8th ID, 28th ID, 161st ID
  XXth Army Corps (Materna)
    162nd ID, 256th ID
  XLIInd Army Corps (Kuntze)
    87th ID, 102nd ID, 129th ID
  Reserve: 403rd Sec.Div.

Panzer Group 3 (Hoth)
  Vth Army Corps (Ruoff)
    5th ID, 35th ID
  VIth Army Corps (Förster)
    6th ID, 26th ID
  XXXIXth Panzer Corps (Schmidt)
    7th Pz, 20th Pz, 14th Mot.Div., 20th Mot.Div.
  LVIIth Panzer Corps (Kuntzen)
    12th Pz, 18th Pz, 19th Pz

In addition, the following command organizations and units were held in reserve directly by Army Group Center or by the OKH in the Army Group Center area.

Second Army, XXXVth Army Corps, XLth Panzer Corps, LIIIrd Army Corps, 15th ID, 110th ID, 197th ID, 293rd ID, Lehrbrigade 900

The Units of Army Group Center, October 2, 1941

Second Army (von Weichs)
  LIIIrd Army Corps (Weisenberger)
    56th ID, 31st ID, 167th ID
  LXIIIrd Army Corps (Heinrici)
    52nd ID, 131st ID
  XIIIth Army Corps (Felber)
    260th ID, 17th ID
  Reserve: 112th ID

Second Panzer Army (Guderian)
  XXXIVth Army Corps (Metz)
    45th ID, 134th ID
  XXXVth Army Corps (Kempfe)
    95th ID, 296th ID, 262nd ID, 293rd ID
  XLVIIIth Panzer Corps (Kempff)
    9th Pz, 16th Mot.Div., 25th Mot.Div.
  XXIVth Panzer Corps (Geyer von Schweppenburg)
    3rd Pz, 4th Pz, 10th Mot.Div.
  XLVIIth Panzer Corps (Lemelsen)
    17th Pz, 18th Pz, 29th Mot.Div.

Fourth Army (von Kluge)
  VIIth Army Corps (Fahrmbacher)
    197th ID, 7th ID, 23rd ID, 267th ID
  XXth Army Corps (Materna)
    268th ID, 15th, 78th ID
  IXth Army Corps (Geyer)
    137th ID, 263rd ID, 183rd ID, 292nd ID

Panzer Group 4 (Hoepner), Subordinated to Fourth Army
  XIIth Army Corps (Schroth)
    34th ID, 98th ID
  XLth Army Corps (Stumme)
    10th Pz, 2nd Pz, 258th ID
  XLVIth Panzer Corps (von Vietinghoff)
    5th Pz, 11th Pz, 252nd ID
  LVIIth Panzer Corps (Kuntzen)
    20th Pz, SS *"Das Reich"* Mot.Div., 3rd Mot.Div.

(continued)

The Units of Army Group Center,
October 2, 1941 (Continued)

Ninth Army (Strauss)
    XXVIIth Army Corps (Wäger)
        255th ID, 162nd ID, 86th ID
    Vth Army Corps (Ruoff)
        5th ID, 35th ID, 106th ID, 129th ID
    VIIIth Army Corps (Heitz)
        8th ID, 28th ID, 87th ID
    XXIIIrd Army Corps (Schubert)
251st ID, 102nd ID, 256th ID, 206th ID
    Reserve: 161st ID

Panzer Group 3 (Hoth), Subordinated to Ninth Army
    LVIth Panzer Corps (Schaal)
        6th Pz, 7th Pz, 14th Mot.Div.
    XLIst Panzer Corps (Reinhardt)
        1st Pz, 36th Mot.Div.
    VIth Army Corps (Förster)
        110th ID, 26th ID, 6th ID

Note: From July 3 to July 29, 1941, the "Fourth Panzer Army" existed under the command of Field Marshal von Kluge. This unit was composed of Panzer Groups 2 and 3 and the IXth and XXth army corps. The OKH believed this new command arrangement would further its goal of reaching Moscow as rapidly as possible in 1941.

Notes

INTRODUCTION

1. See P. Frank, "The Changing Composition of the Communist Party," in *The Soviet Union since the Fall of Khrushchev* (London, 1975), pp. 96–120; F. Hough and M. Fainsod, *How the Soviet Union Is Governed* (Cambridge, Mass., 1979), p. 574.
2. See the comment about this thesis in M. Florinsky, *Russia: A History and an Interpretation* (2 vols.; New York, 1964), vol. I, pp. 215–216.
3. For example, see V. Kluchkevsky, *A History of Russia* (5 vols.; London, 1926), vol. IV.
4. Florinsky, *Russia,* vol I, pp. 421–422.
5. An interesting commentary on the phenomenon of the modern Soviet officer, can be found in R. Gabriel, *The New Red Legions: An Attitudinal Portrait of the Soviet Soldier* (Westport, Conn., 1980), p. 86.
6. See E. Tarle, *Napoleon's Invasion of Russia, 1812* (New York, 1942).
7. Florinsky, *Russia,* vol. II, p. 1352.
8. F. Fischer, *Germany's Aims in the First World War* (New York, 1967), p. 13; H. Holborn, *A History of Modern Germany,* (3 vols; New York, 1959–1969), vol. III, p. 375; D. Treadgold, *Twentieth-Century Russia* (Chicago, 1964), p. 103.
9. N. Stone, "Field-Marshal Paul von Hindenburg," in *The War Lords* (London, 1976), p. 52.

CHAPTER 1
PRE-WAR SOVIET DEFENSE PLANNING AND STRATEGY

1. R. Garthoff, *Soviet Military Policy: A Historical Analysis* (New York, 1966), p. 34. See also J. Erickson, *The Soviet High Command: A Military-Political History 1918-1941* (London, 1962), p. 31.

2. For example, see G. Kennan, *Decision to Intervene* (Princeton, 1959).

3. For a good account of Frunze's theories, see W. Jacobs, *Frunze: The Soviet Clausewitz, 1885-1925* (The Hague, 1969).

4. V. Sokolovsky, *Soviet Military Strategy,* 3rd ed., trans. H. Scott (Stanford, 1957), pp. 121-122.

5. For a good description of the Soviet General Staff and its history, see H. and W. Scott, *The Armed Forces of the USSR* (Boulder, Colo., 1979), pp. 102-113.

6. M. Zakharov, "O teorii glubokii operatsii," *Voenno-istoricheskii zhurnal,* Oct. 1970, pp. 13-14.

7. *50 let vooruzhennihk sil SSSR* (Moscow, 1968), p. 215; G. Isserson, "Razvitie teorii Sovetskogo operativnogo iskusstva v 30-e gody," *Voenno-istoricheskii zhurnal,* March 1965, pp. 52-60.

8. M. Garder, *A History of the Soviet Army* (New York, 1966), p. 75.

9. Isserson, "Razvitie teorii operativnogo iskusstva v 30-e gody," *Voenno-istoricheskii zhurnal,* March 1965, p. 60.

10. L. Shapiro, "The Great Purge," in *The Soviet Army,* ed. B. H. Liddell Hart (London, 1956), p. 69.

11. H. Thomas, *The Spanish Civil War* (New York, 1961), p. 316.

12. K. Kolganov, *Razvitie taktiki Sovetskoi Armii v grody Velikoi Otechest-vennoi voiny, 1941-1945 gg.* (Moscow, 1958), pp. 106-107.

13. See *Voprosy strategii i operativnogo iskusstva v Sovetskikh voennykh trudakh,* ed. A. Siniaev (Moscow, 1965), pp. 613-615.

14. For a good overview of the Soviet economy on the eve of the war, see G. Kravchenko, *Ekonomika SSSR v gody Velikoi Otechestvennoi voiny, 1941-1945 gg.* (Moscow, 1970).

15. Ibid., pp. 74-75.

16. See J. Lundstrom, "The Soviet Mechanized Corps," in *Panzerfaust,* Sept./Oct. 1972, pp. 4-5. See also F. Halder, *Kriegstagebuch* (3 vols; Stuttgart, 1962-1964), vol. II, p. 267; Liddell Hart, *History of the Second World War* (New York, 1970), pp. 158-159.

17. B. Mueller-Hillebrand, *Das Heer, 1933-1945* (3 vols.; Frankfurt/M., 1954-1956), vol. II, p. 106.

18. J. Erickson, *Soviet Command and Control: Past, Present and Future* (unpublished manuscript supplied by the Center for Strategic Technology, Texas A & M University, Sept. 1980), p. 69; A. Seaton, *The Russo-German War, 1941-1945* (New York, 1971), pp. 588-589.

19. Kravchenko, *Ekonomika SSSR,* pp. 202-213; W. Boelke, *Deutschlands Rüstung im Zweiten Weltkrieg: Hitlers Conferenzen mit Albert Speer, 1942-1945* (Frankfurt/ M., 1969), pp. 22-25; A. Milward, *The German Economy at War* (London, 1965), pp. 28-53.

20. H. Guderian, "Russian Strategy in the War", in *The Red Army*, ed. B. H. Liddell Hart (New York, 1956), pp. 130–131; S. Westphal, *Heer in Fesseln: aus den Papieren des Stabchefs von Rommel, Kesselring und Rundstedt* (Bonn, 1952), p. 80; J. Erickson, *The Soviet High Command*, pp. 576–577; W. Laqueur, *Russia and Germany: A Century of Conflict* (London, 1965), p. 261.

21. A. Samsonov, *Velikaia bitva pod Moskvoi, 1941–1942* (Moscow, 1958), p. 184.

22. Gehlen, *The Service* (New York, 1972), p. 26.

23. Siniaev, *Voprosy strategii*, pp. 22, 112 ff.; Savkin, *Osnovnye printsipi taktiki*, pp. 59–60; Zakharov, "O teorii glubokoi operatsii," *Voenno-istoricheskii zhurnal*, Oct. 1970, pp. 13–20; S. Kozlov, *O Sovetskoi voennoi nauke* (Moscow, 1964), pp. 187–188.

24. A. Clark, *Barbarossa* (New York, 1965), pp. 29–30; Erickson, *The Soviet High Command*, pp. 576–577. See also Ivanov, "Sovetskaia strategiia," *Vsemirno-istoricheskaia pobeda sovetskogo naroda, 1941–1945 gg.*, ed. A. Grechko (Moscow, 1971), p. 208.

25. V. Sokolovsky, *Soviet Military Strategy* (New Jersey, 1963), p. 256; Platonov, *Vtoraia mirovaia voina, 1939–1945 gg.* (Moscow, 1958), p. 166.

26. N. Pavlenko, "Reshaiushchaia rol SSSR i ego vooruzhennykh sil v razgrome germanskogo imperializma," *Voenno-istoricheskii zhurnal*, Jan. 1960, p. 26.

27. Isserson, "Razvitie teorii operativnogo iskusstva," *Voenno-istoricheskii zhurnal*, March 1965, p. 52.

28. See Anfilov, *Bessmertnyi podvig; issledovanie kanuna i pervogo etapa Velikoi Otechestvennoi voiny* (Moscow, 1971), pp. 129–130, 145.

29. S. Zaloga, "Organization of the Soviet Armored Force, 1939–1945," preliminary unpublished study 1981, pp. 2–4.

30. Ibid., p. 107. See also V. Vorobev, *Boevoi put Sovetskikh Vooruzhennykh Sil* (Moscow, 1960), p. 283; *Istoriia Velikoi Otechestvennoi voiny Sovetskogo Soiuza, 1941–1945 gg.* (6 vols.; Moscow, 1960–1965), vol. II, pp. 40–41; M. Dorofeev, "O nekotorykh prichinakh neudachnykh deistvii mekhanizirovannykh korpusov v nachalnom periode Velikoi Otechestvennoi voiny," *Voenno-istoricheskii zhurnal*, March 1964, pp. 34–36.

31. Isserson, "Razvitie teorii operativnogo iskusstva," *Voenno-istoricheskii zhurnal*, March 1965, p. 60; Hilger, *The Incompatible Allies: A Memoir-History of German-Soviet Relations, 1918–1941* (New York, 1953), p. 330.

32. Zhukov, *The Memoirs of Marshal Zhukov* (London, 1971), pp. 183–186; M. Kazakov, *Nad kartoi bylykh srazhenii* (Moscow, 1971), pp. 51–56; Anfilov, *Bessmertnyi podvig*, pp. 138–144.

33. Anfilov, *Bessmertnyi podvig*, p. 141.

34. Ibid., pp. 138–139; Kazakov, *Nad kartoi bylykh srazhenii*, pp. 53–54.

35. Anfilov, *Bessmertnyi podvig*, p. 175; A. Fedorov, *Aviatsiia v bitve pod Moskvoi* (Moscow, 1971), pp. 15–17. See also Erickson, *The Soviet High Command*, p. 581.

36. B. Kolchigin, "Mysli ob ispolzovanii armii prikrytiia v nachalnom periode Velikoi Otechestvennoi voiny," *Voenno-istoricheskii zhurnal*, April 1961, p. 36.

37. Zhukov, *Memoirs*, p. 184.

38. See G. Komkov, "Sovetskie organy gosudarstvennoi bezopasnosti v gody Velikoi Otechestvennoi voiny," *Voprosy istorii,* May 1965, p. 27.

39. Kazakov, *Nad kartoi bylykh srazhenii,* p. 55; Anfilov, *Bessmertnyi podvig,* p. 175.

40. Anfilov, *Bessmertnyi podvig,* p. 147.

41. Kazakov, *Nad kartoi bylykh srazhenii,* p. 57.

42. *Memoirs,* p. 185.

43. Kazakov, *Nad kartoi bylykh srazhenii,* pp. 58–59.

44. Zhukov, *Memoirs,* p. 186.

45. Ibid., p. 187; Anfilov, *Bessmertnyi podvig,* p. 147; Kazakov, *Nad kartoi bylykh srazhenii,* p. 62.

46. B. Wolfe, *Khrushchev and Stalin's Ghost* (New York), p. 172; I. Deutscher, *Stalin: A Political Biography* (London, 1949), pp. 471–472.

47. *Memoirs,* p. 248.

48. See V. Anfilov, *Nachalo Velikoi Otechestvennoi voiny* (Moscow, 1962), pp. 41–43.

49. H. Picker, *Hitlers Tischgespräche im Führerhauptquartier* (Stuttgart, 1965), p. 472. Using the USSR 1939 and 1959 census data, it can be calculated that approximately 3 million Soviet Jews perished in territories occupied by the Germans during the war. After the Molotov–Ribbentrop pact in August 1939, the word *Jew* disappeared from the Soviet press and nothing was written about the Nazi anti-Jewish excesses in Europe. There were, therefore, few Jews who saw the need to evacuate the western part of the Soviet Union even after 22 June 1941. See the articles by G. Aronson and A. Goldstein in *Russian Jewry, 1917–1967* (New York, 1969), pp. 88–122, 171–208.

50. A. Hillgruber, *Hitlers Strategie: Politik und Kriegführung, 1940–1941* (Frankfurt/M., 1965), pp. 510–530; H. Greiner, *Die oberste Wehrmachtführung, 1939–1943* (Wiesbaden), pp. 370–371.

51. For the text of the Commissar Decree see H.-A. Jacobsen, "The Kommissarbefehl and Mass Executions of Soviet Prisoners of War," in *Anatomy of the SS State,* ed. H. Krausnick (London, 1968), pp. 507–534.

52. *The Trial of German Major War Criminals: Proceedings of the International Military Tribunal Sitting at Nuremberg Germany,* part 4 (London: HMSO, 1946), pp. 17–18.

53. See Zhukov, *Memoirs,* pp. 232–233; and Anfilov, *Bessmertnyi podvig,* p. 186. See also *June 22, 1941; Soviet Historians and the German Invasion,* ed. V. Petrov (Columbia, S. C., 1968), p. 205; Kazakov, *Nad kartoi bylykh srazhenni,* p. 66.

54. For some details of Pavlov's arrest, see A. Eremenko, *Na zapadnom napravlenni* (Moscow, 1959), pp. 20–21.

55. *Kolganov, Razvitie taktiki Sovetskoi Armii,* pp. 320–321; Radzievskii, "Razvitie taktiki sukhoputnykh voisk," *Vsemirno-istoricheskaia pobeda,* p. 230.

56. Army Group Center captured Soviet documents in July 1941 that ordered the employment of this tactic by the front-line forces. See Second Army, Ia., "KTB Teil I," 15 July 1941, 16690/1, National Archives Microfilm Publication T-312, roll 1654, frame 000038 (hereafter cited as T-312/1654/00038).

This order was actually transmitted by Zhukov to the fronts on 27 June. See Zhukov, *Memoirs*, pp. 256–257.

57. G. Weinberg, "The Yelnia–Dorogobuzh Area of the Smolensk Oblast," in *Soviet Partisans in World War II*, ed. J. Armstrong (Madison, Wis., 1964), pp. 406–413; K. De Witt and W. Moll, "The Bryansk Area," ibid., p. 468; H. Bergen, "Encirclement and Annihilation of the Russian 32nd Cossack Division, 6 and 7 August, 1941," (unpublished study by Dept. of the Army, Office of the Chief of Military History, Washington, D.C., 1947), National Archives MS., D–075, p. 2.

58. H. Greiffenberg, "Battle of Moscow, 1941–1942," (unpublished study by Historical Division, HQ U.S. Army Europe, Foreign Military Studies Branch, 1948), National Archives MS., no. T–28, p. 91. Greiffenberg was the chief of staff for Army Group Center.

59. Ibid., p. 212.

60. Ibid., p. 231; *Istoriia Velikoi Otechestvennoi voiny*, vol. II, p. 20; Anfilov, *Bessmertnyi podvig*, p. 188; Lestev, "Doneseni upravleniia politpropagndy zapadnogo fronta glavnomu upravleniiu politpropagandy Krasnoi Armii o boevykh deistviiakh voisk fronta," *Voprosy istorii*, August 1961, pp. 98–99. See also S. Bialer, *Stalin and His Generals* (New York, 1969), p. 208; J. Erickson, *The Road to Stalingrad: Stalin's War with Germany* (London, 1975), vol. 1, p. 102.

61. See *50 let Vooruzhennykh Sil SSSR*, p. 235; Anfilov, *Bessmertnyi podvig*, pp. 114–115; B. Mueller-Hillebrand, *Das Heer*, vol. II, p. 107.

62. Anfilov, *Bessmertnyi podvig*, p. 115; Vorobev, *Boevoi put*, p. 207; Platonov, *Vtoraia mirovaia voina*, pp. 177–178.

63. See Erickson, *The Road to Stalingrad*, pp. 62–63. See also G. Blumentritt, "Commentary to the Battle of Moscow during the Winter of 1941–1942," (unpublished study by Historical Division, HQ U.S. Army Europe, Foreign Military Studies Branch, 1948), appendix to National Archives MS., T–28, pp. 292–293.

64. Zhukov, *Memoirs*, p. 196.

65. Ibid., p. 250; Anfilov, *Bessmertnyi podvig*, p. 174. See also Panzer Group 2, Ia., "KTB Nr. I," vol. I, 22 June 1941, 25034/1, T–313/80/7318385.

66. Platonov, *Vtoraia mirovaia voina*, p. 177.

67. Zhukov, *Memoirs*, p. 211.

68. Ibid., pp. 228–229; Guderian, "Russian Strategy in the War," in *The Red Army*, pp. 130–131.

69. Zhukov, *Memoirs*, p. 211.

70. Reports from Russian prisoners captured by the Second Army confirmed that Marshal Timoshenko was in personal command of the attacks against the southern flank of Army Group Center from the direction of Gomel. See Second Army, "KTB Teil I," 16 July 1941, T–312/1654/0041.

71. On 15 July 1941 a curious event occurred that has not yet been adequately explained. On that date the German LIIIrd Army Corps discovered a map concealed in a Komsomol house on the Bobruisk–Rogachev road. This map was described as a "high command war game exercise organized by Marshal Timoshenko." The map was dated February 1941 and showed that as the

German armored units crossed the Dnepr north of Rogachev, they would be hit by a pincers attack from the southeast direction, from Zhlobin–Rogachev, and toward the southwest through Mogilev. The two groups were to converge at Bobruisk. The southeast wing of the attack was to have at least twenty rifle divisions and a cavalry corps. As will be seen, these forces described on the map were virtually identical to those actually encountered by the Germans in Timoshenko's counterattack in July. Curiously also, the BBC announced that same night that Timoshenko's counterattack had begun north of the Pripet Marshes, which would drive back the German armies. See LIIIrd Army Corps, "KTB I," 15 July 1941, T-313/1310/000086. The map episode was described in a U.S. Army Historical Division Special Staff Study "Peculiarities of Russian Warfare," MS T-22, June 1949, pp. 17–18. This particular document contains an English language version of Timoshenko's map. Extracts from this study were included in Department of the Army Pamphlet no. 20-230, "Russian Combat Methods in World War II," 1950, pp. 8–12. Who the German participants were who took part in the original Historical Division study are not known. Also, neither is known the whereabouts of the original Soviet map, if it still exists, nor who the Soviet participants in the war game were besides Marshal Timoshenko. It is also open to speculation how the map appeared at that location and why the Germans knew to search that particular house. This author believes the war game was held away from Moscow in February in order to keep the real operations plan a secret from all (including Pavlov) but a few senior officers. See also Kolganov, *Razvitie taktiki Sovetskoi Armii,* pp. 90–93; Krasilnikov, "O strategicheskom rukovodstve v Velikoi Otechestvennoi voiny," *Voenno-istoricheskii zhurnal,* June 1960, p. 9.

72. Zhukov, *Memoirs,* p. 230.

73. Ibid., p. 218; Anfilov, *Bessmertnyi podvig,* p. 174.

74. V. Zemkov, "Nekotorye voprosy sozdaniia i ispolzovanniia strategicheskikh reservov," *Voenno-istoricheskii zhurnal,* Oct. 1971, pp. 13–14.

75. Ibid., p. 13; *Istoriia Velikoi Otechestvennoi voiny,* vol. II, p. 35.

76. A. Seaton, *Stalin as Warlord* (London, 1976), pp. 101–103; J. Erickson, *The Road to Stalingrad: Stalin's War with Germany* (London, 1975), pp. 72–73.

77. Fedorov, *Aviatsia v bitve pod Moskvoi,* pp. 22–24; *Istoriia vtoroi mirovoi voiny, 1939-1945* (12 vols.; Moscow, 1973–1980), vol. IV, pp. 35–36.

78. Wolfe, *Khrushchev and Stalin's Ghost,* pp. 172–174.

79. Zhukov, *Memoirs,* p. 230.

80. Ibid., p. 230.

81. Ibid., pp. 220–221.

82. See N. Voznesensky, *The Economy of the U.S.S.R. during World War II* (Washington, D.C., 1948), pp. 22–24. For more recent commentaries on the evacuation of Soviet industries, see "Tankovaia promyshlennost" in *Sovetskaia voennaia entsiklopedia* (8 vols., Moscow: Voennoe Izdatelstvo, 1976-1980), vol. VII, pp. 662–664; *Istoriia vtoroi mirovoi voiny, 1939-1945* (12 vols., Moscow: Voennoe Izdatelstvo, 1973–1980), vol. IV, pp. 149–162.

83. V. Kravtsov, "Krakh nemetsko-fashistskogo plana 'Barbarossa'," *Voenno-istoricheskii zhurnal,* Dec. 1968, p. 44. See also Zhukov, *Memoirs,* p. 217,

and P. Sokolov, "Opyt kommunisticheskoi partii po ispolzovaniiu liudskikh resursov v gody voiny," *Vsemirno-istoricheskaia pobeda,* p. 445.

84. See *50 let Vooruzhennykh Sil SSSR,* pp. 277-278; *Istoriia Velikoi Otechestvennoi voiny,* vol. II, p. 69.

85. W. Goerlitz, *Generalfeldmarschall Keitel; Verbrecher oder Offizier?* (Göttingen, 1961, p. 274).

CHAPTER 2
GERMAN PLANS FOR THE INVASION OF THE USSR

1. F. Halder, *Kriegstagebuch,* vol. II, pp. 30–34.

2. For the background of the discussion of when Hitler decided to attack the Soviet Union see G. Weinberg, "Der deutsche Entschluss zum Angriff auf die Sowjetunion," *Vierteljahrshefte für Zeitgeschichte,* vol. I (Oct. 1953), 301–315; H. Seraphim and A. Hillgruber, "Hitlers Entschluss zum Zngriff auf Russland," ibid., vol. II (July 1954), pp. 240–254; H. R. Trevor–Roper, "Hitlers Kriegsziele," ibid, vol. VIII (April 1960), pp. 123–133. For the Soviet point of view see Petrov, *June 22, 1941: Soviet Historians and the German Invasion,* p. 25.

3. B. Leach, *German Strategy against Russia, 1939–1941* (Oxford, 1973), pp. 59–60; H. Greiner, *Die oberste Wehrmachtführung,* pp. 292–293.

4. On July 24, 1960, the general staff Intelligence Department reckoned Soviet strength in western Russia at ninety rifle and thirty-three cavalry divisions, plus twenty-eight mechanized brigades. See Hillgruber, *Hitlers Strategie,* p. 213; H. Uhlig, "Das Einwirken Hitlers auf Planung und Führung des Ostfeldzuges," *Das Parlement,* supplement, 16 March 1960, p. 165; B. Von Lossberg, *Im Wehrmachtführungsstab: Bericht eines Generalstabsoffizier* (Hamburg, 1949), pp. 137–138; P. Leverkuehn, *German Military Intelligence* (London, 1954), p. 157; D. Proektor, *Agressia i Katastrofa* (Moscow, 1968), p. 178.

5. See Halder, *Kriegstagebuch,* vol. II, pp. 34, 37 for the Kinzel report. For the Greiffenberg–Feyerabend report see ibid., p. 39. See also Hillgruber, *Hitlers Strategie,* p. 220; Leach, *German Strategy,* p. 97; G. Buchheit, *Soldatentum und Rebellion: die Tragödie der deutschen Wehrmacht* (Rastatt, 1961), p. 285.

6. Uhlig, "Das Einwirken Hitlers," *Das Parlement,* supplement, 16 March 1960, p. 170.

7. For an interesting commentary on the Halder–Brauchitsch relationship, see H. Schall–Riacour, *Aufstand und Gehorsam: Offizierstum und Generalstab im Umbruch: Leben und Wirken von Generaloberst Franz Halder, Generalstabschef, 1938–1942* (Wiesbaden, 1972), p. 126.

8. Halder, *Kriegstagebuch,* vol. II, p. 46.

9. Ibid., p. 50.

10. W. Warlimont, *Inside Hitler's Headquarters,* (New York, 1964), pp. 138–139.

11. O. Jacobsen, *Erich Marcks: Soldat und Gelehrter* (Göttingen, 1971), pp. 90 ff.

12. E. Marcks, "Operationsentwurf Ost," August 1940, 21-g-16/4q, T-84/271/902-923.

13. A. Philippi, "Das Pripjetproblem," *Wehrwissenschaftliche Rundschau,* supplement, March 1956, pp. 69–72.

14. J.F.C. Fuller, *The Second World War, 1939–1945* (New York, 1949), pp. 116–117; G. Buchheit, *Hitler der Feldherr* (Rastatt, 1958), pp. 211–212. Buchheit describes the Marcks plan as similar in concept to Moltke's at Metz in 1870. According to him, Marcks intended for the Wehrmacht to stand on the defensive on a broad front between Riga and the upper Dnepr, while a

strong southern force should push to the Don and then turn north, forcing the Soviets to fight a battle with reversed fronts.

15. See O. Jacobsen, *Erich Marcks,* pp. 166–199.

16. Halder, *Kriegstagebuch,* vol. II, p. 51; Hillgruber, *Hitlers Strategie,* p. 227. The official Soviet history of the war criticizes the Marcks plan for failing to take into consideration the danger to the flanks of the Central Army Group. See *Istoriia Velikoi Otechestvennoi voiny,* vol. I, p. 353.

17. K. Tippelskirch, *Geschichte des Zweiten Weltkrieges* (Bonn, 1956), p. 107.

18. See *Kriegstagebuch des Oberkommandos der Wehrmacht* (hereafter sited as *Kriegstagebuch OKW),* ed. P. Schramm (4 vols.; Frankfurt/m., 1961–1965), vol. I, pp. 266–267; "Protokol doprosa generala githerovskoi armii Waltera Warlimonta," *Niurnbergskii protsess nad glavnymi nemetskimi voennymi prestupnikami* (7 vols; Moscow, 1957–1961), vol. II, p. 634; A. Philippi and F. Heim, *Der Feldzug gegen Sowjetrussland, 1941 bis 1945* (Stuttgart, 1962), p. 29.

19. *Kriegstagebuch OKW,* vol. I, p. 82; Greiner, *Die oberste Wehrmacht-führung,* p. 322; Uhlig, "Das Einwirken Hitlers," *Das Parlement,* supplement, 16 March 1960, p. 173; Philippi and Heim, *Der Feldzug,* p. 43; Hillgruber, *Hitlers Strategie,* pp. 222 n., 230. For an English translation of the Lossberg study, see Leach, *German Strategy,* pp. 255–262.

20. There are those, however, who consider Moltke's teachings no longer relevant in the age of modern warfare. See O. Jacobsen, *Erich Marcks,* pp. 97–98.

21. G. Thomas, "Die wehrwirtschaftlichen Auswirkungen einer Operation im Osten," In *Geschichte der deutschen Wehr-und Rüstungswirtschaft, 1918–1945,* ed. W. Birkenfeld (Boppard am Rhein, 1966), pp. 266–267; Philippi and Heim, *Der Feldzug,* p. 43; Proektor, *Agressia i Katastrofa,* p. 195. See also R. Suchenwirth, *Command and Leadership in the German Air Force* (New York, 1970), pp. 169–170.

22. W. Goerlitz, *Paulus and Stalingrad* (New York, 1963), pp. 24–25.

23. Halder, Kriegstagebuch, vol. II, p. 90.

24. *Trial of the Major War Criminals before the International Military Tribunal* (42 vols.; Nuremberg, 1947–1949), vol. VII, pp. 253–261; "Zaiavlenie Paulusa Sovetskomu Pravitelstvu," *Niurnbergskii protsess,* vol. II, pp. 594–597; Philippi and Heim, *Der Feldzug,* pp. 30–31.

25. See Halder, *Kriegstagebuch,* vol. II, p. 176; Buchheit, *Hitler der Feldherr,* p. 212.

26. Halder, *Kriegstagebuch,* vol. II, pp. 266–267.

27. H. Guderian, *Panzer Leader* (London, 1952), pp. 142–143; Uhlig, "Das Einwirken Hitlers," *Das Parlement,* supplement, 16 March 1960, pp. 172–173.

28. R. Gehlen, *The Service,* p. 50.

29. Hillgruber, *Hitlers Strategie,* p. 214. This author notes that the Germans were not the only ones who underestimated the military potential of the USSR. The British and the American strategic planners shared in many respects the German viewpoint about the Red Army.

30. B. H. Liddell Hart, *Strategy* (New York, 1967), pp. 241–243; Leach, *German Strategy,* pp. 120–121.

31. See P. Bor, *Gespräche mit Halder* (Wiesbaden, 1950), p. 75.

32. *Kriegstagebuch OKW*, vol. I, pp. 208–209; *Trial of the Major War Criminals,* vol. XXVIII, 1799–PS, pp. 393–395.

33. See Philippi, "Das Pripjetproblem," *Wehrwissenschaftliche Rundshau,* supplement, March 1956, p. 73; OKH/Gen.Stb.d.H./Op.abt, (I), 15 Feb. 1941, H22/219, T–78/335/6291500.

34. The exact words that Hitler used have not been preserved and, curiously enough, Halder does not include a transcript of this conference in his war diary. A paraphrase of Hitler's comments are, however, to be found in the *Kriegstagebuch OKW,* vol. I, p. 209. The comment in question reads: "Der Führer erklärt sich mit den vorgetragenen operativen Absichten einverstanden. . . ."

35. Philippi and Heim, *Der Feldzug,* p. 67; Hillgruber, *Hitlers Strategie,* pp. 366–367; Buchheit, *Hitler der Feldherr,* p. 169; Goerlitz, *Paulus and Stalingrad,* p. 107.

36. For the importance of the south of the Soviet Union in German economic planning, see Thomas, "Die wehrwirtschaftlichen Auswirkungen," *Geschichte der deutschen Wehr-und Rüstungswirtschaft,* pp. 515–532; G. Kravchenko, *Ekonomika SSSR v gody Velikoi Otechestvennoi voiny,* p. 40. See also G. Blau, "The German Campaign in Russia; Planning and Operations, 1940–1942" (Department of the Army Pamphlet no. 20–261a, March 1955), p. 174.

37. A. Milward, *The German Economy at War,* pp. 12–13. For the vicissitudes in German-Soviet economic cooperation, see Hilger, *The Incompatible Allies,* pp. 321–327; J. Schnurre, "Second Memorandum on the Status of German-Soviet Trade Relations," 15 May 1941, *Nazi-Soviet Relations, 1939–1941* (Washington, 1948), p. 252. Schnurre was the head of the Economic Policy Division IV (Eastern Europe) of the Reich Foreign Ministry.

38. See Thomas, "Die wehrwirtschaftlichen Auswirkungen," *Geschichte der deutschen Wehr-und Rüstungswirtschaft,* pp. 243–245, 529; *Kriegstagebuch OKW,* vol. I, pp. 257–258.

39. Halder, *Kriegstagebuch,* vol. II, p. 454. Here, in absolute terms, Halder refused to allow economic considerations to interfere with any military operations.

40. Goerlitz, *Paulus and Stalingrad,* pp. 99–120.

41. Philippi and Heim, *Der Feldzug,* p. 35.

42. In point of fact, on paper a Soviet rifle division was comparable to the German infantry division in numerical strength, but actually had greater overall firepower. See K. Kolganov, *Razvitie taktiki sovetskoi armii v gody Velikoi Otechestvennoi voiny,* p. 68.

43. Goerlitz, *Paulus and Stalingrad,* p. 120.

44. Philippi and Heim, *Der Feldzug,* pp. 35–36.

45. *Hitlers Weisungen für die Kriegführung,* ed. W. Hubatsch (Frankfurt/M., 1962), pp. 84–88; *Hitler's War Directives,* ed. H. R. Trevor-Roper (London, 1964), pp. 49–52.

46. See Leach, *German Strategy,* pp. 121.

47. Halder, *Kriegstagebuch,* vol. II, pp. 463–469.

48. Ibid., p. 45; Philippi, "Das Pripjetproblem," *Wehrwissenschaftliche Rundshau,* supplement, March 1956, p. 17; *Kriegstagebuch OKW,* vol. I, p. 1137.

49. Halder, *Kriegstagebuch,* vol. II, p. 267 n.; *Kriegstagebuch OKW,* vol. I, p. 235; Greiner, *Die oberste Wehrmachtführung,* p. 386.

50. See Uhlig, "Das Einwirken Hitlers," *Das Parlement,* supplement, 16 March 1960, p. 178. In a letter to Uhlig in 1952 Heusinger stated that it was his impression that from the very start Army Group South was too weak to carry out its mission.

51. See *Kriegstagebuch OKW,* vol. I, p. 297.

52. Within a month these figures were raised to 121 rifle and 25 cavalry divisions, plus 32 mechanized brigades. Within two months the general staff increased the estimate again to 171 rifle and 36 cavalry divisions, plus 40 mechanized brigades. See "Sonderakte Jodl," Operative Entscheidungen, 1941, "Barbarossa," "Anlage 3a.," Op. abt. IN Nr. 050/41, "Angaben über die Rote Armee. Stand 15.1.41," Bundesarchiv-Militararchiv, Freiburg (hereafter cited as BA–MA), RW 4/v. 78 (OKW/1570); *Kriegstagebuch OKW,* vol. I, p. 353; Greiner, *Die oberste Wehrmachtführung,* p. 386.

53. *Trial of the Major War Criminals,* vol. XXVI, 873-PS, pp. 399–401; N. Rich, *Hitler's War Aims: Ideology, the Nazi State and the Course of Expansion* (New York, 1973), p. 210.

54. Tippelskirch, *Geschichte des Zweiten Weltkrieges,* p. 175.

55. B. H. Liddell Hart, *The Other Side of the Hill* (London, 1951), p. 251; Hillgruber, *Hitlers Strategie,* pp. 505–507; A. Kesselring, *The Memoirs of Field Marshal Kesselring* (London, 1953), p. 85; Guderian, *Panzer Leader,* p. 245; Buchheit, *Hitler der Feldherr,* p. 218.

56. See G. Just, *Alfred Jodl; Soldat ohne Furcht und Tadel* (Hannover, 1971), p. 97.

57. Philippi and Heim, *Der Feldzug,* p. 47.

58. Halder, *Kriegstagebuch,* vol. II, pp. 351, 353; *Kriegstagebuch OKW,* vol. I, pp. 274–276; Goerlitz, *Generalfeldmarschall Keitel: Verbrecher order Offizier?,* p. 246; Gehlen, *The Service,* p. 26; A. Heusinger, *Befehl im Widerstreit* (Tübingen, 1950), p. 130; Kesselring, *Memoirs,* pp. 86–87; E. Manstein, *Verlorene Siege* (Frankfurt/M., 1969), p. 179; Picker, *Hitlers Tischgespräche,* pp. 486–487.

59. *Nazi-Soviet Relations,* p. 252.

60. Halder, *Kriegstagebuch,* vol. II, p. 426; W. Haupt, *Heeresgruppe Mitte* (Dorheim, 1968), p. 21.

61. J. Bengtson, *Nazi War Aims* (Rock Island, Ill., 1962), pp. 7, 21.

62. *Kriegstagebuch OKW,* vol. I, pp. 257–258; Greiner, *Die oberste Wehrmachtführung,* pp. 343–344; G. Reitlinger, *The House Built on Sand* (New York, 1960), p. 64; F. Hinsley, *Hitler's Strategy* (Cambridge, Mass., 1951), pp. 130–131.

63. *Hitler als Feldherr,* pp. 35–37. See also P. Kleist, *Zwischen Hitler und Stalin, 1939–1945* (Bonn, 1950), p. 128; "Adolf Hitler to the Regent of Hungary," *Documents on German Foreign Policy* (Washington, 1962), Series D, XII, no. 661, pp. 1070–1071.

64. Zhukov, *Memoirs,* p. 227; Kravchenko, *Ekonomika SSSR v gody voiny,* p. 91.

65. Speer, *Inside the Third Reich,* pp. 53–54; Dallin, *German Rule in Russia,* p. 20 ff.; Milward, *The German Economy at War,* p. 131.

66. G. Ritter, *The German Resistance: Carl Goerdeler's Struggle against Tyranny* (New York, 1958), p. 152; F. von Schlabrendorff, *Offiziere gegen Hitler* (Frankfurt/M., 1959), pp. 54–61; Schall-Riacour, *Aufstand und Gehorsam,* pp. 9–10, 96; R. O'Neill, *The German Army and the Nazi Party, 1933–1939* (London, 1966), pp. 162–163.

CHAPTER 3
RACE TO THE DNEPR

1. Haupt, *Heeresgruppe Mitte,* p. 21; Philippi and Heim, *Der Feldzug,* p. 52; H. Pottgiesser, *Die deutsche Reichsbahn im Ostfeldzug, 1939–1944* (Neckargemünd, 1960), pp. 21–23.

2. Halder, *Kriegstagebuch,* vol. III, p. 40; R. Hoffman and A. Toppe, "Consumption and Attrition Rates Attendant to the Operations of German Army Group Center, June 22–December 31, 1941," (unpublished study by Historical Division, HQ U.S. Army, Europe, Foreign Military Studies Branch, 1953), National Archives MS., no. P-190, pp. 68–69; "21 Juni: Zahlenmässige Übersicht über die Verteilung der deutschen Divisionen und Heerestruppen," in *Kriegstagebuch OKW,* vol. I, p. 1286.

3. Halder, *Kriegstagebuch,* vol. III, p. 7.

4. Ibid., vol. II, p. 466; Guderian, *Panzer Leader,* pp. 149–150; H. Hoth, *Panzer-Operationen: die Panzergruppe 3 und der operative Gedanke der deutschen Führung, Sommer 1941* (Heidelberg, 1956), p. 48.

5. Guderian, *Panzer Leader,* p. 149; Hoth, *Panzer-Operationen,* p. 49 and n.

6. For an interesting commentary on this, see K. Macksey, *Kesselring: the Making of the Luftwaffe* (New York, 178), p. 197.

7. Halder, *Kriegstagebuch,* vol. III, pp. 5–8; Guderian, *Panzer Leader,* p. 148; Anfilov, *Bessmertnyi podvig,* p. 52.

8. *Istoriia Velikoi Otechestvennoi voiny,* vol. II, pp. 29–30; *SSSR v Velikoi Otechestvennoi voine, 1941–1945; kratkaia khronika* (Moscow, 1970), p. 18; *KPSS o vooruzhennykh silakh Sovetskogo Soiuza; sbornik dokumentov, 1917–1958,* ed. V. Malin (Moscow, 1958), p. 357; Anfilov, *Bessmertnyi podvig,* pp. 273–274.

9. E. Röhricht, *Probleme der Kesselschlacht; dargestellt an Einkreisungs-Operationen im Zweiten Weltkrieg* (Karlsruhe, 1958), p. 28.

10. Hofmann and Toppe, "Consumption and Attrition Rates of Army Group Center," National Archives MS., no. P-190, pp. 68–69; Guderian, *Panzer Leader,* p. 143.

11. L. Addington, *The Blitzkrieg Era and the German General Staff, 1865–1941* (New Brunswick, N.J., 1971), p. 189; Liddell Hart, *The Other Side of the Hill,* pp. 174–175. Liddell Hart was for many years the leading advocate of tracked versus wheeled transport vehicles and he believed that the German failure to heed this warning was one of the main reasons for their defeat in Russia.

12. 9th Army, Ia., "KTB-Ostfeldzug-Nr. 2 'Russland,' " 22 June 1941, 14855/2, T-312/281/7841883; VIIth Army Corps, Ia., "KTB Nr. 5b," 22–24 June 1941, 17263/1, T-314/346/000612–000620; *Kriegstagebuch OKW,* vol. I, p. 411.

13. Halder, *Kriegstagebuch,* vol. III, p. 5.

14. Panzer Group 2, "KTB I," 25 June 1941, T-313/80/7318422. See also G. Fischer, *Soviet Opposition to Stalin: A Case Study in World War II* (Cambridge, Mass., 1952), pp. 4–5.

15. *Kriegstagebuch OKW,* vol. I, p. 417.

16. Halder, *Kriegstagebuch,* vol. III, pp. 8–9.

17. Ibid., p. 10; vol. II, p. 267.

18. Anfilov, *Bessmertnyi podvig*, pp. 215–216. See also Hoth, *Panzer-Operationen*, pp. 53–57.

19. Hoth, *Panzer-Operationen*, p. 60.

20. Ibid., p. 62.

21. Ibid., p. 61–63.

22. Anfilov, *Bessmertnyi podvig*, pp. 222–223.

23. Dorofeev, "O nekotorykh prichinakh neudachnykh deistvii mekhanizirovan-nykh korpusov," *Voenno-istoricheskii zhurnal*, March 1964, p. 36; *Voiska protivovozdushnoi oborony strany*, ed. M. Anaimanovich (Moscow, 1968), pp. 69–78.

24. Anfilov, *Bessmertnyi podvig*, pp. 266–268.

25. Eremenko, *Na zapadnom napravlenii*, p. 17.

26. Ninth Army, "KTB 2," 27 June 1941, T–312/281/7841939.

27. Halder, *Kriegstagebuch*, vol. III, p. 14. See also Field Marshal von Bock, "Tagebuchnotizen Osten I," 25–26 June 1941, 21-g-16/4P-5, T–84/271/000297–0003000.

28. Halder, *Kriegstagebuch*, vol. III, pp. 10, 15.

29. *Kriegstagebuch OKW*, vol. I, p. 420; Halder, *Kriegstagebuch*, vol. III, p. 15.

30. Halder, *Kriegstagebuch*, p. 22.

31. See A. Turney, *Disaster at Moscow: von Bock's Campaigns, 1941–1942* (Albuquerque, 1970), p. 5; U. von Hassell, *The von Hassell Diaries, 1938–1944: the Story of the Forces against Hitler inside Germany* (New York, 1947), p. 130. See also W. Goerlitz, *The German General Staff; its History and Structure, 1657–1945* (London, 1953), p. 476; J. W. Wheeler-Bennett, *The Nemesis of Power: The German Army in Politics, 1918–1945* (London, 1953), pp. 678–680.

32. Halder, *Kriegstagebuch*, vol. III, pp. 24–25.

33. Guderian, *Panzer Leader*, pp. 166–167.

34. Halder, *Kriegstagebuch*, vol. III, p. 13; Kesselring, *Memoirs*, p. 90; B. Telpukhovskii, *Velikaia Otechestvennaia voina Sovetskogo Soiuza, 1941–1945; kratkii ocherk* (Moscow, 1959), p. 51; Anfilov, *Bessmertnyi podvig*, pp. 275–276.

35. Anfilov, *Bessmertnyi podvig*, pp. 224, 268; Platonov, *Vtoraia mirovaia voina*, p. 187.

36. J. Lemelsen, *29. Division* (Bad Nauheim, 1960), p. 109; J. Baritz, "Belorussia and the Kremlin's Strategic Plans," *Belorussian Review*, vol. VI (1958), p. 87.

37. Lemelsen, *29. Division*, pp. 114–115.

38. See Ninth Army, "KTB 2," 27 June 1941, T–312/281/7841937–7841939; Vth Army Corps, Ia., "KTB 2, Nr. I," 28–29 June 1941, 17647/1, T–314/245/000073–000080; Halder, *Kriegstagebuch*, vol. III, p. 30; G. Blumentritt, "Moscow," *The Fatal Decisions*, ed. S. Friedin and W. Richardson (New York, 1956), p. 57; Panzer Group 2, "KTB I," vol. I, 29 June 1941, T–313/90/7318461–7318462.

39. *SSSR v Velikoi Otechestvennoi voine*, p. 25; Anfilov, *Bessmertnyi podvig*, p. 365.

40. Compare Guderian, *Panzer Leader,* p. 160 and Panzer Group 2, "KTB I," vol. I, 30 June 1941, T-313/80/7318469-7318470.

41. K. Macksey, *Guderian Creator of the Blitzkrieg* (New York, 1976), p. 119.

42. Panzer Group 2, "KTB I," vol. I, 2 July 1941, T-313/80/7318492.

43. See Guderian, *Panzer Leader,* pp. 161-162.

44. Panzer Group 2, "KTB I," vol. I, 4 July 1941, T-313/80/7318511.

45. See Wheeler-Bennett, *The Nemesis of Power,* pp. 647 f. See also Guderian, *Panzer Leader,* pp. 269-370.

46. Halder, *Kriegstagebuch,* vol. III, p. 23; *Kriegstagebuch OKW,* vol. I, pp. 422-423.

47. Halder, *Kriegstagebuch,* vol. III, pp. 24-25.

48. Panzer Group 2, "KTB I," vol. I, 3 July 1941, T-313/80/7318500.

49. Ibid., 7 July 1941, 7318539.

50. Anfilov, *Bessmertnyi podvig,* pp. 392-393.

51. Panzer Group 2, "KTB I," vol. I, 7 July 1941, T-313/80/7318542-7318600.

52. See Anfilov, *Bessmertnyi podvig,* pp. 370.

53. Panzer Group 2, "KTB I," vol. I, 11 July 1941, T-313/80/731591.

54. Ibid., 7 July 1941, 7318542.

55. *Panzer* Group 2, "KTB I," 8 July 1941, vol. I, T-313/80/7318558-7318559; Second Army, "KTB I," 8-12 July 1941, T-312/1654/000016-000021. See also, Halder, *Kriegstagebuch,* vol. III, pp. 40, 43, 48; *Geschichte der 3. Panzer-Division; Berlin-Brandenburg, 1933-1945* (Berlin, 1967); pp. 128-129; O. Munzel, *Panzer Taktik; Raids gepanzerter Verbände im Ostfeldzug, 1941-1942* (Neckargemünd, 1959), pp. 96-97; Anfilov, *Bessmertnyi podvig,* pp. 392-393.

56. Panzer Group 2, "KTB I," 8 July 1941, vol. I, T-313/80/7318550; Ninth Army, "KTB 2," 30 June 1941, T-312/281/7841954.

57. Halder, *Kriegstagebuch,* vol. III, p. 29.

58. Hoth, *Panzer-Operationen,* p. 72; Halder, *Kriegstagebuch,* vol. III, pp. 28-29.

59. Hoth, *Panzer-Operationen,* p. 74.

60. Halder, *Kriegstagebuch,* vol. III, p. 34.

61. Ibid., pp. 42-43.

62. I. Zhukov, *Liudi 40-x godov, liudi v brone* (Moscow, 1969), pp. 43-46.

63. V. Butkov, "Kontrudar 5-go mekhanizirovannogo korpusa na lepelskom nepravlennii (6-11 iiulia, 1941 goda)," *Voenno-istoricheskii zhurnal,* Sept. 1971, pp. 61-64; Anfilov, *Bessmertnyi podvig,* pp. 392-393.

64. Halder, *Kriegstagebuch,* vol. III, p. 55; Hoth, *Panzer-Operationen,* p. 79.

65. Halder, *Kriegstagebuch,* vol. III, p. 67; Hoth, *Panzer-Operationen,* p. 86.

66. Halder, *Kriegstagebuch,* vol. III, p. 73.

67. Krausnick, *Anatomy of the SS State,* pp. 521-522; S. Datner, *Crimes against POWs: Responsibility of the Wehrmacht* (Warsaw, 1964), p. 78.

68. Halder, *Kriegstagebuch,* vol. III, pp. 38-39.

69. Ibid., p. 52.

70. Ibid., pp. 53-54.

71. See W. Nehring, *Die Geschichte der deutschen Panzerwaffe, 1916 bis 1945* (Berlin, 1969), pp. 234, 247; Halder, *Hitler als Feldherr,* pp. 37–38; Blumentritt, "Moscow," *The Fatal Decisions,* p. 73.

72. Halder, *Kriegstagebuch,* vol. III, p. 65.

73. Ibid., pp. 64–75, 68.

74. Ibid., p. 82.

75. H. Guderian, "Flank Defense in Far Reaching Operations," (unpublished study by Historical Division, HQ U.S. National Archives MS., no. T–11, pp. 70–71.

76. Lemelsen, *29. Division,* p. 120.

77. Ibid., p. 122; M. Lukin, "V Smolenskom srazhenii," *Voenno-istoricheskii zhurnal,* July 1979, p. 49.

78. Lemelsen, *29. Division,* p. 125.

79. Lukin, "V Smolenskom srazhenii," *Voenno-istoricheskii zhurnal,* July 1979, p. 50.

80. Lemelsen, *29. Division,* pp. 126–135.

81. Hoth, *Panzer-Operationen,* p. 87.

82. Ibid., pp. 92–93.

83. Anfilov, *Bessmertnyi podvig,* pp. 455–456.

84. Hoth, *Panzer-Operationen,* p. 97; Panzer Group 2, "KTB I," vol. I, 18 July 1941, T–313/80/7318667–7318668.

85. 10th Panzer Division, Ia., "KTB Nr. 5," 16 July 1941, 22340/1, T–315/561/000325; Eremenko, *Na zapadnom napravlenii,* pp. 56–47.

86. 10th Panzer Division, Ia., "KTB Nr. 5," 19 July 1941, T–315/561/000353.

87. Ibid., 19 July 1941, 000367.

88. See 10th Panzer Division, "KTB Nr. 5," 20 July 1941, T–315/561/000381. See also Guderian, *Panzer Leader,* p. 190; 10th Panzer Division, "KTB Nr. 5," 22 July 1941, T–315/561/000409.

89. See 10th Panzer Division, "KTB Nr. 5," 21 July 1941, T–315/561/000394.

90. Panzer Group 2, "KTB I," vol. I, 20 July 1941, T–313/80/7318689.

CHAPTER 4
BATTLES FOR THE UPPER DNEPR

1. Cheremukhin, "Na smolensko—moskovskom strategicheskom napravlenii," *Voenno-istoricheskii zhurnal,* Oct. 1966, p. 3.

2. Anfilov, *Bessmertnyi podvig,* p. 384.

3. Zhukov, *Memoirs,* pp. 251–252.

4. Anfilov, *Bessmertnyi podvig,* p. 384.

5. Zhukov, *Memoirs,* pp. 255–256.

6. Eremenko, *Na zapadnom napravlenii,* p. 46.

7. Ibid., p. 65; A. Gorbatov, *Years off My Life* (New York, 1964), pp. 157–165.

8. *Istoriia Velikoi Otechestvennoi voiny,* vol. II, p. 65; Eremenko, *Na zapadnom napravlenii,* pp. 46–47.

9. Anfilov, *Bessmertnyi podvig,* p. 448.

10. Zhukov, *Memoirs,* p. 274.

11. *Istoriia Velikoi Otechestvennoi voiny,* vol. II, p. 35.

12. "Tankovaia promyshlennost' " in *Sovetskaia voennskaia entsiklopediia,* vol. VII, pp. 662–664.

13. Zaloga, "Organization of the Soviet Armored Force, 1939–1945," p. 5; Erickson, *The Road to Stalingrad,* pp. 132–134.

14. *Istoriia vtoroi mirovoi voiny,* vol. IV, pp. 283–284.

15. J. Sloan, "Soviet Units in World War II: New Data from Soviet Sources," in *History Numbers and War,* vol. 1, no. 3, Fall 1977, pp. 163–164; Zaloga, "Organization of the Soviet Armored Forces," pp. 5–6.

16. *Kriegstagebuch OKW,* vol. I, p. 428. See also Röhricht, *Probleme der Kesselschlacht,* pp. 46–59 and Philippi, "Das Pripjetproblem," *Wehrwissenschaftliche Rundshau,* supplement March 1956, pp. 41–42; Uhlig, "Das Einwirken Hitlers," *Das Parlement,* supplement, 23 March, 1960, p. 185.

17. *Kriegstagebuch OKW,* vol. I, p. 584; Philippi, "Das Pripjetproblem," *Wehrwissenschaftliche Rundshau,* supplement, March 1956, p. 51.

18. Anfilov, *Bessmertnyi podvig,* pp. 449–450.

19. *Istoriia Velikoi Otechestvennoi voiny,* vol. II, p. 68. See Panzer Group 2, "KTB Nr, I," vol. I, 14 July 1941, T–313/80/7318622.

20. Panzer Group 2, "KTB Nr. I," vol. I, 16 July 1941, T–313/80/7318639–7318640; Guderian, *Panzer Leader,* p. 176; *Istoriia Velikoi Otechestvennoi voiny,* vol. II, p. 68.

21. Hoth, *Panzer-Operationen,* p. 97.

22. Panzer Group 2, "KTB Nr. I," vol. I, 20 July 1941, T–313/80/7318684.

23. P. 179.

24. Panzer Group 2, "KTB Nr. I," 21 July 1941, T–313/80/7318699.

25. Ibid., 7318738; Guderian, *Panzer Leader,* p. 182.

26. Panzer Group 2, "KTB Nr. I," vol. I, 25 July 1941, T–313/80/7318699; O. Weidinger, *Division Das Reich* (Osnabrück, 1969), pp. 427–434.

27. Zhukov, *Memoirs,* p. 274; *SSSR v Velikoi Otechestvennoi voine,* p. 47.

28. Cheremukhin, "Na smolensko-moskovskom strategicheskom napravlenii, " *Voenno-istoricheskii zhurnal,* Oct. 1966, pp. 31–39.

29. Zhukov, *Memoirs,* pp. 274–275; *Istoriia Velikoi Otechestvennoi voiny,* vol. II, p. 72; K. K. Rokossovskii, *Soldatskii dolg* (Moscow, 1968), pp. 31–39; Von Bock, "Tagebuchnotizen Osten I," 19 July 1941, T–84/271/000378– 000379, 000385.

30. Hoth, *Panzer-Operationen,* pp. 100–101; Anfilov, *Bessmertnyi podvig,* p. 461; Eremenko, *Na zapadnom napravlenii,* p. 65.

31. *Memoirs,* pp. 92–93.

32. Panzer Group 2, "KTB Nr. I," vol. I, pp. 16–17 July 1941, T–313/80/ 7318639–7318657.

33. Second Army, "KTB Teil I," 16 July 1941, T–312/1654/000041.

34. Ibid., 000046–000049. See also Zhilin, *Vazhneishie operatsii Velikoi Otechestvennoi voiny, 1941–1945gg.* (Moscow, 1956), pp. 85–86.

35. Von Bock, "Tagebuchnotizen Osten I," 18–19 July 1941, T–84/271/000342– 000344.

36. Panzer Group 2, "KTB Nr. I," vol. I, 19 July 1941, T–313/80/7318678.

37. Second Army, "KTB Teil I," 21 July 1941, T–313/1654/000057.

38. Panzer Group 2, "KTB Nr. I," vol. I, 21 July 1941, T–313/80/7318698– 7318699.

39. Von Bock, "Tagebuchnotizen Osten I," 21 July 1941, T–84/271/000350.

40. Panzer Group 2, "KTB Nr. I," vol. I, 22 July 1941, T–313/80/7318708.

41. Second Army, "KTB Teil I," 24–26 July 1941, T–312/1654/000070–0074; Von Bock, "Tagebuchnotizen Osten I," 24 July 1941, T–84/271/000354.

42. Second Army, "KTB Teil I," 28 July 1941, T–312/1654/000074–000077.

43. Ibid., 30 July 1941, 000079–000080.

44. Von Bock, "Tagebuchnotizen Osten I," 13 July 1941, T–84/271/000327.

45. Ibid., 000328.

46. For a good commentary on combat conditions in the area south of Lake Ilmen see C. W. Sydnor, *Soldiers of Destruction: The SS Death's Head Division, 1933–1945* (Princeton, 1977), pp. 184–207.

47. Von Bock, "Tagebuchnotizen Osten I," 13 July 1941, T–84/271/000333.

48. Hoth, *Panzer-Operationen,* p. 99.

49. Panzer Group 3, Ia., "KTB Nr. I," 19–20 July 1941, 14837/2, T–313/225/ 7489084–7489093.

50. *Kriegstagebuch OKW,* vol. I, pp. 436–437.

51. Panzer Group 3, "KTB Nr. I," 20 July 1941, T–313/225/7489093; Hoth, *Panzer-Operationen,* p. 98.

52. Halder, *Kriegstagebuch,* vol. III, p. 99.

53. *Panzer-Operationen,* p. 99.

54. Von Bock, "Tagebuchnotizen Osten I," 21 July 1941, T–84/271/000350. See also von Bock, "Tagebuchnotizen Osten—Vorbereitungszeit," 21 May and 4 June 1941, BA-MA, 22/7, pp. 18–19, 20–21 and Turney, *Disaster at Moscow,* pp. 54–55.

55. Halder, *Kriegstagebuch,* vol. III, p. 100. See also Halder, *Hitler als Feldherr,* p. 39.

56. Von Bock, "Tagebuchnotizen Osten I," 24 July 1941, T-84/271/000354–000355.

57. Guderian, *Panzer Leader,* p. 182.

58. Von Bock, "Tagebuchnotizen Osten I," 27 July 1941, T-84/271/000375; Panzer Group 2, "KTB Nr. I," vol. I, 29 July 1941, T-313/80/7318788.

59. Von Bock, "Tagebuchnotizen Osten I," 27 July 1941, T-84/271/000375.

60. Panzer Group 2, "KTB Nr. I," 20 July 1941, T-313/80/7318685.

61. Ibid., 7318720, 7318738.

62. Von Bock, "Tagebuchnotizen Osten I," 28 July 1941, T-84/271/000377.

63. Panzer Group 2, "KTB Nr. I," vol. I, 14 July 1941, T-313/80/7318619.

64. See von Bock, "Tagebuchnotizen Osten I," 9 July 1941, T-84/271/000323–000324; Panzer Group 2, "KTB Nr. I," vol. I, 28 June 1941, T-313/80/7318453.

65. Guderian, *Panzer Leader,* p. 185.

CHAPTER 5
THE PAUSE OF ARMY GROUP CENTER

1. 10th Panzer Division, "KTB Nr. 5," 24–25 July 1941, T–315/561/000423–000427. See also P. Carrell, *Hitler's War on Russia: The Story of the German Defeat in the East* (London, 1964), pp. 93–97; T. Shabad, *Geography of the U.S.S.R.; a Regional Survey* (New York, 1951), p. 134.

2. 10th Panzer Division, "KTB Nr. 5," 25 July 1941, T–315/561/000430.

3. See ibid., 26 July 1941, 000437–000439.

4. IXth Army Corps, Ia., "KTB 7," 27 July 1941, 19067/1, T–314/405/000561–000565.

5. Ibid., 28 July 1941, 000567–000568; Panzer Group 2, "KTB Nr. I, vol. I," 25 July 1941, T–313/80/7318744.

6. Eremenko, *Na zapadnom napravlenii,* p. 62.

7. See von Bock, "Tagebuchnotizen Osten I," 5 August 1941, T–84/271/000389–000390.

8. IXth Army Corps, "KTB 7," 28–29 July 1941, T–314/405/000569–000571.

9. 10th Panzer Division, "KTB Nr. 5," 30 July 1941, T–315/561/000468.

10. IXth Army Corps, "KTB 7," 30 July 1941, T–313/405/000573.

11. IXth Army Corps, "KTB 7," 31 July 1941, T–313/405/000578; Panzer Group 2, "KTB Nr. I," vol. I, 28 July 1941, T–313/80/7318781.

12. See XXth Army Corps, Ia., "KTB I," 6–8 Aug. 1941, 20178/1, T–314/651/000178–000180; IXth Army Corps, "Anlage II, KTB 7," 8 July 1941, 19067/3, T–314/406/000260.

13. XXth Army Corps, "KTB I," 11 Aug. 1941, T–314/651/000188.

14. Von Bock, "Tagebuchnotizen Osten I," 12 August 1941, T–84/271/000403–000404. See also G. Kleinfeld and L. Tambs, *Hitler's Spanish Legion: The Blue Division in Russia* (Carbondale, Ill., 1979), pp. 46–48.

15. H. Krausnick, "The Persecution of the Jews," *Anatomy of the SS State,* p. 64.

16. XXth Army Corps, "KTB I," 13 Aug. 1941, T–314/651/000196–000198.

17. Ibid., 14 August 1941, 000198.

18. Halder, *Kriegstagebuch,* vol. III, p. 147.

19. Panzer Group 2, "KTB Nr. I," vol. I, 4 Aug. 1941, T–313/80/7318854.

20. See *Panzer Leader,* p. 190.

21. Von Bock, "Tagebuchnotizen Osten I," 14 Aug. 1941, T–84/271/000405–000406.

22. Halder, *Kriegstagebuch,* vol. III, p. 177.

23. Von Bock, "Tagebuchnotizen Osten I," 14 Aug. 1941, T–84/271/000406.

24. Ibid., 15 Aug. 1941, 000407; Panzer Group 2, "KTB Nr. I," vol. I, 14 Aug. 1941, T–313/80/7318979–7318980. See also *Panzer Leader,* pp. 194–195.

25. IXth Army Corps, "KTB 7," 15–16 Aug. 1941, T–314/405/000623–000625.

26. XXth Army Corps, "KTB I," 17 Aug. 1941, T–314/651/000206.

27. Ibid., 000208; IXth Army Corps, "KTB 7," 18 Aug. 1941, T–314/405/000627–000628.

28. XXth Army Corps, "KTB I," 20 Aug. 1941, T–314/651/000216–000218.

29. IXth Army Corps, "KTB 7," 22 Aug. 1941, T–314/405/000636.

30. See Fourth Army, "KTB Nr. 9," 22 Aug. 1941, 13616/1, T–312/143/681631.

31. IXth Army Corps, "KTB 7," 23–26 Aug. 1941, T–314/405/000638–000644.

32. Ibid., 27–28 Aug. 1941, 000646; Fourth Army, "KTB Nr. 9." 26–27 Aug. 1941, T–312/143/681636–681640.

33. "AOK 4 der Oberbefehlshaber, A.H. Qu., an Heeresgruppe Mitte," Fourth Army, Ia., "Anlagen A, KTB Nr. 9," 28 Aug. 1941, BA–MA 13715/1.

34. C. Gallenkamp, "Nachtkämpfe," (unpublished study by Historical Division, HQ U.S. Army Europe, Foreign Military Studies Branch, 1950), National Archives MS, no. P–054b, Project 40, pp. 14–18.

35. "Personliche Eindrücke im Jelnja-Bogen (25.8 und Nacht 25./26.8 1941)," Fourth Army," Anlagen A, KTB Nr. 9," 27 Aug. 1941, BA–MA 13715/1; Fourth Army, "KTB Nr. 9," 26 Aug. 1941, T–312/143/681634–681635.

36. Fourth Army, "KTB Nr. 9," 26 Aug. 1941, T–312/143/681635.

37. Zhukov, *Memoirs,* pp. 287–289.

38. Ibid., p. 391.

39. Ibid., pp. 292–293.

40. G. Khoroshilov and A. Bazhenov, "Elninskaia nastupatelnaia operatsiia 1941 g.," *Voenno-istoricheskii zhurnal,* Sept. 1974, pp. 75–81.

41. IXth Army Corps, "KTB 7," 30–31 Aug. 1941, T–314/405/000647–000650.

42. IXth Army Corps, "Anlage II, KTB 7," 2 Sept. 1941, T–314/406/000767.

43. IXth Army Corps, "KTB 7," 31 Aug. 1941, T–314/405/000569–000571; XXth Army Corps, "KTB I," 31 Aug. 1941, T–314/651/000234.

44. XXth Army Corps, "KTB I," 2 Sept. 1941, T–314/651/000238.

45. Zhukov, *Memoirs,* p. 291.

46. Fourth Army, "KTB Nr. 9," 2 Sept. 1941, T–312/143/681686–681687; "Entwicklung der Lage, die zur Aufgabe des Jelnja-Bogens führte, in Einzelheiten," Fourth Army, "Anlagen A, KTB Nr. 9," 9 Sept. 1941, BA–MA 13715/2, p. 7.

47. Von Bock, "Tagebuchnotizen Osten I," 2 Sept. 1941, T–84/271/000438; Halder, *Kriegstagebuch,* vol. III, pp. 211–212.

48. IXth Army Corps, "KTB 7," 2–3 Sept. 1941, T–314/405/000656–000658; XXth Army Corps, "KTB I," 3 Sept. 1941, T–314/651/000242–000243.

49. IXth Army Corps, "KTB 7," 5–6 Sept. 1941, T–314/405/000662–000663; XXth Army Corps, "KTB I," 4 Sept. 1941, T–314/651/000250.

50. Zhukov, *Memoirs,* p. 293.

51. Ibid.

52. "Bericht über die Frontfahrt des O.B. vom 30.8.41.," Fourth Army, "Anlagen A, KTB Nr. 9," 30 Aug. 1941, BA–MA 13715/2. Here are listed the casualties up to August 30 of the three army corps of the Fourth Army which were not actually in the salient at that time, although some of their divisions had fought there. For reports on the losses of various units actually within the salient for the better part of the time from late July to early September see "Entwicklung der Lage, die zur Aufgabe des Jelnja-Bogens führte, in Einzelheiten," ibid., 9 Sept. 1941; "Gen Kdo. IX. AK, Abt. IIa.,

dem AOK 4," ibid., 4 Sept. 1941; "Der Kommandierende General des IX. AK an der 4. Armee, Herrn Generalfeldmarschall v. Kluge, 7 Sept. 1941," ibid.; "Kurzer Bericht über den Einsatz der 263. I.D. im Jelnja-Bogen," ibid., 6 Sept. 1941. The 263rd Infantry Division was in the salient twelve days from 17-29 August and lost 49 officers and 1,167 men. The XLVIth Panzer Corps lost 3,615 men in the salient between 22 July and 3 August, or about three hundred men per day. See Panzer Group 2, "KTB Nr. I," vol. I, 5 Aug. 1941, T-313/80/7318770. See also H. Geyer, *Das IX. Armeekorps im Ostfeldzug, 1941* (Neckargemünd, 1969), p. 201.

53. See A. Seaton, *The Battle for Moscow, 1941-1942* (London, 1971), p. 169; Haupt, *Heeresgruppe Mitte,* pp. 106-107.

54. Zhukov, *Memoirs,* p. 293.

55. Second Army, "KTB Teil I," 28 July 1941, T-312/1654/000077.

56. Guderian, *Panzer Leader,* pp. 184-185; W. Meyer-Detring, *Die 137. Infanteriedivision; im Mittelabschnitt der Ostfront* (Petzenkuchen, Austria, 1962), p. 52.

57. Meyer-Detring, *Die 137. Infanteriedivision,* p. 52.

58. "AOK 4 der Oberbefehlshaber, A.H. Qu., an Heeresgruppe Mitte," Fourth Army, "Anlagen A, KTB Nr. 9," 9 Sept. 1941, BA-MA 13715/2; M. Fretter-Pico, *Missbrauchte Infanterie: deutsche Infanteriedivisionen im osteuropaischen Grossraum, 1941-1944* (Frankfurt/M., 1957), pp. 5-6.

59. Panzer Group 2, "KTB Nr. I," 28 July 1941, T-313/80/7318781; IXth Army Corps, "KTB 7," 31 July 1941, T-314/405/000578; Guderian, *Panzer Leader,* p. 193.

60. IXth Army Corps, "KTB 7," 2 Aug. 1941, T-314/405/000584. See also A. Schmidt, *Geschichte der 10. Division; 10. Infanterie-Division (mot.), 10. Panzer-Grenadier-Division, 1933-1945* (Bad Nauheim, 1963), pp. 103-105.

61. Panzer Group 2, "KTB Nr. I," vol. I, 11 July 1941, T-313/80/7318589; Guderian, *Panzer Leader,* pp. 188, 212.

62. Panzer Group 2, "KTB Nr. I," vol. I, 3 August 1941, T-313/80/7318845; IXth Army Corps, "KTB 7," 3 Aug. 1941, T-314/405/000591.

63. IXth Army Corps, "KTB 7," 5 Aug. 1941, T-314/405/000600.

64. Ibid., 6 Aug. 1941, 000606-000607.

65. Guderian, *Panzer Leader,* p. 193.

66. Von Bock, "Tagebuchnotizen Osten I," 10 Aug. 1941, T-84/271/000400-000401. See also Halder, *Kriegstagebuch,* vol. III, pp. 170-171.

67. Halder, *Kriegstagebuch,* vol. III, pp. 163-164.

68. Von Bock, "Tagebuchnotizen Osten I," 1 Aug. 1941, T-84/271/000390-000391; Halder, *Kriegstagebuch,* vol. III, p. 157.

69. Von Bock, "Tagebuchnotizen Osten I," 6 Aug. 1941, T-84/271/000391.

70. *Panzer Leader,* p. 193.

71. Von Bock, "Tagebuchnotizen Osten I," 7-8 Aug. 1941, T-84/271/000391, 000397-000398.

72. Ibid., 9 Aug. 1941, 000398.

73. Ibid., 9-13 Aug. 1941, 000398-000404; Panzer Group 2, "KTB Nr. I," vol. I, pp. 11-13, Aug. 1941, T-313/80/7318934-7318962; Guderian, *Panzer Leader,* p. 195.

74. Panzer Group 2, "KTB Nr. I," vol. I, 16 Aug. 1941, T-313/80/7319000.
75. Second Army, "KTB Teil I," 13 Aug. 1941, T-312/1654/000130.
76. Ibid., 14 Aug. 1941, 000135.
77. Ibid., 14–15 Aug. 1941, 000136–000144; Platonov, *Vtoraia mirovaia voina,* p. 211.
78. Second Army, "KTB Teil I," 16 Aug. 1941, T-312/1654/000145.
79. Ibid., 17 Aug. 1941, 000153.
80. Guderian, *Panzer Leader,* p. 196.
81. See Panzer Group 2, "KTB Nr. I," vol. I, 20 Aug. 1941, T-313/80/7319042.
82. Ibid., 7319033.
83. p. 196.
84. Von Bock, "Tagebuchnotizen Osten I," 16 Aug. 1941, T-84/271/000409–000410.
85. Second Army, "KTB Teil I," 18 Aug. 1941, T-312/1654/000159–000160.
86. Ibid., 19–20 Aug. 1941, 000164–000168.
87. Von Bock, "Tagebuchnotizen Osten I," 19–21 Aug. 1941, T-84/271/000412–000415.
88. *Kriegstagebuch OKW,* vol. I, pp. 466, 468.
89. Halder, *Kriegstagebuch,* vol. III, p. 180; Hoth, *Panzer-Operationen,* p. 122.
90. *Kriegstagebuch OKW,* vol. I, p. 474; Manstein, *Verlorene Siege,* pp. 201–203; Tippelskirch, *Geschichte des Zweiten Weltkrieges,* p. 193.
91. Von Bock, "Tagebuchnotizen Osten I," 15 Aug. 1941, T-84/271/000407–000408; Halder, *Kriegstagebuch,* vol. III, pp. 179–180; Hoth, *Panzer-Operationen,* pp. 122–123.
92. Von Bock, "Tagebuchnotizen Osten I," 30 July and 2 Aug, 1941, T-84/271/000380, 000385; Halder, *Kriegstagebuch,* vol. III, pp. 167–168; von Knobelsdorff, *Geschichte der niedersächsischen 19. Panzer-Division* (Bad Nauheim, 1958), pp. 98–107.
93. Von Bock, "Tagebuchnotizen Osten I," 9 Aug. 1941, T-84/271/000399; Halder, *Kriegstagebuch,* vol. III, pp. 165–166; *Kriegstagebuch OKW,* vol. I, p. 461.
94. Von Bock, "Tagebuchnotizen Osten I," 12 Aug. 1941, T-84/271/000403.
95. *Istoriia Velikoi Otechestvennoi voiny,* vol. II, p. 74; Rokossovskii, *Soldatskii dolg,* pp. 39–41.
96. Von Bock, "Tagebuchnotizen Osten I," 20 Aug. 1941, T-84/271/000413; *Kriegstagebuch OKW,* vol. I, pp. 470–471.
97. *Kriegstagebuch OKW,* vol. I, 472–474.
98. Ibid., pp. 474–479; Von Bock, "Tagebuchnotizen Osten I," 26 Aug. 1941, T-84/271/000426; XXIIIrd Army Corps, Ia., "KTB Nr. 8," 22–25 Aug. 1941, BA-MA RH 24-23/42 (13677/10); XLth Army Corps, Ia., "KTB Nr. 3," 22–26 Aug. 1941, BA-MA 31093/1; LVIIth Panzer Corps, Ia. "KTB Nr. I," 20–24 Aug. 1941, BA-MA 15683/1; Hoth, *Panzer-Operationen,* p. 123.

CHAPTER 6
HITLER VERSUS THE GENERALS

1. Halder, *Hitler als Feldherr,* pp. 37–38; Hoth, *Panzer-Operationen,* pp. 107–108; Manstein, *Verlorene Siege,* pp. 173, 305–306; Nehring, *Die Geschichte der deutschen Panzerwaffe,* pp. 125, 132, 228; Tippelskirch, *Geschichte des Zweiten Weltkrieges,* p. 198; Westphal, *Heer in Fesseln,* p. 80; Buchheit, *Hitler der Feldherr,* pp. 169, 231–235; Hillgruber, *Hitlers Strategie,* p. 225; R. Hofmann, "Die Schlacht von Moskau, 1941," in *Entscheidungsschlachten des Zweiten Weltkrieges,* ed. by H. Jacobsen and J. Rohwer (Frankfurt/M. 1960), pp. 143–144; Philippi and Heim, *Der Feldzug,* pp. 67–71; J. Fest, *Hitler: eine Biographie* (Frankfurt/M., 1973), p. 889; T. Higgins, *Hitler and Russia: The Third Reich in a Two-Front War, 1937–1943* (New York, 1966), p. 278; Seaton, *The Battle for Moscow,* pp. 29, 168, 185; Idem, *The Russo-German War, 1941–1945* (New York, 1970), pp. 132, 152.

2. Halder, *Kriegstagebuch,* vol. II, p. 454.

3. *Kriegstagebuch OKW,* vol. I, pp. 208–209.

4. Halder, *Kriegstagebuch,* vol. III, pp. 64–65.

5. Halder, *Kriegstagebuch,* vol. III, pp. 24–25; Guderian, *Panzer Leader,* pp. 166–167.

6. Von Bock, "Tagebuchnotizen Osten I," 21 July 1941, T–84/271/000350.

7. Guderian, *Panzer Leader,* p. 183.

8. Halder, *Kriegstagebuch,* vol. III, pp. 103–107.

9. Ibid., pp. 106–107.

10. Ibid., pp. 117–118.

11. *Hitler's War Directives,* pp. 85–88.

12. Ibid., pp. 89–90.

13. *Kriegstagebuch OKW,* vol. I, p. 1034.

14. Ibid., vol. I, p. 1035.

15. Ibid., vol. I, p. 1035.

16. Von Bock, "Tagebuchnotizen Osten I," 25 July 1941, T–84/271/000358–000369. See also *Kriegstagebuch OKW,* vol. I, pp. 1035–1036.

17. Von Bock, "Tagebuchnotizen Osten I," 26–27 July 1941, T–84/271/000371–000375.

18. Panzer Group 2, "KTB Nr. I," vol. I, 28 July 1941 T–313/80/7318775.

19. Halder, *Kriegstagebuch,* vol. III, pp. 122–123.

20. Ibid., p. 124; Manstein, *Verlorene Siege,* pp. 198–99.

21. *Kriegstagebuch OKW,* vol. I, p. 170E. Here the editor of the *Kriegstagebuch OKW,* P. Schramm, remarks that the general staff cooperated closely with the Wehrmacht Operations Staff section chiefs.

22. Ibid., vol. I, pp. 1036–1037; Hoth, *Panzer-Operationen,* p. 112.

23. "Sonderakte Jodl, Operative Entscheidungen, 1941" "Barbarossa," Anlage 8, 29 June 1941, BA–MA RW 4/v. 78 (OKW/1570); *Kriegstagebuch OKW,* vol. I, p. 1037.

24. *Kriegstagebuch OKW,* vol. I, pp. 1040–1041.

25. *Hitler's War Directives,* pp. 90–93.

26. Halder, *Kriegstagebuch,* vol. III, p. 134.

27. Ibid., p. 136.

28. *Kriegstagebuch OKW,* vol. I, pp. 1041–1043.

29. See his *Barbarossa,* pp. 98–101. See also O'Neill, *The German Army and the Nazi Party, 1933–1939,* pp. 150–163; Schlabrendorff, *Offiziere gegen Hitler,* pp. 54–55, 95–97.

30. Guderian, *Panzer Leader,* p. 189.

31. Ibid., pp. 189–190; *Kriegstagebuch OKW,* vol. I, p. 1042; Hoth, *Panzer-Operationen,* p. 117.

32. A. Bullock, *Hitler: a Study in Tyranny* (London, 1952), p. 612.

33. *Kriegstagebuch OKW,* vol. I, p. 1043; von Bock, "Tagebuchnotizen Osten I," 4 Aug. 1941, T–84/271/000386–000387.

34. Halder, *Kriegstagebuch,* vol. III, p. 153.

35. Ibid., p. 155.

36. Ibid., p. 121.

37. Ibid., p. 157; von Bock, "Tagebuchnotizen Osten I," 6 Aug. 1941, T–84/271/000390–000391.

38. Halder, *Kriegstagebuch,* vol. III, pp. 159–160. The emphasis occurs in Halder's transcript of the meeting.

39. Ibid., p. 160. See also E. Murawski, *Der deutsche Wehrmachtbericht, 1939–1945* (Boppard am Rhein, 1962), p. 53.

40. *Kriegstagebuch OKW,* vol. I, pp. 1043–1044.

41. Halder, *Kriegstagebuch,* vol. III, pp. 164–165.

42. Ibid., pp. 165, 170.

43. *Hitler's War Directives,* pp. 93–95.

44. See Röhricht, *Probleme der Kesselschlacht,* p. 56.

45. *Hitler's War Directives,* pp. 94–95.

46. Halder, *Kriegstagebuch,* vol. III, p. 175.

47. Ibid., p. 176.

48. *Kriegstagebuch OKW,* vol. I, pp. 1054–1055.

49. *Kriegstagebuch OKW,* vol. I, p. 468; Hoth, *Panzer-Operationen,* pp. 122–123. For the activities of the XXXIXth Panzer Corps in the drive toward Leningrad, see C. de Beaulieu, *Der Vorstoss der Panzergruppe 4 auf Leningrad* (Neckargemünd, 1961), pp. 133 ff.

50 *Kriegstagebuch OKW,* vol. I, pp. 1055–1059.

51. Ibid., p. 1056.

52. Ibid., pp. 1056–1057.

53. *Kriegstagebuch OKW,* vol. I, p. 1057.

54. Ibid., p. 1059.

55. Halder, *Kriegstagebuch,* vol. III, p. 159.

56. *Kriegstagebuch OKW,* vol. I, p. 1059.

57. Halder, *Kriegstagebuch,* vol. III, p. 170.

58. See P. Schramm's introduction to the *Kriegstagebuch OKW,* vol. I, 169E, 184E, 200E.

59. Ibid., pp. 1016.

60. Ibid., pp. 1045–1047.
61. Von Bock, "Tagebuchnotizen Osten I," 25 July 1941, T–84/271/000361–000362.
62. Kesselring, *Memoirs*, p. 93.
63. Halder, *Kriegstagebuch*, vol. III, p. 32.
64. Ibid., p. 176; von Bock, "Tagebuchnotizen Osten I," 14 Aug. 1941, T–84/271/000405–000406.
65. Warlimont, *Inside Hitler's Headquarters*, p. 190.
66. Heusinger, *Befehl im Widerstreit*, pp. 132–135.
67. Warlimont, *Inside Hitler's Headquarters*, p. 190; *Kriegstagebuch OKW*, vol. I, p. 1062.
68. *Kriegstagebuch OKW*, vol. I, pp. 1063–1068.
69. Ibid., p. 1063.
70. Ibid., p. 1066.
71. Halder, *Kriegstagebuch*, vol. III, p. 193.
72. See Kesselring, *Memoirs*, p. 93.
73. *Kriegstagebuch*, vol. III, p. 194; von Bock, "Tagebuchnotizen Osten I," 23 Aug. 1941, T–84/271/000421–000422; Guderian, *Panzer Leader*, p. 198.
74. Guderian, *Erinnerungen eines Soldaten* (Heidelberg, 1951), pp. 179–180.
75. Panzer Group 2, Ia., "KTB Nr. I," vol. II, 24 Aug. 1941, 25034/60, T–313/86/326515–326516.
76. Panzer Group 2, Ia., "Anlage zum KTB vom 23.8.1941," BA–MA RH 21–2/v. 177 (25034/63), pp. 10–11.
77. Von Bock, "Tagebuchnotizen Osten I," 23 Aug. 1941, T–84/271/000421–000422.
78. Panzer Group 2, "KTB Nr. I," vol. II, 24 Aug. 1941, T–313/86/326511–326512; Guderian, *Panzer Leader*, pp. 199–202.
79. Guderian, *Panzer Leader*, p. 200.
80. Ibid., p. 202; von Bock, "Tagebuchnotizen Osten I," 23 Aug. 1941, T–84/271/000421–000422.
81. Halder, *Kriegstagebuch*, vol. III, pp. 194–195.
82. Ibid., pp. 24–25.
83. *Barbarossa*, p. 112.

CHAPTER 7
STALIN AND KIEV, HITLER AND MOSCOW

1. Anfilov, *Bessmertnyi podvig,* p. 448; Artemev, "Nepreodolimaia pregrada na podstupakh k stolitse," in *Bitva za Moskvu,* ed. Institute for Party History of the Moscow Committee of the Communist Party of the Soviet Union (Moscow, 1968), pp. 111–113.

2. Zhukov, *Memoirs,* pp. 287–289.

3. *Istoriia Velikoi Otechestvennoi voiny,* vol. II, p. 71.

4. Eremenko, *Na zapadnom napravlenii,* pp. 71–72.

5. Anfilov, *Bessmertnyi podvig,* p. 472; Zhilin, *Vazhneishie operatsii,* p. 88.

6. Eremenko, *Na zapadnom napravlenii,* p. 78.

7. *Istoriia Velikoi Otechestvennoi voiny,* vol. II, p. 104.

8. Zhilin, *Vazhneishie operatsii,* p. 88.

9. *Istoriia Velikoi Otechestvennoi voiny,* vol. II, p. 98.

10. Zhukov, *Memoirs,* p. 295; Bagramian, *Tak nachinalas voina* (Moscow, 1971), pp. 300–301.

11. Zhukov, *Memoirs,* p. 296.

12. *Istoriia Velikoi Otechestvennoi voiny,* vol. II, p. 104; Zhukov, *Memoirs,* pp. 294–296; Eremenko, *Na zapadnom napravlenii,* pp. 71–72.

13. *Istoriia Velikoi Otechestvennoi voiny,* vol. II, p. 62; Anfilov, *Bessmertnyi podvig,* p. 449.

14. *Istoriia Velikoi Otechestvennoi voiny,* vol. II, p. 104; K. Moskalenko, *Na iugo-zapadnom napravlennii* (Moscow, 1969), p. 61.

15. Eremenko, *Na zapadnom napravlenii,* pp. 85–86; Khoroshilov and Bazhenov, "Elninskaia nastupatelnaia operatsiia 1941 g.," *Voenno-istoricheskii zhurnal,* September 1974, p. 77.

16. Moskalenko, *Na iugo-zapadnom napravlenii,* p. 62.

17. Ibid., p. 68; Bagramian, *Tak nachinalas voina,* pp. 304–305.

18. Bagramian, *Tak nachinalas voina,* pp. 302–303; Moskalenko, *Na iugo-zapadnom napravlenii,* p. 61; von Bock, "Tagebuchnotizen Osten I," 25 Aug. 1941, T-84/271/000424–000425.

19. Bagramian, *Tak nachinalas voina,* p. 306; Guderian, *Panzer Leader,* p. 206.

20. *Istoriia Velikoi Otechestvennoi voiny,* vol. II, pp. 124–125.

21. Guderian, *Panzer Leader,* pp. 207–208.

22. Eremenko, *Na zapadnom napravlenii,* pp. 92–93.

23. Ibid., pp. 97–99.

24. Leverkuehn, *German Military Intelligence,* pp. 178–183.

25. Bagramian, *Tak nachinalas voina,* p. 318.

26. Zhukov, *Memoirs,* p. 298.

27. Guderian, *Panzer Leader,* pp. 213–214; *Istoriia Velikoi Otechestvennoi voiny,* vol. II, p. 106; Bagramian, *Tak nachinalas voina,* p. 218.

28. Von Bock, "Tagebuchnotizen Osten I," 9 Sept. 1941, T-84/271/000448; Guderian, *Panzer Leader,* pp. 214–215.

29. Bagramian, *Tak nachinalas voina,* p. 319.

30. Ibid., p. 325.

31. Ibid., p. 326; Moskalenko, *Na iugo-zapadnom napravlenii*, pp. 82–83.

32. Zhukov, *Memoirs,* pp. 298–299; Moskalenko, *Na iugo-zapadnom napravlenii*, pp. 83–84; Bagramian, *Tak nachinalas voina,* pp. 327–330; *Istoriia Velikoi Otechestvennoi voiny,* vol. II, p. 107.

33. *Istoriia Velikoi Otechestvennoi voiny,* vol. II, p. 107; Moskalenko, *Na iugo-zapadnom napravlenii,* p. 84; *Istoriia Velikoi Otechestvennoi voiny,* vol. II, p. 235; "Budenny, S. M.," in *Bolshaia Sovetskaia Entsiklopediia* (3rd ed.; Moscow, 1970), vol. I, p. 92.

34. Eremenko, *Na zapadnom napravlenii,* p. 95; Moskalenko, *Na iugo-zapadnom napravlenii,* p. 87.

35. Eremenko, *Na zapadnom napravlenii,* p. 95.

36. Von Bock, "Tagebuchnotizen Osten I," 12 Sept. 1941, T–84/271/000451–000452; Guderian, *Panzer Leader,* p. 216.

37. Bagramian, *Tak nachinalas voina,* p. 321.

38. Ibid., pp. 323–324; Moskalenko, *Na iugo-zapadnom napravlenii,* pp. 68–75.

39. Moskalenko, *Na iugo-zapadnom napravlenii,* p. 89.

40. Ibid., p. 89; *Istoriia Velikoi Otechestvennoi voiny,* vol. II, p. 108.

41. Moskalenko, *Na iugo-zapadnom napravlenii,* p. 89.

42. Ibid., pp. 90–91; Bagramian, *Tak nachinalas voina,* pp. 334–338.

43. Bagramian, *Tak nachinalas voina,* p. 335.

44. *Istoriia Velikoi Otechestvennoi voiny,* vol. II, p. 111.

45. Moskalenko, *Na iugo-zapadnom napravlenii,* p. 91.

46. Guderian, *Panzer Leader,* p. 219. According to the Soviet official history, Bagramian reached Kirponos's headquarters on September 16 and the Southwestern Front received confirmation of the retreat order at 11:40 A.M. on September 17. Bagramian notes in his memoirs, however, that due to bad weather his plane did not take off from Poltava until September 17. Moskalenko has recorded that the confirmation was not received until the night of September 18, a version that would agree with Bagramian's account. See *Istoriia Velikoi Otechestvennoi voiny,* vol. II, p. 109; Bagramian, *Tak nachinalas voina,* p. 335; Moskalenko, *Na iugo-zapadnom napravlenii,* p. 91.

47. *Panzer Leader,* pp. 225–226.

48. *Istoriia Velikoi Otechestvennoi voiny,* vol. II, pp. 109–110.

49. Ibid., pp. 110–111; Guderian, *Panzer Leader,* p. 225. See also "Lageorientierung Osten," OKH, Gen.Stb.d.H./Op.abt. (IIb), 27 Sept. 1941, BA–MA H 22/218; Halder, *Kriegstagebuch,* vol. III, pp. 254, 257.

50. Halder, *Kriegstagebuch,* vol. III, pp. 206–207.

51. Zhukov, *Memoirs,* pp. 297–298.

52. Halder, *Kriegstagebuch,* vol. III, p. 207.

53. Ibid., p. 208.

54. Von Bock, "Tagebuchnotizen Osten I," 30 Aug. 1941, T–84/271/000432.

55. Halder, *Kriegstagebuch,* vol. III, p. 208.

56. Von Bock, "Tagebuchnotizen Osten I," 31 Aug. 1941, T–84/271/000433–000435.

57. Ibid., 000433–000434.

58. Ibid., 000422–000423.

59. Halder, *Kriegstagebuch,* vol. III, pp. 200–201.

60. Guderian, *Panzer Leader,* p. 207.

61. Von Bock, "Tagebuchnotizen Osten I," 27 Aug. 1941, T–84/271/000427.

62. Ibid., 000428.

63. Halder, *Kriegstagebuch,* vol. III, pp. 203–204.

64. Ibid., p. 204; von Bock, "Tagebuchnotizen Osten I," 29 Aug. 1941, T–84/271/000429.

65. Von Bock, "Tagebuchnotizen Osten I," 31 Aug. 1941, T–84/271/000434.

66. Fourth Army, "KTB Nr. 9," 30 Aug. 1941, T–312/143/681663; VIIth Army Corps, Ia., "KTB Nr. 5b," 29 Aug.–2 Sept. 1941, BA–MA 17263/1.

67. Fourth Army, "KTB Nr. 9," 31 Aug. 1941, T–312/143/681668–681672; von Bock, "Tagebuchnotizen Osten I," 30 Aug. 1941, T–84/271/000432; Panzer Group 2, Ia., "Anlage zum KTB vom 31 August 1941," BA–MA 21–2/v. 185 (25034/71), p. 13.

68. Halder, *Kriegstagebuch,* vol. III, p. 208; von Bock, "Tagebuchnotizen Osten I," 31 Aug. 1941, T–84/271/000433.

69. Von Bock, "Tagebuchnotizen Osten I," 2 Sept. 1941, T–84/271/000438–000439; Halder, *Kriegstagebuch,* vol. III, pp. 211–212.

70. Von Bock, "Tagebuchnotizen Osten I," 2 Sept. 1941, T–84/271/000438.

71. Panzer Group 2, Ia., "Anlage zum KTB vom 4 Sept. 1941," BA–MA 21–2/v. 189 (25034/75), p. 18.

72. Von Bock, "Tagebuchnotizen Osten I," 2 Sept. 1941, T–84/271/000438–000439; Halder, *Kriegstagebuch,* vol. III, pp. 213–214.

73. Von Bock, "Tagebuchnotizen Osten I," 6 Sept. 1941, T–84/271/000445.

74. Halder, *Kriegstagebuch,* vol. III, p. 215.

75. *Hitler's War Directives,* pp. 96–98. Hitler's original plan to begin the new offensive by mid-September was modified at the request of the OKH.

76. Halder, *Kriegstagebuch,* vol. III, p. 129; H. Plocher, *The German Air Force versus Russia, 1941* (New York, 1965), pp. 146–147.

77. *Kriegstagebuch OKW,* vol. I, p. 1070; "Directive of the High Command of the Wehrmacht," *Documents on German Foreign Policy,* Series D, XIII, no. 388, pp. 623–624. See also M. Steinert, *Hitler's War and the Germans: Public Mood and Attitude during the Second World War* (Athens, Ohio 1977), p. 127.

78. Von Bock, "Tagebuchnotizen Osten I," 10 Sept. 1941, T–84/271/000449.

79. Von Bock, "Tagebuchnotizen Osten I," 11 Sept. 1941, T–84/271/000450.

80. "Lageorientierung Osten," OKH, Gen.Stb.d.H./Op.abt. (IIb), 19 Oct. 1941, BA–MA H22/218; Von Bock, "Tagebuchnotizen Osten I," 17 Sept. 1941, T–84/271/000457–458.

81. *Trial of the Major War Criminals before the International Military Tribunal,* vol. VII, pp. 370–371.

CHAPTER 8
STRATEGY AND TACTICS: A REEVALUATION

1. Von Bock, "Tagebuchnotizen Osten I," 11 Sept. 1941, T-84/271/000450; Halder, *Kriegstagebuch,* vol. III, p. 224.

2. Halder, *Kriegstagebuch,* vol. III, p. 222; K. Reinhardt, *Die Wende vor Moskau* (Stuttgart, 1972), pp. 57, 317. See also Plocher, *The German Air Force versus Russia, 1941,* pp. 234–236. According to this German source, the height of air operations in the Army Group Center area occurred during the period October 22–25. On October 24 Kesselring's Air Fleet 2 managed to put 662 planes in the air, but operations fell off rapidly afterward due to the deteriorating weather and the difficulty of moving fuel supplies forward over the incredibly muddy and badly rutted roads.

3. Röhricht, *Probleme der Kesselschlacht,* pp. 38–45; G. Blumentritt, "Impossible Situations" (unpublished study by Historical Division, HQ U.S. Army Europe, Foreign Military Studies Branch, 1948), National Archives MS., no. B-682, pp. 6–9.

4. Guderian, *Panzer Leader,* p. 235. See also "Weisung für die Fortführung der Operationen der H.Gr. Mitte und Nord," OKH/Gen.Stb.d.H./Op.abt. (I), 13 Oct. 1941, H22/353, T-78/335/291854. Also, compare Guderian, *Panzer Leader,* pp. 226, 234–235 with "Gespräch Chef Heeresgruppe—Chef Panzergruppe am 10.9.41, 21.35 hr.," Panzer Group 2, Ia., "Anlage zum KTB vom 10. Sept. 1941," BA-MA RH21-2/v. 195 (25034/81), pp. 91–92.

5. The old assumptions about Hitler's iron will and stubborn purpose should no longer be given credence. See the commentary by W. Langer, *The Mind of Adolf Hitler: The Secret Wartime Report* (New York, 1972), pp. 201–202; H.-D. Röhrs, *Hitlers Krankheit: Tatschen und Legenden* (Neckargemünd, 1966), pp. 51–52.

6. Moskalenko, *Na iugo-zapadnom napravlenii,* pp. 130–131.

7. Ibid., p. 131; S. Shtemenko, "Nekotorye voprosy strategichskogo rukovodstva vooruzhennymi silame," *Vsemirno-istoricheskaia pobeda,* p. 202; Zhilin, *Vazhneishie operatsii,* p. 107.

8. Zhukov had been sent to Leningrad on September 8, after he had completed his assignment at Yelnia. See his *Memoirs,* p. 297.

9. G. Zhukov, *Marshal Zhukov's Greatest Battles* (New York, 1969), pp. 49–50; *Istoriia Velikoi Otechestvennoi voiny,* vol. II, p. 241; V. Sokolovskii, *Razgrom nemetsko—fashistskikh voisk pod Moskvoi* (Moscow, 1964), pp. 38–39.

10. Röhricht, *Probleme der Kesselschlacht,* p. 45.

11. *Marshal Zhukov's Greatest Battles,* p. 51.

12. Ibid.

13. See Sokolovskii, *Razgrom nemetsko—fashistskikh voisk pod Moskvoi,* p. 29; A. Vasilevskii, "Nachalo korennogo povorata v khode voiny," *Bitva za Moskvu,* pp. 15–16.

14. "Oseniu 1941g.," *Bitva za Moskvu,* p. 51.

15. H.-A. Jacobsen, "The Kommissarbefehl and Mass Executions of Soviet Prisoners of War," *Anatomy of the SS State,* p. 531. A Polish source puts the total number of Soviet POWs dead at 2,800,000–3,000,000. See Datner, *Crimes against POWs,* pp. 225–226.

16. For information about how the defense of Moscow was prepared, see Artemev, "Nepreodolimaia pregrada na podstupakh k stolitse," *Bitva za Moskvu,* pp. 111–126; Sokolovskii, *Razgrom nemetsko—fashistskikh voisk pod Moskvoi,* pp. 57–61; G. Krimanev, "Vklad rabotnikov sovetskogo transporta v pobedy nad fashistskoi Germaniei," *Vsemirno-sitoricheskaia pobeda,* pp. 352–353; I. Pavlovskii, "Sukhoputnye voiska v Velikoi Otechestvennoi voine," ibid., pp. 38–39.

17. *Istoriia Velikoi Otechestvennoi voiny,* vol. II, p. 271.

18. Zhukov, *Memoirs,* pp. 336–337; Anfilov, *Bessmertnyi podvig,* p. 497; Fedorov, *Aviatsia v bitve pod Moskvoi,* p. 261.

19. Artemev was made a deputy commander of the Western Front and was directly subordinate to Zhukov. See Zhukov, *Marshal Zhukov's Greatest Battles,* p. 48; *Proval gitlerovskogo nastupleniia na Moskvu,* ed. A. Samsonov (Moscow, 1966), p. 78.

20. *50 let vooruzhennykh sil SSSR,* pp. 290–291; F. Lisitsyn, "Pervaia udarnaia," *Bitva za Moskvu,* pp. 292–304; A. Beloborodov, "Sibiriaki v velikoi bitve za Moskvu," ibid., pp. 230–231; K. Rokossovskii, "Na volokolamskom napravlenii," ibid., pp. 163–164. See also Zhukov, *Memoirs,* p. 221; Kazakov, *Nad kartoi bylykh srazhenii,* p. 64.

21. Zhukov, *Marshal Zhukov's Greatest Battles,* p. 79; Sokolovskii, *Razgrom nemetsko—fashistskikh voisk pod Moskvoi,* pp. 110–111, 118 ff; *Istoriia vtoroi mirovoi voiny, 1939–1945,* vol. IV, pp. 283–284.

22. Zhukov, *Memoirs,* pp. 351–352; idem., *Marshal Zhukov's Greatest Battles,* pp. 99–100.

23. Samsonov, *Velikaia bitva pod Moskvoi,* pp. 176, 184.

24. Ibid., pp. 189–190; Sokolovskii, *Razgrom nemetsko—fashistskikh voisk pod Moskvoi,* p. 181. See also *Istoriia Velikoi Otechestvennoi voiny,* vol. II, p. 256.

25. Zhilin, *Vazhneishie operatsii,* pp. 34, 101–102; Samsonov, *Velikaia bitva pod Moskvoi,* p. 170.

26. Zhukov, *Marshal Zhukov's Greatest Battles,* p. 100.

27. See Reinhardt, *Die Wende vor Moskau,* pp. 197–243.

28. See ibid., p. 257, n.

29. It was not without reason that Stalin called artillery "the God of War." For a detailed explanation of how the Red Army made use of artillery in combined-arms operations, see H. Gordon, "Artillery," *The Red Army,* pp. 344–353; G. Peredelskii, "Osnovnye printsipy primeneniia artillerii v nastupatelnykh operatsiiakh," *Vsemirno-istoricheskaia pobeda,* pp. 85–87. For a good description of a Russian combined-arms assault in 1943 and the effect of Russian artillery, see F. von Mellenthin, *Panzer Battles: A Study of the Employment of Armor in the Second World War* (Norman, Okla. 1956), p. 247.

30. Kolganov, *Razvitie taktiki sovetskoi armii,* p. 357. See also G. Blumentritt, "The State and Performance of the Red Army, 1941," *The Red Army,* p. 138; F. Bayerlein and N. Galey, "The Armoured Forces," ibid., pp. 307–312.

31. Kolganov, *Razvitie taktiki sovetskoi armii,* pp. 183–184; Radzievskii, "Razvitie taktiki sukhoputnykh voisk," *Vsemirno-istoricheskaia pobeda,* pp. 228–230.

32. J. Erickson, *Soviet Command and Control: Past Present and Future* (unpublished manuscript supplied by the Center For Strategic Technology, Texas

A & M University, 1980), pp. 56–69; *The Russian War Machine, 1917–1945,* ed. S. L. Mayer (Secaucus, N.J., 1977), pp. 190–191.

33. See von Bock, "Tagebuchnotizen Osten I," 20 July 1941, T–84/271/000345-000346; ibid., 22 July 1941, 000352.

34. Guderian's biographer, Kenneth Macksey, blames Halder for pursuing the goal of Moscow while delaying the completion of the Kiev operation. He also blames Hitler for wanting to contain the Briansk pocket and capture Kursk instead of aiding Guderian's drive on Tula. See Macksey, *Guderian,* pp. 152–155. This approach of blaming everyone on the German side except Guderian for the failure of the advance on Moscow ignores the reality of the situation, certainly insofar as the position and strength of the Soviet reserves is concerned.

35. Speer, *Inside the Third Reich,* pp. 303–306; W. Boelke, *Deutschlands Rüstung im Zweiten Weltkrieg* (Frankfurt/M., 1969), pp. 8–9.

36. See S. Golikov, *Vydaiushchiesia pobeda Sovetskoi Armii v Velikoi Otechestvennoi voine* (Moscow, 1954), pp. 25–26; *Partiino-politicheskaia rabota v sovetskikh vooruzhennykh silakh,* ed. A. Khmel (Moscow, 1964), pp. 36–37. See also Hillgruber, *Hitlers Strategie,* pp. 527–528.

37. Haupt, *Geschichte der 134. Infanterie-Division,* p. 27.

38. Fretter-Pico, *Missbrauchte Infanterie,* pp. 29, 41–42, W. Strik-Strikfeldt, *Against Stalin and Hitler: Memoirs of the Russian Liberation Movement, 1941–1945* (New York, 1973), p. 27.

39. See Halder, *Hitler als Feldherr,* p. 44; Blumentritt, "Moscow," *The Fatal Decisions,* p. 73; Guderian, *Panzer Leader,* pp. 266–267. See also Leach, *German Strategy,* pp. 118–123; *The Goebbels Diaries, 1942–1943,* ed. L. Lockner (New York, 1948), pp. 135–136; *Hitler: Reden und Proklamationen,* ed M. Domarus (2 vols., 4 parts; Munich, 1965), vol. IIb: *Untergang, 1941–1945,* pp. 1815–1816.

40. Fretter-Pico, *Missbrauchte Infanterie,* p. 42.

41. This was clearly demonstrated at Yelnia. See Gallenkamp, "Nachtkämpfe," National Archives MS., no. P–054b, Project 40, pp. 14–15. See also V. Chuikov, *The Battle for Stalingrad* (New York, 1964), p. 72.

42. Fretter-Pico, *Missbrauchte Infanterie,* p. 5.

43. "AOK 4 der O.B., an Heeresgruppe Mitte," Fourth Army, Ia., "Anlagen A, KTB Nr. 9," 9 Sept. 1941, BA–MA 13715/2.

44. Von Bock, "Tagebuchnotizen Osten I," 14 Oct. 1941, T–84/271/000488-000489.

45. *Hitler's War Directives,* pp. 116–121.

46. Hofmann, "Die Schlacht von Moskau, 1941," *Entscheidungsschlachten des Zweiten Weltkrieges,* pp. 159–160.

47. See Zhukov, *Marshal Zhukov's Greatest Battles,* p. 77; A. Eremenko, *Protiv falsifikatsii istorii mirovoi voiny* (Moscow, 1958), pp. 14–20; M. Zakharov, "Podvig sovetskikh vooruzhennuykh sil v Velikoi Otechestvennoi voine," *Vsemirno-istoricheskaia pobeda,* p. 24; Zhilin, *Vazhneishie operatsii,* p. 107; Anfilov, *Bessmertnyi podvig,* pp. 46–53; Kolganov, *Razvitie taktiki sovetskoi armii,* pp. 92–93; Proektor, *Agressia i katastrofa,* p. 270.

48. Hofmann and Toppe, "Consumption and Attrition Rates of Army Group Center," National Archives MS., no. p–190, pp. 68–69; E. Middeldorf,

Taktik im Russlandfeldzug: Erfahrungen und Folgerungen (Darmstadt, 1956), pp. 70–71.

49. Middeldorf, *Taktik im Russlandfeldzug,* p. 51; L. Geyer von Schweppenburg, *Gebrochenes Schwert* (Berlin, 1952), pp. 74–75.

50. See V. Kazakov, "Artilleristy v boiakh pod Moskvoi," *Bitva za Moskvu,* pp. 186–193; Zhilin, *Vazhneishie operatsii,* p. 91.

51. See Gen.Stb.d.H./Op.abt., "Chefsachen 1941, Bd, I," 18 Nov. 1941, BA–MA III H/434 Teil 2 (3356/41). See also Middeldorf, *Taktik im Russlandfeldzug,* p. 36.

52. Buchheit, *Hitler der Feldherr,* p. 250.

53. Middeldorf, *Taktik im Russlandfeldzug,* pp. 189–191. See also Buchheit, *Hitler der Feldherr,* p. 235; Philippi and Heim, *Der Feldzug,* pp. 79–80; K. Macksey, *Tank Warfare: A History of Tanks in Battle* (London, 1971), pp. 110–113.

54. V. Belov, *Kogda bushuiut grozi: kaluzhskaia oblast v Velikoi Otechestvennoi voine* (Tula, 1970), pp. 19, 28–29; A. Litvinov, "Pod Serpukhovym," *Bitva za Moskvu,* pp. 313–316.

55. Zhukov, *Marshal Zhukov's Greatest Battles,* p. 34.

56. Idem., *Memoirs,* p. 345.

57. Eremenko, *Protiv falsifilatsii istorii,* p. 30.

Bibliography

UNPUBLISHED SOURCES

Armed Forces High Command, Operations Staff, "Sonderakte Jodl operative entscheidungen 1941, 'Barbarossa,' " RW 4/v. 78 (OKW/1570).

Army High Command, General Staff of the Army. Records June–December 1941, H 22/353. National Archives Microfilm Publication T–78, roll 335.

Army High Command, General Staff of the Army, Operations Staff, "Chefsachen 1941, Bd. I," June–December 1941. III H/434 vol. 2 (3356/41).

Army High Command, General Staff of the Army, Operations Staff, "Lageorientierung Osten," June–December 1941. H 22/218.

Bock, Fedor von, "Tagebuchnotizen Osten—Vorbereitungszeit," May–June 1941. 22/7.

_____. "Tagebuchnotizen Osten I," June–December 1941, 21-g-16/4P-5. National Archives Microfilm Publication T–84, roll. 271.

Marcks, Erich. "Operationsentwurf Ost," August 1940, 21-g-16/4q. National Archives Microfilm Publication T–84, roll 271, frames 902–923.

2nd Army, Operations Staff War Diary, vol. I, June–September 1941, 16690/1. National Archives Microfilm Publication T–312, roll 1654.

4th Army, Operations Staff War Diary, vol. IX, June–December 1941, 13616/1. National Archives Microfilm Publication T–312, roll 143.

4th Army, Operations Staff War Diary, Appendix A of 28 August 1941. 13715/1.

4th Army, Operations Staff War Diary, Appendix A of 9 September 1941. 13715/2.

9th Army, Operations Staff War Diary, vol. II, June–December 1941, 14855/2. National Archives Microfilm Publication T–312, roll 281.

Panzer Group 2, Operations Staff War Diary, vol. I, 22 June–23 August 1941, 250341. National Archives Microfilm Publication T–313, roll 80.

Panzer Group 2, Appendix to Operations Staff War Diary of 10 September 1941. RH 21-2/v. 195 (25034/81).

Panzer Group 2, Operations Staff War Diary, vol. II, 24 August–31 December 1941, 25034/60. National Archives Microfilm Publication T–313, roll 86.

Panzer Group 3, Operations Staff War Diary, vol. I, June–December 1941, 14837/2. National Archives Microfilm Publication T–313, roll 225.

Vth Army Corps, Operations Staff War Diary, vol. I, June–December 1941, 176471/1. National Archives Microfilm Publication T–314, roll 245.

388   Bibliography

VIIth Army Corps, Operations Staff War Diary, vol. Vb, June–September 1941. 17263/1.

IXth Army Corps, Operations Staff War Diary, vol. VII, June–September 1941, 19067/3. National Archives Microfilm Publication T–314, roll 406.

XXth Army Corps, Operations Staff War Diary, vol. I, June–September 1941, 20178/1. National Archives Microfilm Publication T–314, roll 651.

XXIIIrd Army Corps, Operations Staff War Diary, vol. VIII, 22–25 August 1941. RH 24–23/42 (13677/1).

XLth Army Corps, Operations Staff War Diary, vol. III, 22–26 August 1941. 31093/1.

LVIIth Panzer Corps, Operations Staff War Diary, vol. I, 20–24 August 1941. 15683/1.

10th Panzer Division, Operations Staff War Diary, vol. V, June–September 1941, 22304/1. National Archives Microfilm Publication T–315, roll 561.

Bergen, Hans. "Encirclement and Annihilation of the Russian 32nd Cossack Division, 6 and 7 August 1941." Unpublished study by Department of the Army, Office of the Chief of Military History, Washington, D.C., 1947. National Archives MS., no. D–075.

Blumentritt, Guenther. "Commentary to the Battle of Moscow during the Winter of 1941–1942." Unpublished study by Historical Division, HQ U.S. Army, Europe, Foreign Military Studies Branch, 1948. Appendix to National Archives MS., no. T–28.

––––––. "Impossible Situations." Unpublished study by Historical Division, HQ U.S. Army, Europe, Foreign Military Studies Branch, 1948. National Archives MS., no. B–682.

Erickson, John. "Soviet Command and Control: Past, Present and Future." Unpublished study for the Center for Strategic Technology, Texas A & M University, September, 1980.

––––––. "Threat Identification and Strategic Appraisal in Soviet Policy, 1930–1941." Defense Studies, University of Edinburgh, June, 1980.

Gallenkamp, Curt. "Nachtkämpfe." Unpublished study by Historical Division, HQ U.S. Army, Europe, Foreign Military Studies Branch, 1950. National Archives MS., no. P–054b, project 40.

Greiffenburg, Hans. "Battle of Moscow, 1941–1942." Unpublished study by Historical Division, HQ U.S. Army, Europe, Foreign Military Studies Branch, 1948. National Archives MS., no. T–28.

"Pecularities of Russian Warfare." Unpublished Study of Office of the Chief of Military History, 1949. National Archives MS., no T–22.

Scott, Harriet Fast. "Soviet Military Doctrine: Its Continuity—1960–1970." Washington, D.C. Office, Chief of Research and Development, 1971.

––––––. Soviet Military Doctrine: Its Formulation and Dissemination. Stanford Research Institute Menlo Park, California, 1971.

Zaloga, Steven. "Organization of the Soviet Armored Force, 1939–1945." Preliminary study 1981.

PRIMARY WORKS

Anaimanovich, M. A., ed. *Voiska protivo-vozdushnoi oborony strany* (The Forces of the National Air Defense). Moscow: Voennoe izdatelstvo, 1968.

Artemev, P. A. *"Nepreodolimaia pregrada na podstupakh k stolitse"* (The Insuperable Barrier on the Approaches to the Capital). In *Bitva za Moskvu* (The Battle for Moscow), pp. 111–126. Edited by the Institute for Party History of the Moscow Committee of the Communist Party of the Soviet Union. Moscow: Izdatelstvo "Moskovskii rabochii," 1968.

Babadzhanian, A. Kh. "Primenenie bronetankovykh voisk—vazhneishii faktor uvelicheniia tempov nastupatelnykh operatsii" (The Use of Armored Units in the Acceleration of the Pace of Offensive Operations). In *Vsemirno-istoricheskaia pobeda sovetskogo naroda, 1941–1945gg,* (The World-Historical Victory of the Soviet People, 1941–1945), pp. 76–82. Edited by A. A. Grechko. Moscow: Izdatelstvo "Nauka," 1971.

Bagramian, I. Kh. *Tak nachinalas voina* (Thus the War Began). Moscow: Voennoe izdatelstvo, 1971.

————. *Tanki i tankovye voiska* (Tanks and the Armored Forces). Moscow: Voennoe izdatelstvo, 1970.

Beloborodov, A. P. "Sibiriaki v velikoi bitve za Moskvu" (Siberians in the Great Battle for Moscow). In *Bitva za Moskvu,* pp. 230–233.

Baloian, N. P. "Gvardeitsy" (The Guards Divisions). In *Bitva za Moskvu,* pp. 366–376.

Blumentritt, Guenther. "Moscow." *In the Fatal Decisions,* pp. 76–92. Edited by Seymour Freidin and William Richardson. New York: William Sloane, 1956.

————. "The State and Performance of the Red Army, 1941." In *The Red Army,* pp. 134–139. Edited by B. H. Liddell Hart. New York: Harcourt, Brace, 1956.

Boelcke, Willi. *Deutschlands Rüstung im Zweiten Weltkrieg: Hitlers Konferenzen mit Albert Speer, 1942–1945.* Frankfurt am Main: Akademische Verlagsgesellschaft Athenaion, 1969.

Bor, Peter. *Gespräche mit Halder.* Wiesbaden: Limes Verlag, 1950.

Butkov, V. "Kontrudar 5-go mekhanizirovannogo korpusa na lepelskom napravlenii (6 iiulia 1941 goda)" (The Counterattack of the Vth Mechanized Corps toward Lepel, 6 July 1941). *Voenno-istoricheskii zhurnal,* Sept. 1971, pp. 61–64.

Charles de Beaulieu, W. *Der Verstoss der Panzergruppe 4 auf Leningrad.* Neckargemünd: Kurt Vowinckel Verlag, 1961.

Cheremukhin, K. "Na smolensko—moskovskom strategicheskom napravelenii letom 1941 goda" (On The Smolensk–Moscow Strategic Front, Summer 1941). *Voenno-istoricheskii zhurnal,* Oct. 1966, pp. 8–17.

Chuikov, V. I. *The Battle for Stalingrad.* New York: Holt, Rinehart and Winston, 1964.

Churchill, Winston S. *The Second World War.* 6 vols. Boston: Houghton-Mifflin, 1948–1953.

Documents on German Foreign Policy. Series D, 13 vols. Washington, D.C.: GPO, 1949–1964.

Domarus, Max, ed. *Hitler: Reden und Proklamationen.* 2 vols., 4 parts. Munich: Süddeutscher Verlag, 1965.

Eremenko, A. I. *Na zapadnom napravlenii* (On the Western Front). Moscow: Voennoe izdatelstvo, 1959.

_____ . *Protiv falsifikatsii istorii vtoroi mirovoi voiny* (Against the Falsifications of the History of the Second World War). Moscow: Izdatelstvo Inostrannoi Literatury, 1958.

Fretter-Pico, Maximilian. *Missbrauchte Infanterie: deutsche Infanteriedivisionen im osteuropaischen Grossraum, 1941-1944.* Frankfurt am Main: Bernard und Graefe Verlag für Wehrwesen, 1957.

Gehlen, Reinhard. *The Service: The Memoirs of General Reinhard Gehlen.* New York: World Publishing, 1972.

Geschichte der 3. Panzer-Division, Berlin-Brandenburg, 1933-1945. Berlin: Verlag der Buchhandlung Guenter Richter, 1967.

Geyer, Hermann. *Das IX, Armeekorps in Ostfeldzug 1941.* Neckargemünd: Scharnhorst Buchkameradschaft, 1969.

Geyer von Schweppenburg, Leo Freiherr. *Gebrochenes Schwert.* Berlin: Bernard und Graefe Verlag für Wehrwesen, 1952.

Golikov, S. Z. *Vydaiushchiesia pobedy sovetskoi armii v Velikoi Otechestvennoi voine* (The Signal Victories of the Soviet Army in the Great Patriotic War). Moscow: Izdatelstvo Politicheskoi Literatury, 1954.

Gorbatov, A. V. *Years off My Life.* New York: W. W. Norton, 1964.

Greiner, Helmuth. *Die oberste Wehrmachtführung, 1939-1943.* Wiesbaden: Limes Verlag, 1951.

Guderian, Heinz. *Erinnerungen eines Soldaten.* Heidelberg: Kurt Vowinckel Verlag, 1951.

_____ . *Panzer Leader.* London: Michael Joseph, 1952.

_____ . "Russian Strategy in the War." In *The Red Army,* pp. 127-133.

Halder, Franz. *Hitler als Feldherr.* Munich: Münchener Dom Verlag, 1949.

_____ . *Kriegstagebuch.* 3 vols. Stuttgart: W. Kohlhammer Verlag, 1962-1064.

Haupt, Werner. *Geschichte der 134. Infanterie-Division.* Tuttlingen: Werner Groll, 1971.

_____ . *Heeresgruppe Mitte, 1941-1945.* Dorheim: H.-H. Podzun Verlag, 1968.

Heusinger, Adolf. *Befehl im Widerstreit: Schicksalsstunden der deutschen Armee, 1923-1945.* Tübingen: Rainer Wunderlich Verlag, 1950.

Hilger, Gustav. *The Incompatible Allies: A Memoir-History of German-Soviet Relations, 1918-1941.* New York: Macmillan, 1953.

Hoth, Hermann. *Panzer-Operationen: die Panzergruppe 3 und der operative Gedanke der duetschen Führung, Sommer 1941.* Heidelberg: Kurt Vowinckel Verlag, 1956.

Hubatsch, Walther, ed. *Hitlers Weisungen für die Kriegführung.* Frankfurt am Main: Bernard und Graefe Verlag für Wehrwesen, 1962.

Kazakov, M. I. *Nad kartoi bylykh srazhenii* (Over the Maps of Former Battles). Moscow: Voennoe izdatelstvo, 1971.

Kazakov,, V. I. "Artilleristy v boiakh pod Moskvoi" (Artillery Men in the Battles for Moscow). In *Bitva za Moskvu,* pp. 186-193.

Kernmayer, Erich. *Der grosse Rausch: Russlandfeldzug, 1941-1945.* Göttingen: Plesse Verlag, 1962.

Kesselring, Albert. *The Memoirs of Field Marshal Kesselring.* London: William Kimber, 1953.

Kleist, Peter. *Zwischen Hitler und Stalin, 1939-1945.* Bonn: Athenaeum Verlag, 1950.

Knobelsdorff, Otto von. *Geschichte der niedersächsischen 19. Panzer-Division.* Bad Nauheim: Podzun Verlag, 1958.

Konev, I. S. "Osen'iu 1941g." (In the Fall of 1941). In *Bitva za Moskvu,* pp. 35-62.

Kumanev, G. A. "Vklad rabotnikov sovetskogo transporta v pobedu nad fashistkoi Germanei." (The Contribution of the Soviet Transportation Workers in the Victory over Fascist Germany). In *Vsemirno-istoricheskaia pobeda sovetskogo naroda, 1941-1945gg.,* pp. 349-356.

Lemelsen, Joachim, ed. *29. Division.* Bad Nauheim: Podzun Verlag, 1960.

Lestev, Commissar. "Donesnie politpropagandy Krasnoi Armii o boevykh deistviiakh voisk fronta" (A Red Army Political Propaganda Report about the Front Situation). *Voprosy istorii,* August 1961, pp. 98-99.

Lisitsyn, F. Ia. "Pervaia udarnaia" (The 1st Assault Army). In *Bitva za Moskvu,* pp. 292-304.

Litvinov, A. I. "Pod Serpukhovym" (The Battle for Serpukhov). In *Bitva za Moskvu,* pp. 312-322.

Lochner, Louis P., ed. *The Goebbels Diaries, 1942-1943.* New York: Doubleday, 1948.

Lossberg, Bernhard von. *Im Wehrmachtführungsstab: Bericht eines Generalstabsoffiziers.* Hamburg: H. H. Noelke Verlag, 1949.

Lukin, M. "V Smolenskom srazhenii" (In the Battle for Smolensk). *Voenno-istoricheskii zhurnal,* July 1979, pp. 42-54.

Malin, V. N. and Moskovskii, V. P., eds. *KPSS o vooruzhennykh silakh Sovetskogo Soiuza: sbornik dokumentov, 1917-1958.* (The Communist Party and the Soviet Armed Forces: A Collection of Documents, 1917-1958). Moscow: Izdatelstvo Politicheskoi Literatury, 1958.

Manstein, Erich von. *Verlorene Siege.* Frankfurt am Main: Bernard und Graefe Verlag für Wehrwesen, 1969.

Mellenthin, F. W. von. *Panzer Battles: a Study of the Employment of Armor in the Second World War.* Norman: University of Oklahoma Press, 1956.

Meyer-Detring, Wilhelm. *Die 137. Infanterie-Division: im Mittelabschnitt der Ostfront.* Petzenkirchen, Austria: Kameradschaft der Bergmann-Division, 1962.

Moskalenko, K. S. *Na iugo-zapadnom napravlenii* (On the Southwestern Front). Moscow: Izdatelstvo Nauka, 1969.

Murawski, Erich, ed. *Der deutsche Wehrmachtbericht, 1939-1945.* Boppard am Rhein: Harold Boldt Verlag, 1962.

Nehring, Walther. *Die Geschichte der deutschen Panzerwaffe, 1916 bis 1945.* Berlin: Propylaen Verlag, 1969.

Picker, Henry. *Hitlers Tischgespräche im Führerhauptquartier.* Stuttgart: Seewald Verlag, 1965.

Pottgiesser, Hans. *Die deutsche Reichsbahn im Ostfeldzug, 1939–1944.* Neckargemünd: Scharnhorst Buchkameradschaft, 1960.

Radzievskii, A. I. "Razvitie taktiki sukhoputnykh voisk" (The Development of Tactics for the Land Forces). In *Vsemirno-istoricheskaia pobeda sovetskogo naroda, 1941–1945gg.,* pp. 224–231.

Rokossovskii, K. K. "Na volokolamskom napravlenii" (On the Volokolamsk Front). In *Bitva za Moskvu,* pp. 152–174.

_____ . *Soldatskii dolg* (A Soldier's Service). Moscow: Voennoe izdatelstvo, 1968.

Rudenko, R. A., ed. *Niurnbergskii protsess nad glavnymi nemetskimi voennymi prestupnikami* (The Nuremberg Trials ofthe Major German War Criminals). 7 vols. Moscow: Izdatelstvo, Iuridicheskoi Literatury, 1957–1961.

Schlabrendorff, Fabian von. *Offiziere gegen Hitler.* Frankfurt am Main: Fischer Buecherei, 1959.

Schmidt, August. *Geschichte der 10. Division: 10. Infanterie-Division, 10. Panzer-Grenadier Division, 1933–1945.* Bad Nauheim: Podzun Verlag, 1963.

Schramm, Percy, ed. *Kriegstagebuch des Oberkommandos der Wehrmacht.* 4 vols. Frankfurt am Main: Bernard und Graefe Verlag für Wehrwesen, 1961–1965.

Shtemenko, S. M. *Generalnyi Shtab v gody voiny* (The General Staff in the War). Moscow: Voennoe izdatelstvo, 1968.

_____ . "Nekotorye voprosy strategicheskogo rukovodstva vooruzhennymi silami" (Some Questions Regarding the Strategic Guidance of the Armed Forces). In *Vsemirno-istoricheskaia pobeda sovetskogo naroda, 1941–1945gg.,* pp. 196–206.

Siniaev, A. D., ed. *Voprosy strategii i operativnogo iskusstva v sovetskikh voennykh trudakh* (Questions of Strategy and Tactics in Soviet Military Writings). Moscow: Voennoe izdatelstvo, 1965.

Sokolovskii, V. D. *Razgrom nemetsko-fashistskikh voisk pod Moskvoi* (The Destruction of the German-Fascist Army near Moscow). Moscow: Voennoe izdatelstvo, 1964.

_____ . *Soviet Military Strategy.* New York: Crane Russak, Inc., 1975. Edited with analysis and commentary by Harriet Fast Scott. (Stanford Research Institute—SRI).

Sontag, Raymond J. and Beddie, James S., eds. *Nazi-Soviet Relations, 1939–1941: Documents from the Archives of the German Foreign Office.* Washington, D.C.: Department of State, 1948.

Strik-Strikfeldt, Wilfried. *Against Stalin and Hitler: Memoir of the Russian Liberation Movement, 1941–1945.* New York: John Day, 1973.

Thomas, Georg. *Geschichte der deutschen Wehr- und Rüstungswirtschaft, 1918–1943/45.* Edited by Wolfgang Birkenfeld. Boppard am Rhein: Harold Boldt Verlag, 1966.

Timoshenko, S. K. "Iugo-zapadnyi front v bitve za Moskvu" (The Southwestern Front in the Battle for Moscow). In *Bitva za Moskvu,* pp. 97–110.

Tippelskirch, Kurt von. *Geschichte des Zweiten Weltkrieges.* Bonn: Athenaeum Verlag, 1956.

Trevor-Roper, H. R., ed. *Hitler's Table Talk, 1941-1944.* London: Weidenfeld and Nicolson, 1953.

———, ed. *Hitler's War Directives, 1939-1945.* London: Sidgwick and Jackson, 1964.

The Trial of German Major War Criminals: Proceedings of the International Military Tribunal Sitting at Nuremberg Germany. 23 vols. London: HMSO, 1946-1951.

Trial of the Major War Criminals before the International Military Tribunal. 42 vols. Nuremberg: The International Military Tribunal, 1947-1949.

Tri goda Otechestvennoi voiny Sovetskogo Soiuza (Three Years of the Patriotic War of the Soviet Union). Moscow: Sovinformbiuro, 1944.

Vasilevskii, A. M. "Nachalo korennogo povorota v khode voiny" (The Turn of the Tide in the War). In *Bitva za Moskvu,* pp. 11-27.

Voznesensky, N. A. *The Economy of the U.S.S.R. during World War II.* Washington, D.C.: Public Affairs Press, 1948.

Warlimont, Walter. *Inside Hitler's Headquarters, 1939-1945.* New York: Frederick A. Praeger, 1964.

Weidinger, Otto. *Division Das Reich.* Vol. 2. Osnabrück: Munnin Verlag, 1969.

Westphal, Siegfried. *Heer in Fesseln: aus den Papieren des Stabchefs von Rommel, Kesselring und Rundstedt.* Bonn: Athenaeum Verlag, 1952.

Zakharov, M. V. "O teorii glubokoi operatsii" (The Theory of Deep Operations). *Voenno-istoricheskii zhurnal,* Oct. 1970, pp. 10-14.

———. "Podvig sovetskikh vooruzhennykh sil v Velikoi Otechestvennoi voine" (The Exploits of the Soviet Armed Forces in the Great Patriotic War). In *Vsemirno-istoricheskaia pobeda sovetskogo naroda, 1941-1945gg.,* pp. 19-35.

Zhilin, P. A. *Vazhneishie operatsii Velikoi Otechestvennoi voiny, 1941-1945gg.* (The Decisive Battles of the Great Patriotic War, 1941-1945.) Moscow: Voennoe izdatelstvo, 1956.

Zhukov, G. K. *Marshal Zhukov's Greatest Battles.* Foreword by Harrison Salisbury. New York: Harper and Row, 1969.

———. *The Memoirs of Marshal Zhukov.* London: Jonathan Cape, 1971.

SECONDARY WORKS

Addington, Larry H. *The Blitzkrieg Era and the German General Staff, 1865-1941.* New Brunswick: Rutgers University Press, 1971.

Anders, Wladyslaw. *Hitler's Defeat in Russia.* Chicago: Henry Regnery, 1953.

Anfilov, V. A. *Bessmertnyi podvig: issledovanie kanuna i pervogo etapa Velikoi Otechestvennoi voiny* (The Immortal Exploit: an Investigation of the Pre-War and Early War Period). Moscow: Izdatelstvo Nauka, 1971.

_____ . *Nachalo Velikoi Otechestvennoi voiny* (The Beginning of the Great Patriotic War). Moscow: Voennoe izdatelstvo, 1962.

Aronson, Gregor, et al., ed. *Russian Jewry, 1917-1967.* New York: Thomas Yoseloff, 1969.

Baritz, J. "Belorussia and the Kremlin's Strategic Plans." *Belorussian Review* VI (1958), pp. 85-88.

Bayerlein, F., and Galay, N. "The Armoured Forces." In *The Red Army,* pp. 307-322. Edited by B. H. Liddell Hart. New York: Harcourt Brace, 1956.

Bialer, Seweryn. *Stalin and His Generals.* New York: Pegasus Press, 1969.

Belov, V. D. *Kogda bushuiut grozi: kaluzhskaia oblast' v Velikoi Otechestvennoi voiny* (When the Storm Raged: The Kaluga Region during the Great Patriotic War). Tula: Priokskoe knizhnoe izdatelstvo, 1970.

Bezymenskii, L. *Germanskie generaly—s Gitlerom i bez nego* (The German Generals with and without Hitler). Moscow: Izdatelstvo sotsialno-ekonomicheskoi literatury, 1961.

Blau, George. "The German Campaign in Russia; Planning and Operations, 1940-1942." Department of the Army Pamphlet No. 20-261a, March 1955.

Buchheit, Gert. *Hitler der Feldherr: die Zerstörung einer Legende.* Rastatt: Grote Verlag, 1958.

_____ . *Soldatentum und Rebellion: die Tragödie der deutschen Wehrmacht.* Rastatt: Grote Verlag, 1961.

Bullock, Alan. *Hitler: A Study in Tyranny.* London: Oldham Press, 1952.

Carrell, Paul. *Hitler's War on Russia: the Story of the German Defeat in the East.* London: George G. Harrap, 1964.

Carver, Michael, ed. *The War Lords.* London: Weidenfeld and Nicolson, 1976.

Clark, Alan. *Barbarossa: The Russian-German Conflict, 1941-1945.* New York: William Morrow, 1965.

Conquest, Robert. *The Great Terror: Stalin's Purge of the Thirties.* New York: Macmillan, 1968.

Dallin, Alexander. *German Rule in Russia, 1941-1945: a Study of Occupation Policies.* London: Macmillan, 1957.

Dallin, David. *Soviet Espionage.* New Haven: Yale University Press, 1955.

Datner, Szymon. *Crimes against POWs: Responsibility of the Wehrmacht.* Warsaw: Zachodnia Agencia Prasowa, 1964.

Deutscher, Isaac. *Stalin: A Political Biography.* London: Oxford University Press, 1949.

De Witt, K., and Moll, W. "The Briansk Area." In *Soviet Partisans in World War II,* pp. 458-516. Edited by John Armstrong. Madison: University of Wisconsin Press, 1964.

Dinerstein, Herbert. *War and the Soviet Union: Nuclear Weapons and the Nuclear Revolution in Soviet Military and Political Thinking.* New York: Frederick A. Praeger, 1959. (RAND study).

Dorofeev, M. "O nekotorykh prichinakh neudachnykh deistvii mekhanizirovannykh korpusov v nachalnom periode Velikoi Otechestvennoi voiny" (Some Causes of the Failure of the Mechanized Corps in the Early Period of the War). *Voenno-istoricheskii zhurnal,* March 1964, pp. 34–36.

Erickson, John. *The Road to Stalingrad: Stalin's War with Germany,* vol. I. London: Weidenfeld and Nicolson, 1975.

———. *The Soviet High Command: A Military-Political History, 1918–1941.* London: St. Martin's Press, 1962.

Fedorov, A. G. *Aviatsia v. bitve pod Moskvoi* (The Air Force in the Battle for Moscow). Moscow: Izdatelstvo Nauka, 1971.

Fest, Joachim C. *Hitler: eine Biographie.* Frankfurt am Main: Propylaen Verlag, 1973.

Fischer, George. *Soviet Opposition to Stalin: A Case Study in World War II.* Cambridge, Mass.: Harvard University Press, 1952.

Fischer, Fritz. *Germany's Aims in the First World War.* New York, Norton, 1967.

Florinsky, Michael T. *Russia: A History and an Interpretation,* 2 vols. New York: Macmillan, 1953.

Frank, P. "The Changing Composition of the Communist Party." In *The Soviet Union Since the Fall of Khrushchev,* pp. 96–120. Edited by A. Brown and M. Kaser. London: Macmillan, 1975.

Fuller, J.F.C. *The Second World War, 1939–1945.* New York: Duell, Sloan and Pierce, 1949.

Gabriel, Richard. *The New Red Legions: an Attitudinal Portrait of the Soviet Soldier.* Westport, Conn.: Greenwood Press, 1980.

Garder, Michael. *A History of the Soviet Army.* New York: Frederick A. Praeger, 1966.

Garthoff, Raymond. *Soviet Military Policy: A Historical Analysis.* New York: Frederick A. Praeger, 1966.

———. *The Soviet Image of Future War.* Washington, D.C.: Public Affairs Press, 1959.

Goerlitz, Walter. *Generalfeldmarschall Keitel: Verbrecher oder Offizier?* Göttingen: Musterschmidt Verlag, 1961.

———. *The German General Staff: Its History and Structure, 1657–1945.* London: Hollis and Carter, 1953.

———. *Paulus and Stalingrad.* New York: The Citadel Press, 1963.

Goff, James. "The 1940 Soviet Tank Divisions: Geographic Order of Battle," *History Numbers and War,* vol. I, no. 3, (Fall 1977), pp. 167–189.

Gordon, Harold. "Artillery." In *The Red Army,* pp. 344–366.

Higgins, Trumbull. *Hitler and Russia: The Third Reich in a Two-Front War, 1937–1943.* New York: Macmillan, 1966.

Hillgruber, Andreas. *Hitlers Strategie: Politik und Kriegführung, 1940–1941.* Frankfurt am Main: Bernard und Graefe Verlag für Wehrwesen, 1965.

Hinsley, F. H. *Hitler's Strategy.* Cambridge: University Press, 1951.

Hofmann, R. "Die Schlacht von Moskau, 1941." In *Entscheidungsschlachten des Zweiten Weltkrieges,* pp. 139-184. Edited by Hans Jacobsen and Jürgen Rohwer. Frankfurt am Main: Bernard und Graefe Verlag für Wehrwesen, 1960.

Holborn, Hajo. *A History of Modern Germany.* 3 vols. New York: Alfred A. Knopf, 1959-1969.

Horelick, Arnold. *Strategic Power and Soviet Foreign Policy.* Chicago: the University of Chicago Press, 1966.

Hough, Jerry and Fainsod, Merle. *How the Soviet Union Is Governed.* Cambridge, Mass.: Harvard University Press, 1979.

Irving, David. *The Rise and Fall of the Luftwaffe: The Life of Field Marshal Milch.* Boston: Little, Brown, 1973.

Isserson, G. "Razvitie teorii sovetskogo operativnogo iskusstva v 30-e gody" (The Development of the Soviet Theory of Tactics in the 1930's). *Voenno-istoricheskii zhurnal,* Jan. 1965, pp. 39-46 and March 1965, pp. 44-61.

Istoriia Velikoi Otechestvennoi voiny Sovetskogo Soiuza, 1941-1945 (The History of the Great Patriotic War of the Soviet Union, 1941-1945). 6 vols. Edited by Institut Marksizma-Leninizma. Moscow: Voennoe izdatelstvo, 1960-1965.

Istoriia vtoroi mirovoi voiny, 1939-1945 (The History of the Second World War, 1939-1945). 12 vols. Moscow: Voennoe izdatelstvo, 1973-1980.

Ivanov, S. P. "Sovetskaia strategiia v gody Velikoi Otechestvennoi voiny" (Soviet Strategy in the Years of the Great Patriotic War). In *Vsemirno-istoricheskaia pobeda sovetskogo naroda, 1941-1945gg.,* pp. 207-216.

Jacobs, Walter. *Frunze: The Soviet Clausewitz, 1865-1925.* The Hague: Martinus Nijhoff, 1969.

Jacobsen, Otto. *Erich Marcks: Soldat und Gelehrter.* Goettingen: Musterschmidt Verlag, 1971.

Jasny, Naum. *Soviet Industrialization, 1928-1952.* Chicago: The University of Chicago Press, 1961.

Just, Guenther. *Alfred Jodl: Soldat ohne Furcht und Tadel.* Hanover: National Verlag, 1971.

Khmel, A. E., ed. *Partiino-politicheskaia rabota v sovetskikh vooruzhennykh silakh* (Party-Political Work in the Soviet Armed Forces). Moscow: Voennoe izdatelstvo, 1964.

Khoroshilov, G. and Bazhenov, A. "Elninskaia nastupatelnaia operatsiia 1941g." (The Yelnia Offensive Operation in 1941). *Voenno-istoricheskii zhurnal,* Sept. 1974, pp. 75-81.

Kilmarx, Robert A. *A History of Soviet Air Power.* New York: Frederick A. Praeger, 1962.

Kintner, William and Scott, Harriet. *The Nuclear Revolution in Soviet Military Affairs.* Norman: University of Oklahoma Press, 1968.

Kleinfeld, Gerald and Tambs, Lewis A. *Hitler's Spanish Legion: the Blue Division in Russia.* Carbondale, Ill.: Southern Illinois University Press, 1979.

Kluchevsky, V. O. *A History of Russia.* 5 vols. London: J. M. Dent, 1926.

Kolchigin, B. "Mysli ob ispolzovanii armii prikrytiia v nachalnom periode Velikoi Otechestvennoi voiny" (Thoughts about the Use of Screening Forces in the Early Period of the War). *Voenno-istoricheskii zhurnal,* April 1961, pp. 35–37.

Kolganov, K. S. *Razvitie taktiki sovetskoi armii v gody Velikoi Otechestvennoi voiny, 1941–1945gg.* (The Development of Tactics in the Soviet Army during the Great Patriotic War, 1941–1945). Moscow: Voennoe izdatelstvo, 1958.

Komkov, G. "Sovetskie organy gosudarstvennoi bezopasnosti v gody Velikoi Otechestvennoi voiny" (The Organs of Soviet State Security during the Great Patriotic War). *Voprosy istorii,* May 1965, pp. 25–28.

Kozlov, S. N., ed. *O sovetskoi voennoi nauke* (Soviet Military Science). Moscow: Voennoe izdatelstvo, 1964.

Krasilnikov, S. "O strategicheskom rukovodstve v Velikoi Otechestvennoi voine." (About Strategic Guidance in the Great Patriotic War). *Voenno-istoricheskii zhurnal,* June 1960, pp. 6–12.

Krausnick, H., ed. *Anatomy of the SS State.* London: St. James Place, 1968.

Krausnick, H., and Wilhelm, H. H. *Die Truppe des Weltanschauungskrieges: die Einsatzgruppen der Sicherheitspolizei und des SD, 1938–1942.* Stuttgart: Deutsche Verlags-Anstalt, 1981.

Kravchenko, G. S. *Ekonomika SSSR v gody Velikoi Otechestvennoi voiny, 1941–1945gg.* (The Economy of the U.S.S.R. in the Years of the Great Patriotic War). Moscow: Izdatelstvo Ekonomike, 1970.

Kravtsov, V. "Krakh nemetsko-fashistskogo plana 'Barbarossa' " (The Failure of the German-Fascist Plan "Barbarossa"). *Voenno-istoricheskii zhurnal,* Dec. 1968, pp. 41–45.

Langer, Walter. *The Mind of Adolf Hitler: The Secret Wartime Report.* New York: Basic Books, 1972.

Laqueur, Walter. *Russia and Germany: A Century of Conflict.* London: Weidenfeld and Nicolson, 1965.

Leach, Barry. *German Strategy against Russia, 1939–1941.* Oxford: Clarendon Press, 1973.

Leverkuehn, Paul. *German Military Intelligence.* London: Weidenfeld and Nicolson, 1954.

Levytsky, Boris. *The Stalinist Terror in the Thirties: Documentation from the Soviet Press.* Stanford, Calif.: Hoover Institution Press, 1974.

Liddell Hart, B. H. *The German Generals Talk.* New York: William Morrow, 1948.

––––––– , ed. *The Soviet Army.* London: Weidenfeld and Nicolson, 1956.

––––––– . *Strategy.* New York: Frederick A. Praeger, 1967.

Macksey, Kenneth. *Guderian, Creator of the Blitzkrieg.* New York: Stein and Day, 1976.

––––––– . *Tank Warfare: a History of Tanks in Battle.* London: Rupert Hart-Davis, 1971.

Manvell, Roger, and Fraenkel, Heinrich. *The Canaris Conspiracy: The Secret Resistance to Hitler in the German Army.* New York: David McKay, 1969.

Middeldorf, Eike. *Taktik im Russlandfeldzug: Erfahrungen und Folgerungen.* Darmstadt: E. S. Mittler und Sohn Verlag, 1956.

Milward, Alan S. *The German Economy at War.* London: The Athlone Press, 1965.

Mueller-Hillebrand, Burkhart. *Das Heer, 1933–1945: Entwicklung des organisatorischen Aufbaues.* Vol. 2. Frankfurt am Main: E. S. Mittler und Sohn Verlag, 1956.

Munzel, Oscar. *Panzer Taktik: Raids gepanzerter Verbände im Ostfeldzug, 1941/1942.* Neckargemünd: Kurt Vowinckel Verlag, 1959.

O'Neill, Robert J. *The German Army and the Nazi Party, 1933–1939.* London: Cassell and Co., 1966.

Pavlenko, N. G. "Osnovnye napravleniia razvitiia sovetskogo operativnogo iskusstva" (The Basic Course of Development of Soviet Military Tactics). In *Vsemirno-istoricheskaia pobeda sovetskogo naroda, 1941–1945gg.,* pp. 217–223.

_____ . "Reshaiushchaia rol SSSR i ego vooruzhennykh sil v razgrome germanskogo imperializma" (The Decisive Role of the USSR and its Armed Forces in the Destruction of German Imperialism). *Voenno-istoricheskii zhurnal,* Jan. 1960, pp. 23–27.

Pavlovskii, I. G. "Sukhoputnye voiska v Velikoi Otechestvennoi voine" (The Land Forces in the Great Patriotic War). In *Vsemirno-istoricheskaia pobeda sovetskogo naroda, 1941–1945gg.,* pp. 36–42.

Petrov, V., ed. *June 22, 1941: Soviet Historians and the German Invasion.* Columbia: University of South Carolina Press, 1968.

Philippi, A. "Das Pripjetproblem." *Wehrwissenschaftliche Rundschau,* supplement, March 1956.

Philippi, A. and Heim, Ferdinand. *Der Feldzug gegen Sowjetrussland, 1941 bis 1945.* Stuttgart: W. Kohlhammer Verlag, 1962.

50 let vooruzhennykh sil SSSR (The 50th Anniversary of the Armed Forces of the USSR). Moscow: Voennoe izdatelstvo, 1968.

Platonov, S. P., ed. *Vtoraia mirovaia voina, 1939–1945gg,: voenno-istoricheskii ocherk* (The Second World War, 1939–1945: a Military-Historical Study). Moscow: Voennoe izdatelstvo, 1958.

Plocher, Hermann. *The German Air Force versus Russia, 1941.* New York: Arno Press, 1965.

Proektor, D. M. *Agressiia i katastrofa: vysshee voennoe rukovodstvo fashistskoi Germanii vo vtoroi mirovoi voine* (Aggression and Catastrophe: The German High Command in the Second World War). Moscow: Izdatelstvo Nauka, 1968.

Reinhardt, Klaus. *Die Wende vor Moskau: das Scheitern der Strategie Hitlers im Winter 1941/42.* Stuttgart: deutsche Verlags-Anstalt, 1972.

Reitlinger, Gerald. *The House Built on Sand: The Conflicts of German Policy in Russia, 1939–1945.* New York: Viking Press, 1960.

Rich, Norman. *Hitler's War Aims: Ideology, the Nazi State, and the Course of Expansion.* New York: Norton, 1973.

Ritter, Gerhard. *The German Resistance: Carl Goerdler's Struggle against Tyranny.* New York: Frederick A. Praeger, 1958.

Roehricht, Edgar. *Probleme der Kesselschlacht: dargestellt an Einkreisungs-Operationen im Zweiten Weltkrieg.* Karlsruhe: Condor-Verlag, 1958.

Roehrs, Hans-Dietrich. *Hitlers Krankheit: Tatsachen und Legenden.* Neckargemünd: Kurt Vowinckel Verlag, 1966.

"Russian Combat Methods in World War II." Department of The Army Pamphlet no. 20-230, 1950.

Samsonov, A. M., ed. *Proval gitlerskogo nastupleniia na Moskvu* (The Collapse of Hitler's Offensive toward Moscow). Moscow: Voennoe izdatelstvo, 1966.

_____ . *Velikaia bitva pod Moskvoi, 1941-1942* (The Great Battle of Moscow, 1941-1942), Moscow: Izdatelstvo Nauka, 1958.

Savkin, V. E. *Osnovnye printsipy operativnogo iskusstva i taktiki* (The Fundamentals of Tactics and Operational Principles). Moscow: Voennoe izdatelstvo, 1972.

Schall-Riacour, Heidemarie G. *Aufstand und Gehorsam: Offizierstum und Generalstab im Umbruch: Leben und Wirken von Generaloberst Franz Halder, Generalstabschef, 1938-1942.* Wiesbaden: Limes Verlag, 1972.

Scott, William. *The Armed Forces of the USSR.* Boulder, Colo.: Westview Press, 1979.

_____ . *Soviet Sources of Military Doctrine and Strategy.* New York: Crane Russak, 1957.

Seaton, Albert. *Stalin as Warlord.* London: B. T. Batsford, 1976.

_____ . *The Battle for Moscow, 1941-1942.* London: Rupert Hart-Davis, 1971.

_____ . *The Russo-German War, 1941-1945.* New York: Frederick A. Praeger, 1971.

Seraphim, H., and Hillgruber, Andreas. "Hitlers Entschluss zum Angriff auf Russland," *Vierteljahrshefte für Zeitgeschichte* II (July 1954), pp. 240-254.

Shabad, Theodore. *Geography of the U.S.S.R.: a Regional Survey.* New York: Columbia University Press, 1951.

Sloan, John F. "Soviet Units in World War II: New Data from Soviet Sources," *History Numbers and War,* vol. 1, no. 3, (Fall 1977), pp. 160-181.

Sokolov, P. V. "Opyt kommunisticheskoi partii po ispolzovaniiu liudskikh resursov v gody voiny" (The Experience of the Communist Party in the Use of Manpower in the War Years). In *Vsemirno-istoricheskaia pobeda sovetskogo naroda, 1941-1945gg.,* pp. 439-446.

Sovetskaia voennaia entsiklopediia (The Soviet Military Encyclopedia). 8 vols. Moscow: Voennoe izdatelstvo, 1976-1980.

SSSR v Velikoi Otechestvennoi voine, 1941-1945: kratkaia khronika (The USSR in the Great Patriotic War, 1941-1945: a Short Chronology). Moscow: Voennoe izdatelstvo, 1970.

Stein, George H. *The Waffen SS: Hitler's Elite Guard at War, 1939-1945.* Ithaca: Cornell University Press, 1966.

Steinert, Marlis G. *Hitler's War and the Germans: Public Mood and Attitude during the Second World War.* Athens, Ohio: Ohio University Press, 1977.

Suchenwirth, Richard. *Command and Leadership in the German Air Force.* New York: Arno Press, 1970.

Sukhomlin, A. V. *Suvorovskii sbornik.* Moscow: Izdatelstvo Akademii Nauk SSSR, 1951.

Sydnor, Charles W. *Soldiers of Destruction: The SS Death's Head Division, 1933-1945.* Princeton, N.J.: Princeton University Press, 1977.

Tarle, Eugene. *Napoleon's Invasion of Russia, 1812.* New York: Oxford University Press, 1942.

Telpukhovskii, B. S. *Velikaia Otechestvennaia voina Sovetskogo Soiuza, 1941–1945: kratkii ocherk* (The Great Patriotic War of the Soviet Union, 1941–1945: A Short Study). Moscow: Izdatelstvo Politicheskoi Literatury, 1959.

Thomas, Hugh. *The Spanish Civil War.* New York: Harper and Row, 1961.

Treadgold, Donald. *Twentieth Century Russia.* New York: Rand McNally, 1964.

Trevor-Roper, H. R. "Hitlers Kriegsziele." *Vierteljahrshefte für Zeitgeschichte* VII (April 1960), pp. 123–133.

Turney, Alfred W. *Disaster at Moscow: von Bock's Campaigns, 1941–1942.* Albuquerque: University of New Mexico Press, 1970.

Uhlig, H. "Das Einwirken Hitlers auf Planung und Führung des Ostfeldzuges." *Das Parlement,* supplement, 16 March 1960.

Vorobev, V. F. *Boevoi putsovetskikh vooruzhennykh sil* (The Battle Road of the Soviet Armed Forces). Moscow: Voennoe izdatelstvo, 1960.

Weinberg, Gerald. "Der deutsche Entschluss zum Amgriff auf die Sowjetunion." *Vierteljahrshefte für Zeitgeschichte* I (Oct. 1953), pp. 301–318.

———. "The Yelnia-Dorogobuzh Area of the Smolensk Oblast." In *Soviet Partisans in World War II,* pp. 389–457.

Wheeler-Bennett, John W. *The Nemesis of Power: The German Army in Politics, 1918–1945.* London: Macmillan, 1953.

Wolfe, Bertram D. *Khrushschev and Stalin's Ghost.* New York: Frederick A. Praeger, 1957.

Wolfe, Thomas. *Soviet Strategy at the Crossroads.* Cambridge, Mass: Harvard University Press, 1970.

Yale, Wesley. *Alternative to Armageddon: The Peace Potential of Lightning War.* New Brunswick, New Jersey: Rutgers University Press, 1970.

Zemkov, V. "Nekotorye voprosy sozdaniia i ispolzovaniia strategicheskikh reservov" (Some Questions about the Creation and Use of Strategic Reserves). *Voenno-istoricheskii zhurnal,* Oct. 1971, pp. 13–16.

Zhukov, I. *Liudi 40-x godov: liudi v brone* (Men of the 1940's: Men in Armor). Moscow: Izdatelstvo "Sovetskaia Rossiia," 1969.

INDEX